Command on the Western Front

PEN & SWORD MILITARY CLASSICS

We hope you enjoy your Pen and Sword Military Classic. The series is designed to give readers quality military history at affordable prices. Pen and Sword Classics are available from all good bookshops. If you would like to keep in touch with further developments in the series, including information on the **Classics Club**, then please contact Pen and Sword at the address below.

Published Classics Titles

Forthcoming Titles

PEN AND SWORD BOOKS LTD
47 Church Street • Barnsley • South Yorkshire • S70 2AS

Tel: 01226 734555 • 734222

E-mail: enquiries@pen-and-sword.co.uk • **Website:** www.pen-and-sword.co.uk

Command
on the
Western Front

The Military Career of
SIR HENRY RAWLINSON
1914–18

Robin Prior
and
Trevor Wilson

PEN & SWORD MILITARY CLASSICS

For Megan

First published in Great Britain in 1992 by Blackwell Publishers
Published in 2004 in this format by
PEN & SWORD MILITARY CLASSICS
an imprint of
Pen & Sword Books Limited
47 Church Street
Barnsley
S. Yorkshire
S70 2AS

Copyright © Robin Prior and Trevor Wilson, 2004

ISBN 1 84415 103 4

The right of Robin Prior and Trevor Wilson to
be identified as Authors of this Work has
been asserted by them in accordance with
the Copyright, Designs and Patents Act 1988.

A CIP record for this book
is available from the British Library.

Printed and bound in Great Britain by
CPI UK

Pen & Sword Books Limited incorporates the imprints of
Pen & Sword Aviation, Pen & Sword Maritime, Pen & Sword Military,
Wharncliffe Local History, Pen & Sword Select,
Pen & Sword Military Classics and Leo Cooper

For a complete list of Pen & Sword titles please contact:
PEN & SWORD BOOKS LIMITED
47 Church Street, Barnsley, South Yorkshire, S70 2AS, England.
E-mail: enquiries@pen-and-sword.co.uk
Website: www.pen-and-sword.co.uk

Contents

Acknowledgements

During the six years of preparation of this work, the authors have incurred many debts. Primarily, they wish to express their gratitude to the Australian Research Council, whose generous grant enabled Robin Prior to devote three years of full-time research to the book.

The authors also wish to thank the following research institutions for granting access to materials in their archives: in London, the Public Record Office, the National Army Museum, the Imperial War Museum, and the Liddell Hart Centre at King's College; in Woolwich, the Royal Artillery Institution; in Edinburgh, the National Library of Scotland; in Cambridge, Churchill College; and in Canberra, the Australian War Memorial. The Barr Smith Library at the University of Adelaide and the Bridges Library at University College, Canberra, have managed to secure much elusive and essential material.

Robin Prior expresses his gratitude to Professor Brian Bond and King's College, London, for offering research facilities in 1984. And Trevor Wilson wishes to thank the President and Fellows of Magdalen College, Oxford, for appointing him to a visiting fellowship in 1987.

Many individuals have contributed to the preparation of this book. The following must be singled out: Professor Alan Gilbert for his enthusiastic support of the project and for furthering Robin Prior's application to undertake additional research in London; Irene Cassidy for tracking down many valuable documents often from the vaguest of references; Elizabeth Greenhalgh and Pauline Green for their inexhaustible patience in preparing the manuscript for the publishers; Terry Norman and Keith Jeffrey for their generosity in making General Congreve's diary available; and Gordon Baker for his comments on various chapters of the manuscript.

In addition, the authors wish to thank Her Majesty the Queen for permission to quote from the Wigram papers in the Royal Archives, Windsor

Castle; the family of the late Earl Haig for permission to quote from his papers in the National Library of Scotland; and especially Mr M. A. F. Rawlinson for permission to quote from the letters and diaries of Lord Rawlinson of Trent.

Particular reference must be made to the contribution to this book of Mr Paul Ballard of the Department of Geography at University College, Canberra. Mr Ballard unstintingly placed his cartographical skills at the authors' disposal, and translated their amateurish sketches into the forty-or-so splendid maps which appear here. The gratitude of Robin Prior and Trevor Wilson knows no bounds.

The principal dedication of this book will be found on another page. Trevor Wilson would also like to dedicate his contribution to this work to his colleagues and students at Marshall University, West Virginia, in the fall of 1989; and in particular to the members of the Mycroft Group – Paul Rakes, Jeff Bevins, Stephen Fisher, and John Barker.

Note The translations from German documents in this book are the work of Beate Josephi and Eleanor Hancock. A first draft of the index was prepared by Elizabeth Greenhalgh.

PART I

Prelude

I

Apprenticeship

I

This book is an account of Sir Henry Rawlinson's career as a military commander on the Western Front from late 1914 to November 1918. That is, it covers both the long years of stalemate from the opening of 1915 to the end of 1917 and the dramatic months of 1918 during which the static war gave way to measured advance. It seeks to establish what role this commander played in devising battles, what responsibility attaches to him when all did not go well, and how great was his contribution to the ultimate success of British arms.

Studies of the conduct of warfare on the Western Front are numerous. But studies of the conflict at those levels of command occupied by Rawlinson are not. The fighting in France and Belgium has largely captured attention at two levels. One is the level of high command. This embraces grand strategy: the conflict between generals and politicians, or between 'Westerners' and 'Easterners'. To say that the topic has been exhausted would be to miss the point. In large measure the topic never existed. The struggle was play-acting, springing from the reluctance of sensitive men to acknowledge military necessity. As far as Britain was concerned, the war would be fought on the Western Front or it would be abandoned. None of the political masters who decried the actions of the generals wished to call off the war. Hence they could do little but wring their hands and dispatch additional men and weapons to the cauldron.

A second sort of writing about the war on the Western Front has enjoyed great currency. It concerns the participants on the ground: the experiences of the fighting men, as related in memoirs or poetry or imaginative literature. The appeal of this aspect of the war is not to be wondered at. The experience of the fighting man in the First World War was so intense, and often so atrocious, that it is bound to excite strong sentiments: amazement that individuals could endure so much and dismay that human-kind should be reduced to such transactions.

But the war as seen by the occupants of the trenches was not the war seen whole. The struggles of individuals and small companies were not necessarily a reflection of what was occurring over an entire battlefield. They could not reveal whether the purposes of one side or the other were being advanced. What was more, the endeavours of the fighting men, though certainly the most poignant, were not necessarily the most import-ant element in deciding whether the day of battle would go well or ill. That might already have been determined by the actions and decisions of politicians and bureaucrats, of industrial entrepreneurs, of skilled and unskilled labourers, of military technocrats, and of the red-tabbed soldiers who planned the battles even though they did not participate in them.

This book deals with one of the participants who devised operations but never came within range of the enemy's guns. It looks at military command below the level of grand strategy but decidedly at the level where some of the key decisions in prosecuting warfare would be made: for, as Paul Kennedy has recently proposed, 'it was at the tactical level in this war . . . that the critical problems occurred.'[1] If a study of war at this level lacks the emotive content both of the struggles between com-manders and politicians and of the experiences undergone by those placed at the cutting-edge of warfare, it may be thought to possess other merits. It lays bare the actual course of the war. And it makes clear why stalemate persisted for so long and yet eventually gave way to a different sort of war, in which one side made discernible progress while the other lost its capacity to resist.

There are various reasons for choosing Sir Henry Rawlinson as the subject of this case study. In the course of the Great War he saw command at several key levels, principally those of corps commander and Army commander. From the outset he was (and except where death intervened he remained) a close associate of diversely important individuals such as Lord Kitchener, Sir Henry Wilson, and Sir Douglas Haig. Between 1915 and 1918 he participated in several momentous episodes of battle. For example he exercised a major command in what is generally deemed the blackest day of the British army in modern war (1 July 1916), and he presided over what is habitually described as the Black Day of the German army in the Great War (8 August 1918). And he bestowed

---

[1] Paul Kennedy, 'Britain in the First World War', in Allan R. Millett and Williamson Murray (eds), *Military Effectiveness*, vol. 1 (London: Unwin Hyman, 1988), p. 330.

upon posterity a formidable quantity of written material about his part in the war. In sum, if a study of Rawlinson does not exhaust the subject of command on the Western Front, it may be thought exhaustive enough. Or to put that another way, one may doubt whether much of additional moment will emerge from expounding all aspects of the subject and not just Rawlinson's segment of it.

II

In no sense is this a biography. Nor is it an account of Rawlinson's entire military career. The former would be decidedly dull; for, along with Haig, French, Plumer, Byng, and most other prominent figures in the British military hierarchy during the First World War, Rawlinson personally was of no great interest. (Henry Wilson, almost alone among this company, may be thought to have possessed an arresting personality, if of a rather repellent sort.) A book embracing Rawlinson's whole military career would be obliged to deal rather sketchily with so varied a selection of topics as to lack real unity or continuity. For except in the artificial world of the biography, hunting dacoits (rebel bands) in Burma, seeking to rupture the German lines on the Somme, supervising the evacuation of Archangel, and maintaining Britain's military presence in India really do not belong in the same volume.

Nevertheless it is appropriate briefly to sketch in Rawlinson's career in the years prior to the emergence of stalemate on the Western Front. He was the son of a famous Assyriologist whose success in deciphering a particular Persian cuneiform inscription was rated second in importance only to the translation of the Rosetta Stone. The senior Rawlinson – whose given name was also Henry – in addition saw military service in India and came to hold strong views on the menace to Britain's position of Russian penetration into Afghanistan. (His strictures against 'allowing Russia to work her way to Kabul unopposed' have a decidedly contemporary ring. The context, however, is hardly similar. What Rawlinson père feared was that the Russians intended to establish themselves in Kabul 'as a friendly power prepared to protect the Afghans against the English.') These opinions secured the favour and friendship of a future commander-in-chief in India, Frederick (later Lord) Roberts, who would advance the young Henry Rawlinson's service career.

The Rawlinson who figures in this study was born in 1864 and educated at Eton, where his enthusiasm for sports assured him of a comfortable passage. He entered Sandhurst just before turning 19 and was soon seeing service in India – interrupted in 1886–7 by an interlude hunting dacoits in Burma. In 1889, on the illness (soon followed by the death) of his mother, he returned to England, where he took upon himself the care of his ageing father, and also entered into wedlock. (The marriage endured for the rest of his life. It yielded no offspring.) He entered staff college, where he profited greatly from the teaching skills and engaging personality of the military historian G. F. R. Henderson. If the main concern of the British army in the 1890s remained the defence of India, Henderson's course of instruction took his students to regions more appropriate to the struggle that was to occur two decades later: to the battles of the American Civil War, and to the Prussian campaign against France in 1870–1.

Rawlinson was particularly impressed by a tour of the battlefields of the Franco-Prussian War. With his friend Henry Wilson he returned for a closer inspection, followed by a visit to the military establishments of France and Germany. Some of his conclusions are instructive. For the military machine of Germany, in particular, he conceived a considerable admiration. Contrasting it with the British army, he observed: 'We live in watertight compartments, the infantry know nothing about the artillery, nor the artillery anything about the infantry, the cavalry nothing about either. In the big [German] garrisons like Metz the troops are always working together, and their brigades and divisions are realities, not paper organisations like ours are.'[2] This concern at the way in which Britain's forces compartmentalized what should have been interlocking arms was reinforced when, in 1894, he visited Malta. There he inspected a number of modern British battleships and cruisers. While accepting that naval and military gunnery served different purposes, he noted presciently: 'in some things they [the navy] have a good deal to teach us, particularly in the use of optical instruments, many of which could be adapted to use in the field. It is the old story of watertight compartments. It is no one's business to pool experience.' Soon after, a visit to Gibraltar reinforced his conviction that military artillery had much to learn from naval.

In 1895 Rawlinson graduated (with the rank of brigade-major) to Aldershot, where he established a reputation as a staff officer of promise. His capacities were soon put to the test. In January 1898 either chance or sound management found him in Cairo, where his wife had been directed for her health. Just then Kitchener was launching his expedition against Khartoum, and proved in need of a staff officer to manage the influx of troops. Rawlinson got the job, so for the first time occupying a responsible

---

[2] The direct quotations from Rawlinson in this chapter and the next are all derived from Sir Frederick Maurice, *The Life of General Lord Rawlinson of Trent* (London: Cassell, 1928), chapters 2 to 6.

position during a major military episode. Kitchener habitually operated with a less-than-sufficient staff, and hence during the culminating march on Khartoum Rawlinson was working at full stretch. On him devolved much of the job of transferring fresh arrivals to the front and banding them into the newly created division which Kitchener had deemed appropriate for his enlarged forces. The favourable impression Rawlinson thus created would soon stand him in good stead.

A year after Khartoum, Britain entered its longest and most testing colonial war, that against the Boers of South Africa. Rawlinson, equipped with some books on that country along with Henderson's famous study of Stonewall Jackson, was soon on his way to take up a staff appointment. In short order he found himself besieged in Ladysmith, where he formed a strong appreciation for the enemy's skill with artillery. So of one Boer victory he observed:

> What surprised me most at Lombard's Kop was the Boer artillery. Their field-guns have more range and power than ours, and their shooting was amazingly accurate. This is an eye-opener to our gunners... [who] think too much of their horses and not enough of their guns.

Rawlinson's insight into artillery matters soon began contributing significantly to the defence of Ladysmith. Before the trap had closed he had managed to have some long-range naval guns brought into the town, to the good fortune of the defenders.

Ladysmith was relieved at the beginning of March 1900. By then Rawlinson's long-term benefactor, Roberts, had taken command in South Africa, with Kitchener as his Chief of Staff. Rawlinson, to his considerable satisfaction ('It will be a joy to be with Bobs and Kitchener once more'), was promptly appointed to their staff, joining their mess and living in Roberts's house 'which is spacious and comfortable'. This called forth the contented comment: 'so I have kept up my practice of falling on my feet.' (It added to his satisfaction that the company was shortly joined by his good friend Henry Wilson.) Rawlinson was soon thoroughly occupied in assembling into a coherent force the widely dispersed bodies of troops, of various types and origin, which were to accomplish the advance on Pretoria. This served to provide him with the experience of expanding a self-contained peacetime army into the altogether larger force which a particular war might require.

In November 1900, assuming the war to be as good as over, Roberts returned to Britain, leaving Kitchener in command. Rawlinson also went home, but not for long. The Boers resorted to an effective form of guerilla warfare, and Rawlinson promptly re-embarked to join Kitchener's staff.

(This, he noted somewhat laconically, was 'a great shock to my wife'; however, 'she has taken it like a soldier' – probably the highest praise he could bestow on a person of either sex.) Initially he was engaged in the same staff duties as under Roberts, but Kitchener – responding to some powerful hints from Rawlinson – soon gave him a command in the field. Rawlinson seems thoroughly to have enjoyed the brief episodes of action which this provided, even though on one of them he became – if only for a matter of minutes – the prisoner of two Boers who had shot his horse from under him.

From this phase of the war in South Africa, Rawlinson emerged with a reputation as an efficient commander in the field.

> K. has been very nice to me and very complimentary [he wrote on 2 January 1902]. He is going to . . . give me a big column of 2,000 men to hunt de Wet in the Orange River Colony . . . Altogether my paper strength will be 2,400 mounted men, 6 guns, and 8 pom-poms. I am going up in the world.

Rawlinson commanded one of four columns (among the other commanders was Julian Byng, who would conclude the Great War directing an Army on Rawlinson's left) which in the following weeks pressed the Boers hard. By 27 February he was writing: 'This has been a great day. We had hemmed in the greater part of de Wet's commando, and this morning they sent in to negotiate a surrender.' Rawlinson was promptly transferred to the Western Transvaal, where matters had not been going so well for the British. There his column was part of a force under Ian Hamilton's direction which inflicted on the Boers their last defeats of the war.

The Boers finally abandoned the struggle in May 1902, and Rawlinson said farewell to his forces in mid-June, summing up 'what we had done together':

> Since I took over command on April 1, 1901, we have marched 5,211 miles, and we have halted in 276 camps. The casualties we have inflicted on the Boers come to 64 killed, and 87 wounded. We have taken 1,376 prisoners, 3 guns, 1,082 rifles, and 68,600 rounds of ammunition. There have been no regrettable incidents, and our own casualties have been 12 killed and 42 wounded.

It was a very different war, in scale as well as mobility, from that in which he would next find himself engaged.

Rawlinson sought to draw the military lessons which the fighting in South Africa had to offer. His observations suggest a fair level of military sagacity. The volunteer soldier was to be preferred to the conscript, he wrote, and more attention should be paid to the training in peacetime of volunteer bodies. (His views here would later be abandoned under the pressure of Lord Roberts's campaign for peacetime military conscription.) Of the various elements in the British army, the infantry, Rawlinson concluded, 'remains the only arm that can decide the issue of battle.' (As weapons 'increase in range and power', he noted presciently, the cavalry should be 'trained to fight on foot' – an oblique way of saying that they should cease to function as cavalry.) Infantry must therefore be trained to shoot better and faster, must possess well-equipped machine-gun companies, and must learn better to co-operate with the artillery.

Not all of Rawlinson's reflections on the Boer War were blessed with this degree of sense. He could still take a romantic view of conflict in which victory would go to the side possessing the superior willpower. So his concluding dictum read: 'The moment when a battle seems to be lost is the moment to refuse to accept defeat and to attack with every available man and gun.'

On his return to Britain Rawlinson was assigned, under Roberts's benevolent direction, first to the newly created department of education at the War Office, then as commandant of the staff college – at a time when its courses were becoming both broader in scope and more adapted to military realities. He spent three years there, after which he was given command of an infantry brigade at Aldershot. Then, on his promotion to major-general, he spent four years commanding a division on Salisbury Plain. He travelled much. Business took him to Canada (briefly he toyed with the idea of forsaking the peacetime army for a business career in North America). Invitations from Kitchener took him to India and the Far East (on the latter journey he travelled via Germany and Russia). And the threat implicit in German railway construction towards the Belgian frontier took him to the valley of the Sambre to observe these ominous developments.

All the time Rawlinson was seeking to divine the lessons to be learned from recent wars and current changes. With the aid of his travels, he pondered on the Russo-Japanese War and the military establishments of Germany and Japan. He continued to keep abreast of developments in artillery, and to stress the importance of equipping British infantry with ample machine-guns. After witnessing the peacetime manoeuvres of the Japanese army he wrote:

The Japs have six machine-guns per regiment, and nearly always employ them massed. This is practically the same as the machine-gun company which I have been advocating for our infantry brigades. The result, in the Japanese Army, is that their machine-guns are far better handled than are ours, better use is made of ground, and

there is more initiative in their machine-gun officers, because they
feel they are of importance, and are understood.

He also observed the superior manner in which the Japanese, as against
the British, employed their engineers so as to have them functioning closely
with the infantry.

Yet for all his seeking after wisdom, Rawlinson proved sadly astray in his
reading of one of the lessons of the Russo-Japanese War. After studying
the ground of the battles of Port Arthur, Mukden, and Liao-yang, he
concluded that the slow progress of the Japanese to victory in these actions
was attributable to lack of enterprise and an excess of deliberation: 'It is to
Japanese caution, rather than to trenches, that I ascribe the length of the
battle.' Few among the military establishments of Western Europe would
have felt cause to challenge this ominous miscalculation.

Yet notwithstanding this misjudgement, it is fair to say that when war
came to Europe in 1914 Rawlinson was well equipped to exercise command
in battle. He had directed troops under fire, and shown capacity as a staff
officer of a force rapidly expanding under pressures of war. Although
it remains customary to write him off as one of the First World War's
outmoded cavalry officers (so an historian in the *Canadian Defence Quarterly*
for autumn 1988 speaks of 'cavalry generals Haig and Rawlinson'),[3] he
was in truth a commander of infantry with a developing appreciation of
the effect modern weaponry must have in reducing the role of horse-
soldiers in battle. Certainly he had failed to appreciate the stopping-power
of entrenched defenders against even the most devoted attackers, and had
overrated the ability of morale to overcome material obstacles. Nevertheless
he showed commendable concern for that facet of war which was to loom
so large in the endeavours of the British army during the Great War: the
marriage of infantry with ample fire power – in particular the fire power
of machine-guns and artillery. (Shortly before the outbreak of war, he
even revealed an appreciation of the part which aeroplanes were likely
to play in any coming conflict.) Rawlinson, in sum, was an obvious and
appropriate choice for responsible command in the British army which
burgeoned in Western Europe in the weeks following the declaration of
war in 1914.

---

[3] Brereton Greenhous, '... It was chiefly a Canadian battle', *Canadian Defence Quarterly*, 18
(Autumn 1988), p. 78.

2

Into Battle, August–December 1914

I

As chance had it, on 1 August 1914 Rawlinson was not employed. Having handed over command of his division a few months earlier, he was on half pay and without official occupation. The outbreak of war terminated this spell of inactivity, although not in a manner he found particularly agreeable. Instead of being given a command in the field, he was appointed Director of Recruiting at the War Office. At least this renewed his association with Kitchener, who just then was entering the government as Secretary of State for War. Kitchener, foreseeing a war of three years' duration, determined to raise a mass army by voluntary means. Rawlinson readily endorsed Kitchener's view that the war would not end speedily and that the 'new armies' – which would require a year at least to train and equip – would be needed on the battlefield before victory came in sight. That judgement brought Rawlinson into friendly disputation with Henry Wilson, who even after the fighting had bogged down on the Aisne in September clung to the view that with 'a big effort' the war would be over by Christmas and that Kitchener's 'ridiculous armies' would never see battle.

Rawlinson soon made the transition – for which he ached – from the War Office to the battlefield. At first it was intended that he should take command of two divisions being assembled in Britain out of regular army troops drawn from colonial stations. But just then the commander of 4 Division in France suffered injury and Rawlinson was sent out to replace him. This gave him a first, albeit brief, glimpse of stalemated trench warfare as it had developed on the Aisne. That appointment also proved short-lived. At the beginning of October he was summoned to GHQ to hear that Kitchener had another task for him. This was to take command of a force (consisting of 7 Division, one of the 'overseas' divisions for whose formation he might have had responsibility, and the 3rd Cavalry Division) which was being landed on the southern Belgian coast. Its destination was Antwerp, which was still holding out against the Germans but was in danger of being cut off.

From the outset this was a Cinderella undertaking. Joffre, the French commander-in-chief, entirely disapproved of the project. So did Sir John French, commander of the British Expeditionary Force (BEF), who in addition resented Rawlinson's being accorded an independent command within French's own patch of territory. Anyway, the attempt to save Antwerp was doomed by the time Rawlinson reached the scene. The Belgian forces were much demoralized. The French were attempting to turn the German right flank on the Western Front proper and so had no surplus troops for a separate operation. And the Germans had brought to Antwerp their monster artillery, earlier employed to demolish the Liège forts. Rawlinson himself visited Antwerp briefly, but his troops were still well distant from the city when the Belgian authorities decided to evacuate it.

The force, consisting of one infantry and one cavalry division under Rawlinson's direction, was now renamed IV Corps and placed within the jurisdiction of Sir John French (a situation which Rawlinson found preferable to that of trying to serve several masters). It was ordered back to Roulers in western Belgium, where it joined up with the BEF as a whole. Meanwhile French's army had been moved from the Aisne in central France to Belgium in the hope of finding open country and an opportunity to turn the German flank. But no such opportunity awaited it. The enemy were in the process of assembling an imposing body of men and guns in order to strike at the port of Calais. The BEF constituted their principal obstacle.

II

Rawlinson's 7 Division reached Ypres on 14 October, 'rather tired after their wet march', and with orders to set off again at 6 a.m. Rawlinson was not sure where they were expected to go, and was somewhat alarmed at 'a big gap of from 8 to 10 miles on my left, between me and the Belgian Army. If this is not filled tomorrow, we shall be liable to get in a mess.' Nor was this the extent of his worries. On his right, his troops were in advance of the neighbouring III Corps. Rumours of a further retreat by the Belgians well to his left, and of impending movements towards his flanks by the Germans, also did not reassure him. These misgivings were not shared by Sir John French, who brought strong pressure to bear on Rawlinson to push forward to Menin, in a south-eastern direction. Given that this could well expose his flank and rear to oncoming German forces, Rawlinson, on 18 October, chose to make haste somewhat slowly. That brought upon him strong representations from the command to get a move on. Nevertheless, Rawlinson failed to increase his pace.

His caution proved fortuitous. For on 19 October, as 7 Division was about to advance towards Menin, 'heavy German columns came down on my flank from the east.' Rawlinson extricated his force from a potentially dangerous position 'with 150 casualties'. This display of sound judgement brought upon him the severe disfavour of Sir John French. At a meeting between the corps commanders and their chief on 20 October, Rawlinson found Sir John 'very cold to me, and evidently still angry about Menin.'

The events of the next few days did not serve to heal the breach. Rawlinson was little more than a helpless spectator as his overextended 7 Division bore the brunt of the German assault. 'We are only hanging on by our eyelids,' he related on 25 October, 'our losses in the last two days have been 100 officers and 2,000 men, exclusive of the Wiltshire Regiment... Most of our troubles and losses have come from being on such a wide front. We have to take up these wide fronts in order to get our flanks far enough out to avoid envelopment by the Germans. We want more men, and always more men.'

Rawlinson's manner of conveying such sentiments to his chief proved less than felicitous. In a telegram to Sir John he concluded with an observation that 'when the 8th Division arrives, it will be easier to hold a front of eight miles.' This aroused Sir John's ire, as Rawlinson discovered when he endeavoured to call on his chief at GHQ: 'He thought this [observation] cheeky, and would not see me. Archie Murray [French's Chief of Staff] gave me a long talking to, and said that my wire had given Sir John a sleepless night, because, of course, there was truth in what I said.' Simultaneously Rawlinson received a note from Sir William Lambton, French's military secretary, telling him he must apologize 'and eat humble pie' if he wanted to retain his command, adding: 'I think your telegram is rather impertinent, not to say improper, and don't wonder at the anger; but don't you be a fool, and climb down.' Rawlinson hastened to send a note of apology, and received a conciliatory reply: 'We have always been great friends; let us remain so.' But clearly these events rankled with Sir John. In his official dispatch published in November, he commented adversely on Rawlinson's reluctance to advance towards Menin. While stating that Rawlinson's lack of action was 'probably wise', he held that it had facilitated the rapid reinforcement of the enemy force around Menin and 'thus rendered any further advance impracticable':[1] a backhanded way of saying that Rawlinson's actions were not wise at all. It was plain that

[1] Sir John French, *Despatches* (London: War Office, 1915), p. 42.

his opening weeks of command on the Western Front had left Rawlinson insecurely placed, at any rate as long as Sir John French remained in charge of Britain's forces.

Late in October Rawlinson's cavalry division was transferred to the cavalry corps under Allenby. With only one division (the 7th) left under his hand, his job as a corps commander appeared in danger of disappearing. So he was more than happy to act on a suggestion from Henry Wilson and repair to England to assemble 8 Division which would provide a second element to his corps. (Wilson wanted him to give it 'a darn good lecturing' on how to fight and how to dig and where to dig.) While in London he took the opportunity – which he would not neglect on subsequent occasions – to call on persons of importance: in this instance Kitchener (already at odds with some of his Cabinet colleagues), the King, and Lord Roberts. (The last-named, a few weeks later, was to die of pleurisy while visiting the front.) The authorities were much exercised about a possible German invasion of Britain, causing Rawlinson to wonder whether they would allow his new division to leave the country. (Wilson wrote him at the time wishing that Kitchener would get over his invasion fright: 'It is pitiable.') However, by 6 November Rawlinson was back at GHQ, accompanied by his reinforcements.

Much had happened in his absence. The battle of Ypres had reached a crisis on 31 October, when his 7 Division was battered almost out of existence. So grave had the situation become that Henry Wilson was anticipating the loss of Ypres, and finding comfort only in the fact that 'we shall get a narrower front, which we must get somehow, as we are not able to hold a line of thirty-five miles with about five or six divisions.' Wilson's pessimism, like his optimism earlier, proved unwarranted. If British forces were diminishing under the German onslaught, the toll of casualties being imposed on the enemy was proving greater than the German command felt able to accept. The offensive ground to a halt. The town of Ypres – and therefore the Channel ports – remained in Allied hands.

Rawlinson's IV Corps settled down near Neuve Chapelle for the winter: 'one of the wettest winters', as Rawlinson recorded, 'in Flanders for the last 20 years', and in consequence exceptionally disagreeable for trench-dwellers. 'This is only January 9,' Rawlinson wrote, 'and we have already had the whole of the rain which in normal years falls up to the end of February.' Rawlinson availed himself of the opportunity to take stock. In the western theatre, he wrote privately, the moment was not at hand for 'a serious push'. 'Our time is not yet ... I have always contended that this will be a long, and not a short, war.' Not before the spring would the Allies be ready to do 'big things': 'Rifles, equipment, clothing, etc., have all got to be made', and that could not be done 'in a month, nor in six months.' 'Most important of all', he added with commendable prescience, 'is artillery ammunition. We are *all* short of it, even Germany.'

The position then, he concluded, was that the two sides were facing each other along a line of 400 miles, and were losing on each side at least 2,000 men a day ('our little British Army loses about 200 to 300 a day'). 'So long as we maintain our general line we have nothing to fear.' But there could be no question of driving the Germans out of France and Belgium 'with our present numbers and existing shortage of artillery ammunition.' There might be small pushes, but it must await Kitchener's mass army and the last classes of the French soldiers before 'we can undertake the big offensive.' 'That may be next year.'

Events would prove Rawlinson's cautious timetable to err, anyway as far as the British contribution was concerned, on the side of optimism.

PART II

Neuve Chapelle,
March 1915

3

The Plan

I

Rawlinson was to participate in some of the key battles fought by the BEF in 1915. In order to make sense of those events, it is necessary to provide an outline of how the British army was organized.

At the commencement of 1915 the BEF, under its commander-in-chief Sir John French, was divided into a First and Second Army each with its subordinate corps and divisions.

The key component in this organization was the division. As in most European armies of the time, a British division constituted a self-contained

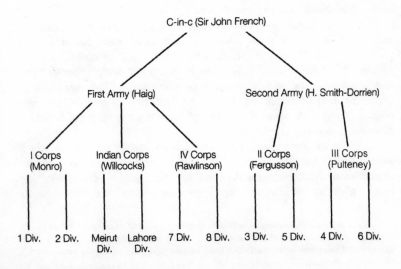

fighting unit. It had its own field artillery (consisting of eighteen 18 pounders, six 4.5 inch howitzers, and six 60 pounders), twenty-four machine-guns, and transport in the form of horses and – to a lesser extent – trucks. A division consisted of approximately 19,000 men. About 12,000 of these were infantry and 4,000 artillery. The remainder were transport, medical, headquarters, and support staff. Typically the division was commanded by a Major-General.

A division was itself subdivided into three brigades, each made up of four battalions. A battalion consisted of about 1,000 men, and was further broken up into companies, platoons, and sections.

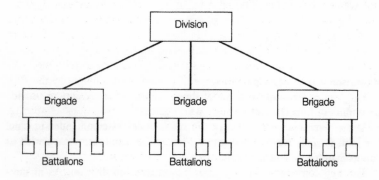

A division almost always fought as an entity. This was not the case with the higher formations of corps and Armies.

A corps consisted of a number of staff officers grouped together to administer the two or more divisions placed under their direction for a particular battle. It was the corps commander's job to co-ordinate the actions and plans of these divisions in battle, to supply direction to them, and to interpret the wishes of the Army commander. The corps was an important level of command, for all the field artillery outside divisional control, along with some of the heavy artillery supporting the attacking divisions, was under corps control.

On a similar pattern, an Army was a headquarters staff under which were placed a number of corps.[1] An Army commander was directly responsible to the commander-in-chief for the conduct of a battle, and usually it was at this level that the outline plan of attack was drawn up. As

---

[1] In order to distinguish between the British army in general and its component Armies, the capital letter will be used for the latter: so 'Army' always refers to one of the two or three or four or five Armies into which the British army became subdivided as the war proceeded.

divisions moved in and out of corps in accordance with circumstances, so corps moved in and out of Armies. The Army commander only controlled directly the heaviest of the artillery, along with the aircraft allotted to spot for these weapons. He might or might not command a reserve of troops to employ as the battle developed.

II

By January 1915, the commanders of Britain's military forces (like those of the other European powers) were confronting a world both unfamiliar and scarcely hospitable. The opening months of war, admittedly, had not proved entirely barren. In terms of thwarting the enemy's larger designs, a measure of success had rewarded the Anglo-French endeavours. Western Europe had not fallen to the Germans, even though most of Belgium and a part of France had. But this ambiguous achievement presented the commanders of France and Britain with a difficulty.

The potency of earthwork trenches as a form of defensive had halted movement on the Western Front. It was far from clear how – with the weaponry available at that time – the armies of either side could proceed from standstill to forward movement. Yet plainly the combatants could not stay where they were. The Germans would not have achieved their purpose until they had overrun France. The French and British could not contemplate terminating hostilities short of expelling the invader from the soil of France and Belgium.

Among those who had to grapple with the practical consequences of this impasse, if hardly at the highest level, was Sir Henry Rawlinson. Neither the teaching of staff college nor the experience of battle on the veldt could provide him with much guidance. To his credit, he had derived from past operations both a healthy regard for the interdependence between infantry and artillery and some experience in rapidly expanding a military force under the demands of battle. But this was something short of an education in the great problems confronting those, at whatever level, exercising authority on the Western Front. By what means, and employing what resources, might an attacking force penetrate the barrier of trench defences and force its occupants into large-scale retreat?

III

Rawlinson, as already related, was commander of the IV Corps of the BEF, consisting of two divisions (7 and 8). By the opening of 1915 it constituted

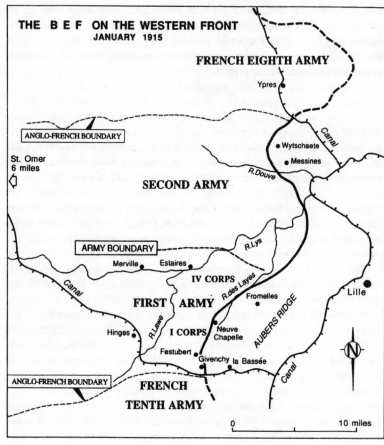

THE B E F ON THE WESTERN FRONT
JANUARY 1915

FRENCH EIGHTH ARMY

Ypres

ANGLO-FRENCH BOUNDARY

St. Omer
6 miles

Wytschaete

Messines

R.Douve

Canal

SECOND ARMY

ARMY BOUNDARY

R.Lys

Merville   Estaires

IV CORPS

R.des Layes

Fromelles

Lille

FIRST   ARMY

Canal

R.Lawe

Hinges

I CORPS

Neuve
Chapelle

AUBERS RIDGE

Festubert

Givenchy la Bassée

ANGLO-FRENCH BOUNDARY

FRENCH

TENTH ARMY

Canal

N

0   10 miles

Note   by March 1915, I Corps replaced in front line by Indian Corps.

MAP I

part of Douglas Haig's First Army, and occupied the northern sector of
that Army's front in a low-lying part of Flanders. The region consisted
largely of water meadows intersected by numerous drainage ditches and
canals. The water table was so close to the surface that deep digging was
impossible. Hence the British position consisted of shallow trenches, protected by earth and sandbag breastworks. During winter the trenches were
never dry and in early January Rawlinson reported that 50 per cent had
been evacuated due to flooding.[2] With the spring, however, the ground

[2] Rawlinson Diary 10/1/15, Rawlinson Papers 1/1, Churchill College, Cambridge

began to dry, and Haig was moved to contemplate ways of improving the tactical position on his front. His choice was an attack on the village of Neuve Chapelle. This happened to fall within the sector occupied by IV Corps, thus involving Rawlinson in the first set-piece offensive against an entrenched adversary delivered by the British army in the Great War.

There were good, though minor, tactical reasons for capturing Neuve Chapelle. The enemy trenches in front of the village formed a salient which jutted into the British position, thus enabling the Germans to bring enfilade fire against the right and left of the IV Corps line. Capturing the village would straighten the British line and eliminate the enfilade fire. By the same token, because the German position did form a salient, it was vulnerable to any convergent artillery fire which IV Corps could direct against it.

On 6 February, Haig ordered Rawlinson to develop proposals for the capture of Neuve Chapelle, adding: 'I [hope] to be ready for the operation in about 10 days.'[3] This unrealistic timetable indicated how much the commanders still had to learn. As Rawlinson realized, the state of the ground would not allow offensive operations to be undertaken for some weeks.[4] Also the planning process must prove more protracted and painful than Haig had anticipated.

This was true even though the German defences protecting the Neuve Chapelle salient were rudimentary (at least by later standards) and had little depth. The main feature was a front line breastwork made of earth and sandbags, built up 4 feet from the ground and approximately 5 feet thick. Protecting it was a double row of barbed wire, supported on 'knife rests'. The wire varied in depth from 6 to 15 feet.[5] Behind the German front line were various small communication trenches. There was also Neuve Chapelle village. This was in ruins, although the church tower still stood; and there had been no attempt by the Germans to fortify the houses. Nevertheless, it constituted something of an obstacle to an attack. Beyond the village lay a shallow trench dug by the BEF itself during its retreat in late 1914. (It was known to the British as the Smith-Dorrien trench.) And a small stream, the Layes Brook, ran behind the front. This was thought by

(hereafter CC). There are two Rawlinson diaries in existence. One consists largely of a list of the people he met during the day and the meetings he attended. It is held by the National Army Museum, Chelsea, London (hereafter NAM) and will be referred to as 'Rawlinson Short Note Diary'. The more detailed diary containing Rawlinson's reflections on events is the one referred to above. Hereafter it will be cited as 'Rawlinson Diary'.

[3] Haig Diary 6/2/15, Haig Papers, National Library of Scotland.
[4] Rawlinson Diary 8/2/15.
[5] Brigadier E. C. Anstey, 'The History of the Royal Artillery 1914–1918'. (Unpublished draft in the Royal Artillery Institution, Woolwich.)

the British to be a major obstacle in the sector which faced the still-wooded
Bois du Biez.[6]

Rawlinson had good information regarding most of these defences.
Some of it had been gathered by observation from high points behind the
British front.[7] But a substantial contribution had been made by a major
innovation in warfare – aerial photography. Although the cameras used
at this time were crude and the methods employed primitive (sometimes
a camera was hand-held by the observer), the results were encouraging. So
by 22 February Haig was speaking of 'the wonderful maps of the enemy's
trenches which we now had as the result of the aeroplane reconnaissances . . .
[enabling us] to make our plans very carefully beforehand and with full
knowledge of how the enemy's trenches run, his communication trenches
etc.'[8]

By 7 March the Royal Flying Corps (RFC) had photographed the
German position from the front line to a depth of 700 to 1,500 yards.
Between 1,000 and 1,500 maps assembled from these photographs were
issued to each corps and to the artillery.[9] Nevertheless, a key component of
the German defences seems to have escaped the attention of the British
commanders. About 1,000 yards behind the German front was a series of
concrete strongpoints designed to hold machine-gun nests once battle had
been joined. They had been built in early February and sited to sweep the
flat ground immediately behind the German front. In the event of the
British making a breach in the enemy's front line, these were the points
on which the defence was to pivot.[10]

There remained the question of the Germans' weaponry and manpower.
Rawlinson and Haig knew that the enemy artillery on the first day of battle
would be weak. The Germans possessed only six 4-gun batteries in the
area under attack, although these could be reinforced by others from the
flanks.[11] The commanders also estimated that the salient was held by only
2,000 German infantry, against an attacking force of 12,000. But they
were aware that this numerical advantage would be short-lived – GHQ

---

[6] Information on the German defences at Neuve Chapelle has been taken from two works
by Captain G. C. Wynne, both based on German Regimental sources: *If Germany Attacks: The
Battle in Depth in the West* (London: Faber, 1940), pp. 20–2 and 'The Other Side of the Hill:
no. XVII: Neuve Chapelle 10th–12th of March, 1915', *Army Quarterly*, 37 (1938–9), pp.
30–46.

[7] Haig Diary 18/2/15.

[8] Ibid. 22/2/15.

[9] 'Memorandum On The Attack on Neuve Chapelle by First Army', n.d., IV Corps War
Diary March 1915, WO 95/708.

[10] Wynne, *If Germany Attacks*, p. 22. Wynne claims that the existence of these strongpoints
was known to British GHQ, but we can find no evidence to support this.

[11] Ibid.

calculated that the enemy could bring in another 4,000 men within 12 hours of the attack and 16,000 all told by the evening of the second day.[12] So speed was of the essence of any successful offensive.

IV

Rawlinson's response to his very first directive to produce a plan of attack was somewhat odd. He did not attempt to come up with an outline plan himself, but passed the whole problem to his two divisional commanders. One of them, General Capper, did not (as far as can be discovered) ever respond. But General Davies, in charge of 8 Division, did produce a 'Memorandum on the Attack of Neuve Chapelle'.[13] Rawlinson deemed it 'well and carefully worked out',[14] but his actions belie this judgement. He rejected each of its principal aspects. So where Davies proposed a series of sapping operations, Rawlinson substituted what he called 'bombard and storm', whereby the enemy trenches would be pounded by artillery after which the infantry would overwhelm them on a broad front. Rawlinson made it clear that a decisive predominance of artillery would be needed:

> An undertaking such as that which is under consideration depends for its success almost entirely on the correct and efficient employ-ment of the artillery. It is primarily an artillery operation and if the artillery cannot crush and demoralise the enemy's infantry by their fire effect the enterprise will not succeed.[15]

This was highly prescient. Indeed in these few remarks Rawlinson indicated the principal feature of battles on the Western Front during the next four years. What remained to be seen, on this as on subsequent occasions, was whether principle and practice would march hand in hand.

Apart from the method to be employed, Rawlinson did not here set forth any particular plan for the Neuve Chapelle operation. Yet from Haig's point of view it was becoming urgently necessary that one reach him. For on 8 February a new factor had entered the situation. Sir John French requested that his two Army commanders, Haig and Sir Horace Smith-Dorrien, provide plans for offensive operations.[16] Haig was no

[12] GHQ, 'Special Order of the Day', 9/3/15; GHQ, 'Movement of German Reserves', 8/3/15 in 'Neuve Chapelle – Operations', WO 158/181.
[13] See IV Corps War Diary Jan–Feb 1915, WO 95/707.
[14] Rawlinson, 'Remarks on VIIIth Division Scheme' in ibid.
[15] Ibid.
[16] Haig Diary 9/2/15.

doubt anxious that such operations should be conducted on his front, rather than on that of Smith-Dorrien's Second Army. Yet Smith-Dorrien could propose an attack of considerable tactical importance, namely the capture of the Wytschaete–Messines Ridge. Against this, the storming of an insignificant village in order to straighten the line might well seem not worthy of consideration.

Haig's first step, therefore, was to increase the scope of Rawlinson's operation so as to include objectives whose capture, it might seem, would have far-reaching consequences. He also held out the possibility of joint action with the French. The attack would take Neuve Chapelle in the first rush and would then push forward to the Aubers Ridge. From there the enemy's position around La Bassée could be seriously threatened and an advance on the mining area south of Lille made in conjunction with the French. He held that this was far superior to any operation which might be mounted on Second Army's sector:

> In my opinion it is better to advance from this front rather than from Ypres, because we can directly co-operate with the French about Arras which is the main theatre ... The French will not co-operate at Ypres and if we drive back the enemy from Ypres we soon come up against a strong position on the Lys, and then the forts of Lille.[17]

The scope of the whole operation had thus considerably widened since Haig first requested a plan from Rawlinson. Whether the resources at IV Corps's disposal, while possibly sufficient for an attempt at straightening the line, were adequate for a thrust towards Lille was not a matter which appeared to be engaging Haig.

Haig's next step was to call a conference for 15 February of his corps commanders, Rawlinson (IV Corps) and Willcocks (Indian Corps). At the conference he announced that the attack would be carried out by their units and explained the extended nature of operations envisaged: 'I asked Corps Commanders to give me a written statement by Saturday [20 February], showing how they proposed to carry out the orders I had given them'.[18]

Additional urgency was promptly added by the intervention of the French. On 16 February Joffre informed GHQ that he intended assaulting Vimy Ridge, and he suggested British co-operation in the form of an attack on Aubers Ridge to his left.[19] At this point the large Anglo-French operation foreshadowed by Haig became a real prospect.

[17] Ibid. 12/2/15.
[18] Ibid. 15/2/15.
[19] Sir James E. Edmonds and Captain G. C. Wynne, *Military Operations: France and Belgium, 1915*, vol. 1 (London: Macmillan, 1927), pp. 70–1.

V

Rawlinson responded to Haig's call for proposals regarding extended operations by producing two papers: 'Note on the Attack on Neuve Chapelle' and 'Points for Consideration in the attack on Neuve Chapelle'.[20] Neither, in truth, addressed the wider objectives. As if nothing had changed since 6 February, Rawlinson proposed a two-phase plan in which Neuve Chapelle village would be isolated by the IV and Indian Corps on the first day and then subjected to converging attacks on the second. In the days preceding the attack, the artillery would be assembled at night and registered on the targets a few guns at a time in order to conceal the concentration that was taking place. Each battery would be allocated specific objectives. The opening bombardment was 'not to exceed half an hour'. He concluded: 'It is of the first importance that all concerned should be fully aware that the enterprise is to be carried through to a successful issue at all costs.'

What these papers lacked, apart from appreciation of the wider enterprise, was specifics. They contained no proposals about the actual employment of infantry: which units were to make the initial attack, at what hour they were to go over the top, or how their movements were to be integrated with what Rawlinson had deemed the all-important role of the artillery. Haig was quick to point out these deficiencies. He replied to Rawlinson:

> [Your two papers] deal with the general principles on which an attack on any defended locality protected by trenches & obstacles shd be conducted – please put forward a scheme for this particular operation . . . I hope to discuss your scheme at the conference at Merville on Monday 22nd inst. So please get to work on it at once.[21]

Rawlinson promised to do his best in 'the limited time available'. But he then made a point which must have raised serious doubts in Haig's mind as to whether any detailed scheme would ever be forthcoming: 'Of course I have thought over all these matters but have not discussed them with any of my subordinates for I deem secrecy to be of the first importance.'[22] Haig, by contrast, deemed the production of a plan to be of the first importance, as he indicated to Rawlinson in no uncertain terms: 'It is absolutely necessary to take some of your subordinates into your confidence in this matter in order to have their detailed proposals for carrying out your orders . . . I think the C.O. of a Battalion ought to be trusted to keep a secret!'[23]

[20] These documents are in the Rawlinson Papers, National Army Museum, 5201/33/17.
[21] Haig to Rawlinson 19/2/15 in 'Neuve Chapelle: Report on Operations', WO 158/374.
[22] Rawlinson to Haig 19/2/15 in ibid.
[23] Haig to Rawlinson 19/2/15 in ibid.

Under this impetus, on the following day a specific plan for the capture of Neuve Chapelle was sent to Haig. But rather than emanating from IV Corps, it consisted of a second attempt by General Davies of 8 Division, to which Rawlinson appended covering notes. In the first phase of the offensive, two brigades would attack to the left of Neuve Chapelle. By a complicated manoeuvre the more rightward brigade would execute a 90 degree turn during the attack and form a line facing the village from the north. The left brigade would protect its flank. A similar procedure was to be carried out by the Indian Corps on the other side of Neuve Chapelle. A pause would then follow to regroup, and Neuve Chapelle would be captured on the second day by a converging movement of IV Corps from the north and the Indian Corps from the south.[24]

To this document Rawlinson contributed comments on such matters as the problem of finding suitable cover for the large concentration of artillery, the strength of the attacking brigades, the means of dealing with difficulties in digging forming-up trenches for the assault troops, and various administrative matters. While admitting that 'the scheme put forward by General Davies may seem somewhat complicated', he urged that it be accepted as a basis for discussion.[25] Nothing was said about subsequent operations towards Aubers Ridge.

Haig forthwith made it clear that he regarded this plan as open to serious objections. The first phase called for a change of direction in mid-attack, a dangerous and complicated manoeuvre. The second phase involved two considerable forces of troops approaching each other 'blind' from either side of a village. He also raised objection to the pause preceding the attack on the village. This would lose the element of surprise and give the Germans time to convert some of the houses into machine-gun nests. The attacking troops would be so close to the village that heavy artillery could not be used to bombard it with any safety, and meantime they would be exposed to counterattacks from a number of different directions, perhaps simultaneously.[26] Thus he rejected the Davies plan and passed the problem back to Rawlinson.

What happened on the following day is not altogether clear, although it appears that Rawlinson once more endeavoured to elicit schemes from his two divisional generals – one of whom (Capper) had seemingly not so far come forward with anything. This brought upon Rawlinson a stinging rebuke from Haig, on account of the conduct of the divisional generals ('If

---

[24] Untitled plan in 8 Division War Diary, Sept 1914–Mar 1915, WO 95/1671.

[25] Rawlinson, 'The attack on Neuve Chapelle', 21/2/15, 'Neuve Chapelle: Report on operations', WO 158/374.

[26] Haig Diary 22/2/15.

any Commander did not do what was required, he would be dismissed'), the dissipation of the decision-making process ('If each problem is to be given to two Commanders where are we to stop?'), and the tardiness of the whole proceeding ('the time for setting schemes had passed').[27]

Haig's strictures had an immediate effect. Rawlinson in co-operation with 8 Division produced a paper that day (23 February) which would form the basis of the plan finally adopted for the attack on Neuve Chapelle. For the complicated two-phase, two-day plan which Haig had rejected, it substituted a direct attack on the village by IV and Indian Corps, designed to capture it in one day. This direct attack, in Rawlinson's view, had the merits of simplicity, enhanced co-operation between IV Corps and the Indian Corps, reduced the danger of loss of direction, eliminated the possibility of casualties caused by converging British attacks, and greatly simplified artillery support.[28] In adopting these tactics Rawlinson was almost certainly following lines laid down by Haig at a conference a few days previously; for in his diary Haig noted contentedly that the attack was 'now to be carried out as I wished in a simple common sense way'[29] – in itself a powerful expression of displeasure regarding the earlier proposals sent him by Rawlinson.

What all this shows is that Rawlinson, in the planning stage of his first battle, had acquitted himself less than satisfactorily. He had shown good sense concerning fundamental principles: most of all the principle that infantry movements required powerful artillery support. But he had proved tardy in his own formulation of a plan embodying this principle, and had been content to promulgate the questionable schemes of a subordinate. This had brought from his commander a well-merited rebuke – without which it seems uncertain that he would ever have formulated a serviceable plan at all.

VI

An acceptable scheme had now been produced. Three important matters remained to be settled: co-ordination of the attack with the French, the duration of the artillery bombardment, and the nature of operations after the capture of Neuve Chapelle.

The matter of co-ordinating the attack with the French was soon re-

[27] Ibid. 23/2/15.
[28] 'Notes on attack on Neuve Chapelle,' 25 Brigade War Diary Oct 1914–Aug 1915, WO 95/1724.
[29] Haig Diary 25/2/15.

solved. There was to be no French attack in this sector. Joffre had cooled
on the idea of assaulting Vimy Ridge. He proceeded to make his part in the
operation conditional on the relief by the British of the French IX Corps in
the Ypres salient. Sir John French deemed this relief impossible, owing
to lack of troops. Joffre thereupon withdrew his participation, apart from
offering the British some flanking artillery fire. This development deflected
Haig not at all, even though he had recommended his offensive to Sir John
partly on the basis of French support.[30]

A matter more under the control of the British was the artillery bombardment. It was realised that its effectiveness was crucial to the success of the
plan. Yet the experts differed markedly about the duration of the bombardment required before the infantry should go forward. Haig's artillery
adviser, Major-General Mercer, thought a bombardment of four days
might be necessary. Haig considered three hours to be adequate. And
Rawlinson opted for just 30 minutes.[31]

Rawlinson had good reason for choosing a brief bombardment. Compared
with slow, spasmodic shelling, a sharp hail of missiles was more likely to
deny, to those defenders it did not kill, the opportunity for recovery before
the attackers moved in. The question was whether the preferred form of
bombardment was feasible, in terms of guns and shells available. On 24
February Haig received calculations regarding the number of shells that
had been required to destroy a section of enemy trench facing I Corps.[32]
These were passed on to Rawlinson and his artillery experts for analysis.
Taking into account the number of guns available and their rate of fire, he
was able to show that the required quantity of shells could be delivered
by a hurricane bombardment of short duration.[33] Mercer and Haig, meanwhile, were coming to much the same conclusion.

The matter was settled at a conference on 5 March, which opted for
an artillery plan in four parts. First, drawing on experiments in the use of
shells against barbed wire of the type confronting IV Corps, it was decided
on a wire-cutting bombardment lasting for the remarkably short time of 10
minutes. Then, for 35 minutes, the artillery would pound the enemy
trenches. Thirdly, several batteries would then drop a curtain of fire to the
east of Neuve Chapelle village to prevent German reinforcements from
reaching it. (Thus was born the artillery 'barrage' – literally a 'barrier'.)[34]

---

[30] R. Holmes, *The Little Field-Marshal: Sir John French* (London: Cape, 1981), pp. 269–70.

[31] For Haig and Mercer see Haig Diary 10/2/15. For Rawlinson see 'Remarks on VIIIth
Division Scheme', IV Corps War Diary Jan–Feb 1915, WO 95/707.

[32] Haig Diary 24/2/15.

[33] 'Artillery Problem of Neuve Chapelle', IV Corps War Diary Mar–Apr 1915, WO
95/708.

[34] Edmonds, *1915* vol. 1, p. 78, n. 2.

Finally, as the British infantry – having overrun the German trenches – were approaching Neuve Chapelle itself, the village would be bombarded for 25 minutes.

So far all Rawlinson's planning had been confined to the capture of the village. He was being noticeably reticent about subsequent operations towards Aubers Ridge. As the day of battle approached Haig became concerned at this oversight. At a meeting between the two men on 2 March Haig expressed disapproval with the limited purpose of the IV Corps plan. He pointed out that 'our objective was not merely the capture of Neuve Chapelle. Our existing line was just as satisfactory for us as if we were in Neuve Chapelle!' (So much for the straightening of the line which had been the entirely sufficient objective of Haig's original plan.) Haig went on: 'I aimed at getting to the line Illies–Herlies'[35] – that is, Aubers Ridge.

At a conference on 5 March Haig reported that Rawlinson and Davies 'thought it would be well to stop for the day after reaching the East edge of the village. I said "no" . . . our advance must be as rapid as possible'.[36] In his address to the conference Haig felt obliged to emphasize the far-reaching nature of the objectives to be attained:

> The advance to be made is not a minor operation. It must be understood that we are embarking on a serious offensive movement with the object of breaking the German line and consequently our advance is to be pushed vigorously. Very likely an operation of considerable magnitude may result.
>
> The idea is not to capture a trench here, or a trench there, but to carry the operation right through; in a sense surprise the Germans, carry them right off their legs, push forward to the Aubers . . . ridge with as little delay as possible, and exploit the success thus gained by pushing forward mounted troops forthwith.[37]

He did introduce one qualification. In order to meet enemy counter-attacks, captured ground must be placed in a state of defence even while fresh advances were being prepared. In other words, fresh formations would be required to carry forward advances from positions which had been secured by the original attacking force.

This conference at last drove Rawlinson to act on the matter of wider objectives. On 6 March, with the battle just four days away, he asked his divisional commanders for the first time to examine the possibility of an advance beyond Neuve Chapelle to Aubers Ridge. Even then there was

---

[35] Haig Diary 2/3/15.
[36] Ibid. 5/3/15.
[37] 'Notes on Conference on 5/3/15' in IV Corps War Diary Mar–Apr 1915, WO 95/708.

little urgency – the divisions were to give him their views in writing by the night of the 7th.[38]

Rawlinson clearly remained sceptical about the possibility of organizing a rapid advance beyond Neuve Chapelle. On the same day as he wrote to his divisional commanders, he recorded in his diary that Haig desired an advance on Aubers Ridge *'in the event of not very serious opposition.'*[39] Patently, Haig had admitted no such qualification. But Rawlinson then produced yet another reason for delaying the advance once the village had been captured – the need to wait for the Indian Corps to attack the Bois du Biez.[40] Haig would have none of this, telling Rawlinson that 'each attack if boldly pursued would directly help forward the other'.[41] Haig's exhortations had plainly failed to convert Rawlinson into an enthusiast for the larger scheme.

VII

In the days preceding the opening of the offensive, Rawlinson revealed himself an energetic organizer.

On 2 March, the troops designated for the attack were withdrawn from the line into billets around Merville. Here they rehearsed the first phase of the operation and practised moving into specially dug assembly trenches at night.[42] At the same time the tactics and formations to be used in the infantry assault were being formulated. These matters were important, given that the troops were at their most vulnerable during the advance across no-man's-land and their danger could be minimized or increased by the tactics adopted. Although accounts of the battle are hardly exhaustive on this subject, it is clear that the troops were to attack in columns and at a rapid pace,[43] rather than in the slow-moving 'wave' formations unhappily to be employed on a later occasion. The adoption of a suggestion from General Capper of 7 Division that backpacks not be worn indicates the command's concern that its forces advance with speed.[44]

From the outset Rawlinson proved to be aware that to maintain control of the battle he must have at his disposal effective communications. The

[38] Rawlinson Diary 6/3/15.

[39] Ibid. Emphasis added.

[40] Ibid.

[41] Haig Diary 9/3/15.

[42] Edmonds, *1915* vol. 1, p. 82.

[43] See, for example, 23 Brigade – Operation Order No. 42, 9/3/15 in 23 Brigade War Diary, Nov 1914–May 1915, WO 95/1707.

[44] Capper to Rawlinson 21/2/15 in 'Neuve Chapelle: Report on Operations', WO 158/374.

months since December 1914 had demonstrated that this would be extremely difficult to accomplish. His forces would have at their disposal a supply of runners and dispatch riders, but both were terribly at risk in battle. Consequently, the greatest transmitter of messages at this stage of the war was the telephone. But the telephone relied on wires which were vulnerable to artillery fire and which were frequently cut even during 'quiet' periods. Wires could also be disturbed by friendly infantry and cavalry moving towards the line. Given that all these factors would be multiplied many times during a battle, the preservation of communications between one level of command and another was bound to be hazardous. Rawlinson's solution was to order that all wires should be triplicated and also joined across (at intervals) to one another, so maximizing the chances of at least one route remaining open after the wires had received a number of hits. He also instructed that wires be not laid along roads or trenches, which might be registered by German artillery, but across open fields where shells were less likely to fall.[45] Given that the headquarters of the various formations were miles apart, both establishing this communication network and providing the squads to repair it under fire involved an immense amount of labour.

Crucial to Rawlinson's plan, a great artillery concentration proceeded as the day of battle approached. When completed, an arc of 340 guns – constituting the weapons of four divisions plus some heavier guns drawn from England or from other sections of the front – ringed the enemy salient. For this length of front (800 yards opposite IV Corps and 1,200 yards opposite the Indian Corps), this represented one gun for every 6 yards of enemy trench – a truly formidable achievement. It was also a triumph of staff work that the guns and their ammunition were moved into position without alerting the Germans as to what was taking place. To achieve this Rawlinson insisted that all movements be made at night, and that the gun-positions be camouflaged before the arrival of the weapons. Once in place, the weapons were registered on their targets only a few at a time, so as not to arouse suspicion. Despite these precautions, it proved possible to give serious attention to the matter of registration. For the heavy artillery, which would be firing at targets not always visible from the British line, this process was facilitated by the use of spotter planes equipped with wireless. Another device was the accurate fixing by survey of the position of Rawlinson's heavy batteries, in order to facilitate 'shooting from the map'.

It is further evidence of Rawlinson's expertise that, for the first time, the distinctive qualities of particular guns and types of ammunition were

[45] Rawlinson, 'Remarks on VIIIth Division Scheme'.

taken into account in selecting the targets against which they were to be employed. Thus Rawlinson allocated most of the 18 pounders with their shrapnel ammunition to wire-cutting. Heavier pieces, such as the 4.5 inch and 6 inch howitzers firing high explosive, were directed to batter down enemy trenches and breastworks, their plunging fire being particularly destructive against this type of defence. The heaviest artillery (15 inch, 9.2 inch howitzers, 4.7 inch, and 60 pounder guns) were reserved for selected targets such as Neuve Chapelle village and enemy command positions, or were employed as counter-batteries to silence German guns on the Aubers Ridge. Of the 340 guns available, 37 were allocated to counter-battery purposes.[46]

VIII

Rawlinson's accomplishments, then, in the preliminary stages of the battle (which were the stages where command could make its largest contribution) were clearly impressive. Despite the huge concentration of artillery and other preparations, secrecy had been maintained. The assault troops had been removed from the line, rested, trained, and concentrated behind the front with a minimum of dislocation. At the same time a substantial (for the time) communications network had been created.

Wherever technical innovation was becoming available, Rawlinson brought it into play. Survey was used to fix the position of the heavy batteries, aerial photography was employed extensively, the RFC was drawn in to locate enemy batteries, and counter-battery fire was made an important part of the initial artillery plan. Rawlinson tried hard to obtain efficient trench mortars, and it was hardly his responsibility that his troops went into battle with obsolete models.

Yet all this was accompanied by some disturbing features. They concerned what action was to be taken once Neuve Chapelle village had fallen. The ambiguities and uncertainties which obtained here underscored the fact that Rawlinson was clearly sceptical of his ability to organize a rapid advance from Neuve Chapelle on to Aubers Ridge. As late as 6 March he had been arguing for a pause once the village had been captured. This meant that all his attention was focused in the planning stage on that single objective. The artillery fire plan, like the detailed instructions to the infantry, was solely designed to effect this result. No precise directives were being provided for the operations that lay beyond the capture of Neuve Chapelle.

[46] Edmonds, *1915* vol. 1, Appendix 16, pp. 190–1.

This would not have mattered had Rawlinson been in control of the whole operation. But it was likely to prove very important given that Haig, who was in control, was insisting on 'an operation of considerable magnitude', 'not to capture a trench here or a trench there' but to 'carry [the enemy] right off their legs' and 'exploit the success thus gained' by sending in the cavalry; something for which Rawlinson was making few plans and in which he seemed to possess no belief.

4

The Technical Framework

At this point some technical explanation is necessary. As we have seen, Rawlinson placed great emphasis on the role of artillery in the forthcoming battle. Hence it is important to establish the precise state of artillery development by 1915. It will also be helpful to discover whether other weapons were available to the infantry which would assist in quelling the enemy defences.

The artillery piece in Rawlinson's day was a means by which an explosive charge or a cluster of shrapnel bullets could be delivered from long distance to the near proximity of the target. But the limiting factor in its effectiveness was contained in the words 'near proximity'. Artillery weapons employed in the Great War were not precision instruments. If 100 shells were fired successively from the same gun, set at a fixed range, under identical conditions of weather and wind, all shells would not fall in the same place. On the contrary, they would fall within what came to be designated the 50 per cent zone of the gun – that is, 50 per cent of all shells fired under the above conditions would fall within this area.

This zone varied in length and breadth for different guns and for the same gun firing at different ranges. Thus for the 4.5 inch howitzer (one of the most common of the British field artillery pieces), the 50 per cent zone at a range of 3,000 yards was a rectangle 29 yards long by 2 yards wide. For the same gun firing at 5,000 yards, the zone increased to 52 yards long by 8.8 yards wide.[1] For a 60 pounder gun at 5,000 yards the zone was 39.3 by 4.4 yards.[2] The zone was much longer than it was wide because shells in transit did not deviate appreciably to left or right but did vary greatly in the distance they might travel.

[1] For these figures see Great Britain: War Office, *Range Table for 4.5" Howitzer*, June 1916, p. 4.
[2] Great Britain: War Office, *Range Table for 60 pr Gun*, October 1916, pp. 4–5.

It needs to be recalled that an average trench was only a few yards wide. Hence it was no easy matter arranging for a large quantity of shells to land within a trench, so killing and maiming its occupants, or in near proximity to it, so causing its walls to subside.

At the time of Neuve Chapelle, trench destruction was undertaken in two stages. First the gun was 'ranged' or 'registered' on the target. This was carried out as follows. The commander of a battery of guns would send forward an officer (known as the Forward Observation Officer or FOO) who would be in communication with the battery by telephone. Each gun of the battery would in turn fire a ranging shot. The FOO would inform the battery if the shot was short of the target, over it, or to the side. The battery would make the appropriate adjustment and fire another shot. This process continued until a shell found the target. Thereupon readings of range, elevation of the gun barrel, and strength of the charge used, all would be noted down. The gun would then fall silent until the time of the bombardment, when it would be reset on those readings and firing resumed in earnest. As indicated, this did not mean that every shell would hit the target. It merely ensured that the target had been fixed within the 50 per cent zone of the gun, and that as long as a large enough quantity of shells was dispatched then a sufficient number would fall on or near the target to cave in the trench and incapacitate its occupants.

All gunners in 1915 were familiar with this method, which had been used by European armies since the invention of long-range artillery. The only refinement developed by the time of Neuve Chapelle was the linking of all FOOs to their batteries by telephone. Crude though it was, the system worked well enough if certain conditions held. The most critical condition was that the FOO could witness the fall of shot and identify it as belonging to his particular battery. That is, the method could not be used for targets well behind the enemy line which could not be seen from some point within the British positions. This was a particular disadvantage when the ground was flat and featureless, as it was at Neuve Chapelle. Other factors could also prevent the FOOs from obtaining a clear view of shell bursts. The most common were atmospheric – mist, fog, dust, or low cloud.

Where direct observation from the ground was not available, then other methods, separately or in combination, must be employed to direct shells on to their targets; in particular, the use of maps and aircraft.

Pre-war artillery experts had become well aware that in a future conflict they might be called upon to fire on targets not visible from the ground. One method developed to facilitate this was 'shooting from the map'. If the target and the gun could be accurately located on a map, then bearings from one point to the other could be measured and the gun laid along that bearing. This gave the line. The range could be found by measuring the distance between gun and target on the map. Thus the theory of map shooting was available in 1915. But, as was recognized, difficulties existed in applying it. As a pre-war artillery manual put it: 'This [map shooting] is an excellent method when a large-scale ordnance map is available, as would be the case in home defence.'[3] The problem was that on the Western Front the British found that no large-scale maps existed. In fact the last detailed survey of the area had been undertaken by Napoleon.[4] This did not pose insuperable difficulties for a small area like Neuve Chapelle. For it was not necessary to map the district in every detail. All that was necessary was to know the exact relationship between the gun and its target. So an attempt would be made to fix the exact position of batteries on the earth's surface by trigonometrical survey and then endeavour to fix targets within the German line by the same method. A chart could then be drawn up giving the exact bearings and ranges from the gun to the target.

To facilitate this process of survey, a small team was sent out from England in January 1915. Before the battle of Neuve Chapelle, they had established on the map the positions both of the British siege and heavy batteries and of 'all prominent points in the German area.'[5] When the 'prominent points' coincided with artillery targets, reasonably accurate shooting would follow. Thus in the case of Neuve Chapelle it was evident that the town of Aubers, the Bois du Biez, and Neuve Chapelle village would need to be and could be accurately bombarded. But many desirable targets, such as German artillery pieces or machine-guns in concrete strongpoints or in the ruins of isolated houses, were not in prominent locations at all – indeed, they had often been specifically placed to conceal them from the British line. In early 1915 methods did not exist whereby these positions could be accurately located by survey. The best that could be done was to use existing maps, inaccurate and small in scale though they were, and to supplement these by aerial observation.

Aircraft had first been used in September 1914 to assist British artillery on the Aisne. They could do this in two ways. If equipped with a wireless transmitter, they could be used as aerial FOOs to register artillery on targets hidden from direct observation. Alternatively, the German positions could be photographed from the air and the results transferred to maps as an aid to map shooting. Both functions were performed for the army by the

---

[3] Brevet-Colonel B. A. Bethell, *Modern Guns and Gunnery* (Woolwich: Cattermole, 1910), p. 227.

[4] Lt.-Col. H. St J. L. Winterbotham, 'Geographical and survey work in France, especially in connection with artillery', *Journal of the Royal Artillery*, 46 (1919), p. 157.

[5] Edmonds, *1915* vol. 1, p. 83.

RFC at Neuve Chapelle.[6] But both at this stage of the war were severely limited in their effectiveness.

Thus although enemy batteries could be registered from the air, they might then move to another location and so force the process to be repeated; something which, given the limited availability of aircraft operating with wireless, was not always possible. As far as aerial photographs were concerned, they had many shortcomings as an aid to artillery which were only partially realized at the time. When aerial photographs were transposed to maps, errors could be caused by the variation in, or the uncertainty of, the scale of the photographs resulting from variations in the height from which they were taken. Distortions could be caused by the angle of the camera in relation to the surface photographed (angles were certain to vary when the cameras were hand-held), the types of lens used, and the fact that a curved surface (the earth) was being rendered as a flat surface on a photograph.[7]

These factors could lead to considerable defects in the maps produced. Some maps made at this time contained errors of 150 yards, rendering them virtually useless for artillery purposes.[8] Moreover, even when these problems were realized they were not always easy to correct. On British-held territory, photographs could be checked against what was eventually a detailed trigonometrical grid. This was not possible in the case of enemy-held territory, where only the most prominent features could be surveyed. A further factor limited the effectiveness of the photographs. The definition obtained by the early cameras was just not good enough to allow some features of the enemy defences to be identified.[9]

Other factors told against the accuracy of artillery fire, be it direct or indirect. For example, wind speed and other atmospheric conditions might be different at the time the bombardment came to be fired from what had obtained when registration was undertaken. (Such variations were more than likely in the case of the Neuve Chapelle battle, given that – for the purpose of maintaining secrecy – some guns had been registered as many as ten days before the bombardment.) If the weather had been calm when the gun was registered but a strong following wind was blowing on the day of battle, the majority of shells in the actual bombardment were likely to

[6] H. A. Jones, *The War In The Air* vol. 2 (London: Hamish Hamilton, 1969), pp. 91–3. (This is a reprint of the 1928 edition of the British official history.)

[7] Great Britain: War Office: General Staff, *Geographical Section, Report on Survey on the Western Front 1914–18* (London: War Office, 1920), p. 33.

[8] Ibid., p. 21.

[9] Ibid., pp. 34–5. See also Colonel R. M. StG. Kirke, 'Some aspects of artillery development during the First World War on the Western Front', *Journal of the Royal Artillery*, 101 (1974), p. 135.

descend well past the target. Yet in battle conditions it would be difficult for the FOOs to send back adjustments to their particular batteries because of the problem of distinguishing their own shell bursts from those of other guns firing at the same target. Further, the whole communication system might break down should enemy fire sever the telephone link between the FOO and the battery.

If differing strengths of wind could produce variations in the flights of shells, so could variations in air temperature and barometric pressure. The higher the temperature and air pressure, the thinner the air and the further a shell would travel. Again, slight variations in the weights of shells or the diameter of their driving bands could cause considerable differences in their range, as could the temperatures of the propellant and the types of fuse.[10] Equally, inaccuracies could be caused by variations in guns. A worn barrel might reduce the range of a gun quite severely. On the other hand brief bouts of continuous firing could actually increase the range of a gun by causing the muzzle to turn up. (This was not fully understood until late in 1916.) To add to the problems thus created, there was no uniformity in these variations. Guns which had fired about the same number of rounds might be subject to quite different rates of wear. This meant that individual adjustments had to be made for each gun.

In 1915 only some of the foregoing difficulties were recognized. What was more, such knowledge as existed was unevenly spread through the military profession. For example, pre-war gunnery manuals did make the point that atmospheric conditions must be taken into account in ranging guns, and even contained calculations of the adjustments in range made necessary by variations in temperature and speed of wind.[11] Nevertheless, this wisdom had failed to impose itself upon a section of artillery officers even at the highest level. When the BEF arrived in France some artillery-men lamented the lack of good information about the weather in the area in which they were operating. The RFC promptly offered to make available their statistics on wind velocity to 'assist [the heavy artillery] in the calibra-tion of their guns.' The response from Major-General Du Cane, then artillery adviser to GHQ, was that 'we cannot make any use of this in-formation.'[12] ('Meteor' telegrams to the artillery were not established on a regular basis until 1916.)

Du Cane's response is indicative of a major stumbling block in the way

---

[10] Mark Severn, *The Gambardier: Giving some Account of the Heavy and Siege Artillery in France 1914–18* (London: Benn, 1930), p. 95.

[11] Bethell, *Modern Guns and Gunnery*, pp. 14–15.

[12] Anstey, History of the Royal Artillery 1914–1918, p. 341.

of 'scientific' gunnery. Before the war the Royal Regiment of Artillery was by no means a unified service. It was split into at least three factions, which in ascending order of social status were the Royal Garrison Artillery, the Royal Field Artillery, and the Royal Horse Artillery. It happened that the low-status Garrison Artillery employed the most scientific methods. For this branch manned the heavy coast defence batteries and such siege artillery as the British army possessed, and at the long ranges for which these guns were employed adjustments for weather were essential. But these methods were rather despised by the other two factions. In part this was because anything that smacked of science was foreign to the social grouping from which the officers of the Field Artillery and the Horse Artillery were drawn (it has been suggested that the attitude of these officers was that 'the artillery would really be a good show if it wasn't for the confounded gun').[13] In part it was because these men were not among the gunners habituated to firing at targets they could not see.

When war came and the Field Artillery and the Horse Artillery were required to shoot indirectly, it transpired that old habits died hard. There were many cases of battery commanders who simply refused to assimilate the new information and techniques as they became available. This problem was compounded by the fact that most of the new senior artillery appointments made in France went to the more socially acceptable officers from the Field Artillery and the Horse Artillery. Many of these officers (of whom Du Cane was representative) resisted change; and although some of them such as Uniacke and Budworth (who was to become Rawlinson's artillery commander in 1916) became enthusiastic supporters of the new methods, 'it was generally believed that had there been more Garrison Gunners in senior posts the tactical possibilities of the new gunnery would have been perceived sooner.'[14]

In operational terms this meant in early 1915 that the artillery was not likely to hit, with any certainty or regularity, a target that could not be seen. At best, then, the artillery at this time was a flawed weapon of infantry support. Yet what other weapons could the infantry call on to supplement the big guns in knocking out such obstacles as concrete machine-gun posts or defended trenches? In early 1915 the answer was practically none. The only weapon carried by the ordinary infantryman was the Lee-Enfield rifle. In defence, this weapon in the hands of experts could produce such a hail of fire that even a score of riflemen could stop a company of attacking

---

[13] S. Bidwell and D. Graham, *Fire-Power: British Army Weapons and Theories of War 1904–1945* (London: Allen and Unwin, 1982), pp. 100–1.

[14] Ibid., p. 101.

troops. Yet in offence the rifle was of little utility. It could hardly be fired at the run, and in an attack on an entrenched or concealed enemy it could not be brought to bear on its targets. The only other weapon available to the infantry was the hand grenade. But in 1915 these devices were few in number, they were unreliable, and, as names such as 'jam pot' and 'hairbrush' indicate, they were often home made.[15] Grenades were weapons primarily designed for fighting *within* trenches, their short range making them unsuitable for attacks on strongpoints. At Neuve Chapelle an innovation in the attack was the decision to carry across no-man's-land several heavy machine-guns behind the attacking infantry. These guns, however, were earmarked for defence: they were sent forward to assist entrenching troops in beating off German counterattacks. This was for good reason. Heavy machine-guns were too cumbersome to be used with facility by the spearhead of an attack.

One other weapon was being developed at this time which could be useful in an offensive – the trench mortar. Rawlinson was, in fact, in the forefront of the development of this weapon. In January he had placed his brother, Toby, in charge of an unofficial programme to develop trench mortars. By the end of the month he reported that 'the results were eminently satisfactory.'[16] He hoped to be able to establish a factory at Versailles to produce mortar shells, the weapons themselves being supplied by the French. Later he ordered 100 mortars for IV Corps.[17] Unfortunately the only mortars the French felt able to offer dated back to the reign of Louis Philippe.[18] There is no evidence that they were used successfully, and in any case they were too heavy to be carried by advancing infantry. Light trench mortars would later prove an extremely useful weapon in the destruction of strongpoints, machine-guns, and other small targets where a short-range, high explosive charge was needed. At this stage, however, efficient designs were yet to be developed.[19]

The conclusion from this technical exposition is fairly evident. The infantry had no weapons at their disposal with which to subdue the obstacles to an advance. The way must be made clear for them by action of the artillery, neutralizing at least enough of the enemy's defences to enable the foot soldiers to get forward without prohibitive loss. To this extent Rawlinson was entirely justified in the vital role he was assigning to artillery

[15] Edmonds, *1915* vol. 1, pp. 7–8.
[16] Rawlinson Diary 29/1/15.
[17] Ibid. 13/2/15.
[18] Edmonds, *1915* vol. 1, p. 8.
[19] Major N. Hudson, 'Trench Mortars in the Great War', *Journal of the Royal Artillery*, 47, 1920, p. 17.

in the coming attack. What was less certain was that in all circumstances even the artillery could suppress the defences so thoroughly as to lay open the way for the infantry. Only the events of the day would resolve that question.

5

Day One

I

Haig had fixed 10 March as the day of battle, providing the weather was fine. On the 9th rain fell and there was an occasional flurry of snow. But towards evening the sky cleared and at 10 p.m. the First Army issued the order for the attack to proceed.[1]

On receiving this order the men of the three attacking brigades began the five or six mile march to the front. This march was uncomfortable in the biting cold, and the final approach over boggy meadow was tiring. However, Rawlinson's administrative arrangements worked smoothly. A hot meal was provided at the halfway point, and before dawn the men were concentrated in the assembly trenches immediately behind the British line.[2] By 6.30 a.m. the leading battalions were deployed ready for the attack. On the left was 23 Brigade and in the centre 25 Brigade, both from Rawlinson's 8 Division. On their right was the Garhwal Brigade from Willcocks's Indian Corps.

At 7.30 a.m. the bombardment started. By later standards it would be considered puny, but to the attacking troops it was impressive enough:

---

[1] Unless otherwise stated the information used in the following three chapters comes from two documents. The first is: 'Report On The Operations Of The IV Army Corps From The 10th To The 14th March, 1915 Inclusive' which is contained in 'Neuve Chapelle: Report on Operations', WO 158/374. This document contains telegrams received and sent by IV Corps HQ during the five days of the battle. The second document is: 'Narrative – Operations About Neuve Chapelle' in the IV Corps War Diary Jan–Feb 1915, WO 95/707. This contains narratives of the battle compiled by IV Corps, divisions, brigades, battalions, and specialist formations such as artillery and signals. Only direct quotations from these sources will be specifically footnoted.

[2] Edmonds, *1915* vol. 1, pp. 89–90.

the village, the neighbouring trenches, and the whole German position selected for attack were blotted from sight under a pall of
smoke and dust. The earth shook and the air was filled with the
thunderous roar of the exploding shells. To the watching thousands
the sight was a terrible one: amidst the clouds of smoke and dust
they could see human bodies with earth and rock, portions of houses,
and fragments of trench hurtling through the air.[3]

Thirty-five minutes later the guns switched from the German front line
and placed a curtain of fire to the east of Neuve Chapelle, seeking thereby
to prevent the Germans from reinforcing their forward position. At that
moment the first of the 12,000 assault troops climbed the specially placed
ladders and moved as fast as the boggy ground would allow towards the
German line.

At Rawlinson's advanced HQ at Estaires, five miles behind the front,
the conclusion of the bombardment must have seemed anticlimactic.
There was little to be done until information on the progress of the attack
arrived from the front. Rawlinson knew that in the first few hours such
information would be sparse. In fact until 10 a.m., by which time the
attack had been under way for two hours, the information received by
Rawlinson was sketchy and incomplete.

At 8.25 a.m., Rawlinson learned that the two leading battalions of 25
Brigade had taken the German front line. (It was captured at 8.15.) Then
at 9.50 he was informed that one of these battalions (the Rifle Brigade)
had entered Neuve Chapelle and was holding the main street. This was
very satisfactory progress. However, one unsatisfactory aspect must be
noticed. The Rifle Brigade had captured this line at 8.50. At 8.59 Brigade
HQ had been informed. Yet it took an hour for the message to reach
Rawlinson, even though as yet there were no breaks in the signal network.

The situation regarding the second of his attacking brigades, the 23,
was much less encouraging. The first news came at 8.35 when Rawlinson
was told that the leading battalions of the brigade had reached the enemy
breastworks under 'considerable hostile fire'.[4] This made Rawlinson uneasy. So at 9.30 he sent a liaison officer to Brigade HQ to learn more
about the situation. He soon had further cause for apprehension. At 10
a.m., 8 Division reported that one of the leading battalions, the Middlesex,
'had failed to gain the enemy's line of trenches and was asking for further
artillery support', while on their right the other battalion, the Scottish

[3] Major Herbert A. Stewart, *From Mons to Loos: Being the Diary of a Supply Officer*
(Edinburgh: Blackwood, 1916), p. 233.
[4] IV Corps Report, WO 158/374.

Rifles, 'had been only partially successful.'[5] The first crisis of the battle
had arrived.

Nevertheless such assistance as Rawlinson might have provided was
already being rendered. The re-bombardment of the German trenches
had been asked for by 23 Brigade as early as 8.58, had been ordered by 8
Division at 9.40, and had commenced at 9.50 – that is before Rawlinson
received confirmation that the brigade was in difficulty. All he could now
do was to hope that the re-bombardment would be successful.

In fact 23 Brigade was in more trouble than Rawlinson had cause to
realize. When the Middlesex and the Scottish Rifles left their trenches
at 8.05, they found themselves facing sections of uncut wire and unbombarded trench. Enemy machine-gun and rifle fire caused hundreds
of casualties in a matter of minutes. As some of the leading columns of
the Middlesex were still endeavouring to find gaps in the wire, two more
attacks were initiated by the remainder of the battalion. These met with
the same fate as the first. Only on the extreme right of the attack did
some parties of the Scottish Rifles (supported by a follow-up battalion,
the 2 Devonshire) enter the German trenches.

The cause of failure is not far to seek. The German trench-dwellers
had not been neutralized, and their barbed wire was intact. The reason
was that the two howitzer batteries responsible for bombarding this section
of trench had arrived from England only on 9 March. The light had been
poor and time was short, with the result that the FOOs had not accurately
registered the guns on the German trench. Consequently on the 10th
most of their shells landed behind the German front line. In a subsequent
report on the action this much was recognized by the artillery.[6] However,
the same report stated that the wire-cutting on the front of 23 Brigade
was 'very satisfactory'.[7] This was far from being the case. There are
many well-documented instances of men reaching the wire only to find
themselves unable to proceed.[8] Obviously, for reasons which are obscure,
the 18 pounder batteries detailed to cut the wire on this sector had also
failed. Their want of success is underscored by the fact that when the
re-bombardment was ordered, it included 18 pounder batteries to cut
the wire and not just howitzers to destroy the trenches.[9]

While Rawlinson awaited news of this re-bombardment, he turned his

[5] Ibid.

[6] 8 Division HQ Royal Artillery, 'Remarks on Experiences on 10th–13th March', 21/3/15,
in 8 Division War Diary Sept 1914–Mar 1915, WO 95/1671.

[7] Ibid.

[8] For example see John Baynes, *Morale: A Study of Men and Courage: The Second Scottish
Rifles at the Battle of Neuve Chapelle* (London: Cassell, 1967), pp. 68–9.

[9] 8 Division HQ Royal Artillery, 'Remarks', as in footnote 6 above.

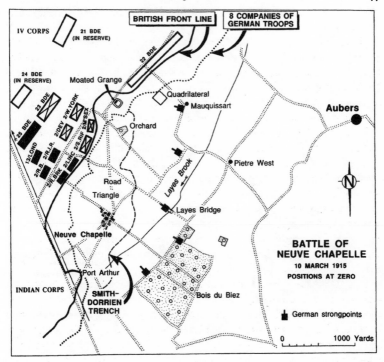

MAP 2

attention to the more hopeful activities of 25 Brigade. From that quarter news continued to be good. At 10.10 a.m. he learned that the Rifle Brigade had advanced beyond Neuve Chapelle almost to the line of the Smith-Dorrien trench. But he had as yet heard nothing about the progress of the Indian Corps on his right. This raised the possibility that the Rifle Brigade might be unsupported on either flank. Rawlinson therefore ordered 8 Division HQ to secure the road triangle to the north of Neuve Chapelle so as to give flanking support to the Rifle Brigade at least on their left. At the same time he drew Davies's attention to the importance of capturing the supposed strongpoint at the orchard, lest that might further delay the already-stalled advance of 23 Brigade.

The first order, concerning the road triangle, was in fact unnecessary. Indeed it demonstrated Rawlinson's comparative impotence at this stage of the battle. The Royal Irish Rifles of 25 Brigade had entered the road triangle an hour before Rawlinson's order was issued and, although suf-

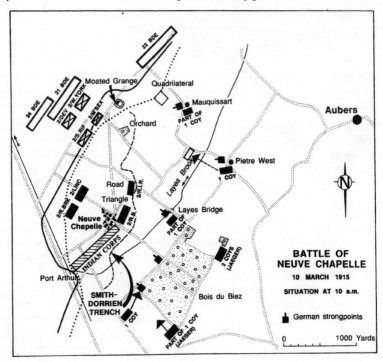

MAP 3

fering from flanking machine-gun fire, had secured their objective by
9.30 and had joined up with the Rifle Brigade on their right. Yet neither
Rawlinson nor 8 Division HQ was aware of this movement until at least
1 p.m. Rawlinson's second order concerning the orchard was to have
important consequences which will be examined later.

At this point (10.40 a.m.) 7 Division, which had yet to enter the fray,
asked permission to send forward its 21 Brigade. That formation had
just reached the British front line from which 23 Brigade had attacked.
According to a later account, Capper, the divisional commander, was
convinced that there was 'no opposition on this section of his front' and
that the way was clear for 21 Brigade to go forward.[10] If this was indeed
Capper's belief at the time, he was under a serious misapprehension. As
we have seen, the attack by 23 Brigade had failed and its survivors were

[10] The account is that of Haig in his comments on a draft of the official history July 1925.
See Cab 44/19.

pinned down in front of the German trenches. Rawlinson, fortunately for his troops, knew enough about the actual situation to hold back 21 Brigade 'until the situation on the left [that is, on the front of 23 Brigade] should improve.'[11]

At 11.15 a.m., IV Corps's liaison officer returned from 23 Brigade HQ with information confirming that the situation on this sector remained critical. Rawlinson promptly did two things. He extended the scope of the supporting bombardment. And he ordered one of his reserve brigades (24th) to follow the path of the successful 25 Brigade, but only as far as the former German front line. There, presumably, it was to attack the flank of the enemy forces holding up 23 Brigade.

As it happened, by the time both these orders were issued events had outrun them. By 11.15 a.m. the Middlesex battalion of 23 Brigade had accomplished its task. The shaken German defenders surrendered to parties of British troops advancing along the enemy trench lines, thereby enabling the remainder of the Middlesex to traverse no-man's-land and occupy the trenches in front of the orchard. So by 11.20 a.m. the whole of the German front line facing IV Corps was in British hands.

Rawlinson's priority now was to capture the supposed German strong-point at the orchard. But once more events were moving too fast for him. Before the reserve 24 Brigade, which Rawlinson was proposing to employ, could be apprised of the situation, 23 Brigade – whose original objective the orchard was – had organized their own attack. In fact they would have gone forward a good half an hour before they did but for fire from British artillery which had been ordered by 8 Division to beat off a (nonexistent) counterattack from the orchard.[12] When the guns finally ceased, 23 Brigade advanced on the orchard and occupied it at 12.30 p.m. It was undefended. The supposed strongpoint was merely a cluster of trees.

The 23 Brigade, like the 25th, had now attained its objectives, and could await the action of other of Rawlinson's forces. All now seemed ready for the second-phase advance: the capture of Aubers Ridge.

II

While Rawlinson's attention had been focused on the difficulties of 23 Brigade, had he been missing a considerable opportunity to advance even further on his right, from whence success had come at the outset? Since

[11] IV Corps Report, WO 158/374.
[12] 8 Division HQ Royal Artillery, 'Remarks', WO 95/1671.

9.30 a.m. the leading units of 25 Brigade (the Rifle Brigade and the Royal Irish Rifles) had been occupying a position to the east of Neuve Chapelle close to the line of the Smith-Dorrien trench. Behind them in close reserve were the remaining two battalions of the brigade (the 2 Lincolns and the 2 Royal Berkshires). Casualties in the Royal Irish Rifles had been severe (217 killed and wounded), but the other three battalions were in good shape. The brigade was concentrated, they were in touch with the Indian troops on the right, and there were few Germans in sight. Yet they had no orders to advance: only to entrench the captured line and await the advance on Aubers Ridge by the Indian Corps on their right and 24 Brigade on their left. That there was scope for independent action occurred at least to Lt.-Col. Stephens, the commander of the Rifle Brigade. During the morning he sent a message to Brigade HQ 'saying that there seemed to be v[ery] few of the enemy in front of us and asking if a further advance was to be made.'[13] The answer was unequivocal. There was to be no advance until the stalled 23 Brigade attained its objectives.

As noted earlier, Rawlinson was not aware until 1 p.m. that the situation on the front of 25 Brigade was so favourable. So the earliest he could have ordered an unanticipated advance by this brigade was just after 1 p.m. But by then Rawlinson was expecting a general advance along the whole front. Even had the thought occurred to him, there appeared to be no reason for ordering forward just one brigade.

Rawlinson's critics (such as Alan Clark) have suggested that, had 25 Brigade been sent forward at the time requested by Stephens, a great success would have followed.[14] Correspondingly they have condemned the rigid chain of command which ensured that Rawlinson's subordinates were in no position to seize such opportunities as presented themselves. In so doing they ignore the fundamental question: supposing an advance had been attempted by 25 Brigade at 9–9.30 a.m. on 10 March, would it have been the walkover they imply? For the answer we have to examine the German response to the sudden capture of Neuve Chapelle.

Of the eight German companies holding the section of line attacked, five had either been wiped out by the bombardment or overrun, two continued to hold up the Indian Corps on the extreme right of the British attack, and one had stopped the Middlesex and Scottish Rifles of 23 Brigade on the extreme left. While the bombardment was still in progress, however, two German reserve companies supported by machine-guns had occupied two concrete strongpoints. By 9 a.m., when the Rifle Brigade of 25 Brigade was moving through Neuve Chapelle, the German company

[13] Rifle Brigade Narrative, WO 95/707.
[14] Alan Clark, *The Donkeys* (London: Hutchinson, 1961), p. 54.

at one of these strongpoints (Pietre West) had also occupied a disused trench between Pietre West and the former German front line. At the same time a third company of Germans was sent to the south of the Bois du Biez to block any British attempt to outflank the wood from that direction. And by 9.30 a.m. – the earliest that 25 Brigade could have launched a concerted advance from Neuve Chapelle – more reinforcements had arrived. About two companies and two machine-guns from the Jäger Battalion in reserve reached the northern end of the Bois to protect two field guns which had escaped the bombardment. The remainder of this battalion (about 100 men and two machine-guns) moved to the south-east corner of the Bois in order to reinforce the defenders already sent to that area.[15]

By 9.30 a.m., therefore, five and a half German companies and eight machine-guns faced approximately twenty British companies and three or four machine-guns. There can be little doubt that, despite their numerical superiority, the British would have found such opposition too formidable to permit an advance over open ground. Admittedly they were facing only pockets of resistance, which in later years they would develop the techniques and weaponry to subdue. But, as our technical explanation has shown, in 1915 the British infantry did not possess the weapons with which to eliminate the obstacles they now faced, neither was the artillery capable (least of all in early morning mist) of eliminating such small targets. And even supposing it had been possible to subdue the defenders in the immediate area of Neuve Chapelle, this would not have been the end of the matter. There were seven more German companies with machine-gun support between the Bois and the line for which the British were making.[16]

In short, the supposed opportunity which had beckoned Stephens of 25 Brigade appears on inspection to have been little or no opportunity at all.

III

The fall of the orchard to 23 Brigade had finally cleared the situation on the British left wing and completed the first phase of the operation: the

---

[15] The movement of German reserves at Neuve Chapelle is based on three works by G. C. Wynne, *If Germany Attacks*, pp. 31–3; 'Reflections on Neuve Chapelle, March 1915', in *The Fighting Forces*, 12 (1935), pp. 497–503 (especially pp. 501–3); and 'The other side of the hill: no. XVII'.

[16] Wynne, *If Germany Attacks*, map facing p. 23.

overrunning of Neuve Chapelle village. Of this Rawlinson was apprised by 1.10 p.m. He thereupon set in motion the second phase of the attack. He ordered his two reserve brigades, 21 and 24, to advance on Aubers Ridge, concerting this movement with the Indian Corps on his right.

A difficulty promptly presented itself. The 21 Brigade was indeed ready to set forth, and had been available since early morning. But 24 Brigade was not ready, and for good reason. In the planning for the battle, it had been assigned two conflicting roles. One has just been mentioned: participating in the second-phase advance on Aubers Ridge. The other involved action during the first phase, as a reserve force for 8 Division. Its units were to participate in local emergencies, plug gaps in the line, attack strongpoints which had escaped the bombardment, and even (in the case of one battalion) carry out quite menial tasks such as carrying stores and digging communications trenches across captured territory.

In consequence, at the time 24 Brigade was called on to spearhead (along with 21 Brigade) the attack on Aubers Ridge, it was scattered all over the battlefield. Some of its units had seen considerable fighting. One, for example, had been employed by General Davies (the divisional commander) to fill a gap which had developed between the left of 25 Brigade and the right of 23; and Rawlinson himself had employed another to help out the beleaguered 23 Brigade and assist the attack on the orchard. In total, three of the brigade's five battalions had participated in the first phase of the battle, a fourth had engaged in digging trenches and carrying stores, while the fifth was well behind the British line in reserve.

At 1.30 p.m., as if unaware of all this, Rawlinson ordered that 24 Brigade be collected for an advance. He simultaneously informed Haig that instructions for an attack by 24 and 21 Brigade would be issued in half an hour to come into effect at 2.30. Needless to say, no advance occurred at 2.30. Rawlinson's orders did indeed reach the headquarters of the two brigades at 2 p.m. But whereas 21 Brigade was in a position to move almost immediately, the battalions of 24 Brigade were so dispersed that it would take until 3.30 to assemble them. In addition, Rawlinson's order only specified that the brigades assemble for an advance. He considered that the order to commence the assault could not be given until the Indian Corps were ready on his right. On enquiry at 1.35, Rawlinson found that the Indian Corps was not ready. Willcocks would not commence until the entire German line in his area had been captured. This was only accomplished at 2.30, as Rawlinson was informed 25 minutes later.[17] So it was not until 3 p.m. that the order to advance was issued to divisional headquarters.

---

[17] First Army War Diary 10/3/15, WO 95/154.

It is a minor puzzle that, although Haig was impatient for the advance on Aubers to begin, he did not, when he was informed that Rawlinson was waiting for the Indian Corps, tell him to proceed immediately. This would have been consistent with his pre-battle exhortation that attacks by one corps 'would directly help forward the other'. But in this instance he did nothing. Either the whole line would advance or none of it.

Yet more puzzling is Rawlinson's timetable for the attack. His orders were issued to the divisions at 3 p.m. They designated that the bombardment and advance were to commence just 30 minutes later. Yet the experience of the day had shown that no order had passed from division to battalion in 30 minutes – the time-lag was at least an hour, and this sometimes extended to two.

In the event the attacking brigades did not receive Rawlinson's orders at all. For, by the time these missives reached their destinations, the brigades were already on the move. The reason was as follows. By 3.30, both brigades were concentrated and in a state to advance. Then a mishap befell them. The artillery bombardment arranged by IV Corps to cover their attack descended not on its designated targets (a series of strongpoints) but on the troops it was intended to assist. This spurred both brigadiers to action. Although still without orders, they decided to try and concert an advance.

At 3.30 a liaison officer was sent from 21 to 24 Brigade asking when they intended moving. He happened to cross with an officer sent from 24 to 21 Brigade bearing a similar enquiry. Simultaneously a message reached 24 Brigade from 8 Division HQ to the effect that 21 Brigade was already on the move. Before this information could be digested, however, 24 Brigade's liaison officer returned with the news that 21 Brigade was not advancing. Meanwhile 21 Brigade had heard that 24 Brigade had moved off and sent a message to their battalions to deploy. A few minutes later the most rightward battalion of 21 Brigade reported that the 24th had not in fact moved. But by that time some battalions of the 21st were already attacking.

The result of this fiasco was that from about 4 p.m. until darkness fell two hours later, battalions of the two brigades made various uncoordinated attempts to advance on Aubers Ridge. It would not be rewarding to describe these movements, and anyway no clear picture can be gained even by the closest reading of the battalion narratives. What can be said is that the attempted advance had to traverse flat, boggy ground, intersected by a maze of trenches and drainage ditches, and to do so in failing light, unsupported by artillery, and in the face of a hail of fire from German strongpoints. It is remarkable that any ground at all was gained.

Rawlinson, not surprisingly, was having difficulty following the course of the attack. He was not aided by several misleading reports from 7 and 8 Divisions. He was told by Capper at 4.45 p.m. that 21 Brigade was advancing. Yet it is doubtful if more than one battalion was attacking at this time. Other reports between 5 and 6 p.m. indicated that 21 Brigade was progressing 'all right' and that the Germans were 'coming out of their trenches and surrendering in groups.'[18] Neither statement bore any relation to the facts.

News from 8 Division headquarters was just as misleading. Davies reported 24 Brigade as approaching Pietre West at 6.50 p.m., whereupon Rawlinson ordered that the brigade must take the village that evening. There was never any chance that this could be accomplished: Pietre West was one of the strongest German centres of resistance, 24 Brigade was not advancing as a unified body (and anyway was not within a quarter of a mile of the village), its units were intermixed, and it was almost pitch-dark. Luckily for the brigade, by the time Rawlinson's directive to take the village had reached the front line, other messages had arrived calling off the attack for the day and ordering the consolidation of ground already gained.

Events on the front of the Indian Corps from 3.30 p.m. of that day should be noted. On the left of the corps, no movement was made because 25 Brigade remained halted waiting for 24 Brigade. On its right, the situation around Port Arthur having been cleared up, some forward movement proved possible. The Layes Brook was crossed and in the gloom of late afternoon some isolated battalions approached the Bois du Biez. But flanking fire from Layes Bridge and the arrival of German reinforcements in the wood forced these troops back and they took up positions for the night on the west bank of the Layes Brook. The first day at Neuve Chapelle was over.[19]

IV

What can be said about Rawlinson's exercise of command on the first day of his first major battle? In truth 10 March provides a good example of how little influence a commander could bring to bear on such an occasion. As we have seen, many of the important decisions during the day were taken at the divisional or brigade level without reference to Rawlinson. Thus 23 Brigade, which fared so disastrously in the opening minutes of the battle, had taken the appropriate action to extricate itself before

---

[18] IV Corps Report, WO 95/374.
[19] Edmonds, *1915* vol. 1, pp. 111–13.

Rawlinson could intervene. And 24 Brigade was used by Davies as he thought fit to rectify situations of which, in some cases, Rawlinson was not even aware.

In other instances the interval required for Rawlinson's orders to reach the front meant that by the time of their arrival they were irrelevant. Examples of this are Rawlinson's instructions to attack positions which had already been captured. The time factor also applied in reverse. By the time Rawlinson realized that 25 Brigade had been completely successful and was concentrated for an advance, the opportunity to order it to proceed (whether or not this was ever his intention) had long since passed. Other orders issued by Rawlinson were simply incapable of implementation in the conditions prevailing at the front. We may instance his attempt to have 24 Brigade attack the orchard, and the attempt to co-ordinate the advance of 21 and 24 Brigades to capture the German strongpoints in front of them.

How then did Rawlinson influence the battle? Two main areas may be identified. Primarily, his influence lay in the part he had already played in making the original plan. As we have seen, this influence was not as great as it might have been owing to Rawlinson's inexperience and the guidance that had to be provided by Haig. Nevertheless, Rawlinson took the decision at the outset to use the artillery to crush the German defences, and this proved of real moment given that it enabled his forces to capture Neuve Chapelle village without suffering excessive casualties.

The second respect in which Rawlinson influenced the battle on the first day is less to his credit. The reserves were clearly misused, with the result that the attempt to employ 24 Brigade in the second phase of the advance was a fiasco. Rawlinson blamed Davies, claiming that he was responsible for using the brigade piecemeal to remedy local emergencies. Yet it was Rawlinson's plan which had assigned to this brigade the incompatible roles of spearheading the advance on Aubers Ridge and acting as a divisional reserve. The responsibility correspondingly lay with him. Further, Rawlinson's action during the first phase in ordering the brigade to attack the orchard indicates that he was just as prepared as Davies to use it against immediate objectives rather than preserve it for the second-phase advance.

In addition to these two major (if dissimilar) contributions by Rawlinson on the first day, a minor contribution remains to be noticed. Rawlinson acted felicitously regarding Capper's attempt prematurely to employ the second reserve brigade, the 21st. Capper had not grasped the seriousness of the situation on the front of 23 Brigade. Had he sent in the 21st at the point he proposed, confusion and a large number of casualties would almost certainly have resulted.

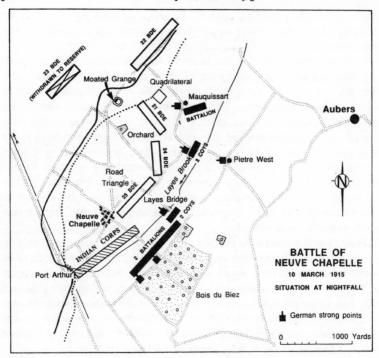

MAP 4

In the aftermath of 10 March, Rawlinson was in no doubt that a considerable success had been achieved. He wrote in his diary:

> We have had a grand day – our plans succeeded admirably... Douglas Haig is certainly pleased and we have received the congratulations of Sir John French. Altogether things have gone quite as well as I expected... The great point is that we have now proved that a line of trenches can be broken with suitable Art[iller]y preparation combined with secrecy.[20]

This was a just assessment. But it gave rise to a further 'great point'. Once the enemy's front line had been overrun, subsequent attacks must be delivered against defences which had not been registered by the artillery. And these operations, once initiated, would be yet more difficult to control than action on the first day. The 11th of March would reveal whether these large matters were being fully appreciated.

[20] Rawlinson Diary 10/3/15.

6

Day Two

I

As was usual during this period of the war, all major attacks ceased at night. The hours of darkness were devoted to sorting out battalions which had become intermixed in the course of battle, establishing as exactly as possible the position of the front line, and settling plans for the morrow. By 1 a.m. on 11 March Rawlinson was able to establish the position of his attacking brigades with some accuracy. In the early morning he issued his orders for the coming day. The main advance on Aubers Ridge was to be made by 20 Brigade, brought forward from reserve. Its right would be protected by 24 Brigade, its left by the 21st.[1] The Indian Corps would advance in concert with it.[2]

The Germans, meanwhile, had not been idle. No less than 13 companies of troops from local reserve had entered the line.[3] In addition artillery reinforcements of seven field batteries and four and a half heavy howitzer batteries had been brought forward.[4] And, further back, 4,000 men were being concentrated at Aubers – the advance regiments of the 6th Bavarian Reserve Division.[5] Moreover, the Germans were constructing new defensive positions. On the first day of battle, their defences behind the front line consisted only of some concrete strongpoints and hastily improvised positions. During the night these were converted into

---

[1] For these operation orders see IV Corps War Diary Mar–Apr 1915, WO 95/708 and 7 Division War Diary Feb–May 1915, WO 95/1628.
[2] First Army Telegram 10/3/15, in First Army War Diary Dec 1914–Mar 1915, WO 95/154.
[3] Wynne, *If Germany Attacks*, pp. 34–5.
[4] Edmonds, *1915* vol. 1, p. 118.
[5] *Der Weltkrieg* vol. 7 (Berlin: Mittler, 1931), p. 58. (The German Official History.)

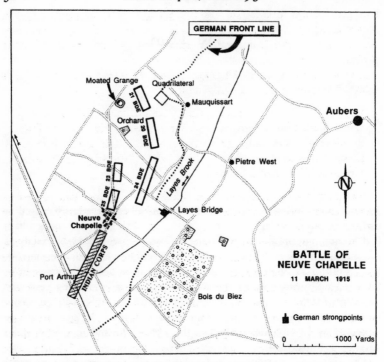

MAP 5

a more defensible line. On the right, breastworks were constructed between Mauquissart and the Layes Bridge road, and the whole line was
wired. On the left, a new line was constructed in front of the Bois du
Biez. There was a gap between these positions, but it was covered by a
strongpoint at the Layes Bridge. During the night additional machine-
guns were brought forward and German reinforcements distributed along
the line.[6]

In sum, by the morning of 11 March the British were confronting well-
prepared positions and twice the number of German troops which had
opposed them at the outset of battle.

II

Rawlinson had ordered his three attacking brigades (from left to right,
21, 20, and 24) to advance at 7 a.m., preceded by a 15 minute bom-

[6] Edmonds, *1915* vol. 1, p. 119.

bardment. These orders had reached the battalions in plenty of time, so a reasonably co-ordinated attack was possible. At the appointed time six battalions – two from each brigade – set off towards the German positions.

The result was a fiasco. All along the line the attack was stopped in its tracks. The experience of 24 Brigade was typical:

> Impossible to leave trenches. Artillery bombardment was ineffective. Breast work from [Pietre West to Layes Bridge] untouched. Tried to advance ... but only got a few yards ... attack driven back by heavy rifle and cross machine-gun fire ... No prospect of going forward without artillery support.[7]

It was plain what had gone wrong. Rawlinson's artillery had missed its targets completely. Against unsubdued defences, his infantry stood no chance of advancing.

This was not a situation that was easy to correct. The misty weather, combined with the initial uncertainty of the FOOs regarding the precise location of newly dug German trenches, meant that further bombardments were likely to prove equally ineffectual. Further, communications between the British front and rear were proving even more hazardous than on the previous day owing to the enhanced enemy artillery. The Germans were now constantly bombarding the British positions, thereby cutting telephone lines almost continuously, especially between battalions and brigades. One result was that it took two hours for Rawlinson to learn that the attacks had failed. Just after 9 a.m., 7 Division reported being held up by fire from houses at Moulin de Pietre (it was actually fire from Mauquissart) and 8 Division reported a similar problem at Pietre West. Rawlinson's response was to order a re-bombardment of these two points. This availed nothing. In the first case the artillery was firing on the wrong position. And in the second it proved incapable of hitting the target.

Rawlinson was quick to grasp the problem. He reported to First Army HQ 'that owing to mist and fog, there was difficulty in getting accurate artillery observation, and progress was accordingly slow.'[8] But he seemed at a loss to resolve the problem. The only course he managed to propose was the seemingly barren one of yet another re-bombardment.

In the event this third bombardment did not take place. Before the artillery could deliver it, a crisis threatened on the right flank. The Germans were reported to be massing for a counterattack from the Bois du Biez.

---

[7] 24 Brigade Narrative 11/3/15, WO 95/707. The abbreviations used in the original have been expanded to make the account intelligible.

[8] IV Corps Report 11/3/15, WO 158/374.

All guns were immediately turned on this position. As it happened, no attack was under contemplation by the enemy. But at least this flurry saved the left of the British line from an immediate repetition of the futile endeavours already made.

III

It was now mid-morning, and any hope of a further advance at this late stage had apparently departed. Rawlinson, however, would not recognize this. Indeed during this period he became yet more insistent that attacks should be pressed home.[9] When informed that progress was difficult given the ineffectiveness of the artillery, his response was obtuse. He directed that the German strongpoints opposite the British 'should be captured without further delay; lose no time in getting guns on to them and assaulting the buildings with infantry.'[10]

The divisional commanders, by contrast, were becoming concerned that lives were being thrown away without prospect of a result. They determined not to attack until a thorough artillery preparation had been arranged. The 8 Division stated that they would not be ready to go forward until 2.15 p.m. The 7 Division could not even meet this deadline – 3 p.m. was the earliest they could advance. Indeed Davies, commanding 8 Division, seemed reluctant to attempt any further movement. After Rawlinson's instructions had been considered he responded: 'that the 24th Brigade was in an uncomfortable position; that the ground was very open and exposed, and that the brigade might not be able to take [Pietre West].'[11] Rawlinson was not impressed. Davies was informed: 'The Corps Commander said that it [Pietre West] must be taken.'[12]

As anticipated by the divisional commanders, the endeavours of the three attacking brigades achieved no substantial purpose. So on the right, where the Rifle Brigade was supposed to go forward in conjunction with the Indian Corps, no forward movement was ever set in train. Both formations announced attacks, cancelled them, reinstated them, and then cancelled them a second time, each unit waiting for the other to move first.

On their immediate left, 24 Brigade was supposed to attack at 2.15 p.m.,

---

[9] Rawlinson sent messages to the divisions to this effect at 11.15 and 11.22 a.m., and 12.10, 12.15 and 12.19 p.m. See ibid.

[10] Ibid.

[11] Ibid.

[12] Ibid.

after an artillery bombardment of half an hour. But the brigadier (Carter) had received insufficient time to co-ordinate the advance of his frontline battalions with this bombardment. So the best he could do was to instruct two companies of the Worcesters, who were close by in reserve, to carry out the advance, hoping that neighbouring troops from the brigade would go forward with them. This desperate expedient failed. The Worcesters did not reach the front until 2.22 p.m. – seven minutes after the bombardment had ceased. They attacked alone, and in the words of their major were 'swept away after going 50 yards.'[13]

A message from the Worcesters reached another battalion of 24 Brigade, the 2 Northants. It indicated that the Worcesters were about to attack and appealed to the Northants to do the same. Significantly, the answer that came back was: 'No it is mere waste of life; the trenches have not been touched by art[illery] . . . A frontal attack will not get near them . . . impossible to go 20 yards much less . . . 200 yards.'[14] Nor did the Northamptonshires take part in any other attacks that day. So one result of Rawlinson's persistence was to cause a regular battalion to refuse to participate in his purposeless operations.

On the left of 24 Brigade, the operations of 21 Brigade also went awry. Here a bombardment of one hour had been arranged. But at 3 p.m., when the infantry was supposed to go forward, the artillery had so obviously failed to locate the German defences that the attack was cancelled. This order did not reach many of the forward battalions, but so bad had communications become that the original order to attack had not reached them either. Some isolated companies did try to improve their position, but essentially the line remained where it had been in the morning.

IV

It is hard to disagree with Rawlinson's comment in his diary that 11 March was 'not a satisfactory day'.[15] When the positions of the leading brigades were finally located, it was found that the line had hardly advanced at all. Yet Rawlinson and Haig were loath to conclude that the German defences were now too strong for any further advance. Instead Rawlinson criticized Davies for not acting vigorously enough.[16] Haig also blamed Davies, but the extended his strictures to the rank and file:

---

[13] 24 Brigade Narrative 11/3/15, WO 95/707.
[14] Ibid.
[15] Rawlinson Short Note Diary 11/3/15.
[16] Ibid.

'In fact the troops had done nothing.'[17] The truth was otherwise. What seems particularly lamentable is that Rawlinson, who before the event had stressed the vital nature of artillery in the attainment of success, persisted in ordering attacks on 11 March on no less than nine occasions despite clear evidence that his guns could not hit their targets.

[17] Haig Diary 11/3/15.

7

Day Three

I

Rawlinson's orders for operations on 12 March were almost identical with those for the 11th. The objectives were the same. The offensive was to be prosecuted with 'the utmost vigour'.[1]

The Germans, yet again, had not been dragging their feet. But on this occasion, instead of continuing to improve their defences, they seized the opportunity to repeat the misjudgements of their British counterparts. Since the arrival, the day before, of 6 Bavarian Reserve Division and 86 Brigade from XIX Corps, the Germans had been preparing a counter-attack. To their misfortune the local corps commander, von Claer, chose to launch it at dawn on 12 March, before the appearance of substantial artillery reinforcements.[2] The bombardment which preceded the attack was just as inaccurate as recent British efforts, and it left its targets substantially untouched. Ten thousand German troops then went over the top. Despite the shortcomings of the bombardment they pressed forward devotedly, and at a few points the British line was entered. Nevertheless, 'eventually the counter-attack failed on the entire front, and whereas on the 10th the German casualties had been about one-fifth of those of the British, the proportion on this day was reversed.'[3] At 7 a.m., two hours after it had commenced, the attack was abandoned. German dead lay in rows in front of the British positions.

[1] IV Corps Report 12/3/15, WO 158/374.
[2] Wynne, *If Germany Attacks*, p. 38.
[3] Ibid., p. 40.

II

Rawlinson, at IV Corps HQ, was slow to learn that these important events were taking place. Because it was anticipated that the 12th would be misty, his own 7 a.m. attack had already been postponed until 10.30 'to give time for accurate bombardment'.[4] While preparations were in train, the first reports of German activity began arriving. The earliest, at 7.29, came from the Indian Corps, stating that the Germans were counter-attacking at Port Arthur. Thirty minutes later 8 Division reported a similar attack to the east of Neuve Chapelle, and by 8.35 Rawlinson knew that the Germans had attacked from the Layes Bridge, Pietre West, and a maze of trenches known as the Quadrilateral in front of Mauquissart.

These messages did not deter Rawlinson from going ahead with pre-parations for his own attack. Probably he was encouraged by statements from the Indian Corps that the attack on their front had been driven back and by 8 Division's claim that the German advance 'had been easily repulsed'.[5] (That these statements were hardly accurate is evident from the post-battle reports of these divisions, which speak of 'severe fighting at close quarters'.)[6] However, it seems likely that not even the divisional headquarters themselves realized until later how devoted the counter-attacks had been, or how hard their troops had been pressed in some areas. For not only were the reports from the battalions taking at least three hours to arrive, but ironically – because of the heavy fighting – they contained few details.

By mid-morning news began reaching Rawlinson of the substantial German reinforcements which had arrived during the 11th. At 9.45 a prisoner stated that he was part of a division from Lille (in fact the 6th Bavarian Reserve Division) which had now reinforced the German VII Corps. Later another prisoner said corps reserves had been brought up for the specific purpose of retaking Neuve Chapelle. It was now clear that the 16,000 German reinforcements that GHQ Intelligence had calculated would arrive on the battlefield within 48 hours were already present. That is, the numerical superiority of the British – which had not brought them success on the 11th – was plainly diminishing. So on the 11th a potential force of 48,000 British troops (although nothing like that number could be deployed at the 'sharp end' of the small length of front being attacked) had failed to advance against 4,000 German troops. Now on the 12th, as

---

[4] IV Corps Report 12/3/15, WO 158/374.

[5] Ibid.

[6] 7 Division, 'Narrative of Operations in the neighbourhood of Neuve Chapelle', 7 Division War Diary Feb–May 1915, WO 95/1628.

Rawlinson had cause to know, less than 48,000 British troops were confronting 20,000 Germans. Yet he did not hesitate to order a new series of attacks.

Haig did little to restrain him. His Chief of Staff rang IV Corps HQ at 9 a.m. and asked if the artillery had registered all points due to be attacked.[7] Rawlinson replied that he was not sure. Haig, seeming to have learnt at least one lesson from the experiences of the 11th, postponed the attack for a further two hours.[8] But this was as far as his restraining hand went.

The new start-time of 12.30 p.m. found only three of the four brigades designated for the operation in a position to undertake it. The exception was 24 Brigade on the centre right. Earlier in the morning (about 7 a.m.) two battalions of this brigade, the Northants and the Worcesters, had followed up a failed German counterattack and had occupied several houses in Pietre West. But they were unsupported and soon came under shelling from their own artillery. (It was ironical that only during the occupation of Pietre West by their own troops did the British artillery at last find the range.) Hence at about 10 a.m., under severe counterattacks, these British forces were driven back with heavy casualties to their own line. Carter, the brigade commander, therefore refused to order them forward to take part in the 12.30 p.m. attack. The morning operation by these battalions, nevertheless, was to have an influence on the subsequent course of the battle.

By contrast with 24 Brigade, the attack by the 25 Brigade on the right started according to plan. It failed utterly. A message sent by the brigade at 12.45 reported that the attack was held up by fire from the Layes Bridge. What followed exemplified Rawlinson's inability to make an effective intervention once battle had started. The division received this message at 1.10 p.m.; Rawlinson did not receive it until 2.15. At 2.25 he arranged for the artillery to bombard Layes Bridge, and firing commenced 20 minutes later. But no second attack followed. The battalions had earlier reached the decision that as 'the enemy trenches were well wired & very strongly held with many m.g's [machine-guns] . . . a fresh attack could not succeed in daylight.'[9]

It remains to consider the attack on the left by 20 and 21 Brigades of 7 Division. Here fortunes were mixed. Two of the battalions of 20 Brigade, having not received the message postponing the attack until 12.30 p.m., had gone forward two hours earlier, with lamentable results. The other

[7] First Army War Diary 12/3/15, WO 95/154.
[8] Ibid.
[9] 25 Brigade Narrative 12/3/15, WO 95/707.

battalions in this brigade, by contrast, attacked at the rescheduled hour and against an area (the complex of German trenches called the Quadrilateral) which had been accurately bombarded by the artillery. The position was overrun and 400 prisoners taken. That constituted the sole success in this sector. As the narrative of 21 Brigade relates: 'Remainder of line could make no progress owing to heavy enfilade fire which our guns could not reduce to silence.'[10]

On the right of IV Corps the Indian Corps advanced to the Layes Brook with little loss. But observing that 25 Brigade was stalled, and being under intense enfilade machine-gun fire from Layes Bridge, they did not press the advance. No further attacks were made on this corps's section of the front.[11]

III

At IV Corps HQ, Rawlinson was receiving a quite distorted view of events on his sector. In the early afternoon he was told that Pietre West had been captured, the Quadrilateral had fallen, 'that the Germans were surrendering in large numbers', and that 20 Brigade was advancing.[12] Only the second of these was correct.

Rawlinson passed on this inaccurate information to Haig,[13] who was quite overwhelmed by it. After ascertaining from GHQ the availability of cavalry, at 3.06 p.m. he telephoned orders to the corps commanders for a further advance – 'The 4th and Indian Corps will push through the barrage of fire regardless of loss'[14] – by cavalry as well as infantry. Rawlinson, as it happened, was with Capper at 7 Division HQ when Haig's order reached him. He had by this time received a more accurate account of the situation, and could have informed Haig that no roads were clear for the cavalry and that the situation was not as favourable as it had been reported. But Rawlinson still went ahead and ordered further attacks by the infantry, telling them 'to push on vigorously at all costs'.[15]

Better sense prevailed among Rawlinson's subordinates. By the time 7 Division had prepared orders for the new attack, its commanders knew that their troops had achieved no success apart from the capture of the

[10] 21 Brigade Narrative 12/3/15 in ibid. The abbreviations in the original have been expanded to make the account intelligible.

[11] Edmonds, *1915* vol. 1, pp. 141–2.

[12] IV Corps Report 12/3/15, WO 95/374.

[13] First Army War Diary 12/3/15, WO 95/154.

[14] Ibid.

[15] IV Corps Report 12/3/15, WO 158/374.

Quadrilateral. Capper, the divisional commander, thereupon sent a strongly worded message to Rawlinson stating that his troops were exhausted and had suffered considerable losses. He advised consolidating the line captured and making a fresh attack on the 13th. To this Rawlinson agreed.[16]

The 8 Division was not so fortunate. Carter, commander of the shattered 24 Brigade, once more refused to order them forward. But units from 25 Brigade made a further attempt. In the sour comment of the commander of the Rifle Brigade: 'The 2nd attack failed in exactly the same way as the first, but with even more cas[ualties].' He offered four reasons. One was the nature of the ground, with ditches running obliquely to the line of advance. The second was the excessive distances to be covered, obviating 'any possibility of rushing the enemy's trenches'. The third was the fact that the enemy 'had been strongly reinforced, was well dug in and had many m.g's.' Finally, the attackers' artillery bombardment had been ineffective, 'probably from want of knowledge of the exact pos[itio]n of these new enemy trenches.' 'Under these conditions', he concluded, 'it was impossible for the inf[antry] to succeed,' but this did not prevent large numbers of men being 'thrown into the attack.'[17]

Even now, Rawlinson was not prepared to accept the lessons of two days of failure. He ordered a new series of attacks, to be made by the three brigades of 8 Division – even though these brigades has been in the line for three days. The attacks were to take place at night. That is, Rawlinson was contemplating sending forward these exhausted and depleted formations in the dark across boggy and shell-cratered ground against a line whose exact position was unknown and which his artillery had conspicuously failed to hit in the light.

Happily for his troops, two hours later wiser counsels prevailed and the order for further attacks was cancelled. But this was not quite the end of the day's operations. The cancellation order reached 25 Brigade but not 24 or 23. Carter of the 24th, again showing rare independence, declared his brigade 'stone cold' and refused to participate.[18] By contrast, Pinney of the 23rd, which had been held in reserve most of the day and so was the freshest of the 8 Division brigades, spent most of the night collecting his men for an attack. Only the extreme difficulty of this task delayed the operation until 1.30 a.m. on the 13th. At that time a few companies of the 2 Devons advanced on Pietre West with no success. Five minutes later a message (timed over three hours earlier) arrived from 8 Division cancelling the attack.

[16] 7 Division, 'Narrative of Operations', WO 95/1628.
[17] Rifle Brigade Narrative 12/3/15, WO 95/707.
[18] 24 Brigade Narrative in ibid.

8

Summing Up

I

The high command was now prepared to recognize what had been obvious to some of the brigadiers for the last two days. So on 13 March, Haig ordered Rawlinson to consolidate the ground gained. The battle of Neuve Chapelle was over. What had been achieved? British forces had captured the village of Neuve Chapelle. And they had straightened their line. But these less-than-considerable accomplishments had been secured at great cost. Total casualties were 11,652. In IV Corps alone the figures were over 7,500, of whom over 2,000 had been killed.[1] Only on account of the German policy of attempting to regain all ground lost did the balance sheet of casualties come out at least reasonably even.[2]

What is to be said of Rawlinson's handling of his first offensive battle? The major charge levelled against him has usually been that he missed an opportunity to turn initial success into something more substantial. This does not stand up to scrutiny. It has become evident in the course of the narrative that no opening for a substantial advance ever presented itself. Perhaps on occasion his forces might have pushed a little further forward than they did, but before long they were bound to run into German reinforcements and strongpoints powerful enough to halt their progress.

The real criticism to be made is in fact the precise opposite of that just mentioned. Far from failing to seize opportunities to press forward, Rawlinson sought to exploit openings that were never offering.

It will be remembered that, in the planning stage, Rawlinson had wanted to halt the battle after the capture of the village. This reflected

[1] Edmonds, *1915* vol. 1, p. 151.
[2] *Der Weltkrieg*, vol. 7, p. 59.

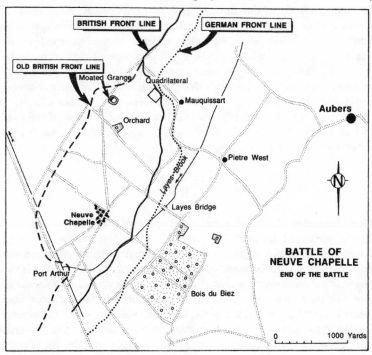

MAP 6

a recognition of the difficulty of providing fire support for his troops beyond this point. He was, however, overruled by Haig, who insisted on an advance to Aubers Ridge. Yet when battle was joined Rawlinson seemed just as determined as Haig to press on. In fact there is no evidence that Rawlinson dissented from any of Haig's decisions to keep the battle going. This applied even to 12 March, by which time Rawlinson had good information that there was no prospect of any further advance. Indeed Rawlinson spent most of the battle ordering, or trying to order, a series of increasingly futile attacks against increasingly strong defences.

How do we account for this? It seems insufficient to speculate that, as long as Haig kept ordering attacks, Rawlinson felt bound to carry them out. In that case at least some note of dissent would have entered his diary or correspondence. More probably, Rawlinson's judgement was affected by the extent of his success on the first morning of the battle. He can hardly have been unaware that a major component of that success was a heavy and accurate artillery bombardment, such as could not be repeated on subsequent days. But he may have felt that, against improvised defences and an enemy who had sustained heavy losses, a less convincing bombardment would facilitate a further advance by the infantry. If so, this was a serious miscalculation which Rawlinson seemed slow to recognize. It would indeed prove much easier for a defending force, even after an initial setback, to create adequate defences and call in sufficient reinforcements than it would be for the attackers seeking a further advance to deliver the sort of bombardment that might subdue these. Rawlinson's dictum of 'bombard and storm' would be validated by his own attempt, consequent upon early success, to disregard it.

II

Notwithstanding that Neuve Chapelle was applauded by his superiors, Rawlinson almost forfeited his command by coming out on the wrong side of an argument with one of his divisional generals. While viewing the battle as a success 'from which [the Germans] will not recover in a hurry', Rawlinson was concerned at the 'failure to press on in the early stages of the attack.'[3] He attributed responsibility for this to Davies, commander of 8 Division. Davies, he claimed, had dissipated his reserves around the battlefield in the first stage of the operation, with the result that they were not to hand to carry out the advance from Neuve Chapelle to Aubers Ridge. As he wrote in his diary: 'I have not been pleased with Joey Davies who has not handled his men well in action and I told him today that he would be relieved of his command.'[4] The next day Rawlinson met Haig, who also adjudged Davies 'much too slow' in pushing forward from Neuve Chapelle. They agreed that Davies should go home.[5]

Meanwhile Rawlinson, always an assiduous correspondent, had been spreading the news of his 'victory' to his influential friends in England. In the next few days Sclater (the Adjutant-General), Kitchener, and the King (via his aide-de-camp (ADC) Clive Wigram) were all informed of Rawlinson's success.[6] Further, in two of these letters (to Sclater and Kitchener) Rawlinson made it quite clear that even more ground would have been captured but for the inaction of Davies. Kitchener transmitted

---

[3] Rawlinson Diary 13/3/15.

[4] Ibid.

[5] Haig Diary 12–14/3/15.

[6] Rawlinson to Sclater 14/3/15; Rawlinson to Kitchener 15/3/15; Rawlinson to Wigram 16/3/15, Rawlinson Papers, NAM, 5201/33/17. Unless otherwise stated, all Rawlinson correspondence in this chapter comes from this file.

this criticism of Davies to H. H. Asquith, the Prime Minister, who commented that 'the whole operation, successful tho' expensive as it was, just failed of being the most brilliant success in the whole war thro' the mishandling at a critical moment of *one* Division. The General (quite a good man, Davies) has been sent home.'[7]

Asquith's closing comment was premature. After being confronted with his impending dismissal, Davies began collecting evidence in his own defence. This made it quite evident that Rawlinson himself had involved the reserve battalions in the fighting of the early stages, so ensuring that they would not be immediately available for the advance on Aubers Ridge. Davies forwarded this material to Rawlinson. To his credit, Rawlinson immediately sent on Davies's letter to Haig and accepted responsibility for the delay in advancing from the village. On receiving this message, Haig, who had just recommended to French that Davies was unfit to hold an active command, momentarily waxed furious with Rawlinson.[8] But by the time of a conference between Haig and French, the First Army commander's wrath seems in a measure to have abated. The conference agreed that Rawlinson had 'behaved badly' to Davies. Initially French took the view that Rawlinson should be sent home. But – presumably on account of arguments from Haig – it was decided that Rawlinson should be warned that any further attempt to blame subordinates for his own failings would result in the loss of his corps.[9] Haig conveyed this message to Rawlinson, making it clear whom Rawlinson had to thank for the retention of his command.[10]

It promply became clear that one person whom Rawlinson did not have to thank for retention of his post was Sir John French, who showed no inclination to allow the matter to die down. A friend reported to Rawlinson that the incident was being discussed widely in London. Not only the blame for mishandling 24 Brigade but also responsibility for the heavy losses suffered by IV Corps during the whole operation were being laid at Rawlinson's door.[11] That the source of these aspersions was GHQ seemed confirmed by the appearance of French's dispatch on the operation. This document stated categorically that the failure to push on rapidly from Neuve Chapelle was instrumental in limiting the success of the operation,[12] and singled out for comment Rawlinson's inability to bring his reserves more speedily into action.

---

[7] Asquith to Venetia Stanley 18/3/15, in H. H. Asquith, *Letters to Venetia Stanley*, edited by Michael and Eleanor Brock (Oxford: Oxford University Press, 1982), p. 488. Asquith's italics.

[8] Haig Diary 16/3/15.

[9] Ibid. 17/3/15.

[10] Rawlinson Diary 17/3/15.

[11] ? to Rawlinson 28/3/15, Rawlinson Papers, 1/2, CC.

[12] *The Despatches of Lord French* (London: Chapman and Hall, 1917), p. 239.

Rawlinson responded with vigour to these mounting charges. He sought to demonstrate that the heavy casualties were the result not of tardiness on the first day but of the ensuing attempts to accomplish a wide-ranging advance. He told Kitchener that the criticisms being directed against himself were ill-informed, adding:

> If we had not tried to do too much our losses would have been one quarter what they were & we should have gained just as much ground[,] but the idea of pushing through the Cav[alr]y which has just been seized hold of by our leaders, all Cav[alr]y Officers, was the origin of our heavy losses.[13]

This passage, although clearly directed primarily against French, might seem also to embrace Sir Douglas Haig. For not only did it criticize 'Cavalry Officers' but its clear implication was that the attack had gone wrong once Rawlinson's proposal for the capture of Neuve Chapelle had been converted into something much larger. But when, three weeks later, Rawlinson conveyed similar views to the King (via Wigram), he was careful to single out French as the author of the operation's shortcomings. After detailing the 'many inaccuracies' in French's dispatch on Neuve Chapelle, Rawlinson observed:

> It would have been better to have stopped after capturing the Village which only cost us 2,300 casualties instead of hammering on for three days & gaining no more ground[,] but Sir John was obsessed with the idea of getting the Cav[alr]y through to operate against the enemy's line of communications. The time for this is not yet.[14]

At the end of April the Davies affair and its subsequent recriminations receded, as preparations intensified for the coming offensive on Aubers Ridge. In itself the affair was pretty trivial. Yet it deserves attention in the present context on account of its effect on relations between Haig and Rawlinson. Initially, Haig noticeably cooled towards Rawlinson, and his visits to IV Corps HQ became less frequent. Yet in the longer run what mattered was that Rawlinson had fallen out of favour with French and was beholden to Haig. That, willy-nilly, converted Rawlinson into the sort of subordinate commander whom Haig was disposed to employ.

The affair has another significance. It reveals an ambivalence in Rawlinson's attitude to operations on the Western Front. Before the event, and after it when criticized by his commander-in-chief for failing to press on from Neuve Chapelle, Rawlinson was strongly of the opinion that attacks on the Western Front could at best achieve only limited results.

---

[13] Rawlinson to Kitchener 1/4/15.
[14] Rawlinson to Wigram 22/4/15.

He espoused the view that the capture of Neuve Chapelle village was the most this operation ever had to offer, and that the devotion of men and resources to wider objectives amounted to a squandering of lives. Even if the cavalry had got through, he wrote to Wigram on 22 April, 'they would not I fear have been able to effect much & would have suffered very heavily.'[15]

Yet if this was Rawlinson's view before and after the operation, it was one he failed to express while the battle was in progress. On 10, 11, and 12 March he appeared as eager as Haig – with whom lay the responsibility for extending the objectives of the attack beyond Rawlinson's original proposal – to push on past Neuve Chapelle to Aubers Ridge and the broad fields beyond. And he proposed sacking Davies for his supposed part in thwarting this further progress. That is, once battle was joined Rawlinson made no attempt to function as a restraining hand on the 'Cavalry Officers' who, in one guise or another, would be in overall command of the British army for the remainder of the war.

[15] Ibid.

PART III

Aubers Ridge to Loos,
May–December 1915

9

Aubers Ridge: The Plan

I

In the weeks following Neuve Chapelle, Rawlinson strove to divine the lessons of that episode and to derive from them a coherent theory for further trench-warfare battles. This was no easy matter. From this one experience, varying and even contradictory messages could be drawn. Nor were the lessons that did seem to emerge necessarily applicable to subsequent actions. There was a further difficulty. Military commanders – Rawlinson among them – were capable of forgetting some of the truths they had managed to seize upon.

The most important insight derived by Rawlinson from Neuve Chapelle was that the German line could be broken by a sufficient artillery bombardment. Writing to Kitchener soon after the battle, Rawlinson commented:

> the lessons we have learned at Neuve Chapelle are...that it is always possible by careful preparation and adequate Art[iller]y support by heavy Howitzers to pierce the enemy's line provided always that his wire entanglements can be cut by the fire of our field guns, and it can always be so cut if it is visible and not protected by earthworks.[1]

In the next few days he repeated this point in other correspondence.[2]

This conclusion, that if assailed by sufficient artillery fire the enemy's front line could be 'pierced', became the basis of Rawlinson's tactical ideas. The real problem, as he saw it, was what to do next. Initially, under

[1] Rawlinson to Kitchener 15/3/15, Rawlinson Papers, NAM, 5201/33/17. All Rawlinson correspondence in this chapter is from this source.
[2] Rawlinson to Sclater 21/3/15; Rawlinson to Derby 23/3/15.

the influence of the Davies affair, he concentrated on swift exploitation of the initial breakthrough. As he told Kitchener: 'It was I think our failure to press forward rapidly in the first instance that prevented us from gaining more ground.'[3] However, further reflection and the appearance of more detailed reports on Neuve Chapelle caused a change. He now thought that 'we had tried to do too much.'[4]

> I think it was a mistake to go on hammering at the enemy's defences all through the 11, 12 & 13. It cost us 5,000 men & we gained nothing. Had we been content with the capture of the village & stopped at the end of the 1st day our losses would have been only 2,300 & we should have killed twice that number of Germans.[5]

He concluded: 'when the enemy has been able to man his second line of defence it is waste of life to attack him until the heavy guns are able to pulverise these localities.' In line with this emphasis on the role of artillery, Rawlinson was unable to believe that the cavalry could provide the means of rapid exploitation: 'He [Haig] expects to get the Cav[alr]y through with the next push but I very much doubt if he will succeed in doing more than lose a large number of gallant men without effecting any very great purpose.'[6]

From the conclusion that a break into the enemy's line did not hold out the prospect of cheap exploitation by the infantry or any sort of exploitation by the cavalry, Rawlinson derived the principle of 'bite and hold'. He explained it most clearly in a letter to Wigram late in March:

> What we want to do now is what I call, 'bite and hold'. Bite off a piece of the enemy's line, like Neuve Chapelle, and hold it against counter-attack. The bite can be made without much loss, and, if we choose the right place & make every preparation to put it quickly in a state of defence[,] there ought to be no difficulty in holding it against the enemy's counter attacks & inflicting on him at least twice the loss that we have suffered in making the bite . . . it of course entails the expenditure of a good deal of Art[iller]y ammunition which we have not got.[7]

Rawlinson realized that there was a difficulty with this policy. He wrote to Kitchener concerning it:

---

[3] Rawlinson to Kitchener 15/3/15.
[4] Rawlinson to Kitchener 1/4/15.
[5] Rawlinson to Kitchener 21/4/15.
[6] Rawlinson Diary 14/3/15.
[7] Rawlinson to Wigram 25/3/15.

it does not of course result in any decisive victory which could affect the final issue of the war & it only very slowly forces the enemy's line back towards their own frontiers. The time for breaking up the trench line is still some distance away. Before we bring this about we shall have to make the Germans extend their front for another 500 or 600 miles across Austria & thus oblige them to weaken their defensive power.[8]

This passage makes abundantly clear both the strengths and shortcomings of the proposed method. 'Bite and hold' was not only entirely sensible but probably the only successful form of warfare which lay open to Britain. But it constituted an admission that the war would have to be fought in a quite undramatic way employing scientific gunnery and meticulous planning. There would be little room for rapid infantry advances, let alone the sweep and dash associated with the cavalry. And a war conducted by such means would not be brief. Many military figures, journalists, politicians, and members of the general public were unlikely to embrace these uncomfortable truths.

Rawlinson's formulation of his views contained both inconsistencies and bizarre aspects. On the key issue of the quantities of fire power that bite and hold would require his judgement wavered alarmingly. To Wigram he remarked that huge amounts of artillery would be needed for its implementation. Yet soon after he told Kitchener that 'it does not need much ammunition.'[9] And still later Wigram was informed that bite and hold attacks could be made every week, 'with due economy in ammunition'.[10] Given that at Neuve Chapelle it had been necessary to assemble almost every available British gun and round of ammunition to penetrate one weak German line, there seemed no justification for Rawlinson's backtracking on this matter.

Then there was the 'Eastern' dimension to Rawlinson's plan. No doubt oppressed by an awareness that bite and hold would not bring a 'decisive victory' (that is, a speedy end to the war), he slipped easily into believing that it must be accompanied by some grandiose operation in the Balkans. His views here were far from specific. It made no sense to oblige the Germans to extend their front 'another 500 or 600 miles across Austria' if the Franco-British line had to be extended a like distance. So presumably Rawlinson was anticipating the formation of a coalition of Balkan countries eager to challenge the military might of the Central Powers. He

[8] Rawlinson to Kitchener 1/4/15.
[9] Ibid.
[10] Rawlinson to Wigram 22/4/15.

failed to assess the likelihood that Romania, Greece, and Bulgaria would sink their internecine hatreds if promised a small complement of British troops to aid their peasant armies and their ox-drawn, ill-equipped artillery in making battle with one of the most formidable armies in the world. Events would soon reveal that when offers of this kind were made the Balkan countries wisely declined them. Rawlinson would eventually see the futility of this aspect of his policy and concentrate his thoughts on Belgium and France.

Yet whatever its inconsistencies and misjudgements, Rawlinson's bite and hold policy went to the heart of the matter of waging war on the Western Front. If the cavalry was useless, only the infantry could force the enemy back. But the infantry itself could not get forward until its opponents had been thoroughly subdued by ample and well-directed artillery fire. And once the initial objectives had been taken, operations would have to halt while the artillery was moved forward and brought to bear on fresh objectives. Rawlinson was not alone in perceiving this: some other commanders were thinking along similar lines.[11] But it was Rawlinson who first, and most lucidly, formulated the policy of the limited objective.

Something more, however, needs to be said. First, the men exercising the highest command over Britain's forces were not inclined to fall in with Rawlinson's (inherently gloomy) line of reasoning – anyway at this stage of the war. Second, Rawlinson himself would prove anything but a single-minded advocate for the artillery-dominated policy which, momentarily, he had come to embrace. The battle of Aubers Ridge, in painful fashion, bears this out.

II

French preparations for a large spring offensive in Artois made it almost inevitable that the British would be called upon to attack the German line again – if only to prevent the movement of German reserves from the British sector to the French. But this suited the mood of the British commanders admirably. Rawlinson, believing that in a well-executed bombardment he had found the means of overwhelming the German front line, was in the van of enthusiasts for a new attack. He reported that his divisions 'have their tails right over their backs now & are spoiling to get at the Germans again.'[12] Even the wounded, he suggested (in what was

[11] General Du Cane also advocated a bite and hold policy after he had studied the lessons of Neuve Chapelle. See his 'memo on Neuve Chapelle' in 'General Staff: Notes on operations', WO 158/17.

[12] Rawlinson to Sclater 21/3/15.

surely an unhappy turn of phrase), were 'dying' to return to the line.[13]

Haig had initially intended to resume the operation at Neuve Chapelle without waiting for the French offensive. However, it transpired that the British had used almost all of their artillery ammunition during the three days of that battle, so that stocks had fallen to a few dozen rounds per gun. Further action would have to wait upon the accumulation of new supplies.

Nevertheless, planning for the new operation began immediately. On 14 March Haig announced that it was his intention to use 7 Division 'to take the enemy's front system of trenches [in front of Fauquissart], and hold them and the immediate flanks. The Canadians will then advance through the gap which has been made, and push on as quickly as possible to Aubers. Gough's detachment [2 Cavalry Division] will be in readiness to follow the Canadians on the first favourable opportunity.'[14] Haig, unlike Rawlinson, evidently still regarded rapid exploitation of a break-in as possible and the cavalry as even now having a place in trench warfare. But he had learned one lesson from Neuve Chapelle. Regarding the use of infantry, it was a mistake to employ the troops who had carried out the break-in to exploit the success.

Yet notwithstanding this improvement, Haig's tactics were plainly far removed from bite and hold, and Rawlinson was unhappy with them. He regarded the area of attack chosen by Haig as unpromising: 'the Germans are rather strong there and they have four lines of trenches.' He thought the battle would 'cost a lot of lives and I much doubt if we will get the cavalry through.' Later he complained that the operation presented a 'much greater problem than Neuve Chapelle for the enemy is prepared and has been digging and wiring for all they are worth.'[15]

As originally designed, Haig's plan was not destined to be carried out. While British preparations were going forward, Joffre supplied GHQ with the details of his proposed attack. The northern flank of that operation was to be at Loos. Sir John French therefore insisted that Haig move the main thrust of his attack somewhat to the south so as to bring it into line with Joffre's plan.[16] Haig agreed. But he also proposed that his initial scheme for an operation to the north of Neuve Chapelle should still go ahead. In this way there would be two attacks by British forces, and these would converge on Aubers Ridge.[17]

[13] Rawlinson Diary 16/3/15.

[14] Haig Diary 14/3/15.

[15] See Rawlinson Diary 18, 19, 25 March 1915.

[16] Brigadier-General Sir James E. Edmonds, *Military Operations: France and Belgium 1915*, vol. 2 (London: Macmillan, 1928), Appendix 4, pp. 429–30.

[17] Haig Diary 5/4/15.

The final arrangement saw the more southerly of Haig's two attacks assigned to I Corps and the Indian Corps, on a front of 2,400 yards. To the north, Rawlinson's IV Corps would attack opposite Fromelles. At the outset the two British operations would be separated by some 7,000 yards. They were to converge on Aubers Ridge but not halt there: a series of further objectives was stipulated to the east of the ridge. That is, the idea of an unrestricted operation still obtained: with (in the words of First Army's operations plan) 'two Cavalry Corps and three infantry divisions ... being held in readiness ... to exploit any success.'[18]

For this operation Rawlinson had at his disposal three divisions. There were the two original divisions of his corps, 7 and 8, now reconstituted after their blood-letting at Neuve Chapelle. And there was the 2nd Cavalry Division of General Gough, which would be employed for exploitation. (The Canadian Division, which had figured in Haig's original plan, had meanwhile departed to take over a section of the Ypres salient from the French.)

This time Rawlinson did not delegate the planning of the operation to his divisional commanders. He and his staff set about the task in co-operation with the staff of 8 Division (which was to spearhead the attack). Although Rawlinson complained that Davies was 'not very helpful or imaginative',[19] a plan was soon produced. The 8 Division's 25 Brigade, on the left, and 24 Brigade, on the right, were to punch a hole in the German defences and advance as far as Fromelles. On the left the 25 Brigade would then form a defensive flank, while on the right 24 Brigade would mop up the German defenders trapped between itself and the Indian Corps advancing simultaneously from the south. Thereupon 8 Division was to halt and 7 Division pass through it to a further position (Don-Bauvin), where it would line up with I Corps which in like manner was following up the advance of the Indian Corps. After that, exploitation would be the task of the cavalry, which would raid further east as opportunity provided.[20]

In appearance this scheme reflected Haig's penchant for a wide-ranging offensive rather than Rawlinson's concept of bite and hold, which would have confined the operation – at least in the first instance – to the advances by 8 Division and the Indians. However, the actual operation orders issued by Rawlinson bespoke more his own approach than Haig's. In a note before the battle Rawlinson cautioned his divisional commanders that it would take hard fighting to reach the designated objectives. He

---

[18] First Army Operation Order 6/5/15, quoted in Edmonds, *1915* vol. 2, p. 431.
[19] Rawlinson Diary 9/4/15.
[20] Rawlinson to Haig 22/4/15 in IV Corps War Diary Mar–Apr 1915, WO 95/708.

had no intention of feeding in more troops once determined opposition had been reached. At that point:

> It will ... be better to wait a little so as to re-organize the infantry, re-establish communication between artillery and infantry, and get the artillery on to the fresh targets. Therefore we must be prepared for operations lasting several days.[21]

That is, Rawlinson would contemplate advancing to the final objectives only in a series of bite and hold operations.

How Haig would have reacted had he been aware of this directive must remain unknown. However, it is the case that just before the battle Haig seemed to recognize that only an operation of limited scope was possible. He complained to French that he had not sufficient troops to 'reap decisive results', and that securing Aubers Ridge would be the most that could be achieved. He went on to say that fresh infantry divisions would be needed to carry out exploitation beyond the ridge and that 'the Cavalry Corps will not suffice, because hostile infantry will be found, for certain, in prepared positions in rear.'[22] This statement did not necessarily signify that Haig had been converted to the notion of limited-objective operations. But he was clearly saying that, on this occasion anyway, his forces were insufficient to achieve any large result.

III

It would be reasonable to expect that, in planning and execution, Aubers Ridge would prove an advance on Neuve Chapelle. In some, rather minor, respects this was indeed the case. In the respect which Rawlinson himself had proclaimed of greatest importance it was the reverse of true.

No doubt learning from Neuve Chapelle, for this next operation Rawlinson was at pains to ensure that the forces designated to follow up the break-in were not involved in the initial stages of the attack. Further, he endeavoured to overcome the various problems of communication and control which were likely to develop once battle had been joined. Recognizing the difficulty of establishing the exact position of infantry who had penetrated the German front, he arranged for aeroplanes fitted with wireless to monitor their movements. So attacking infantry were furnished with white strips of cloth to indicate their position to 'contact

---

[21] Note by Rawlinson 10/4/15 in ibid.
[22] Haig Diary 30/4/15.

patrols' in the air, and with coloured flags to signal their whereabouts to the artillery.[23]

Nevertheless, in the most telling aspect of all, the message of Neuve Chapelle was thrust aside. This concerned the artillery bombardment. Both Haig and Rawlinson had initially made the Neuve Chapelle bombardment their point of departure. They were agreed that the length of front attacked 'will depend on the number of extra guns placed at his [Rawlinson's] disposal, especially of 6" siege howitzers, which are specially useful for destroying the enemy's front trenches, as they are very accurate, and throw a large shell.'[24] So in mid-April it was decided that 8 Division's attack would be on a front of 600 yards,[25] the area that could be covered by the 6 inch howitzers available.

But the principle of making the length of front to be attacked proportional to the heavy artillery available was soon abandoned. In the ensuing weeks the front was extended first to 1,000 yards and then to 1,500 yards, without any further batteries of 6 inch howitzers being added to the artillery.[26]

Neither Rawlinson nor Haig offered any explanation for this curious decision. Yet it represented a considerable retreat from the type of bombardment used at Neuve Chapelle. At that battle the German trench line had been bombarded entirely by heavy guns – either 6 inch howitzers or 4.7 inch guns. And this fire had been overlaid along most of the trench line by 4.5 inch howitzers.[27] The extension of the front of attack at Aubers Ridge to 1,500 yards meant that such an intensity of fire could not be duplicated, let alone improved upon. Only 600 yards of the front under attack could be dealt with by the 6 inch howitzers. The remaining 900 yards would be bombarded only by the much lighter 4.5 inch howitzers, or in some cases even by the ludicrously inadequate 18 and 13 pounders firing only shrapnel.[28]

There was another important difference between the bombardment at Neuve Chapelle and that at Aubers Ridge. At Aubers Ridge a much higher percentage of guns was directed not against the German front line but against strongpoints behind it. This may have reflected an attempt to apply a lesson learned from Neuve Chapelle, where such strongpoints

---

[23] See 8 Division Narrative, IV Corps War Diary May 1915, WO 95/709 and 8 Division operation order No. 30, 5/5/15, 8 Division War Diary Apr–July 1915, WO 95/1672.

[24] Haig Diary 8/4/15.

[25] Ibid. 15/4/15.

[26] See ibid. 19/4/15 and Edmonds, *1915* vol. 2 (maps), map 4.

[27] Edmonds, *1915* vol. 1 (maps), map 3.

[28] Edmonds, *1915* vol. 2 (maps), map 4.

had held up the British after the capture of their initial objectives. Yet by devoting a smaller percentage of guns to the destruction of the German front trenches, Rawlinson was diminishing still further the instrument of early success at Neuve Chapelle.

This diversion of a proportion of heavy guns from the enemy's front line to his rearward strongpoints creates a statistical complication. For it means that, in order to calculate the relative weight of the initial bombardment at Aubers Ridge compared with that at Neuve Chapelle, it is not sufficient to take into account just the length of front attacked and the number of guns employed against it. In these terms – that is, guns per yard of front under attack – the British at Neuve Chapelle had one gun for every 6 yards, while at Aubers Ridge the figure was one gun for every 8 yards. But when the figures embrace only those guns actually bombarding the German front line, a significantly different result is obtained: one gun per 30 yards at Neuve Chapelle; one gun per 50 yards at Aubers Ridge.[29]

Yet even this does not fully represent the diminution in intensity of the preliminary bombardment at Aubers Ridge. When we look at weight of shell falling on the enemy front line, it transpires that while at Neuve Chapelle 5 lb. of shell was directed at every yard of trench, at Aubers Ridge only 2 lb. was used.[30] Nor is this the end of the matter. At Neuve Chapelle the British were attacking only a single major trench line. At Aubers Ridge they were for the most part combating a trench system, consisting of three lines each a short distance apart. If this did not have the effect of tripling the length of front needing to be bombarded (because a shell missing one trench might land in another), it at least doubled the length.

The statistical conclusion of the foregoing is quite startling. For the initial attack, in terms of weight of shell falling on actual trenches the bombardment preceding the infantry attack at Aubers Ridge possessed only one fifth of the intensity of that employed at Neuve Chapelle. To understand the significance of this, it is only necessary to stress a single point. The British had done only one thing well at Neuve Chapelle. They had fired a crushing artillery bombardment which had facilitated an initial advance by their infantry. At Aubers Ridge, the artillery bombardment was certain to be a good deal less than crushing.

[29] These figures have been obtained by comparing the Neuve Chapelle and Aubers Ridge bombardment maps in the map volumes of the official history.

[30] For the respective weights of shell used in the First World War see I. V. Hogg and L. F. Thurston, *British Artillery Weapons and Ammunition 1914–1918* (London: Ian Allen, 1973). The numbers of shells used in each battle are in the official history.

IV

Other factors – only some of which had been in evidence at Neuve Chapelle – told against the effectiveness of the preliminary bombardment. First there was the weather. The days before the battle, when the registration of the guns was taking place, were misty, thus hampering the FOOs and aeroplanes in providing accurate reports. Then on the day of battle the weather suddenly cleared, so rendering most of the previous registrations inappropriate because of the changed atmospheric conditions.[31]

As at Neuve Chapelle, the terrain made accurate registration difficult. The ground was very flat and observation points few. But the Aubers Ridge bombardment suffered a further disadvantage not in evidence at Neuve Chapelle: by early May large numbers of trees had come out in leaf, making observation of the fall of shot in some areas almost impossible.[32]

The wear on the guns also made firing less accurate than two months before. Most of the guns used at Aubers Ridge had seen duty at Neuve Chapelle. The comparatively large number of rounds fired in the earlier battle had worn the gun barrels, with a deleterious effect on accuracy, to an extent not encountered before by British artillery commanders. Wear was most severe in the older type of guns such as the 4.7 inch. But the main weapons of the field artillery, the 18 pounder and the 4.5 inch howitzer, had also deteriorated and the battery commanders of this arm of the artillery were even less likely to make the appropriate adjustments than their fellow officers in the heavy artillery.[33]

Another factor hampered accurate registration. In response to the German gas attack in the Ypres salient on 22 April, much of the field artillery of 7 Division (along with the division itself) moved to that sector. They did not see action there, but were not returned to Rawlinson's command until 4 May. That gave 7 Division's artillery an insufficient five days in which to carry out registration.[34]

The plan for Aubers Ridge, in consequence, hinged on an artillery bombardment which would not only be employing relatively much less weight of metal than at Neuve Chapelle but would be firing it far less accurately. The British command, however, seemed blissfully unaware of all this. Rawlinson wrote with seeming satisfaction on 5 May: 'I think things look hopeful for our breaking the line . . . The guns are well regis-

---

[31] Rawlinson Diary 7/5/15; Haig Diary 7/5/15; Peter Mead, *The Eye in the Air* (London: HMSO, 1983), p. 68.

[32] Edmonds, *1915* vol. 2, p. 19.

[33] Ibid., p. 33.

[34] Rawlinson Short Note Diary 3/5/15.

tered and we have enough.'[35] It would be interesting to know on what basis Rawlinson had formed that judgement.

V

The infantry plan devised for Aubers Ridge also departed in some respects from that used at Neuve Chapelle. On the earlier occasion, the infantry had attacked directly across no-man's-land against a consecutive front line and with no large gaps between the various formations making the assault. At Aubers Ridge, three battalions of 24 Brigade attacking to the north of the Layes Brook were required to execute a 45 degree turn to the left after leaving their trenches and then make an oblique dash across no-man's-land to the German breastworks.[36] This was a complicated manoeuvre which would expose the brigade to heavy enfilade fire. In fact it was a similar manoeuvre to that suggested by Rawlinson in one of his earlier Neuve Chapelle schemes. Then Haig had vetoed it. But this time the Army commander offered no dissent.

Furthermore, there was to be a gap between these three battalions of 24 Brigade and its remaining battalion, the 2 Northants, which was to attack the German salient from the orchard.[37] This battalion, too, would be exposed to enfilade fire from the unattacked section of the German front. Special precautions could have been taken to neutralize the German defenders not directly attacked, by employment against them of the heaviest British ordinance. Nothing of the sort was undertaken. The bombardment of this part of the German front was assigned to 4.5 inch howitzers in one section, 18 pounders in another, and nothing at all in the section immediately to the left of the 2 Northants attack.[38]

This situation was duplicated on the left of the British attack. There a somewhat smaller gap existed between the 13 London Battalion and the remaining battalions of the 25th Brigade. In this instance the unattacked section of front was to be shelled only by weak 13 pounders.[39]

VI

This survey of the planning for Aubers Ridge renders inescapable a disturbing conclusion. It had seemed reasonable to assume that Rawlinson's

[35] Rawlinson Diary 5/5/15.
[36] 8 Division Narrative, IV Corps War Diary May 1915, WO 95/709.
[37] Ibid.
[38] Edmonds, *1915* vol. 2 (maps), map 4.
[39] Ibid.

direction of battles on the Western Front would follow a straightforward pattern. The commander would take good note of what had gone well and what had gone astray in any operation, and for the next occasion would seek to enhance the former aspects and diminish the latter. Such a proceeding would not necessarily ensure that each fresh operation would go better than its predecessor. A later attack might run into difficulties of terrain or weather which had been absent from the earlier. And the enemy also would be drawing conclusions from each experience, and so might devise new forms of defence which would more than offset any improvements in Rawlinson's methods of attack. But at least it might be assumed that the British conduct of operations would be on an ascending scale of competence.

Such an interpretation has generally been deemed applicable to the battle of Aubers Ridge. The British, it has been supposed, were seeking to repeat there what they had done well at Neuve Chapelle while avoiding the earlier operation's shortcomings. But in the event they were stymied by the response of the Germans, whose greatly enhanced defences denied Rawlinson even the partial success of Neuve Chapelle.

What is evident from our scrutiny of Rawlinson's plan for Aubers Ridge is that this benevolent interpretation will not stand. No doubt the Germans were learning from Neuve Chapelle. In crucial respects the British command, quite manifestly, was not. Far from doing better at Aubers Ridge what they had done well at Neuve Chapelle – namely the artillery bombardment – they were on the later occasion doing it extremely badly. Even more alarmingly, Rawlinson revealed no awareness of this deterioration in the quality of his preparations. Nor was wisdom being thrust upon him from above. Whereas Haig had called Rawlinson to order before Neuve Chapelle over the matter of inappropriate infantry tactics, the First Army commander imposed no restraining hand at Aubers Ridge.

It appears, then, that the exercise of command on the Western Front was not a consistent process of learning. To the misfortune of those required to carry out these operations, lessons already mastered might then go disregarded and have to be learned all over again.

10

The Battle

I

At 5 a.m. on 8 May – a fine and clear but somewhat chilly morning – the IV Corps bombardment opened. Several battalions noted that it was rather ragged: 'noise nothing like as bad as one had been led to expect, and general opinion seemed to be that bombardment was not so intense as at N.C.'[1] The assault battalions were also acutely aware of another factor. The British artillery was firing short, so that shells were dropping among the infantry waiting to attack. Particularly badly hit were the men of 24 Brigade: first they were showered with shrapnel from the wirecutting 18 pounders; then heavier shells from the 4.5 inch and 6 inch howitzers fell among them. And the left of 25 Brigade fell victim to the notoriously unreliable 4.7 inch guns, which were supposed to be firing on strongpoints well behind the German line. In this way the attacking troops sustained a substantial number of casualties even before leaving their trenches, and a quantity of the less-than-adequate supply of artillery ammunition had gone to waste.

Then, as the British troops left their trenches and advanced into no-man's-land, they were shot down by the unsubdued machine-guns and riflemen in the German line. Particularly heavy casualties were inflicted on those battalions trying to advance on the flanks of the several gaps in the attack. So on the front of 24 Brigade, 2 Sherwood Foresters reported eight machine-guns firing from the section of trench between their attack and that of 2 Northants.

[1] See 1/6 Scottish Rifles Narrative 9/5/15 in IV Corps War Diary May 1915, WO 95/709. All quotations in this chapter come from this source unless specified otherwise.

Only in three places, widely separated, were small lodgements made in the German front. On the left, 13 Londons had detonated two mines under the German trenches. Attacking immediately after the explosions a few platoons forced their way into the enemy positions. In the centre, a more substantial force from the Rifle Brigade passed over the German front line and established themselves not far short of the Rouges Bancs. On the extreme right, 2 Northants, though suffering severe casualties, managed to place about 30 men near the tip of the salient in the enemy line.

In their endeavours to reinforce these isolated groups 8 Division was to endure an agonizing day. In general, the bombardment had failed to subdue the German frontline machine-guns, which now exacted a heavy toll on the follow-up battalions. To their fire was added that of the many machine-gun strongpoints behind the German front which the bombardment had failed even to locate. This hail of fire soon halted all British attempts to leave their own trenches.

The troops thus denied the opportunity to go over the top were by no means out of danger. IV Corps's counter-battery fire had proved even more ineffectual than its bombardment of the German front system. And the German artillery was present at Aubers Ridge in much greater strength than it had been at Neuve Chapelle. Unhindered by British shelling, the German gunners brought down a rain of shrapnel and high explosive on the British front line and the assembly trenches just to its rear. Casualties immediately began to mount. They were substantially increased by the crowding in the British trenches caused by the 'conveyor belt' system designed by Rawlinson to feed a continual flow of troops into the British attack. In the circumstances of a failed offensive, this system added to the casualties and confusion as the rearward battalions became intermixed with the survivors and wounded of the first attack. The deadliness of the German fire is graphically illustrated by the case of the 2 Devons. Although this battalion took no part in any attack on this day, they suffered 242 casualties (about 30 per cent of the battalion). All occurred during their approach to the British front line.

In the event it proved impossible substantially to reinforce the small groups of men who had actually managed to advance. Haig and Rawlinson attempted to arrange a second attack at noon. This proved impossible. Then an afternoon attack was mooted. It too never took place. Finally at a conference with the corps commanders Haig decided that 7 Division should attack at dawn on the 10th.[2] Gough, now in command of the division, reconnoitred the front and soon came to the conclusion that, such

[2] Haig Diary 9/5/15.

was the chaos in the trenches, his division would not be able to relieve 8 Division in time. With Rawlinson's concurrence he recommended that the attack be cancelled. This was accepted by Haig.[3] During the night those troops who had got forward and were still alive were evacuated.

The I and Indian Corps had also gained no ground on their respective fronts. The total casualties for the day were just over 11,000 (4,500 in IV Corps alone). The total ground gained was nil.

II

What had gone wrong on the IV Corps front? Perhaps the most facile explanation was Rawlinson's: that the troops were to blame. In his diary he recorded:

> I fear that the E Lancs and some Battalions of the 25 Brigade got cold feet and did not advance with the dash they ought to have done in the first instance ... The E Lancs did not gain the enemy's trenches – it is doubtful if they tried very hard.[4]

As the East Lancs suffered 454 casualties out of a total of about 1,000 engaged, this would seem to be an unreasonable and unreasoning conclusion.

There were other causes of failure. The one usually given is that the Germans had considerably strengthened their front trench system. This was certainly true. Since Neuve Chapelle the enemy had doubled or in some areas trebled the thickness of their breastworks, to 15–20 feet. The breastworks were also heightened to 6–7 feet. The wire entanglements in front of the main line had been thickened and stouter wire had been employed. Further, sections of wire were sunk in a trench in front of the parapet, from where it could not be seen from the British line. At intervals of 20 yards, machine-gun emplacements protected by steel sheeting had been set up, and only a direct hit from a heavy shell could remove these. Further, the attacking forces were up against a larger number of defenders than at Neuve Chapelle. At the earlier battle a German regiment held 3,000 yards of front, at Aubers Ridge only 2,000 yards.[5]

Yet it is unlikely that the abysmal failure of the Aubers Ridge operation sprang from these enhancements in the German defences. More significant was the markedly inferior type of attack which the British were delivering. By adopting an infantry plan which involved complicated manoeuvres in no-

[3] Ibid. 10/5/15.
[4] Rawlinson Diary 10/5/15.
[5] 'Observations on the operations', 8 Division War Diary Apr–June 1915, WO 95/1672.

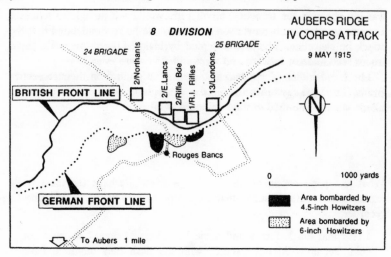

MAP 7

man's-land and allowed gaps between the attacking formations, the British commanders ensured that infantry casualties would be maximized should the bombardment prove ineffective. And this the lamentably weak bombardment certainly did.

Had Rawlinson again brought to bear a bombardment of the intensity employed at Neuve Chapelle, there is good reason to believe that he would have repeated his success at Aubers Ridge. For if we take note of the two points where, at this second operation, lodgements were made in the German line (setting aside the small success which the mines facilitated on the left), it transpires that both lay in the sectors bombarded by the 6 inch howitzers – the weapons which had contributed so largely to the conquest of the enemy front line at Neuve Chapelle. So it is not surprising to find the official narrative by one of the groups which enjoyed initial success at Aubers Ridge, the 2 Northants, stating: 'the enemy trenches . . . had been breached by our art[illery].'

It is fair to speculate that, had Rawlinson's forces been able on 9 May to bombard the entire front of attack with 6 inch howitzers, a different situation would have obtained. But owing to the paucity of such guns, this would only have applied to a frontage of 600 yards – which had been Rawlinson's first suggestion. This was of course a very narrow front, and would have exposed all the attacking troops to enfilade fire. But at least directly ahead of them they would have been encountering a more or less neutralized enemy and thus would have had a greater chance of securing a substantial lodgement.

Whether any further advance could have been made is too speculative even to consider. But had not another yard of ground been gained, Aubers Ridge would still have managed to duplicate the minor success of Neuve Chapelle, instead of resulting in abject failure.

In sum, when Haig and Rawlinson failed to apply at Aubers Ridge the principles of bombardment established at Neuve Chapelle, they threw away all chance of making even a break-in, let alone a substantial advance.

11

Givenchy

I

The period between the battle of Aubers Ridge in May and the battle of Loos in September was one of frustration and disappointment for Rawlinson. After Aubers Ridge, Rawlinson reached the conclusion that only attacks on a wide front after a prolonged bombardment would achieve success.[1] But he was relegated to the role of spectator while Haig scored a partial success using these methods at Festubert in mid-May.

Meanwhile his relations with Sir John French continued to be poor. Although Rawlinson had been 'thrilled' by the political crisis in Britain[2] which saw the formation of the first wartime coalition government, he was aware that the 'shells scandal' which had helped to precipitate the crisis had been based on information leaked by French in order to imperil Kitchener's position.[3] This intelligence Rawlinson passed on to Kitchener via the latter's military secretary, Brinsley Fitzgerald.[4] A few weeks later Rawlinson heard from a French liaison officer with IV Corps 'that Joffre & French H.Q. were much put out with Sir J French for his stupidity & obstinacy.'[5] What incident had aroused Joffre's ill humour is not clear, but Rawlinson saw it as his duty to inform Kitchener of the rift. He recorded disingenuously in his diary: 'I wrote to Fitzgerald to tell K [about the matter], as if the question

[1] Rawlinson to Fitzgerald 11/5/15, Rawlinson Papers 5201/33/17, NAM.
[2] Rawlinson Diary 20/5/15.
[3] Ibid. 24/5/15. Following the failed attack at Aubers Ridge, a report (inspired by Sir John French) appeared in British newspapers claiming that the setback was the consequence of a lack of shells and holding Kitchener to blame. This 'shells scandal' played a part in Asquith's decision to form a wartime coalition government.
[4] Rawlinson to Fitzgerald 24/5/15, Rawlinson Papers 5201/33/17, NAM.
[5] Rawlinson Diary 12/6/15.

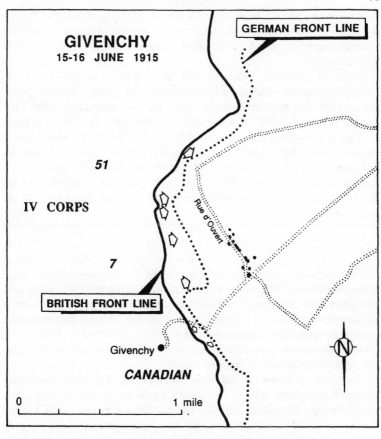

GIVENCHY
15-16 JUNE 1915

GERMAN FRONT LINE

51

IV CORPS

Rue d'Ouvert

7

BRITISH FRONT LINE

Givenchy

CANADIAN

0   1 mile

MAP 8

of Sir John French's removal again comes up they may wish to know Joffre's feelings. It is far too serious a matter to allow any personal considerations to stand in the way.'[6] Clearly, if Sir John retained his command it would be no fault of Sir Henry's.

Rawlinson was soon given further reason for antipathy towards French. As divisions of Kitchener's recruits arrived on the Western Front, the decision was taken to form a Third Army. Rawlinson was the senior general, but French passed him over. Command of the new army went to Sir Charles Monro, who had been in charge of I Corps. Rawlinson commented on this:

[6] Ibid. 24/6/15.

'Monro passes over my head to get III Army. I didn't think with Sir John at the head of affairs they would select me ... suppose I cannot expect fair treatment with Sir John & old Robertson against me. I must await my time & be patient.'[7]

Rawlinson's continuing disfavour at GHQ tied him more closely to Haig. For it was Haig who had saved his command after Neuve Chapelle. And it was to Haig that he must look for future useful employment in the First Army. Further, if Sir John's career should go awry then Haig would be more than likely to succeed him. This would mean that Rawlinson would have a supporter at GHQ instead of an antagonist. It would also mean that the command of an army would again fall vacant, with Rawlinson this time in a good position to secure it. So it is not surprising that from this time on Rawlinson was Haig's man, or that he proved eager for the removal of Sir John French.

II

It was unfortunate for Rawlinson that the next employment he was offered was a most unpromising operation indeed, an attack on the Rue d'Ouvert in the area of Givenchy. This straight road, lined for the most part with solid two-storey houses, had been one of the objectives in the battle of Festubert. Despite repeated attempts, the trenches in front of the Rue d'Ouvert had on that occasion remained in German hands.

The battle of Festubert had closed on 25 May. Two days later Joffre explained to Haig his intention to launch a general offensive in early June. He asked for a British diversionary attack at the same time. Joffre wanted this to be in the direction of Loos, but Haig considered the area so unpromising that he sought and gained permission once more to attack the Rue d'Ouvert.[8] To carry out this attack Rawlinson's IV Corps was moved south and reconstituted. It now consisted of the Canadian and 7 Divisions and a Territorial Division, 51 (Highland).

On 29 May, Rawlinson moved his headquarters from Merville to Hinges and during the next few days reconnoitred the area over which his attack was to be made. He did not like what he saw:

> it is a pretty stiff nut for us to crack. It will cost us many thousands of lives before we are in possession of it unless we get an unlimited amount of ammunition to smash the place to pieces before we go in.[9]

[7] Ibid. 13/7/15.
[8] Haig Diary 27/5/15.
[9] Rawlinson Diary 4/6/15.

There is no evidence that Rawlinson conveyed these views to Haig. Rather, he set about devising a plan and ensuring that his divisions were trained for their task. Rawlinson felt particularly concerned about the poor staff work of the Highland Division, which was to carry out the northern section of the attack: eventually he sent Dallas, his own COS, to help them prepare their orders.[10] In Rawlinson's view 'their officers are not good, too few gentlemen amongst them.'[11] These strictures were unwarranted. The un-gentlemanly Highlanders would soon prove as willing as any of Rawlinson's regular divisions to sacrifice themselves in futile attacks.

Never during the course of the war was Rawlinson more pessimistic about an operation he was required to carry out. In the two weeks before the battle his diary is littered with references to the hopelessness of the task. His despair deepened when on the eve of battle Haig insisted on being provided with plans for further advances once the Rue d'Ouvert had been captured. Rawlinson commented:

> I wrote out some orders at night and showed them to him in the morning. They are in the form of a pious aspiration rather than anything that is likely to be actually carried into effect for we are not going to capture the Rue d'Ouvert as easily as he appears to think. The new photos taken on the afternoon of the 12th of the enemy's trenches show that the Boshes have been working like beavers and have constructed many new works which will give us trouble – they have strengthened their wire to an alarming extent and it is doubtful if we shall be able to cut it satisfactorily... My opinion is that we shall be very lucky if we get the Rue d'Ouvert after three days hard fighting and 5,000 casualties.[12]

It is indicative of Rawlinson's failure to convey these views to his chief that, at the same time, Haig was writing in optimistic terms about the outcome of the battle and describing the wire-cutting as quite satisfactory.[13]

After three postponements ordered by GHQ as a result of the con-stantly changing date of the French attack, a 48-hour bombardment of the German positions along the Rue d'Ouvert began on 15 June.[14] As had been the case at Festubert, the bombardment was slow and deliberate so that its effect could be carefully observed. In a return to Neuve Chapelle tactics, most of the twenty 6 inch howitzers were used to bombard the

[10] Ibid. 13/6/15.
[11] Ibid. 9/6/15.
[12] Ibid. 13/6/15.
[13] Haig Diary 13/6/15.
[14] Ibid. 15/6/15. For the postponements see entries for 8, 11, 12 June.

German frontline trenches.[15] And for the first time, on one section of the front 4.5 inch howitzers were used to cut the wire.[16] But in the key respect what we are observing is neither a return to Neuve Chapelle nor an advance to something better, but rather a repetition of Aubers Ridge.

At Aubers Ridge 190 guns were employed to bombard a front of 1,500 yards; at Givenchy the figures were only slightly more favourable for the attackers – 211 guns on a front of 1,300 yards.[17] The improvement was not significant. The result, consequently, was a rerun of Aubers Ridge. Several lodgements in the enemy line were made, but wire-cutting had failed on a considerable length of the front so that once more the lodgements were widely separated. Attempts to reinforce the troops in the enemy line were defeated by machine-gun and rifle fire from the great number of German troops untouched by the bombardment. To this fire was added that of the German artillery, which had survived the British counter-batteries virtually unscathed. To make matters worse, those few British troops who had entered the German trenches soon ran out of hand grenades (a large supply of which had been blown up by German artillery on the 15th). They were bombed out by German grenadiers. By nightfall all surviving British troops were back in their own line.[18]

Undeterred by this total failure, Haig ordered further attacks on the 17th, using the Canadian Division to reinforce 7 and 51 Divisions.[19] The result was the same as on the 15th. At a cost of 3,500 casualties IV Corps gained not an inch of ground.[20] What made this failure worse was that their attacks had been defeated by local enemy troops. The Germans had not diverted even a battalion from the French front.

As soon as the battle had ended the reasons for failure were investigated. This brought forth the by now almost obligatory reference to the failings of the troops. So of the Canadians, who had lost 600 men in the action,[21] Rawlinson commented: 'I don't think they meant business.'[22] Alongside such grotesqueries Rawlinson's report, drawn up soon after the battle, contained only one point of substance. However, it was a point possessing wide ramifications for future battles:

[15] IV Corps Operation Order No. 24, 7/6/15, IV Corps War Diary May 1915, WO 95/709.

[16] Edmonds, *1915* vol. 2, p. 94 n. 6.

[17] For the number of guns see IV Corps Operation Order 7/6/15. For the length of front see Edmonds, *1915* vol. 2, sketch facing p. 93.

[18] The above account is based on a IV Corps report 21/6/15 in IV Corps War Diary June–Aug 1915, WO 95/710.

[19] Haig Diary 16/6/15.

[20] Casualty Returns, IV Corps Operations 15–18 June 1915, Rawlinson Papers 1/4, CC.

[21] Ibid.

[22] Rawlinson Diary 17/6/15.

it is evident [the report began] that the hostile trenches are from seven to ten feet deep and that shell-proof dug outs have been constructed some five or six feet below the ground level. Into these the garrisons no doubt withdraw during the artillery bombardment and the success of the attack therefore depends on the ability of our Infantry to reach the hostile parapets before the enemy can leave his dug-outs to man them. The moral[e] effect of the heavy shells is neutralised by this form of semi-permanent fortification which the enemy has had ample time to prepare in the last six months in soil well suited to the purpose at all times of the year.

I much doubt if any kind of artillery fire however accurate and well sustained will have the desired effect unless it is sufficient to bury the garrisons in the deep dug-outs they have now constructed, and this is a matter of chance.[23]

This was an extremely important conclusion, raising the question whether even a bombardment as intense as that employed at Neuve Chapelle would have proved sufficient. It remained to be seen how Rawlinson would respond when faced with similar defensive works in future battles.

In the aftermath of Givenchy Rawlinson feared that he might be called upon to make yet another attempt on the Rue d'Ouvert. When such a course was indeed suggested by the commander of the Canadian Division, Rawlinson replied sharply:

What is the object of our attacks on the Givenchy ridge? A feeling exists that life is being thrown away on objects which are not worth it ... Are we not asking too much of our Infantry?[24]

And in his diary he wrote:

It is a thousand pities that we were allowed to attack the Rue d'Ouvert[,] for any sensible person would have known that we should not take it! We lost 3000 men, fired off a lot of Am[mu]n[ition] & did harm to our morale.[25]

Whether Haig was being excluded from the category of 'sensible persons' can only be guessed. What is noteworthy about so trenchant a comment is that Rawlinson had held similar views in advance of the battle. He had made no representations then to higher authorities.

---

[23] IV Corps report 21/6/15.
[24] Rawlinson to Alderton (GOC Canadian Division) 23/6/15, Rawlinson Papers, 1/4, CC.
[25] Rawlinson Diary 24/6/15.

12

Loos: The Plan

I

Givenchy would prove the last minor operation involving Rawlinson in the course of the war. Indeed, simultaneously with its termination planning was under way at First Army HQ for a large undertaking in co-operation with the French, in which IV Corps would play a major part. The attack would be in the area of the mining town of Loos.

II

At the time of Aubers Ridge back in May, the BEF had consisted of 16 divisions. During the next three months a further 12 divisions were added. So, by August, the British had 11 Regular, 6 Territorial, 7 Kitchener, 2 Canadian, and 2 Indian divisions – in all 900,000 men.[1] Concurrent with this expansion the BEF took over further sections of the front from the French. In June, Haig's First Army extended its line to the south, to include the area from the La Bassée Canal to Loos.

Haig was quick to reconnoitre this new sector of his command. Surprisingly, in view of his later attitudes, he formed the opinion that it was a suitable area for offensive operations. He told Sir John French that he thought it would be best, as soon as Givenchy had been taken, 'to transfer the area of activity to the south side of the [La Bassée] canal, in the direction of Loos.' He reasoned that 'the general features [of the ground] are much more suitable for military operations than where we have been attacking; they are more undulating and country is open.'[2] On closer

[1] Edmonds, *1915* vol. 2, p. 133 n. 1.
[2] Haig Diary 26/5/15.

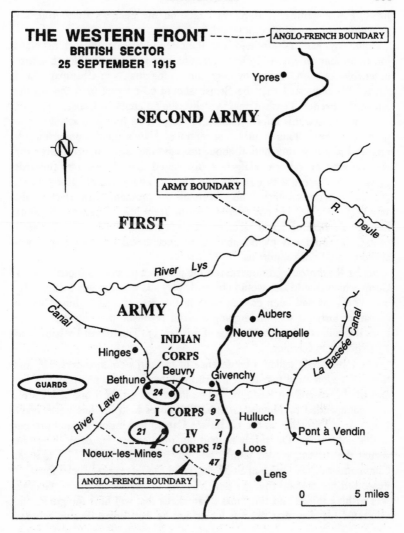

THE WESTERN FRONT ------- ANGLO-FRENCH BOUNDARY
BRITISH SECTOR
25 SEPTEMBER 1915

Ypres

SECOND ARMY

ARMY BOUNDARY

FIRST

R. Deule

River Lys

ARMY

Canal

Aubers
Neuve Chapelle

INDIAN
CORPS

Hinges

La Bassée Canal

Beuvry

Bethune

Givenchy

GUARDS

24

2

River Lawe

I CORPS

9

Hulluch

21

7

IV

1

Pont à Vendin

Noeux-les-Mines

CORPS

15

Loos

47

Lens

ANGLO-FRENCH BOUNDARY

0   5 miles

MAP 12

inspection Haig's opinion became less favourable. He found the country so open that it provided no good artillery positions, and deemed the distance between the opposing lines of trenches too great for anything but a night attack.[3] However, during the next few weeks his opinion fluctuated. By 14

[3] Ibid. 27/5/15.

June he was writing: 'I think an attack on the enemy's front from say [Haisnes] to Loos is quite practical.'[4]

Some days earlier Joffre had communicated to Sir John French his plans for an autumn offensive. Joffre's intention was to make the Noyon salient untenable for the Germans by huge converging attacks in Champagne and Artois. He requested that the British should co-operate in Artois on the left of the French Tenth Army, by delivering an attack at Loos.[5]

French passed this information on to Haig on 19 June and asked him to prepare a plan.[6] This request concentrated Haig's mind wonderfully. It removed any lingering notion about the advantages of attacking over the open ground near Loos. Haig now discovered that 'the country [towards Loos] . . . is covered with coal pits and houses. The towns of Lieven, Lens, etc., run into one another. This all renders the problem of an attack in this area very difficult.' He considered that the front line of trenches opposite Loos to a length of 1,200 yards could be captured. But he added significantly, 'it would not be possible to advance beyond, because our own artillery could not support us.'[7]

So far Rawlinson had not entered the planning process, although the IV Corps which faced Loos would obviously play a key role in any battle there. The IV Corps had been concentrated in this area since late June.[8] Given its earlier losses it was undergoing a major reconstitution. By the time of Loos it would consist of 1 (Regular) Division, 47 (Territorial) Division, and 15 (Kitchener) Division.

On 3 July Haig called a conference of his corps commanders. He told them of his intention to capture a section of the German line opposite Loos and the Hohenzollern Redoubt.[9] (The latter was on the front of I Corps, now commanded by Hubert Gough. This corps held the line north of IV Corps from Vermelles to the La Bassée Canal.) Rawlinson was not present at this conference. On 1 July he had left for London on leave. There he visited the dentist, played tennis, was invested with the KCMG (Knight Commander of the Order of St Michael and St George) at 'Buck House',[10] expressed the opinion that the new Minister of Munitions (Lloyd George) was rushing things and 'may make bad shells that will hurt the guns', and reiterated his view that the war would not be won unless Britain invaded

[4] Ibid. 14/6/15.
[5] Edmonds, *1915* vol. 2, p. 113.
[6] Haig Diary 19/6/15.
[7] Quotations from ibid. 20/6/15 and 22/6/15.
[8] Rawlinson Short Note Diary 2, 5 ,6, 7 July 1915.
[9] Haig Diary 3/7/15.
[10] Rawlinson Short Note Diary 2, 5, 6, 7 July 1915.

Austria from the south in co-operation with the Russians, Bulgarians, and Italians.[11] He returned to France on 8 July.[12]

On arrival at his headquarters he found Barter (the commander of 47 Division and acting corps commander in his absence) at work on Haig's proposal to capture the German trenches opposite Loos. Barter's plan provided for a three-day bombardment followed by a two-division assault from the Béthune–Lens road in the south to the Vermelles–Loos road in the north.[13] Rawlinson approved the plan, with some minor modifications, and passed it on to Haig.

As it happened, on the day that Haig received it he was writing to French deprecating any attack in the Loos area. He put forward instead a further plan to capture Aubers Ridge, and in the course of his exposition made the following observation:

> The resources at my disposal . . . do not permit of an offensive being undertaken on a large scale, such as might lead at once to freedom of manoeuvre, and it is therefore necessary, whilst being prepared for any eventuality in case of success, to limit the offensive to a definite operation within the scope of the force.[14]

Sir John might well have observed that, as Haig had amply demonstrated the difficulty of capturing Aubers Ridge, he could hardly do worse somewhere else. Yet this was not his response. Rather, he accepted Haig's alternative proposal.

However, the British commander-in-chief was soon obliged to reconsider. At an interview with Joffre early in August, Sir John had been pressed to support the operations of the French by attacking on their flank from the La Bassée Canal to Loos. The objective was the capture of Hill 70 and Hulluch.[15] Reluctantly abandoning Haig's Aubers Ridge plan, Sir John assented. But the qualified nature of this assent is evident from his subsequent instructions to Haig: his attack was 'to be made chiefly with artillery and [he was] not to launch a large force of infantry to the attack of objectives which are so strongly held as to be liable to result only in the sacrifice of many lives.'[16]

Haig responded by holding a conference with his three corps commanders

[11] Rawlinson Diary 1/7/15 and 4/7/15.

[12] Rawlinson Short Note Diary 8/7/15.

[13] 'Scheme for the capture of Front Line System of German Trenches between the Bethune–Lens Road . . . and the Vermelles–Loos Road by Major-General Barter 23/7/15', IV Corps War Diary June–Aug 1915, WO 95/710.

[14] First Army to GHQ 23/7/15, First Army War Diary June–July 1915, WO 95/156.

[15] Haig Diary 7/8/15.

[16] Ibid.

at which he called for new plans. In the first instance the objectives of the IV Corps would be the German front line opposite Loos. The I Corps on their left would capture the Hohenzollern Redoubt. The Indian Corps would not participate. The object of these attacks would be to hold the enemy infantry to their positions while the French launched their major offensive to the south. A subsequent advance towards Loos, Hill 70, and Hulluch was mooted 'on the assumption that the progress of the French offensive makes such an attack possible.' A new element was then introduced by Haig. He announced: 'It is anticipated that an ample supply of asphyxiating gas will be available, and its employment in connection with these attacks should be considered.'[17]

For the first time Rawlinson set about studying the problems of attacking the German positions opposite Loos. What he learned did not arouse his enthusiasm. He discovered, as Haig had done already, that to the rear of the British line – where his artillery would have to be assembled – 'the area is open and undulating and is devoid of cover.' Moreover in the area to be attacked 'the mining villages, railway embankments, and "Fosses" [pit-heads] which are numerous throughout the district, have been fortified by the enemy during the last few months with great care and diligence.' His plan was one of extreme caution. He proposed capturing the German front line after a bombardment lasting 'several days'. This would be followed by a pause while the artillery was brought up for the attack on Loos village. The village would be heavily bombarded and then drenched with all the gas that was available.

Rawlinson judged that if these methods were successful it should be possible to carry the village and Hill 70. He pointed out, nevertheless, that the attainment of these objectives would bring the IV Corps up against a German second line of defence, 'Continuous . . . well-constructed and strongly wired', which ran from Lens northward to Cité St Auguste and Hulluch. He saw the capture of this line as a separate operation requiring fresh troops which 'could only be undertaken successfully in conjunction with a vigorous and successful offensive by the French against Lens from the South.'[18]

These cautious plans were almost immediately overthrown by actions of the French and British high commands. On 12 August Joffre wrote to French saying that British support would be effective only 'if it takes the form of a large and powerful attack, composed of the maximum force you have available, executed with the hope of success and carried through to

---

[17] First Army Order 13/8/15, First Army War Diary Aug 1915, WO 95/157.

[18] All quotations from Rawlinson, 'Proposals For The Attack of Loos Village and Hill 70', IV Corps War Diary Sept 1915, WO 95/711.

the end.'[19] To this Sir John reluctantly agreed. He told Haig that he now wished to attack 'on as wide a front as possible, and that he knew that we must have big losses in order to achieve any result.'[20]

Even had Sir John refused to conform to Joffre's wishes, he would soon have discovered that his compliance was required by the British government. On 18 August Kitchener arrived at GHQ. He announced that the situation of the Russians – who had just lost Warsaw and whose armies were falling back in disarray – required the British to attack to the utmost of their power. He '*had decided that we must act with all our energy, and do our utmost to help the French, even though, by so doing, we suffered very heavy losses indeed.*'[21] Haig, whether or not he retained his original doubts, replied that his army was ready to attack. 'All we wanted was ammunition.'[22]

Rawlinson received the news with apprehension. He wrote: 'I fear heavy losses and doubt if we will get through unless the gas turns up trumps which it may do, but we are not very good at these new improvisations.'[23] He had reason to be apprehensive. The operation which had started life as an attempt to capture the German front line, and had then developed into an attack on Loos and Hill 70, now had as its objective the Haute Deule Canal, some two miles to the east of Hill 70.[24] It therefore involved the capture of the German second line, an undertaking that Rawlinson had argued would require fresh troops and a whole new operation. Such an operation could only be prosecuted in the context of a substantial French advance.

Whatever his misgivings, Rawlinson had now to formulate a new plan. He decided that 47 Division would attack to the south of Loos, thereby forming a defensive right flank. The main advance would be assigned to 15 Division, a Kitchener force of which Rawlinson had formed a favourable opinion.[25] It was to capture Loos village and Hill 70, and then to overrun the German second line in the course of reaching the Haute Deule Canal near Pont à Vendin. The 1 Division would be held in reserve. As regards the contribution of the artillery, the infantry attack was to be preceded by a four-day bombardment. In addition, gas was to be used on the entire front of attack (which was also to include 2 and 9 Divisions of I Corps on Rawlinson's left). On 22 August Rawlinson had attended a gas demonstration at St Omer. It had left him distinctly unimpressed. However, after

[19] Joffre to French 12/8/15, quoted in Haig Diary 14/8/15.

[20] Haig Diary 17/8/15.

[21] Ibid. 19/8/15. Underlined in the original.

[22] Ibid.

[23] Rawlinson Diary 20/8/15.

[24] First Army, Plan of Operations 28/8/15, First Army War Diary Aug 1915, WO 95/157.

[25] Rawlinson Short Note Diary 17/7/15.

speaking to the gas experts six days later he became convinced that all would go well.[26]

There remained one aspect of the Loos plan that caused Rawlinson concern. In the final version, a section of German line opposite his own 1 Division and Gough's 7 Division was to be left unattacked. Perhaps remembering Aubers Ridge with its deadly enfilade fire from the un-attacked section of the front, and now convinced that there was a 'good chance of a big success', Rawlinson saw Gough and suggested that this part of the line should also be assaulted.[27] Gough agreed, as did Haig when his approval was sought later in the day.[28] The attack was now to be continuous along the front from Loos to the La Bassée Canal.

This decision was to have an important consequence. Rawlinson and Gough had just incorporated into the initial assault the two divisions hitherto assigned to act as a reserve, so the First Army now had no reserve divisions. The only reserves available would be the three divisions of XI Corps, recently formed by GHQ. (These were the 21 and 24 Kitchener Divisions and the Guards Division.) But these troops were not assigned to Rawlinson or Gough, or even placed under the command of Haig. Sir John French insisted that they remain under his own control.[29] The significance of this arrangement seems to have been lost on Rawlinson. For it is clear that he thought these reserves would form an integral part of his attacking force on the first day of the battle and would enable him to achieve very large results. So in his diary for 14 September he refers to his own troops and the reserve divisions as forcing their way through the German second line by 'sheer weight of numbers'.[30]

It is worth making a comment on the process that has just been re-counted. For it is a process by now becoming uncomfortably familiar. Rawlinson, seeing only the prospect of a modest advance, found himself confronted with a wildly ambitious plan. Yet (in company with Haig in this instance) he managed by stages to cast off the wisdom of bite and hold, and before long was endorsing the visionary proposals of his superiors.

III

As the day of battle approached, Haig, as was so often the case, became certain that a major triumph lay to hand. He urged his corps commanders

[26] Rawlinson Diary 23/8/15, 28/8/15.
[27] Ibid. 28/8/15.
[28] Ibid.
[29] Holmes, *Little Field-Marshal*, p. 300.
[30] Rawlinson Diary 14/9/15.

to push on past the Haute Deule Canal to the plain of Douai, thereby turning a tactical success into a strategic victory.[31] Rawlinson, however, was becoming concerned that even the attainment of the 'tactical success' involved in the capture of the German second line would prove more difficult than he had but recently been anticipating. He noted that the Germans were strengthening their defences, 'especially on their second line which is now wire[d] the whole way along.' And he added: 'I feel in my bones that we shall be very fortunate indeed if we manage to penetrate there. It looks to me as if we may be here for the winter.'[32] Rawlinson now began to define success as the capture of the German first line, and to suggest that just the capture of Loos village would be a triumph – 'a great feather in the cap for IV Corps.'[33]

Evidently a gap was reappearing between Rawlinson's aspirations, which were retreating to about what he had managed to accomplish at Neuve Chapelle, and Haig's. Yet there is no evidence that Rawlinson brought this difference in expectations to the attention of the First Army commander. His dependence on Haig's approval precluded such frankness. Nevertheless, Rawlinson's private view that the IV Corps would be 'very fortunate indeed' to penetrate the German second line should be kept in mind when the 'lost opportunities' at Loos are discussed.

IV

Once the broad outlines of the Loos operation had been decided, detailed planning could begin. To help in this process Rawlinson acquired two staff officers who were to remain with him for almost the rest of the war. Rawlinson had long decided that Dallas, his COS, was inadequate as a planner. On 14 August Dallas was replaced by Brigadier-General A. A. Montgomery, whom Rawlinson had known since his staff college days, and who had been COS to Rawlinson during his brief spell as commander of 4 Division.[34] To command the artillery of 1, 15, and 47 Divisions, Brigadier-General Budworth, artillery commander of 1 Division, was elevated to the position of IV Corps artillery adviser for the duration of the battle.[35]

Three main elements confronted Rawlinson, Montgomery, and Bud-

---

[31] 'First Army Conference on Monday, 6 Sept. 1915', Butler Papers 69/10/1, IWM.

[32] Rawlinson Diary 14/9/15 and 17/9/15.

[33] Ibid. 2/9/15.

[34] See Rawlinson Diary 8/8/15 and 13/8/15 and General A. A. Montgomery-Massingberd, 'The Autobiography of a Gunner', p. 18 (unpublished typescript), Montgomery-Massingberd Papers, Folder 159, Liddell Hart Centre, King's College, London.

[35] Anstey, History of the Royal Artillery 1914–18, p. 95.

worth in planning for the attack on Loos. The first was the quite familiar question of artillery: what resources were available and how were they to be employed? The second was the unfamiliar matter of the use of poison gas. The third fell between the well-known and the little-known: the tactics to be employed by the attacking infantry now that the majority of Rawlinson's soldiers were not products of the old regular army.

The last matter may be dealt with summarily. At Loos, for the first time in a major battle, Rawlinson would be commanding predominantly non-regular troops. In fact he had one Territorial (47), one Kitchener (15), and one Regular (1) division. Given this mixture, what needs to be stressed is that there was virtually no heart-searching about the infantry tactics that should be adopted, and no suggestion that non-regular troops might be incapable of conforming to the relatively sophisticated attack formations of the old army. It seems always to have been assumed that the new divisions would use the same formations as the old. Thus the battalions of 15 and 47 Divisions attacked in columns of platoons on a front of two platoons.[36]

The attacks were to be made at a fast pace and the momentum of the attack was to be maintained at all costs.[37] In other words the formations and tactics adopted by the new divisions at Loos were similar to those used by the regulars at Neuve Chapelle. This point would perhaps not seem remarkable but for the abandonment of such premises on a subsequent occasion.

V

As regards artillery planning for the battle, some positive aspects may be noticed.

One tactical innovation deserves mention. It was arranged that, during the period just preceding the infantry advance and while the gas was being released, the German defences were to be swept by shrapnel. It was hoped thereby that many of the Germans manning the trenches in anticipation of the coming attack would be eliminated.[38]

On the right of the IV Corps sector, observation of the enemy lines was generally good.[39] In addition, concealed positions were available close

---

[36] 'Formation in which 44th Brigade attacked', 44 Brigade War Diary July 1915–July 1916, WO 95/1934; 47 London Division Instructions 5/9/15, 47 Division War Diary Sept 1915, WO 95/2698.

[37] Ibid.

[38] 'The IVth Corps Artillery at the Battle of Loos', Montgomery-Massingberd Papers, Folder 45.

[39] Ibid.

behind the British front for the wire-cutting guns of 15 and 47 Divisions, so that most of the wire could be bombarded at relatively close range.[40] Further, some of the most southerly batteries, located between the Double Crassier and the Loos-Vermelles road, were able to fire virtually along the German trenches rather than at right angles to them. This meant that a much higher proportion of shells would fall within the German lines.

As against these positive aspects, a number of factors were bound to tell against the effectiveness of the artillery preparations for the Loos offensive.

On the left of the IV Corps sector and particularly in the zone of 1 Division, the ground immediately behind the British front was devoid of cover. No concealed positions for the field artillery could be obtained. Accordingly most of the 18 pounders had to be placed well back and attempt to cut the wire at long range. This told against accurate shooting.[41]

The configuration of the ground also meant that certain sections of the German defences could not be directly observed from the British positions. This applied to the northern end of Loos village, Cité St Auguste, and the country between Hill 70 and Hulluch.[42] Bombarding the defences in these areas required the co-operation of spotter planes. Given the shortage of pilots experienced in this work, this meant that the bombardment could be neither as prolonged nor as intensive as in areas open to direct observation.[43] Even some sections of the wire were invisible except from the air, thus preventing accurate assessment of the progress of wire-cutting.[44]

A further difficulty encountered by IV Corps artillery was the siting of the German second line. More will be said about this when the German defences are discussed, but it should be noted that this line had been deliberately positioned beyond the range of British wire-cutting guns and on a reverse slope.[45] Hence it could only be bombarded sporadically, at long range, and without direct observation. Under these circumstances, there was little prospect of removing the wire.

A serious deficiency in the artillery bombardment of one sector sprang from the late decision to add 1 Division to the initial attack, rather than hold it in reserve. Most of the artillery of that division had already been moved to the south to support 47 and 15 Divisions. It was not possible to return more than a few batteries to 1 Division's zone without causing

[40] Edmonds, *1915* vol. 2, pp. 174–5.

[41] IV Corps Artillery at Loos.

[42] Ibid.

[43] E. R. Ludlow-Hewitt to Air Vice-Marshal Brooke-Popham 22/9/26, Official History Correspondence: Loos, Cab 45/120.

[44] Ibid.

[45] Wynne, *If Germany Attacks*, p. 64.

serious dislocation to the bombardment plan. The 1 Division was therefore mainly supported by the reserve batteries of 47 Division equipped with obsolete 15 pounders, and with some 18 pounder batteries of 24 Division recently arrived from England who had no experience in wire-cutting.[46]

In addition to these problems, most of the causes of artillery inaccuracy mentioned in relation to the battles of Neuve Chapelle and Aubers Ridge still applied. Thus the aerial photographs upon which the heavy artillery relied to construct maps of the German positions were often indistinct; no compensation was made for the errors inherent in transposing photographs to maps; insufficient allowance was made for worn guns; and the various meteorological factors mentioned earlier were not given sufficient weight.

Yet the various considerations so far mentioned – some aiding, some hampering the effectiveness of the bombardment – are of minor import when set alongside the really great consideration: that of numbers, both of guns and of shells. What mattered was whether Rawlinson's artillery was in a position to throw at the enemy such a weight of explosive as would suppress the German defences long enough for the attacking infantry to overrun them. The answer is straightforward, and it is plainly in the negative. It is only necessary to compare the artillery resources available for Loos with those employed earlier at Neuve Chapelle for the deficiency in artillery to become painfully evident. At Loos, unlike Neuve Chapelle, there was never any question that detailed calculations would be made of the number of shells needed to destroy a section of trench, or that the guns required to fire that number of shells would be assembled. For the autumn battle it was known from the start that the British would lack both the weapons and the projectiles systematically to destroy the enemy defences.[47]

Altogether on the front of IV and I Corps, 533 guns were concentrated, 255 of which were to support IV Corps. Excluding four light guns which hardly contributed to the bombardment, they consisted of 184 guns in the field artillery, 20 assigned to counter-battery, and 251 in the heavy artillery[48] (see table 12.1). As was customary, these were divided between corps and Army artillery. Budworth, who as we have seen had been designated IV Corps artillery adviser, was in charge of the field artillery. He assigned the 15 and 18 pounders to cut the wire, and the howitzers to bombard trenches and machine-gun posts.[49] The heavy artillery remained under Army control and was commanded by Brigadier-General Franks.

[46] IV Corps Artillery at Loos.

[47] Anstey, History of the Royal Artillery 1914–18, p. 97.

[48] IV Corps Artillery at Loos.

[49] Rawlinson to First Army 9/10/15 (on the artillery lessons at Loos), IV Corps War Diary Oct–Dec 1915, WO 95/712. (Henceforth Rawlinson, Loos Artillery Lessons.)

TABLE 12.1 *Composition of IV Corps artillery at Loos*

	Type of gun	Number
Field artillery	15 pounder gun	32
	18 pounder gun	120
	4.5 inch howitzer	32
		184
Counter-batteries	60 pounder gun	12
	4.7 inch gun	8
		20
Heavy artillery	6 inch gun	2
	8 inch howitzer	8
	9.2 inch howitzer	4
	15 inch howitzer	1
	155 mm (French) howitzer	8
	5 inch howitzer	8
	6 inch howitzer	16
		47
Total		251

These guns were to bombard trenches, strongpoints, fortified houses, and dugouts.[50] In what was a most clumsy arrangement, Franks also commanded the counter-batteries for the whole front.[51]

It will be noticed that the total number of guns (251) available at Loos to support the three divisions of IV Corps was considerably less than the number which had supported the three attacking divisions at Neuve Chapelle (342). Yet the defences that the artillery at Loos were required to subdue were much more extensive and formidable than they had been in the March battle. At Neuve Chapelle the target had been 2,000 yards of trench and its protecting wire. At Loos 36,000 yards of trench on the front of IV Corps required to be dealt with (see table 12.2). In addition, the villages of Loos, Hulluch, and Cité St Pierre which contained many fortified houses and machine-gun posts needed to be bombarded.[52]

Clearly, in terms of guns per yard of enemy trench, the Loos bombardment (one gun to 141 yards) compared most unfavourably with that at

[50] Rawlinson, Loos Artillery Lessons.
[51] Edmonds, *1915* vol. 2, p. 175.
[52] Rawlinson, Loos Artillery Lessons.

TABLE 12.2   *Enemy trench system at Loos*

Position	Length of trench (in yards)
Front line trench	7500
Second line trench	7300
Trenches protecting Loos village	2000
Communication trenches	19200
Total	36000

Neuve Chapelle (one gun to 6 yards). Two factors, certainly, detract somewhat from the force of this comparison. First, the bombardment at Loos lasted for much longer (four spells each of 12 hours, as compared with Neuve Chapelle's one period of only 35 minutes), making it possible for the guns at the later battle to fire many more shells. And second, far more heavy guns were used at Loos than at Neuve Chapelle. The question is whether these two factors were so substantial as to cancel out the unfavourable comparison revealed by the above calculation of guns per yard of front.

This question can be answered by comparing the weight and number of shells which fell on the German trench systems at Neuve Chapelle and at Loos. At Neuve Chapelle, during a bombardment of 35 minutes, 5 shells with a total weight of 288 lbs. fell on each yard of trench under attack. At Loos, in a bombardment spread over 48 hours, only seven-tenths of a shell weighing 62 lbs. fell on every yard of trench. That is, in terms of weight of shell per yard of trench attacked, the Loos bombardment was only one-fifth as heavy as that at Neuve Chapelle; and in terms of number of shells per yard of trench it was only one-seventh as heavy.

Even the wire-cutting guns at Loos were, on a comparative basis, inadequate for the task in hand. At Neuve Chapelle, 26 shells weighing 444 lbs. had been employed against each yard of enemy wire. At Loos, only 8 shells weighing 141 lbs. were available (see table 12.3).

As it happened, the effectiveness of the Loos bombardment in relation to Neuve Chapelle was even less than these figures indicate. The hurricane bombardment at Neuve Chapelle gave the Germans no time to repair damage to either wire or trenches. This was not the case at Loos where the bombardment was fired during daytime over four 12-hour periods. Each night the Germans, despite sporadic British harassing fire, had an opportunity to repair some of the damage inflicted on the previous day. These repaired defences then needed to be destroyed again, so reducing the total impact of the bombardment.

TABLE 12.3 *Comparison of wire-cutting bombardment at Loos with that at Neuve Chapelle*

Factor	Loos	Neuve Chapelle
Period of bombardment	21–25 Sept	10 Mar
Yards of wire per gun	80	22
Weight of shell per yard of wire	141 lb.	444 lb.
Number of shells per yard of wire	8	26

Table derived from 'Neuve Chapelle: Gun Ammunition, Total Rounds Expended on 10/3/15'; IV Corps, 'Ammunition expended, estimated and allotted for operations from 21st to 30th September 1915', Rawlinson Papers 1/4, Churchill College, Cambridge.

VI

The conclusion to be drawn from the foregoing is clear. By themselves, the artillery preparations for Loos were plainly inadequate. Of this the command was well aware. It had therefore taken the decision to complement the artillery bombardment by what, for the BEF, was a new weapon – poison gas. The interaction of the two, it was believed, would suppress the German defences at the moment the infantry was launched into the fray.

What contribution, in the view of the British command, would the gas weapon make to the opening stages of the offensive? At a conference on 6 September, Haig explained to his corps commanders that the gas would be carried by the wind 'in front of the assaulting divisions, and create a panic in the German ranks, or, at least, incapacitate them for a prolonged resistance.' He anticipated that, in favourable circumstances, the advance would be rapid; and, since the gas would be effective up to two miles, he hoped that the enemy's first and second defence systems would be overrun in the first rush.[53]

Haig's suggestion of a panic among the enemy when confronted with gas was little more than a chimera. It was known that opposing the British at Loos were seasoned troops equipped with respirators. So even though these Germans had not previously endured a gas attack, they were clearly prepared to confront a weapon which anyway was losing some of its terrors. It could hardly be assumed that they would respond differently from the Canadians who had stood firm at Ypres.

If the gas would not cause the Germans to panic and abandon their

---

[53] Edmonds, *1915* vol. 2, p. 154.

posts, what of Haig's other expectation? There were grounds for believing that the deleterious effects of gas, if sustained for sufficient time, would incapacitate the occupants of machine-gun posts even when they were wearing gas masks.[54] And it seemed probable that the gas would counter the protection provided to German frontline and support garrisons by the deep dugouts they would be occupying. (Since Givenchy, these dugouts were becoming a feature of the German defences.) The British command knew that the German dugouts were 'so well protected that it would be scarcely worthwhile trying to destroy them [by artillery].'[55] But it was also known that the dugouts could not be made gas-tight, and it was expected that the gas, being heavier than air, would soon penetrate into these positions, either killing the garrisons or driving them to the surface where an intense shrapnel barrage would fall on them.[56] There was a further function which gas might perform for the British, to which Haig did not appear to make reference. Released in combination with smoke, gas would screen the attackers during their transit of no-man's-land.

In the weeks leading up to the offensive, a great deal of thought was given to three matters concerning the most felicitous employment of gas. How should it be transmitted to the enemy? How much of it was required? And under what conditions should it be employed?

The first question was quickly decided. After some unsuccessful experiments with 18 pounder gas shells and gas-filled hand grenades, those methods were abandoned in favour of gas cylinders. These cylinders would be placed in groups in the front trenches. A nozzle and a section of pipe, which would project into no-man's-land, would be attached to each cylinder. When the nozzles were turned on, gas would leave the cylinder under pressure and be propelled towards the German trenches. As for the quantity of gas required, it was concluded that the decisive factor was the length of time it would take for the gas to overpower the German respirators. It was known that the chemicals used in the respirators to absorb and neutralize chlorine would last only 30 minutes, as would the breathing apparatus used by some German machine-gunners. It was concluded that a flow of gas lasting for 40 minutes would render the enemy subject to the deleterious effects of gas for 10 minutes. Thereupon the infantry would attack. There remained the third question, concerning the conditions under which gas might be employed. Once it had been decided that

---

[54] First Army, 'Notes of Conference 24/8/15', First Army War Diary Aug 1915, WO 95/157; Haig Diary 26/8/15.

[55] First Army, 'Notes of Conference 24/8/15'.

[56] First Army, 'Notes In Connection with the Employment of Gas in the Attack', 22/9/15, First Army War Diary Sept 1915, WO 95/158.

the gas must be delivered from cylinders, this question admitted of only one answer. The gas could only be employed in a favouring wind.

These calculations gave rise to serious problems. In short order the British command discovered that there would not be sufficient gas available for a discharge of 40 minutes. The reasons were threefold. First, it transpired that each cylinder would take only 3 minutes to empty instead of the estimated 5 minutes. Second, the front to be attacked had been extended by the inclusion of 1 and 7 Divisions, so reducing the number of cylinders available per yard of front. Third, the output from the factories supplying the gas failed to reach the quantities anticipated.

It was thought that a partial solution to this problem of insufficiency would be provided by supplementing the gas with smoke – the latter an innovation in warfare. Smoke was available in three varieties: smoke candles to be lit in the trenches, smoke bombs which could be fired from the Stokes mortars, and phosphorous grenades which could be thrown into no-man's-land from the British line. Eventually it was decided to employ all three. The plan adopted was that the gas would be released for 12 minutes, followed by 8 minutes of smoke, another 12 minutes of gas, and a final 8 minutes of smoke.[57]

It was anticipated by the command that gas alternating with smoke would be as effective as a continuous flow of gas. The wearing of gas masks over a long period impaired the fighting efficiency of the defenders, and it was expected that enemy troops would not remove their masks during the intervals when smoke was being substituted for gas. Again, smoke would provide concealment just as effectively as gas for the British infantry as they crossed no-man's-land and so would impair the effectiveness of the defence.

Yet in a major respect it was unwarranted to assume that smoke would prove an effective complement to gas. It would not aid in crippling the defenders by exhausting the resistance of their gas masks. As long as only 24 minutes of gas, not 40, were being dispatched, then the German machine-gunners and dugout-dwellers would not fall victims to gas poisoning. The gas weapon, therefore, was ceasing to have the potential to make good Haig's deficiencies in artillery.

There was another problem regarding the use of gas for which the British command had failed to provide a satisfactory answer. This concerned its manner of delivery. A too-powerful wind blowing towards the German trenches might so disperse the gas that it would provide little

---

[57] The information in the preceding paragraphs has been derived from Major-General C. H. Foulkes, *"Gas"! The Story of the Special Brigade* (Edinburgh: Blackwood, 1936), pp. 42–69.

inconvenience to the defenders and inadequate concealment for the at-tackers. An absence of wind, or a wind blowing away from the German trenches, would render the gas weapon quite unusable. That is, in order to launch an attack on the assigned day against subdued frontline defenders, the trinity of Sir John French, Sir Douglas Haig, and Sir Henry Rawlinson had placed themselves in a state of dependence on an element over which they possessed no control.

The realities of the gas situation may now be summarized. Under the most favourable circumstances, it could not be delivered in sufficient quantities actually to incapacitate the Germans. At the very most, gas might diminish the fighting capacity of enemy machine-gunners forced to don gas masks, cause German infantry to leave their dugouts in advance of a shrapnel bombardment, and help to conceal the attackers during the transit of no-man's-land. But for the gas to achieve even this much, it required the presence of a favouring but not boisterous wind. In this respect the British at Loos were not in the happy position of the Germans at Second Ypres back in April. The latter had been engaged in an isolated attack with no strategic implications. Hence they could delay their attack until a favourable wind presented itself. Loos, by contrast, was a small segment of a major operation being launched by the French, who had fixed the day of the attack and were not employing gas. Moreover the British attack was to be preceded by a four-day bombardment. At the time the guns commenced firing, no calculation would be possible as to whether the wind on zero day would be blowing towards or away from the enemy, if indeed it were blowing at all.

There was little the British command could do about this, crucial though gas had become in their calculations. They called in meteorological experts from Britain to aid in forecasting the weather, but that was not going to influence the weather they would actually get. And they prepared an alternative plan for a smaller (and much less viable) attack in case the gas weapon could not be used. But this would constitute an effectual abandon-ment of the scheduled operation. Anyway, the decision whether or not to adhere to the original plan would have to be based on weather observations made the day before the attack. And once a positive decision had been reached, and the machinery set in motion for moving the six attacking divisions into position, the imperatives to allow the attack to proceed on even the most meagre chance of a favourable wind would be very great indeed.

13

Day One

I

On the night of 18 September, the arduous process was set in train of transporting the gas cylinders to the front line. Rawlinson's plan went without a hitch. None of the 2,550 cylinders in the IV Corps sector was dropped by the carriers, nor were the proceedings interrupted by the enemy. By 21 September the gas was in place.[1]

Early on the morning of the 21st the preliminary bombardment commenced. This proved a less than dramatic event. The Germans, contrasting the modest British fire with that of the French to the south, concluded that an attack on the British sector was unlikely.[2] They therefore concentrated most of their artillery against the French. It was this factor, and not the British counter-battery fire (which usually failed to hit the German guns), that accounted for the feebleness of the German artillery response. The ironical outcome was that the British carried out their artillery plan free from harassing fire.[3]

Even so, the British bombardment did not proceed without problems. On the first two days dry conditions caused the exploding shells to kick up so much dust as to render observation of the fall of shot almost impossible. Rawlinson described the air as 'like a London fog so charged with dust was it.'[4] Consequently much shell was wasted, in circumstances where the

---

[1] See IV Corps, 'Proposals for Bringing up Gas Cylinders into the Front Trenches', 28/8/15, First Army War Diary Aug 1915, WO 95/157; Rawlinson to Kitchener 28/9/15, Rawlinson Papers 5201/33/18, NAM.

[2] *Der Weltkrieg* vol. 9 (Berlin: Mittler, 1933), p. 55.

[3] Anstey, History of the Royal Artillery 1914–1918, p. 97.

[4] Rawlinson Diary 23/9/15.

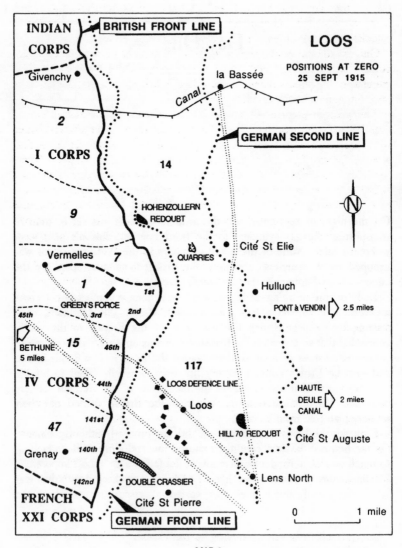

INDIAN CORPS

BRITISH FRONT LINE

LOOS

POSITIONS AT ZERO
25 SEPT 1915

Givenchy

la Bassée

Canal

2

GERMAN SECOND LINE

I CORPS

14

9

HOHENZOLLERN REDOUBT

N

Vermelles

QUARRIES

Cité St Elie

7

Hulluch

1

1st

GREEN'S FORCE

2nd

PONT à VENDIN ⇨ 2.5 miles

45th

3rd

15

46th

BETHUNE 5 miles

IV CORPS

44th

117

LOOS DEFENCE LINE

Loos

141st

HAUTE DEULE CANAL ⇨ 2 miles

47

HILL 70 REDOUBT

Cité St Auguste

Grenay

140th

142nd

DOUBLE CRASSIER

Lens North

FRENCH XXI CORPS

Cité St Pierre

GERMAN FRONT LINE

0   1 mile

MAP 9

supply was already inadequate. On the evening of the 22nd Rawlinson anxiously recorded that 'there is much more to be done yet.'[5] On the 23rd the weather changed, but not for the better. Now rain and low cloud hampered visibility. In addition the wind was gusty and variable, rendering calculations of adjustments for the range extremely difficult.[6]

Only on the 24th did visibility improve. A number of important strongpoints were destroyed and much wire-cutting was accomplished. The intensity of the bombardment increased on this day, a fact that did much to raise the morale of the assault troops.

The greatest element of uncertainty in planning the commencement time lay with the gas. It was for Haig to decide whether circumstances were propitious. At 9.20 p.m. on the 24th he received the final full weather forecast from the meteorological experts. It was favourable – 'wind southerly changing to S.W. or West, probably increasing to 20 miles per hour.'[7] On this basis Haig ordered the troops into the trenches. In the early morning of the 25th it was obvious that the wind had not reached anything like the anticipated velocity. In places it had fallen to 1 mile per hour. Haig asked for another forecast and received the very imprecise statement: 'the wind would probably be stronger just after sunrise [5.30 a.m.] than later in the day.'[8] It was now 3 a.m. If the attack was to go in at dawn he must decide immediately. On the strength of the ambiguously hopeful reference to the probable state of the wind at 5.30 a.m., Haig decided to commence the gas attack at 5.50.[9] The infantry would go over the top at 6.30.

II

Four days before the attack was launched, Rawlinson had moved to his advanced HQ at Vaudricourt, about six miles behind the front. Here he was in contact by telephone with the HQ of the three attacking divisions, as well as with the field artillery, the heavy artillery, the RFC, and the First Army command.[10] At 4 a.m. on 25 September Rawlinson received Haig's orders that the gas attack was to proceed. At 5.50 a.m. an intense artillery

---

[5] Ibid. 22/9/15.
[6] Anstey, History of the Royal Artillery 1914–1918, p. 97.
[7] Haig Diary 24/9/15.
[8] Ibid. 25/9/15.
[9] First Army War Diary 25/9/15, WO 95/158.
[10] IV Corps, 'Report on communications during the fighting at Loos and Hill 70, on 25/9/15 and 26/9/15', IV Corps War Diary Oct–Dec 1915, WO 95/712.

bombardment was opened on the German front line and simultaneously the gas was released. Forty minutes later the infantry went forward.[11]

The outcome of the attack by 47 Division on the right of IV Corps may be briefly summarized. The task assigned to 140 and 141 Brigades was to form a defensive flank to the south between two large slag heaps.[12] Potentially this movement was full of danger. The brigades were required to capture two German defensive positions and advance through a valley vulnerable to flanking fire from Loos village to the north and the outer suburbs of Lens to the south. Nevertheless, by mid-morning the division was able to report that, except on the extreme left where it had become mixed up with 15 Division attacking Hill 70, all objectives had been taken and the line consolidated.[13] Casualties were less than 1,000.[14]

Why was this attack successful? And what light does this throw on the effectiveness of Rawlinson's plan? Three factors contributed significantly to the success. First, when the assaulting brigades arrived at the German front line they found the wire 'completely cut'.[15] That is, the artillery had in this important respect accomplished its task. Second, such was the speed of their advance that many of the German garrisons in the front trench were caught emerging from their dugouts[16] and even the German support battalion just behind the line was found unprepared. The German reserve battalion, situated four miles away, was unable to reach the Loos defence line – which was consequently unoccupied – before the British entered it. (This was a fortunate circumstance for the British. The wire in front of this line was uncut.)[17] Third, on this sector of the front the gas and smoke proved successful in one of its purposes. Not many Germans were killed or even incapacitated by the gas. Indeed a search after the battle recorded only five such cases.[18] What the cloud did accomplish was to screen the British infantry, in the first instance from the German trench-dwellers, and later from the potentially lethal fire from German machine-guns in Loos. The village was still reported to be blanketed in smoke at 1.30 p.m., well after the division had dug itself in.[19]

---

[11] IV Corps, 'Report of Operations 22/9/15–7/10/15', IV Corps War Diary Sept 1915, WO 95/711.

[12] 47 Division, Operation Order No. 19, 20/9/15, quoted in Edmonds, *1915* vol. 2, pp. 457–60.

[13] 47 Division War Diary 25/9/15, WO 95/2698.

[14] Edmonds, *1915* vol. 2, p. 191.

[15] 47 Division War Diary 25/9/15.

[16] Edmonds, *1915* vol. 2, p. 188.

[17] 47 Division War Diary 25/9/15.

[18] 47 Division, 'Report on the use of Gas' by Lt.-Col. Hitchcock, 2/10/15, First Army War Diary Sept 1915, WO 95/158.

[19] 47 Division War Diary 25/9/15.

The gas and smoke, it needs to be added, were not an unqualified success even in this sector. On the extreme right of the British attack the cloud was dispersed by the southerly wind, so providing German machine-guns in the northern suburbs of Lens with a clear view of the British battalions and enabling them to inflict many casualties. But this check was not so severe as to prevent 47 Division as a whole from attaining its objectives.[20]

III

On the left wing of the IV Corps attack, a rather different story was unfolding. This was on the front of 1 Division. The 1 and 2 Brigades of that division were designated to capture the German front line, then take the German second position, and after that push on two and a half miles before halting.[21]

As 5.50 a.m. approached, the wind in the northern section of the IV Corps front increased to two or three miles an hour. But this was not to their advantage. The wind blew from the SSW, whereas the British line on the 1 Division sector bulged and ran towards the north-east. Consequently the right wing of 1 Division was affected both by its own gas and by that released on its right. Probably some 300 men from the leading battalions fell victim to their own gas in the first few minutes of the attack.[22]

The 2nd Brigade on the far right suffered by far the heaviest casualties from the gas. Worse soon followed. The troops from this brigade who remained capable of advancing across no-man's-land found the wire uncut and the German defenders unsubdued. Their attack came to a halt in a hail of machine-gun fire.[23] By contrast, 1 Brigade on their left, despite gas casualties and enfilade machine-gun fire, made a considerable advance. Finding the wire well cut, they overwhelmed the German defenders. So by 9.10 a.m. the three leading battalions of 1 Brigade were occupying positions facing the German second line opposite Hulluch.[24] But by now the battalions were weak, the thick wire in front of Hulluch stood uncut, and there was no sign of 2 Brigade on their right. They decided to dig in.[25]

[20] Edmonds, *1915* vol. 2, p. 188.

[21] 1 Division Operation Order 18/9/15, 1 Division War Diary July–Sept 1915, WO 95/1229.

[22] Edmonds, *1915* vol. 2, pp. 210–12.

[23] 1 Division Messages 25/9/15, 1 Division War Diary July–Sept 1915, WO 95/1229.

[24] Ibid.

[25] Edmonds, *1915* vol. 2, p. 213.

The crucial question which now confronted the command was where to send the substantial reserves on the 1 Division front. (These consisted of the four battalions of 3 Brigade, along with two battalions of what was known as Green's Force.) Initially Rawlinson and Holland, the 1 Division commander, came to the same decision. Green's Force, with 3 Brigade in close support, should make an attack on the unbreached defences holding up 2 Brigade.[26] This was a baffling decision. Rawlinson and Holland were reinforcing failure. Had they chosen to assist the successful 1 Brigade, they could have employed some battalions to aid that brigade in attacking the German second line and others to take from the flanks and rear the German defenders holding up 2 Brigade.

As time passed Rawlinson began to appreciate this opportunity. At 10 a.m., in a telephone conversation, he told Holland: 'it would be as well to ignore the Germans still holding them [2 Brigade] up, and push on ... The Germans in front of 2nd Brigade will then be surrounded and would probably surrender.'[27] This was sound advice, but Rawlinson failed to incorporate it in a definite order. Holland for his part ignored the suggestion and continued to organize a further attack on the front of 2 Brigade. Owing to difficulties in communication, it was midday before Green's Force began its approach march and just after 1 p.m. before it attacked. As it then advanced into uncut wire and against unsubdued machine-guns, the result was predictable. Within a few minutes Green's battalions had ceased to exist as a fighting force.[28]

At this stage Rawlinson at last made his change of opinion felt, prevailing on Holland to adopt a different approach. A small force was sent around the right flank of 1 Division to attack the German defenders from the rear, while 3 Brigade was ordered north to reinforce the remnants of the successful 1 Brigade in front of Hulluch.[29]

It was the movements of 3 Brigade that paid off. Although several battalions suffered heavy casualties, the 2 Welch managed to get behind the enemy holding up 2 Brigade and Green's Force. The Germans, already low on ammunition, promptly surrendered. Over 500 prisoners were taken. It was now 2.20 p.m.[30]

The remainder of 3 Brigade now joined 1 Brigade in front of Hulluch.

[26] 1 Division Messages 25/9/15; 'Telephone Conversations of Lieut-General Sir Henry Rawlinson, Bt K.C.B., K.C.V.O., from the Commencement of the Attack', Rawlinson Papers 5201/33/67, NAM. (Hereafter, Rawlinson, Telephone Conversations.)

[27] Rawlinson, Telephone Conversations.

[28] 1 Division War Diary 25/9/15.

[29] Ibid; Rawlinson, Telephone Conversations.

[30] Edmonds, *1915* vol. 2, p. 219; 1 Division War Diary 25/9/15.

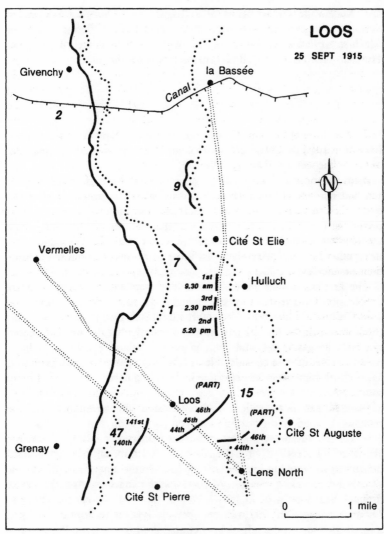

MAP 10 *Progress of the battle*

These troops were almost immediately counterattacked by the reserve battalion of the German regiment holding the front line. The attack was beaten off. But as no support was visible on the right of 1 and 3 Brigades, they abandoned all idea of further operations against the German second

line. Meanwhile the remnants of 2 Brigade and Green's Force at last
managed – at 3.20 p.m. – to overrun the section of the German front line
which so far had withstood them. And by 5.20 they had reached the Lens–
Hulluch road. Hereupon all movement ceased for the day.[31]

IV

Having outlined the events of 25 September on the right (47 Division) and
left (1 Division) of Rawlinson's command, we must now look at the crucial
sector – the centre. The 15 Division, in the centre of IV Corps, had
perhaps the most difficult task. In Haig's scheme of things, which Rawlinson had not actually repudiated, this division had a succession of objectives. First it must capture the German front line and the trenches
protecting Loos, then occupy the village, fight its way up Hill 70, breach
the German second line, and finally press on to the high ground some
three miles beyond.[32] Merely to list these objectives is to throw doubt on
their practicality.

The first major question confronting the operation was the wind. Here
15 Division were both lucky and unlucky. To their advantage, the wind
blew SW to W, which was the required direction. But, particularly on the
front of 46 Brigade (on the left), it blew so slowly that the attacking troops
ran into the gas cloud while still in no-man's-land. Their gas helmets
proving inadequate, 'a considerable number were gassed.'[33] In addition the
smoke in this area was less effective in providing cover than it was further
south.

Neither gas nor artillery had eliminated the defenders. German
machine-gunners and riflemen in several parts of the line poured a heavy
fire into the advancing columns, causing numerous casualties. Moreover
the failure (just related) of 2 Brigade to the north meant that 15 Division's
attack was subjected to intense enfilade fire. On the other hand the gas and
smoke did provide a measure of cover for the attackers. And the British
artillery had done a good job in cutting the wire. In consequence, 15
Division managed, if only with considerable loss, to get forward. By 7.30
a.m. 46 Brigade on the left had penetrated the Loos defence line and had
reached the north of the village. An hour later some of its columns were
advancing up the lower slopes of Hill 70. To their right, 44 Brigade had
found the trenches in front of Loos undefended and had entered the

---

[31] Edmonds, *1915* vol. 2, pp. 220–2; 1 Division War Diary 25/9/15.

[32] IV Corps Operation Order No. 35 quoted in Edmonds, *1915* vol. 2, p. 453.

[33] 46 Brigade 'Operations 25/26th [September 1915]', 46 Brigade War Diary July 1915–
July 1916, WO 95/1948.

village at 7 a.m. An hour later the leading columns of this brigade were on the eastern edge of the village and advancing on the Hill 70 Redoubt. It proved to be unoccupied. Consequently, at 10.10 the commander of 15 Division (McCracken) was able to inform Rawlinson that Hill 70 had been taken and that the reserve brigade (the 45th), which at 9.30 a.m. had moved into the old British front line, was being sent forward in support.[34]

Thus by mid-morning IV Corps seemed on the brink of a considerable victory on the front of 15 Division. Rawlinson certainly thought as much and reported to Haig that 'the enemy was on the run.'[35] But this proved unduly optimistic. The battalions of 44 and 46 Brigades which had captured Hill 70 were much depleted. For example, the two leading battalions of 44 Brigade had suffered over 60 per cent casualties.[36] In addition much intermixing of the brigades had occurred, uncertainty reigned as to who was in overall command, and the hill was under fire from the direction of Lens.[37]

At least two battalion commanders on the spot quickly realized that the brigades were fully extended and that the small number of men on Hill 70 would be hard put to it to consolidate what they had won, let alone attempt an advance on the German second line. But before they could order a halt, large parties of the troops on Hill 70 set off again and were advancing down the far side of the hill towards the sound of firing coming from Lens North. In so doing they were carrying with them on the left some battalions from 46 Brigade who had lost direction and imagined that they were advancing on their objective, Cité St Auguste.[38]

This advance beyond the crest of Hill 70 was soon halted. The German second line was untouched by the bombardment. Thick wire lay in belts in front of it, preventing any attempt to rush it. Several German machineguns from Lens North and Cité St Auguste swept the bare slopes of the hill with a deadly crossfire.[39] No artillery bombardment came to the support of the attacking force, for communication between front and rear had by this time (11 a.m.) completely broken down.[40] There was nothing for the troops on the forward slope of Hill 70 to do but attempt to dig in and await reinforcements.

---

[34] Ibid; 44 Brigade War Diary 25/9/15, WO 95/1934; 15 Division, 'Report on Operations September 21–30th, 1915', 15 Division War Diary July–Sept 1915, WO 95/1911.

[35] First Army War Diary 25/9/15.

[36] Brigadier-General M. G. Wilkinson [CO 44 Brigade] to Edmonds 8/6/26, Official History Correspondence: Loos, Cab 45/121.

[37] Edmonds, *1915* vol. 2, pp. 200–1.

[38] For these details see Wilkinson to Edmonds 8/6/26.

[39] G. C. Wynne, 'The other side of the hill: no. III: the fight for Hill 70: 25th–26th of September, 1915', *The Army Quarterly* 8 (April 1924), pp. 264–5.

[40] IV Corps, 'Report on Communications'.

In the event, German reinforcements arrived first. At 11.30 the British were counterattacked, albeit unsuccessfully, by a German battalion which had been in reserve in Lens.[41] During the next hour elements of three more German battalions arrived in the German line.[42] This placed the forward British troops under the concentrated fire of almost four battalions. Further counterattacks forced the British back on to the reverse slope of the hill. To prevent the loss of more ground, the command threw in 45 Brigade, the only local reserve remaining to 15 Division.[43] Their action stabilized the situation, but that was all. The limit of the British advance at the battle of Loos had now been reached.

How close did the British come to breaking into the German second line on the 15 Division front? Despite a popular view to the contrary, the answer clearly is not very close at all. The 1,500 men who swept over the crest of Hill 70 at about 10.30 a.m. were opposed in the area from Lens North to Cité St Auguste by some 700 to 800 defenders.[44] The gas and smoke had dispersed, the defences were intact and protected by thick belts of wire, the enemy were amply supplied with machine-guns, and their field of fire was unobstructed. There was never any chance that a defending force could be turned out of such positions by the number of British troops available.

V

It was not until after midday on 25 September that Rawlinson began to realize that the situation on Hill 70 was not as favourable as he had earlier thought. At 1 p.m. he informed Haig by telephone: 'news from the 15th Division is not so good. They might be turned off Hill 70. Being pretty heavily attacked.'[45] Haig had no help to offer. The most he could suggest was that Rawlinson's men hold on while the divisions of XI Corps, constituting GHQ reserve, were brought forward.

This would not happen quickly. In seeking to reach the front, 21 and 24 Divisions of XI Corps had to negotiate an area already crowded with troops from IV and I Corps. The wounded moving back and the artillery moving forward hindered them at every turn. It soon became obvious that they would not arrive before nightfall. So the men on the slopes of Hill 70 were required to hold on as best they could; which, in the event, they proved able to do.

---

[41] Edmonds, *1915* vol. 2, p. 204.
[42] *Der Weltkreig* vol. 9, p. 55.
[43] Edmonds, *1915* vol. 2, pp. 204–5.
[44] Wynne, Fight for Hill 70, p. 264.
[45] Rawlinson, Telephone Conversations.

14

Day Two and After

I

Plans had now to be made to employ the reserves on the second day. The man who would make them was not Sir John French, despite the fact that the reserve divisions had initially been placed in GHQ reserve, but Haig. Haig decided that the main attack on 26 September would be made between Hulluch and Loos by four brigades from 21 and 24 Divisions. On their left, General Gough's I Corps, whose 7 and 9 Divisions had been moderately successful on the first day, would (with the aid of a brigade from 24 Division) renew its attack on the German second line. On their right, Rawlinson's 1 Division, which had been visited with such mixed fortunes on 25 September, would attempt to capture Hulluch. As a preliminary to all this, the much-battered 15 Division assisted by a brigade from 21 Division would endeavour to retake Hill 70.[1]

As an exercise in military planning, this scheme of operations had one overriding quality. It was possessed of not a single redeeming feature. If the high command had applied any logic to the situation at the end of 25 September, they would have reinforced the front troops where they stood and attempted no attack on the 26th. During the night of the 25th, as predicted by GHQ, two German divisions arrived in the line.[2] This meant that by the following morning the German second line was more strongly held than their original front line had been on the morning of the 25th. This second line was now to be attacked without the benefit of accurate artillery fire (indeed after a bombardment of only one hour), and without

[1] IV Corps Operation Order 25/9/15, IV Corps War Diary Sept. 1915, WO 95/711.
[2] Edmonds, *1915* vol. 2, pp. 177–8.

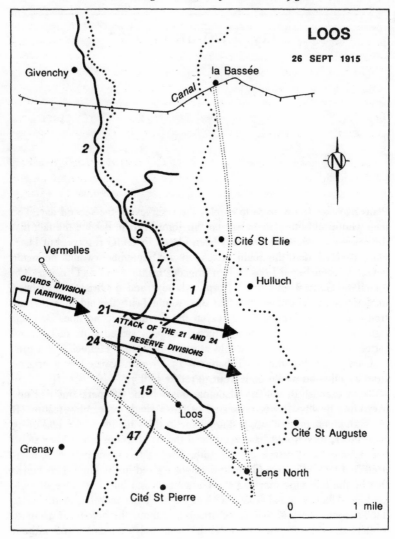

LOOS

26 SEPT 1915

Givenchy

la Bassée

Canal

2

9

Vermelles

Cité St Elie

7

Hulluch

1

GUARDS DIVISION
(ARRIVING)

21

ATTACK OF THE 21 AND 24

24

RESERVE DIVISIONS

15

Loos

Cité St Auguste

47

Grenay

Lens North

Cité St Pierre

0   1 mile

MAP 11

the screening effect of gas and smoke. As for the troops being called on to deliver the attack, they were either exhausted, as in the case of 7, 9, 1, and 15 Divisions, or they were new to the battlefield, as with the 21 and 24 Divisions.

There is no evidence that Rawlinson was reluctant to endorse this operation. Indeed when the commander of 15 Division (McCracken) expressed doubts as to the fitness of his troops to attack yet again, Rawlinson insisted that Haig's plan be carried out.[3]

The results of the actions of 26 September are painful to describe. The reserve 21 and 24 Divisions lost 8,200 men in little over an hour.[4] Confronted by uncut barbed wire and devastating machine-gun and artillery fire, the survivors fled to the rear in a mixture of terror, panic, and confusion. The Guards Division was hastily brought forward to prevent the panic from spreading.

As for Rawlinson's forces, the attacks by IV Corps also failed. Battalions of 3 Brigade were cut down in front of Hulluch.[5] Only one glimmer of success attended IV Corps's effort, and that was soon snuffed out. The 45 Brigade of 15 Division actually obtained a foothold on the summit of Hill 70. But 62 Brigade on its left failed utterly and fled headlong towards Loos, taking some of the 15 Division troops with them. The summit was lost once again, and for a time it seemed that all of Hill 70 and even Loos village might be overrun. But the troops rallied and reoccupied their line of the night before; and there they held firm.[6] The IV Corps was then withdrawn from the line.

II

Even now IV Corps was not quite done with the battle of Loos. Under great pressure from Joffre and Foch, French in the early days of October agreed to renew the offensive. As a precondition, it was deemed necessary to capture the dominating positions of what was known as the Hohenzollern Redoubt and the Quarries to the north of Hulluch. On the right of this operation, Rawlinson's 1 Division – now back in the trenches – was to attack Hulluch in order to straighten the line. Gas and smoke were to be used.[7]

The attack by 1 Division on 13 October was a complete failure. The supply of gas and smoke was insufficient, so that the attacking troops were clearly visible as they approached the German line. There they ran into

---

[3] 15 Division, 'Report on Operations September 21–30, 1915', 15 Division War Diary July–Sept 1915, WO 95/1911.

[4] Edmonds, *1915* vol. 2, p. 342.

[5] Ibid.

[6] 15 Division, 'Report on operations September 21–30'.

[7] Edmonds, *1915* vol. 2, p. 380.

uncut wire. Somehow, soon after the commencement of the attack, a quite inaccurate report reached Rawlinson intimating that 'our infantry have taken enemy's trenches . . . and are now entrenching.' In consequence supporting troops were sent forward. They suffered as heavily as the first wave. By the end of the day 1 Division had sustained 1,200 casualties and were back at their start line. For IV Corps it was an ignominious end to the battle of Loos.[8]

III

Rawlinson did not doubt that the battle could have achieved very much more. In the aftermath of 25 September he argued repeatedly that the nonappearance of the reserves on that first day constituted a great lost opportunity. But for the bungling of Sir John French – who had held the reserve divisions under his own hand – the modest success of the day would, according to Rawlinson, have developed into something much greater. As he wrote to Kitchener on 28 September regarding the events of three days earlier:

> It is very much to be regretted that these two new divisions [21 and 24 Division, XI Corps] could not have been brought up to the battlefield fresh and in time to take full advantage of the first assault delivered by the IVth Corps without giving the enemy time to concentrate against them. Had this been done, and had they delivered their attack between 10.00 and 12.00 am on the morning of the 25th I am quite certain that they would have been successful and that we should have broken through the enemy's second system of defences and been able to send on the cavalry to Pont à Vendin and Carvin.
>
> I am told that the delay was primarily due to Sir John's desire to keep these two divisions in G.H.Q. reserve until the last possible moment. There can be no doubt that this moment was too long delayed and it is doubly to be regretted that this was the case, for in his communique to the French Army, General Joffre lays special stress upon the need for all reserve formations to be well up to move forward to the attack at the same moment as the assault is delivered.[9]

---

[8] The quotation in this paragraph is taken from the IV Corps War Diary 13/10/15, Montgomery-Massingberd Papers, Folder 41. The remaining detail of the action comes from IV Corps, 'Report On The Operation Of The IV Corps During The Period 13th to 21st October, 1915', First Army War Diary Oct 1915, WO 95/159.

[9] Rawlinson to Kitchener 28/9/15, Rawlinson Papers 5201/33/18, NAM. All references to Rawlinson correspondence in this chapter come from this source.

There is an anomaly here. The capture of the enemy's second line and the advance on Pont à Vendin were not operations assigned to the reserves. In the operations orders they had been designated as objectives for Rawlinson's own corps. Pretty clearly, Rawlinson in private took the view that his corps would never attain these objectives unaided. Yet he had made no representations on the matter to Haig or French nor pointed to the fact that he had no reserves of his own. A possible explanation suggests itself, and gains support from his letters to Kitchener. Rawlinson apparently expected that the reserves would be available to him on the first morning of the battle. So we find many entries in his diary before the battle along the following lines:

> The XI Corps is to come up behind me to Noeux-les-Mines and to move forward as soon as my attack goes in. All are to move forward together and force our way through by sheer weight of numbers.[10]

It would also be consistent with his urgent and repeated calls for the reserves on the morning of the 25th, beginning as early as 8.30.[11]

A single entry in Haig's diary suggests that Rawlinson was justified in anticipating that GHQ reserve would be available to him from the outset. Haig wrote: 'the 3 Divisions [of the XI Corps] will I hope be close up in the places where I have arranged to put them [Noeux-les-Mines–Beauvry], and will go forward as soon as any opportunity offers.'[12] As 21 and 24 Divisions did indeed assemble in the places suggested by Haig (the other division, the Guards, was kept further back), this suggests that Rawlinson's expectation of their early movement forward was warranted. Rawlinson therefore may well have accepted his own lack of reserves on the assumption that XI Corps would be readily to hand.

Yet this expectation – irrespective of anything done by Sir John French – was quite unrealistic. Rawlinson had been told at a conference four days before the battle that, on the evening of the 24th, the heads of the columns of 21 and 24 Divisions would be on the line Beuvry–Noeux-les-Mines, about five miles behind the British front line.[13] This referred, it will be noted, only to the leading brigades; the rear brigades would be as much as three miles further back.[14] For these divisions to be concentrated for battle, the rearmost troops would have to march eight miles to the British

---

[10] Rawlinson Diary 14/9/15. See also entries for 4 and 8 September.

[11] Rawlinson, Telephone Conversations. Rawlinson called for the reserves at 8.30 a.m., 9.06, 9.10, 9.41, 11.10, 11.30, and 12 noon, on the 25th.

[12] Haig Diary 23/9/15.

[13] IV Corps, 'Notes of Conference at First Army Headquarters 21st September, 1915', IV Corps War Diary Sept 1915, WO 95/711.

[14] Edmonds, *1915* vol. 2, p. 279.

front. With good march discipline that would take the leading brigade (according to Haig, who in view of his dispute with French was not likely to underestimate) four hours to reach the old German front line. The rear brigades, correspondingly, would arrive at that point about two and a half hours later.[15] That is, the divisions could not have been concentrated for an attack before 1 p.m. And given the chaos of the battlefield, at least another hour would have been required for them to reach the front near Hill 70.

We have already seen that by 2 p.m. the Germans were occupying their second line and the environs of Hill 70 with at least four battalions. And these troops were experienced, fresh, well supplied with machine-guns and artillery support, and with their barbed wire intact. The British reserve divisions were inexperienced, they were bound to be tired, and they would be required to attack across the open. Most important of all, their artillery support would be minimal; for by the early afternoon of 25 September on the 15 Division front, most of the British guns had not been able to get forward, and from their original positions they could not secure direct observation over the area to be attacked. As noted earlier, communications between the FOOs and the batteries had almost completely broken down by this stage. It is plain, therefore, that on the first day the reserve divisions could not have been introduced on to the battlefield in circumstances where their appearance would have made any difference.

In his comments on the battle, Rawlinson made no allowance for these considerations. Even while the battle was still in progress he began claiming that, on the first day, 'golden opportunities' had been lost for want of reserves. Nor did more sober reflection cause him to modify this view. In the months ahead he adhered to his original proposition that French's handling of the reserves on 25 September had cost the British a great victory. This may reflect an inability on his part to reach a dispassionate judgement on military events in which he had been intimately involved. But it needs also to be noted that he had a strong non-military reason for sticking to his original judgement. It provided him with grounds for seeking the dismissal of the British commander-in-chief.

Rawlinson set about that other sort of campaign with a will. We have seen how prompt he was to apprise Kitchener of his hostile judgement on French's conduct. He did not stop there. Other persons of influence were contacted on the same day: the King (through his private secretary Lord Stamfordham), Lord Derby (Director of Recruiting), and Walter Bagot, recently on his staff and now a director of the Ministry of Munitions.[16]

---

[15] Haig to French 21/10/15, Butler Papers 69/10/1, IWM.
[16] Rawlinson to Derby, Stamfordham, Bagot 28/9/15.

(Bagot passed on his communication to Geoffrey Robinson, editor of *The Times*.)[17] To see that his point got home, just one day later Rawlinson wrote again to Kitchener and to Stamfordham (telling the latter 'I send you the enclosed ... which it may interest H.M. to see') restating his case against Sir John.[18]

In the next few weeks Rawlinson discussed the issue with Haig, who proved of an identical view: 'we must have a new C in C before we can win battles.' Later Haig, who was also making his views known to the King, to Asquith, and to other influential figures in England, told Rawlinson: 'he [Haig] has been very loyal to Sir John all along but over the last show he cannot be so. He said Sir John ought to have been removed after the retreat [from Mons]!! and he is right.'

Early in November Rawlinson, who must have been worried that his intrigues were not bearing fruit, took leave in London. There he sought out Lloyd George and impressed upon him that the fiasco of the reserves had been solely Sir John's fault. Significantly Lloyd George asked Rawlinson's opinion of Haig. Rawlinson replied that he was 'the best soldier we had in France.'[19]

By 12 November Rawlinson had decided that it was time for yet plainer speaking. He told Derby:

> If the Cabinet do not take steps soon to strengthen the General Staff at home and to change the command of the Army in France we shall go very near losing this war ...
>
> Now in my opinion the only hope we have of avoiding further strategical mistakes is to appoint Robertson ... to a supreme position at the War Office ... and to appoint Sir John to the command of the troops in the British Isles replacing him here by Douglas Haig. If you do not do this you will continue to have vacillation and indecision at home and no hope of accomplishing any decisive success on the Western front. Cannot you use your influence at home to bring these changes about?[20]

In fact Derby did not possess this degree of influence. But it was not needed. In London, French was also being assailed by Kitchener, Haig, the King, Gough, and Robertson.[21] Late in November, Asquith made up his mind, and by 4 December all the changes suggested by Rawlinson in his letter to Derby were in the process of implementation.

[17] Rawlinson Diary 5/10/15.
[18] Rawlinson to Kitchener and Stamfordham 29/9/15.
[19] For these quotations see Rawlinson Diary 10/10/15, 22/10/15 and 5/11/15.
[20] Rawlinson to Derby 12/11/15.
[21] Holmes, *Little Field-Marshal*, pp. 307–10.

IV

In the event French's supersession did not result in early advancement for Rawlinson. It was all along evident that Haig's elevation to the post of commander-in-chief would render vacant the command of First Army, and on 11 December Haig intimated that if he replaced French he would recommend Rawlinson for this vacancy.[22] Yet when, a week later, Rawlinson went to bid farewell to French, the fallen commander was able to tell him – no doubt with some degree of relish – that he was not to get First Army. Monro was being brought back from Egypt, where he had been overseeing the Gallipoli evacuation, to fill the post.[23] Rawlinson was given temporary command of First Army, but his promotion to permanent Army commander would have to await a new year and the formation of a new Army.

[22] Rawlinson Diary 11/12/15.
[23] Ibid. 18/12/15.

PART IV

The Somme,
1916

15

The Outline Plan

I

In January 1916 the expansion of the BEF made necessary the creation of a Fourth Army. An 'Army', it needs to be stressed, was simply an administrative unit, consisting of about 100 headquarters staff. Corps and divisions were assigned to or removed from it by the commander-in-chief as the exigencies of battle required. In terms of experience, the obvious candidate for the post of commander of the new unit was Rawlinson. And the major obstacle to his advancement, the hostility of Sir John French, had now been removed. On 24 January, Haig informed him that he was to have the command. Rawlinson decided that Montgomery should accompany him from IV Corps to be COS. Major-General Birch from First Army was given to Rawlinson as artillery adviser.[1]

By the opening of the Somme campaign nearly six months later, the BEF had expanded to a force of one and a half million men. Under the commander-in-chief, Douglas Haig, there were now five Armies commanded respectively by Charles Monro, Hebert Plumer, Edmund Allenby, Henry Rawlinson, and Hubert Gough. The last of these Armies was designated not the Fifth but the Reserve Army. It was envisaged as an instrument for exploiting the hoped-for breakthrough to be accomplished by the Fourth Army under Rawlinson. The 5 Armies embraced a total of 12 corps consisting of 38 infantry and 5 cavalry divisions. The Fourth Army, which is our principal subject of concern, consisted of about half a million men divided into 5 corps and 16 divisions.

Weaponry had not changed greatly since the BEF first set foot in Europe. The main additions, as will be seen shortly, were light machine-

[1] Rawlinson Diary 24/1/16 and 1/2/16.

guns and light trench mortars. But if the British army did not possess many new weapons, it had a great many more of the familiar sort. The increase in heavy guns was of particular note, given the role that these were bound to play in an attack upon a trench system. From a modest total of 36 batteries on 1 January 1915, the BEF possessed 191 batteries by 1 July 1916. But whether this constituted a significant accretion of strength – or any accretion at all – would depend on the scale of the undertaking in which they were to be employed.

One noteworthy feature of Britain's army in Europe in mid-1916 was the inexperience of its commanders. The five men who were now Army commanders had, back in 1914, been in charge only of divisions. Most of the present corps commanders had then led infantry brigades. And many of the current divisional generals had started the war commanding battalions. Of all the formation commanders directing the attack in mid-1916, only Haig, Rawlinson, and Gough had exercised real authority at the BEF's last major operation – the battle of Loos just nine months before.

II

Originally Haig had envisaged a British spring campaign launched from the Ypres salient. Indeed Rawlinson had spent the first weeks of his command reconnoitring the ground around Ypres. A plan for an attack had been prepared and submitted to the commander-in-chief.

In the meantime, however, Joffre came forward with the proposal for an Anglo-French offensive astride the River Somme, 30 miles to the south of Loos. In the spring the British were to launch a 'wearing-out' attack to the north of the river to exhaust the German reserves. The main effort would be made some months later by the French to the south of the river.[2]

Haig was not averse to a combined effort by the British and French, nor to the Somme as its locale.[3] But he had no intention of allowing the British army to be used in the subsidiary role proposed by Joffre. He was also opposed to the unco-ordinated nature of Joffre's plan. He suggested a larger British contribution to an offensive taking place simultaneously with the French.[4] To this Joffre agreed. As a result of these negotiations, Haig halted Rawlinson's preparations for a northern attack and ordered him to

---

[2] Brigadier-General Sir James Edmonds, *Military Operations: France and Belgium, 1916* vol. 1 (London: Macmillan, 1932), p. 27.

[3] Robin Prior, *Churchill's 'World Crisis' As History* (London: Croom Helm, 1983), pp. 214–5.

[4] Haig to Joffre 1/2/16, WO 158/14.

shift his headquarters south to the Somme. The British front in that area was held by Allenby's Third Army, and Haig proposed that while Rawlinson would command the three or four corps which would fight the battle he would be placed under Allenby's overall control.[5]

In the event this clumsy arrangement was never put to the test. On 21 February the Germans attacked the French at Verdun. French reserves were rushed to that area. As a consequence the British Third Army took over the sector hitherto occupied by the French Tenth Army. The Fourth Army now took charge of the area between the Third Army and the Somme.[6] Thus Rawlinson's command of the coming battle was to be exercised independently.

By late June, the Fourth Army held a 20-mile front stretching from Fonquevillers on the left to Maricourt (a few miles north of the River Somme) on the right. It consisted of the following corps: VIII (Hunter-Weston), X (Morland), III (Pulteney), XV (Horne), and XIII (Congreve). Between them they embraced 14 divisions.[7]

Rawlinson moved to his new headquarters at Querrieu, near Amiens, and proceeded to make a series of inspections of the front with a view to formulating a plan of attack. In general he thought the area suitable for launching an offensive.

> It is capital country in which to undertake an offensive when we get a sufficiency of artillery, for the observation is excellent and with plenty of guns and ammunition we ought to be able to avoid the heavy losses which the infantry have always suffered on previous occasions.[8]

Of particular note in this passage is Rawlinson's stress on the importance of artillery in securing the infantry against prohibitive losses. It deserves to be kept in mind as we follow the process of preparation for the great battle.

From his reconnaissances Rawlinson realized that the German defences opposite Fourth Army were even more formidable than those which IV Corps had faced at Loos. Once again the Germans had completed two main trench systems. The foremost consisted of 'three lines of trench 150 to 200 yards apart, one for the sentry groups, the second . . . for the front-trench garrison to live in, and the third for the local supports.'[9] But unlike the earlier battle, the enemy on this occasion had incorporated into their front line a succession of fortified villages: Fricourt, la Boisselle, Ovillers,

---

[5] For these details see Rawlinson's Diary, 12 and 21 February 1916.

[6] Ibid. 24/2/16.

[7] Edmonds, *1916* vol. 1, p. 39.

[8] Rawlinson to Wigram 27/2/16, Rawlinson Papers 5201/33/18, NAM. All Rawlinson correspondence in this chapter comes from this file unless otherwise indicated.

[9] The detail of the German defences is taken from Wynne, *If Germany Attacks*, pp. 100–1.

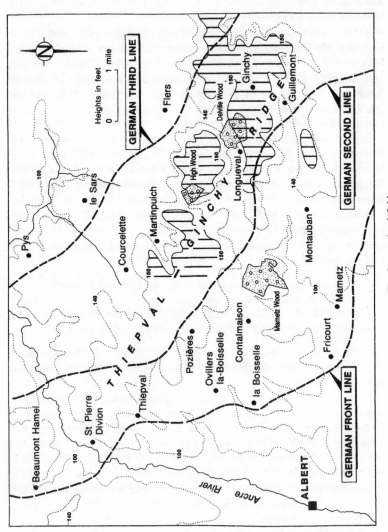

MAP 13   *The Somme battlefield*

Thiepval, and Beaumont Hamel. This system was protected by two belts of wire, each 30 yards wide and 15 yards apart. The second line system, some 2,000–4,000 yards back, was similar in organization to the first, just as strongly wired, and situated on a reverse slope. Of crucial importance to any plan of attack, this second line (as at Loos) lay beyond the range of the main British wire-cutting guns. Between the two main systems were various intermediate positions covering the villages of Montauban, Mametz, Contalmaison, St Pierre Divion, and Beaucourt. (Unknown at this stage to Rawlinson, work was already beginning on a third system about 3,000 yards beyond the second.)

The contemplation of these defences determined Rawlinson to advocate a cautious step-by-step attack for the coming offensive. Before he could draw up a plan, he was taken ill with influenza. During the first week in March his condition worsened and by the 17th he was forced to take two weeks leave in the south of France.[10] On his return he found that Montgomery had drawn up a 'very good' scheme for a bite and hold operation on a wide front.[11] However, he also learned from Kitchener that Haig had in mind a much more grandiose operation, unlimited in its objectives.[12] Rawlinson referred this information to Montgomery and his corps commanders and found that they all favoured a bite and hold operation. So he decided to go ahead and submit Montgomery's scheme, with a few amendments, to Haig. He wrote in his diary:

> I daresay I shall have a tussle with him over the limited objective for I hear he is inclined to favour the unlimited with the chance of breaking the German line.[13]

III

The essence of the Rawlinson–Montgomery plan was as follows.[14] First, Rawlinson defined the area to be attacked. He did this by using two criteria: the number of troops and the number of heavy howitzers likely to be available. He anticipated having at his disposal 17 infantry divisions, of which 10 were to attack, 2 to remain on the defensive, and 5 to be in corps

---

[10] Rawlinson Short Note Diary 17/3/16.

[11] Ibid. 28/3/16.

[12] Rawlinson Diary 30/3/16.

[13] Ibid. 4/4/16.

[14] All quotations in the following paragraphs and other explanatory material are taken from 'Plan For Offensive By Fourth Army', 3/4/16, in IV Army Summary Of Operations, WO 158/233.

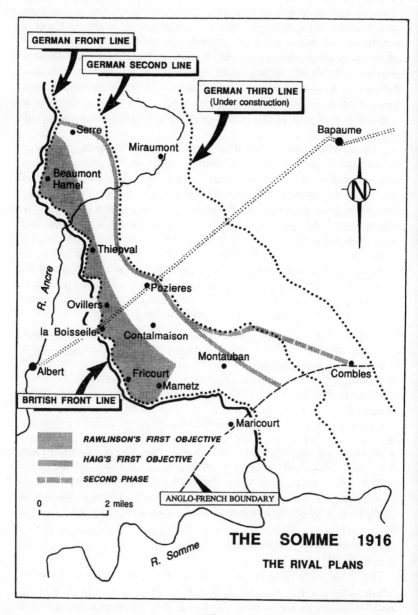

GERMAN FRONT LINE

GERMAN SECOND LINE

GERMAN THIRD LINE
(Under construction)

Bapaume

N

Serre

Miraumont

Beaumont
Hamel

Thiepval

R. Ancre

Pozieres

Ovillers

la Boisseile

Contalmaison

Montauban

Combles

Albert

Fricourt

Mametz

BRITISH FRONT LINE

RAWLINSON'S FIRST OBJECTIVE

HAIG'S FIRST OBJECTIVE

SECOND PHASE

Maricourt

0   2 miles

ANGLO-FRENCH BOUNDARY

THE SOMME 1916

R. Somme

THE RIVAL PLANS

MAP 14

or Army reserve. Using a formula for the attacking divisions of 8 or 9 men per yard, he arrived at a front of attack of 20,000 yards. Happily, 20,000 yards was also the maximum length of front he considered could be dealt with by the 200 heavy howitzers (defined as 6 inch and above) which he would have. After examining a map Rawlinson concluded that a suitable 20,000-yard front of attack would result from establishing one defensive flank on the high ground around Serre in the north and the other on the Montauban–Mametz spur in the south.

Second, Rawlinson turned to the vital subject of the depth to which the attack would seek to penetrate in the first instance. He stated – without elaboration – that with his 200 howitzers he could, on the selected front of 20,000 yards, 'deal effectively' with the enemy defences to a depth of 4,000–5,000 yards. This was highly ambitious; such a distance would encompass not only the first but also the second German trench system. Rawlinson, however, then went on to offer six reasons why his initial attack should not aim for so much. The first three reasons concerned the inexperience of his troops. Rawlinson wrote:

> it must be remembered that neither our new formations nor the old Divisions have the same discipline that obtained in our Army of a year ago.

From this want of experience, in his view, three things followed: raw troops advancing beyond a depth of 3,000 yards would become disorganized and lose direction; once disorganized, they would be hard put to it to reorganize so as to meet a counterattack; finally, should the German second line prove to be well defended and so repulse the first rush, reorganization for a further advance would present a difficulty.

The three further considerations for limiting the depth of advance concerned his artillery resources. First, for most of its length the German second line was situated on a reverse slope; and Rawlinson held that, given the artillery methods then in use, direct observation was particularly necessary for the systematic cutting of the enemy wire. Second, the deeper the projected advance the greater the number of targets with which the artillery would have to deal. Finally, 'it is difficult, if not impossible under these conditions, to assist the infantry with artillery fire against counterattacks in its more distant positions. This latter disadvantage is perhaps the most important of all.'

This is all rather mysterious. In effect, Rawlinson is not qualifying his preliminary claim that he could 'deal effectively' with an area as deep as 4,000–5,000 yards. He is flatly contradicting it. For what he is saying is that owing to the inexperience of his troops and the limitations of the support which his artillery could provide, the German second line might well withstand his attack and his forces succumb to a counterattack.

The upshot of this was that Rawlinson proposed overrunning objectives well short of the German second line. On the northern part of the sector to be attacked, lying between Serre and Pozières, he proposed that Fourth Army in its first endeavour advance to a depth of just 1,000–2,000 yards. Thereby it would overrun the Germans' first set of defences along with certain tactical positions beyond. From here his artillery, once it had been brought forward, would possess good observation over the Germans' second line and could prepare the way for a subsequent attack.

South of Pozières Rawlinson faced a more problematical situation. He planned again to assail only the German first line, along with the defended village of Fricourt, while on his right he would establish a defensive flank between Montauban and Mametz. But in so doing he would not be placing himself in a good position to fire on the German second line. Hence he concluded that he would not assail that line directly. Rather, any further advance would take place in the northern sector, with Contalmaison as its objective. That accomplished, it would then be possible to move forward, swing right, and roll up the German second line in the southern sector.

What is particularly noteworthy about this scheme is that it did not envisage the capture of a large area of German-held territory. Rawlinson's justification for this approach was that:

> It does not appear to me that the gain of 2 or 3 more kilometres of ground is of much consequence . . . Our object rather seems to be to kill as many Germans as possible with the least loss to ourselves . . . [In his view the best way to do that was to] seize points of tactical importance which will provide us with good observation and which we may feel quite certain the Germans will counterattack . . . under disadvantages likely to conduce to heavy losses, which we can only ensure if these tactical points are not too far distant from our gun positions.

In short, bite and hold remained Rawlinson's preferred method.

Two consequent matters were also dealt with. One was the length of the bombardment. The other concerned the use of gas and smoke, which had been a feature of the Loos plan.

As to the first, while acknowledging the stunning effect likely to be achieved by a hurricane bombardment (like that employed at Neuve Chapelle), Rawlinson felt he had no choice but to opt for a methodical artillery fire plan spread over 50–60 hours. In the first place he did not possess the wherewithal for a hurricane bombardment: that is, a sufficient number of guns to deliver in a short period the quantity of shells necessary to cut the wire and demolish the German defences. Also, the number of heavy shells available was so limited that it would be necessary to ensure that as many as possible reached their goals. This meant keeping a continual watch on the German defences to see that the shells were actually arriving on target.

Regarding the second matter, Rawlinson rejected the use of gas on three grounds: the Germans now had efficient gas masks; it was impossible to forecast the direction of the wind on the day of attack; and the assaulting infantry would be hampered by the necessity of themselves wearing gas masks.

All of this may have been true. But it left an important issue unresolved. At Givenchy and Loos, a feature of the German defences had been the deep dugouts constructed below the enemy trenches. Presciently, Rawlinson had written after Givenchy:

> I much doubt if any kind of artillery fire however accurate and well sustained will have the desired effect unless it is sufficient to bury the garrisons in the deep dug-outs they have now constructed, and this is a matter of chance.[15]

This problem was not absent at the Somme. Indeed, Rawlinson was aware that in its chalk soils dugouts of any depth could be constructed.[16] The details of a dugout near Ovillers, 17 feet deep and capable of holding a garrison of 12 men, had been obtained from a prisoner and passed on to him.[17]

If the artillery could not penetrate into these positions, how were they to be suppressed? At Loos, it had been anticipated that the use of gas would have the incidental effect of incapacitating the dugout-dwellers. On that occasion, an insufficient supply of gas and the absence of a favouring wind had thwarted the attempt. This no doubt left Rawlinson disenchanted with gas as an instrument for incapacitating the opposition at the Somme. Yet he had no other solution to offer to the problem of eliminating these well-protected German defenders. The most that Rawlinson could propose in order to lessen the effect of this unsubdued resistance was the concealment of his own forces during their passage of no-man's-land. No doubt he recalled that at Loos 47 Division, thanks to a rapid advance under the concealment provided by a cloud of smoke (along with gas), had caught the Germans still in their dugouts. So after Loos, Rawlinson was enthusiastic

---

[15] Rawlinson to First Army 21/6/15, in IV Corps War Diary Jun–Aug 1915, WO 95/710.
[16] See, for example, 'Information Gained From The Raiding Party On The Night Of [June] 5th', Fourth Army Intelligence Summary 8/6/16, WO 157/171.
[17] 'Extracts from Information given by a prisoner . . . captured opposite Ovillers 17/1/16', Montgomery-Massingberd Papers, Folder 98.

about employing smoke as a means of securing surprise: 'All the reports that I have received from the infantry are strongly in favour of the use of smoke, not only in the shape of candles but also in the way of phosphorus, both as hand grenades and trench mortar bombs.'[18] For the Somme, therefore, Rawlinson proposed to employ smoke 'to the fullest possible extent': 'This will take the form of candles, hand smoke bombs, and 4" Stokes Mortar bombs if the wind is favourable, and 4" Stokes Mortar bombs only if it should be unfavourable.'[19]

At this stage, therefore, Rawlinson was accepting that he could not totally eliminate the opposition, but was hoping that the half measure of a smoke screen would protect his infantry from prohibitive loss.

IV

Rawlinson's plan may be briefly summarized. It provided for an attack by ten divisions on a front of 20,000 yards, preceded by an artillery bombardment of four to five days. The infantry, advancing under the cover of smoke, would seize the German first line and advance beyond it, but would stop well short of the German second line; and on their right they would establish a defensive flank from Maricourt to just north of Mametz. After a pause of about three days, during which time the artillery would be brought up and German counterattacks defeated, a second advance would be undertaken. This would capture the German second line between Serre and Pozières, and to the south the fortified village of Contalmaison. Then the artillery would again be moved forward and a second series of counterattacks beaten off. A further attack to capture the southern section of the German second line beyond Contalmaison could then be contemplated.

Very little of this plan proved pleasing to Sir Douglas Haig. The commander-in-chief criticized it on two main grounds. First, it made no attempt to achieve surprise. Second, it was too cautious. He also told Rawlinson that the southern section of his attack would have to be recast to take into account the actions of the French who would now be operating to the north as well as south of the River Somme.[20]

In order to achieve surprise, Haig rejected Rawlinson's methodical bombardment extending over several days and opted for a 'short intensive bombardment immediately preceding the assault.'[21] As for Rawlinson's

[18] Rawlinson to First Army 5/10/15, First Army War Diary Sept 1915, WO 95/158.

[19] 'Plan For Offensive By Fourth Army', 3/4/16.

[20] Haig to Rawlinson 10/4/16 in 'Battle Of The Somme: Preparations By The Fourth Army', Fourth Army Papers vol. 1, Imperial War Museum. (Hereafter, Fourth Army Somme Preparations.)

step-by-step infantry operations, Haig stated that much larger steps could be taken with much shorter intervals between them. He told Rawlinson that, as first objectives, the Fourth Army should aim in the north for the capture of the entire German second line between Serre and Pozières, and in the south for a line running from Pozières to the ridge north-east of Maricourt. Subsequent advances, made after the briefest possible intervals, would not only complete the capture of the German second line in the southern sector but would also push eastwards to Combles. That is, Haig was envisaging the capture of the German first and second lines (and in the south an advance even beyond) in what was in effect a single operation in two closely adjoining phases.[22]

The rationale for this more ambitious plan was as follows. Haig took the view that a hurricane bombardment lasting just five or six hours would be sufficient to enable the British infantry to storm the German front line. This would create severe disorganization to the German defences, giving his forces the opportunity to rush the German second line before the defenders could recover. Further attacks by the infantry would keep the Germans on the run. The object of killing Germans, he argued, would be better achieved once they had been forced out of their fixed defences. He was also critical of Rawlinson's plan in that it contained no role for the cavalry which he insisted should be kept on hand in order to exploit any 'favourable development'.

Haig acknowledged that this approach involved some risks. But he insisted:

> The risks to be incurred can be foreseen and to a great extent guarded against by careful previous arrangement for providing artillery support, for throwing in reinforcements as required to fill gaps in the line and to cover flanks that become exposed ... and generally, for providing the means of holding what may be gained.

The outstanding feature of Haig's strictures is the manner in which they refused to come to grips with most of Rawlinson's arguments. First, Haig's advocacy of a hurricane bombardment overlooked the fact that no such bombardment was possible. With the limited number of guns available, a short bombardment would be more akin to a stiff breeze than to a hurricane. In order to fire the volume of shells needed to cut the wire, a bombardment of four or five days could not be forgone.

---

[21] Ibid.

[22] The quotations and supporting material in the following paragraphs are in Haig to Rawlinson 13/4/16, Fourth Army Somme Preparations.

Second, Haig's plan to rush the second line contained a number of flaws. The disorganization of the German defenders to which he attached such importance would at most apply only to the frontline garrisons. The German reserves who would be brought forward to man the second line once the attack began were beyond the range where British artillery could severely hamper their movements. There was no reason to anticipate that they would be suffering from severe disorganization, especially as they would be sheltering behind uncut wire which lay outside the reach of the British wire-cutting guns.

Third, Haig's assertion that with 'careful arrangements' artillery support could be provided for the troops advancing on the German second line was largely without foundation. In order to render effective support, a substantial number of guns and howitzers would have to be got forward the moment the infantry attack commenced. Given the crowded state likely to be found in the British rear areas during this period, that was bound to be a protracted business – if indeed it could be managed at all.

Fourth, as regards the cavalry, it was manifest that the maze of trenches and shell holes on both sides of the front constituted unsuitable ground for manoeuvring large numbers of horsemen. And beyond this lay the intact and manned defences of the second German line.

Finally, and most significantly of all, by setting a more distant objective Haig was decreasing by a large factor the intensity of the bombardment which could be brought to bear on the defences under attack. In fact, Haig had just about doubled the number of yards of trench to be bombarded by his heavy howitzers without in any way increasing his supply of howitzers and howitzer ammunition. He was thereby creating the danger that the bombardment would be inadequate to quell even the first German positions, in which case his forces might be denied any success at all.

V

As a result of Haig's criticisms, Rawlinson set about drafting a new plan. He was obviously uneasy with the tactics suggested by the commander-in-chief. He recorded in his diary:

> It is clear that D.H. would like us to do the whole thing in one rush and I am quite game to try but it certainly does involve considerable risks . . . It will be difficult unless we start a panic.[23]

By 19 April his new scheme was complete.

[23] Rawlinson Diary 14/4/16.

I am sending in to G.H.Q. tonight [a] very important memorandum ... On it may possibly depend the tactics of one of the
greatest battles the British Army has ever fought and I fully recognize
the responsibility ... Archie Montgomery drafted most of the memorandum and I added a few paragraphs and polished it up.[24]

The Montgomery–Rawlinson memorandum[25] began by saying that the
new information provided by Haig 'alters to a considerable extent the
situation on which my plan was originally based, and calls for certain
alterations in it in order to enable me to carry out the Commander-in-
Chief's instructions as now laid down.' This seemed to foreshadow a
complete capitulation to GHQ even though the only new information
provided by Haig, concerning the participation of the French north of the
Somme, hardly altered the basis on which Rawlinson's plan had been
made. But what followed was a *mélange* of capitulation and resistance.
So Rawlinson described as 'alluring' Haig's suggestion that the German
second line be rushed, but he nevertheless repeated his original reasons
for rejecting this course. He said that the distances to be covered meant, in
all probability, that the German reserves could man the second line before
the assaulting troops could reach it; that the second line was strong and
well wired; that wire-cutting at extreme distances would present a 'serious
difficulty'; that the provision of artillery support for the infantry if they did
gain a footing in the second line would be extremely difficult; and that
troops without the discipline of the regulars would be vulnerable to disorganization at a very early stage of the battle.

Thus far Rawlinson had firmly restated his case for confining operations
to those laid down in his original plan. And a summary of his objections to
extending the first phase of the operation began in similar vein. He wrote:

It still seems to me that an attempt to attain more distant objectives,
that is to say the enemy's second line system, under the conditions
above described, involves considerable risks.

But what follows is in striking contrast. Rawlinson concluded:

I, however, fully realise that it may be necessary to incur these risks
in view of the importance of the object to be attained. This will,
no doubt, be decided by the Commander-in-Chief, and definite instructions be sent to me in due course.

---

[24] Ibid. 19/4/16.

[25] The quotations and supporting material in the following paragraphs are in 'Memorandum
by Rawlinson' 19/4/16, IV Army Summary of Operations, WO 158/233.

The retreat signified by this passage, after what had seemed a firm statement of the grounds for standing by his original proposal, is worth dwelling upon. For it constituted an amendment to his scheme of the utmost gravity.

If the area to be captured by the infantry's initial advance was to be extended to the depth of the German second line, as stipulated by Haig, then this was bound to imperil the effectiveness of the bombardment upon the enemy's front line. The number of howitzers available to Rawlinson was more or less fixed; so he could only bombard the German second position by considerably reducing his capacity to damage the first. Yet nothing in Haig's exposition addressed this problem. Rawlinson's lame comment that 'it may be necessary to incur these risks in view of the importance of the object to be obtained' simply disregarded the fact that one 'risk' mattered above all others. The British command might overreach itself and thereby fail – at heavy cost – to take even the first defensive positions. This risk Haig was wantonly incurring.

Why did Rawlinson capitulate so easily? In part he may have failed to perceive the extent of the 'risks' to which Haig was subjecting his plan. Indeed, he had played into his chief's hands at the outset by claiming that he possessed the howitzers to 'deal effectively' with the German defences to a depth of 4,000–5,000 yards (which was as far as Haig now insisted his troops should go) and then offering a jumble of reasons for not doing so. Those reasons, as has been indicated, make sorry reading. The first group concerned the inexperience of his troops. On the day this would prove the least of his problems. For the human frames of experienced troops would not prove better able than those of inexperienced troops to withstand enemy machine-guns and artillery if the preliminary bombardment had failed to achieve its purpose. The other group of reasons concerned the problem of taking on 'many more objectives' and the ineffectiveness of artillery fire against enemy defences at long distance. What in effect Rawlinson was doing here was contradicting his claim that he could 'deal effectively' with those defences to a depth of 4,000–5,000 yards. It is to be presumed that Rawlinson, when challenged by Haig, was loath to point out – even if he managed to detect – his own muddle-headedness on this matter.

But another reason suggests itself for Rawlinson's capitulation to Haig's ill-founded amendments to his plan. Rawlinson was engaging in an unhappy act of obeisance to Haig's authority. Between men of equal standing, it would have been incumbent on Rawlinson to point out that the 'importance of the object to be attained' in no way warranted the taking of risks which had not been calculated and might jeopardize the attainment of any objectives whatsoever. But the authority structure of the British army, and Rawlinson's particular relationship with Haig, did not admit of such unequivocal speaking by the Fourth Army commander to the commander-in-chief.

Having given way on this quite vital matter, Rawlinson proved less amenable in some other respects. He seemed to capitulate to Haig in the matter of objectives to be attained once the second line had been captured, agreeing that even after that event further advances could be undertaken. However, in this case appearances were deceptive. For Rawlinson was careful not to specify whether the further objectives would be reached in a single operation or only in a series of operations with intervals between them. He also indicated that before even the first of these additional operations began, 'a considerable number of fresh troops would be required.' In this matter Rawlinson was clearly keeping his options open.

On the issue of cavalry, Rawlinson provided a sop to Haig. He introduced the suggestion that cavalry could well be used in the second phase, but only 'if we succeed in inflicting on the enemy a serious state of demoralization.'

On one matter – the length of the bombardment – Rawlinson clung tenaciously to his original plan. He had already made it plain that there was no question of firing a hurricane bombardment, because he did not possess sufficient guns to deliver the required number of shells in a few hours. Haig had failed to grasp this point, and had discoursed on the superior damage which a hurricane bombardment would render to the defenders' morale. It might have been thought sufficient for Rawlinson to point out that, as a hurricane bombardment lay beyond his powers, its merits as a morale-breaker were beside the point. But once more (it may be speculated) the authority structure of the British army forbade such plain speaking. Hence, although on this occasion Rawlinson stuck to his position, he abandoned the sensible grounds he had first adopted for doing so. Instead of reiterating that a hurricane bombardment was impossible, he discoursed on the irrelevant issue raised by Haig concerning enemy morale, claiming, however, that a lengthy bombardment would render it even greater damage than a hurricane:

> the effect on moral[e] of a long, accurate, bombardment, which will pulverise strong points one by one, gradually knocking in communication trenches [and] prevent[ing] reliefs from being carried out ... will, to my mind, be much greater [than a] hurricane bombardment.

VI

Rawlinson's second memorandum met with a wall of silence from GHQ. On 25 April he noted in his diary:

I can get no decision yet from D.H. as to whether we are to have a Hurricane or a deliberate bombardment but Kiggell tells me he still hangs [*sic*] towards a hurricane. Nor is it yet settled if we are to try and rush right through to the second Pozières line in the first day.[26]

Three more weeks were to elapse before Rawlinson received a reply to these questions. Meanwhile further evidence was arriving which strengthened Rawlinson's view that the Germans could not be rushed out of their fixed positions. On 25 April aerial reconnaissance revealed that a third line of defence was being constructed. Rawlinson ordered more photographs to be taken and himself went on a flight to confirm its existence.[27] The reports placed the matter beyond doubt. By the time the battle opened the third line would be almost complete.[28]

Yet not even these revelations shook the determination of Haig to aim for a distant objective on the first day. On 16 May he informed Rawlinson that the 'Serre-Mira[u]mont spur; Pozières; Contalmaison, and Montauban be the objectives to be attained during the first day's operations ... It is understood that you concur in this view.'[29] It must have been obvious to Haig that Rawlinson did not concur at all, but was being required to comply with the commander-in-chief's wishes.

Only on the question of the length of the bombardment did Haig eventually back down. To the end he remained extremely reluctant to do so. In the margin of Rawlinson's 19 April plan he wrote, with persisting obtuseness:

I do not agree that the moral[e] effect of a 'long & slow' fire is comparable to the same amount of shell fired upon the same spots in say a tenth of the time.

Perhaps when Haig finally came to reply to Rawlinson it had been pointed out to him that the Fourth Army did not have anything like the number of guns to fire 'the same amount of shells' in 'a tenth of the time'. Whatever the reason, Haig in his 16 May memorandum at last conceded the necessity for a prolonged bombardment. He added that the bombardment should be 'continued until the officers commanding the attacking units are satisfied that the obstacles to their advance have been adequately destroyed.'[30] He

[26] Rawlinson Diary 25/4/16.

[27] Ibid. 25, 26, 27 April 1916.

[28] Wynne, *If Germany Attacks*, p. 101.

[29] GHQ to Rawlinson 16/5/16, quoted in Edmonds, *1916* vol. 1 Appendices, Appendix 11, p. 83.

[30] For these quotations see Haig's marginalia on 'Memorandum by Rawlinson 19/4/16' in IV Army Summary of Operations, WO 158/233.

did not go on to indicate how this could be done, given that the date for the attack would have to be set well in advance and co-ordinated with the French.

It is worth remarking upon the sorry condition to which this exchange reduced the plans for the initial Somme attack. Rawlinson had proposed a lengthy bombardment of a limited area. It would eliminate all element of surprise but might neutralize the German defences in the modest sector he intended to seize. Haig had countered by requiring a heavy but brief bombardment (which it lay beyond his capacities to deliver) upon an altogether greater area. Supposedly this would facilitate such a measure of surprise as to throw the German defenders, not only in the first but in the second line of defence, into a state of confusion, and so enable the British infantry to overrun both lines.

In the event Haig was obliged to abandon the pipe dream of a hurricane bombardment, and so to forgo the element of surprise. Yet he insisted on his aim of a deep penetration, even though attacking without the surprise factor to which he had attached such importance. As for the diminution in the effectiveness of the bombardment likely to result from doubling the area upon which the limited supply of howitzer shells must fall, this matter seems never to have entered Haig's calculations or Rawlinson's comments upon them. Rarely can an ambitious operation have been embarked upon on such insubstantial grounds.

16

The Implements

I

In mid-1916 there were three fundamental implements to any military operation. These were cavalry, infantry, and artillery.

Early in their planning for the Somme campaign neither Haig nor Rawlinson had considered that conditions looked promising for the use of cavalry. However, Haig had insisted that Rawlinson include cavalry in his plan in case a 'favourable development' arose.[1] As the day of battle approached, Haig – as was his wont – became more optimistic. Late in May, Kiggell wrote to Gough (who was to command the GHQ cavalry reserve) that the commander-in-chief now saw opportunities to use cavalry for 'a dash on Miraumont' and 'to help the attack on the Pozières heights.'[2]

Later still Haig's plans for the cavalry became yet more ambitious. By mid-June he was dwelling on the great numerical superiority in infantry enjoyed by the British. It was estimated by British Intelligence that the Germans would have 32 battalions in the front line with 65 available for reinforcement during the first six days. In contrast the British were attacking with 164 battalions with another 64 in close reserve. This numerical superiority, Haig thought, meant that the chances of an initial success were good. (The British commander-in-chief was failing to notice that at Loos the superiority in numbers of British infantry had been even greater relatively, yet there had been no striking success.) Haig concluded that action should be taken to build on this potential result by the use of cavalry. He thought that the horse-soldiers should be pushed through north of Pozières to seize Bapaume. The reserve infantry (now also to be placed

---

[1] Kiggell to Gough 1/5/16, GHQ Letters 5 Feb/16 Nov 1916, Fourth Army Papers vol. 5.
[2] Kiggell to Gough 24/5/16, IV Army Summary of Operations, WO 158/233.

under the command of Gough) would then relieve the cavalry there and establish a strong southerly flank. Thereupon the cavalry would turn north and drive the Germans from the Arras salient.[3]

As a result of these flights of fancy, Rawlinson was obliged to issue an operation order incorporating the new objectives.[4] It was also necessary to call a conference of his corps commanders so that the best methods of implementing Haig's instructions could be discussed. However, at this conference Rawlinson indicated that he was by no means an enthusiast for Haig's cavalry schemes. He told his corps commanders:

> An opportunity may occur to push the cavalry through . . . and in this connection I will read you the orders I have received on the subject from the Commander-in-Chief this morning. But before I read them I had better make it quite clear that it may not be possible to break the enemy's line and push the cavalry through at the first rush . . . A situation may supervene later . . . for pushing the cavalry through; but until we can see what is the course of the battle, it is impossible to predict at what moment we shall be able to undertake this, and the decision will rest in my hands to say when it can be carried out.[5]

II

As far as the infantry were concerned, it was Rawlinson's intention that most of the period between the creation of the Fourth Army in February 1916 and the opening of the Somme campaign in July would be spent on training. His policy, so he told Robertson, Chief of Imperial General Staff (CIGS), in April, was to 'keep a good many troops back for training. In the case of the new Divisions this is badly needed.'[6]

This objective, however, proved unattainable. It ran up against the paucity of labour available for preparing an operation involving half a million troops. In anticipation of the battle, the Fourth Army had to construct new roads and upgrade others, lay new railway track, provide accommodation additional to what was available in the small villages, lay

[3] GHQ to Rawlinson 16/6/16, quoted in Edmonds, *1916* vol. 1 Appendices, Appendix 15, pp. 89–90.

[4] Fourth Army: Continuation of Operation Order No. 2, 22/6/16, Fourth Army Operation Orders and Instructions 5 Feb/19 Aug 1916, Fourth Army Papers vol. 7.

[5] 'Report of the Army Commander's remarks at the Conference held at Fourth Army Headquarters, 22 June, 1916', Fourth Army Conferences and Various Source Papers, Fourth Army Papers vol. 6.

[6] Rawlinson to Robertson 8/4/16, Rawlinson Papers 5201/33/18, NAM.

pipe to ensure an adequate supply of water, and establish ammunition dumps. In addition assembly and communication trenches had to be dug and a system of signals cable laid. This last required an enormous effort. The experience of previous battles had shown that only cable buried six feet deep would survive German medium howitzer shells. Accordingly the decision was taken that all cable forward of divisional headquarters be buried at this depth. Eventually 7,000 miles of cable were so buried. This was not the whole of the task. Rearward of divisional headquarters over 43,000 miles of cable were laid overground.[7]

To carry out this work GHQ could offer Rawlinson only five labour battalions, a total of 5,000 men.[8] This force was manifestly inadequate. Rawlinson had little choice but to supplement the labour battalions with the infantry. This – as he well realized – detracted heavily from the training programme. He told Wigram, 'I am hard at work teaching them [the infantry] in schools & in the usual work with their units in the open; but there is an immense amount of labour to get out of them at the same time, chiefly making railways & roads, gun emplacements, trenches of all sorts.'[9] General Maxse (18 Division), one of the most assiduous trainers of troops in the British army (he would become Inspector of Training in 1918), was more explicit about how the labour requirements of the army hampered other activities. He claimed that while theoretically four months had been available to train, in practice: 'manual labour was being required day and night, whenever battalions were out of the trenches. Railways were built, roads created and repaired, tram lines laid, water pipes were put underground, cables were buried 6 feet deep. *No rest and no training for the infantry, except during the 1 week.*'[10] Other units have testified to the 'elaborate, tireless fatigue-duty in all kinds of labour behind the line', resulting – in the case of one unit – in only one week at the end of April being available for training.[11] The end result was summed up by Captain Jack of the 2 Cameronians (8 Division):

> We have done our level best to instruct all ranks and tune them up for the battle ahead. But the very heavy all-nightly and daily fatigues . . . have swallowed up almost all the officers and men who should have been putting the finishing touches to practice for oper-

---

[7] For these points see Edmonds, *1916* vol. 1, pp. 271–80, 286.

[8] Ibid., p. 272.

[9] Rawlinson to Wigram 8/5/16, Rawlinson Papers 5201/33/18, NAM.

[10] Maxse to Montgomery 31/7/16, Montgomery-Massingberd Papers (emphasis added).

[11] Magnus Laurie, *The West Riding Territorials in the Great War* (London: Kegan Paul, Trench, Trubner, 1920), p. 88.

ations, and who in my opinion are still not PROPERLY TRAINED, although full of courage.[12]

Courage, it is fair to surmise, was no substitute for proper training.

Facing the commander of any body of foot soldiers assailing a defended trench system lay an acute problem. How, without inordinate loss, was he to get his infantry across open ground swept by the fire of automatic weapons and artillery? According to a popular view, Rawlinson's response to this question was governed by a preconception which was both unjust to his troops and fatal to their wellbeing. He is said to have believed that, on account of the inexperience of the Kitchener soldiers, it would not be appropriate to employ the infantry tactics used in earlier battles. For if they were sent forward in small columns moving rapidly, they would lose all cohesion. Hence he required the infantry to proceed across no-man's-land at a slow pace and in a series of extended lines or 'waves'. On no account were they to break from this formation, for its whole purpose was to ensure that each wave would arrive at the German line simultaneously. Anyway (this argument goes) the troops were so overburdened with equipment that they would be in no position to make the crossing at speed. For each infantryman – in addition to his rifle – was required to carry 220 rounds of ammunition, two gas helmets, two grenades, a small entrenching spade, two empty sandbags, a water bottle, and rations. This constituted a total weight of 66 lb.[13]

How valid is this account? It does seem that Rawlinson placed no great faith in the initiative and capabilities of the new divisions of which his Fourth Army was largely composed. We have already noted his unfavourable view of the new divisions compared with the regulars of 1915. And in his tactical notes of May 1916 he wrote:

> We must remember that owing to the large expansion of our Army and the heavy casualties in experienced officers, the officers and troops generally do not now possess that military knowledge arising from a long and high state of training which enables them to act instinctively and promptly on sound lines in unexpected situations. They have become accustomed to deliberate action based on precise and detailed orders.[14]

[12] John Terraine (ed.), *General Jack's Diary 1914–1918* (London: Eyre and Spottiswoode, 1964), p. 138.
[13] Edmonds, *1916* vol. 1, pp. 313–14.
[14] 'Fourth Army Tactical Notes', May 1916, quoted in Edmonds, *1916* vol. 1, Appendices, Appendix 18, p. 131.

Yet it does not follow that these preconceptions decided the speed of attack or the formations that Rawlinson laid down for the infantry. They had not done so at Loos, where the inexperienced 15 and 47 Divisions had employed tactics similar to those employed by the regulars at Neuve Chapelle; that is, column formations moving across no-man's-land at speed. Nor do operational records for 1 July 1916 bear out the contention that Rawlinson at the Somme actually imposed slow-moving wave formations upon his infantry.

On the matter of the pace at which the troops should attempt the crossing of no-man's-land the most complete discussion at the planning stage is contained in the Fourth Army Tactical Notes. In that document, with respect to the allocation of objectives, Rawlinson stated *inter alia* that:

> celerity of movement and the necessity of taking immediate and full advantage of the stunning effects [of the bombardment] on the enemy's moral[e] and physical powers are essentially the governing factors ... The assaulting troops must push forward at a steady pace in successive lines, each adding fresh impetus to the preceding line. Although a steady pace for the assaulting troops is recommended, occasions may arise where a rapid advance of some lightly-equipped men on some particular part of the enemy's defences may turn the scale.[15]

What seems most noteworthy about this passage is its ambiguity. Rawlinson, far from imposing a method of proceeding, is not giving his infantry commanders clear directions. His initial exhortation to 'celerity of movement' is promptly cancelled out by a proposal to 'push forward at a steady pace'. (Clearly Rawlinson did not regard these expressions as synonymous. For the 'steady pace' recommended generally for the assaulting troops is explicitly contrasted with 'a rapid advance of some lightly-equipped men' in particular circumstances.) What Rawlinson may have been endeavouring to say here is that the troops should get across no-man's-land with as much celerity as was compatible both with the need to keep formation and with the fact that most of them would not be 'lightly-equipped'. But his way of saying it proved so imprecise that it effectually imposed no manner of proceeding on his corps and divisional commanders.

This seems to explain what is otherwise a curious feature of the infantry attack on 1 July – its lack of uniformity. The abiding image of the first day of the Somme is of British soldiers set up for slaughter: 'the British [lines] rigid and slow, advancing as at an Aldershot parade ... torn and ripped by

[15] Ibid., p. 134.

the German guns.'[16] Yet an investigation of existing evidence does not reveal the attacking units as invariably going to their doom in this way. Rather, the conclusion to be drawn is that each corps, or sometimes each division within a corps, made its own decision about the speed at which it would attempt the crossing of no-man's-land; and that sometimes battalions and brigades, under pressure of actual combat, took the matter into their own hands. Thus we know that in the case of VIII Corps the commander, Hunter-Weston, did specifically warn his troops against advancing at the double, except for short distances such as 20 yards. For, he explained, 'with the heavy weight men will be carrying', moving at the double would be very exhausting.[17] Yet there is evidence that at least some battalions from each of the divisions of VIII Corps attempted to rush the German positions.[18] The same applies to some battalions from every division of X Corps and XV Corps.[19] On the other hand both divisions of III Corps seem to have advanced at a slow walk.[20] (It is notable that the two divisions of this corps sustained the largest number of deaths on 1 July.)[21]

It is clear, then, that Rawlinson did not determine the pace at which, from one end of the front to the other, the infantrymen of Fourth Army attempted the passage of no-man's-land. His observations on this matter were so ambiguous as to leave his corps commanders with a wide discretion. The corps commanders either delegated this decision to those further down the scale or, at least in some instances, had the matter taken out of their hands. The reality of battle imposed further amendments; for there are many occasions where battalions began the attack at a walk but responded to enemy fire by rushing the German positions. Apparently, therefore, it was possible to advance at a good pace carrying 66 lb. of

[16] An eyewitness account by Sir Edward Spears, liaison officer with the French Sixth Army, quoted in his book *Prelude to Victory* (London: Cape, 1939), p. 91.

[17] VIII Corps, 'Notes of Two Conferences Held at Corps Headquarters – 21 & 23/6/16', VIII Corps War Diary Mar–Dec 1916, WO 95/820.

[18] In the 31 Division the Yorks and Lancs battalions and the East Lancs 'rushed'. In 4 Division the 8 Royal Warwicks advanced by a series of rushes. On the right of 89 Brigade of 29 Division some battalions rushed. On the other hand most of 87 Brigade from the same division walked. See A. H. Farrar-Hockley, *The Somme* (London: Batsford, 1964), pp. 113, 115, 118, 120.

[19] For X Corps (32 Division) see Farrar-Hockley, *Somme*, p. 127; Edmonds, *1916* vol. 1, pp. 401–2; 32 Division Weekly Summary of Operations, X Corps War Diary Jul–Dec 1916, WO 95/851; (36 Division) Farrar-Hockley, *Somme*, pp. 130, 132; Edmonds, *1916* vol. 1, pp. 404, 406; Martin Middlebrook, *The First Day on the Somme* (London: Allen Lane, 1971), p. 174. For XV Corps (21 Division) see Edmonds, *1916* vol. 1, pp. 359–60; (7 Division) 'Notes on Attacks Carried Out By 7th Division In July 1916', 7 Division War Diary Jul–Dec 1916, WO 95/1631.

[20] For III Corps see Farrar-Hockley, *Somme*, p. 139; Edmonds, *1916* vol. 1, p. 386.

[21] Ernest W. Bell, *Soldiers Killed on the First Day of the Somme* (Bolton, Lancs: Bell, 1977).

equipment, or else some troops achieved a good pace by abandoning part of their kit.

If Rawlinson did not specify the speed at which his troops should proceed, did he dictate the formations, insisting that the infantry advance in waves? Certainly the Fourth Army Tactical Notes give four illustrations of the 'best formations' and each takes the form of a modified wave. Nevertheless these formations were not insisted upon. Indeed Rawlinson stated: 'There can be no definite rules as regards the best formation for attack.' The most suitable, he suggested, would depend on the ground over which the advance was to be made and the particular objective to be captured. And later in the Notes he suggests that 'small columns, which can make full use of the folds of the ground to cover their advance, are preferable during the preliminary stages of the advance.'[22] In other words, only when the enemy line was being approached should these columns be deployed into waves to ensure that the weight of attack would fall along the entire enemy line.

Given the generality of these instructions, it is not surprising that corps, divisions, and brigades adopted attack formations of their own. Two examples, from 29 Division, will suffice. The 87 Brigade on the left of the attack generally used wave formations. The 1 Royal Inniskilling Fusiliers, by contrast, attacked with platoons in single file. The latter formation was adopted 'because of enemy strong points on the battalion right flank', and was 'designed to offer the least target to machine-guns in enfilade.'[23]

Was Rawlinson, nevertheless, seriously failing his troops by even allowing his subordinate commanders the discretion to send the infantry forward at a slow pace and in wave formations? The answer, almost certainly, is that this matter would not be of great importance except in circumstances where the opposition had been very largely, but not completely, subdued. Only when a small measure of resistance remained would the speed and the formation employed in the crossing of no-man's-land affect the extent of British losses. If no resistance remained, or a great deal of resistance remained, then these matters would count for little.

It is therefore necessary to go on to consider the key question: namely, how was Rawlinson proposing to subdue the German forces arrayed against the attackers? The infantry themselves, it must have been clear, would not possess weapons sufficient to effect the passage of no-man's-land. Indeed, at the time of the Somme offensive, Britain's new armies were only slightly better equipped than had been the regulars at Neuve Chapelle. Late in 1915 the Lewis gun, a machine-gun able to be carried by one man,

[22] All quotations are taken from 'Fourth Army Tactical Notes', pp. 134–6.
[23] Farrar-Hockley, *Somme*, p. 120.

had begun to make its appearance; and it was intended for the Somme that all infantry battalions should have 16 of them. However this number was nowhere near attained by 1 July, when no more than four were held by some battalions.[24] This represented a useful increase in fire power, but not of a sort seriously to threaten well-entrenched defenders. Anyway, on account of the weight of the Lewis guns (27 lb.) its operator and the five-man support team – employed primarily to carry additional drums of ammunition – proved a slow-moving and vulnerable target. Consequently some commanders at the Somme held back their few Lewis gunners to support the mopping-up parties, so providing no additional protection for the leading infantry waves.[25]

In any case, from no-man's-land the Lewis guns did not have the range to take on such major obstacles to the infantry as heavy machine-guns. The Lewis gun was essentially a close-range weapon. If the attackers were finding themselves held up well short of the enemy lines, the Lewis gunners could not help them.

One infantry weapon that had improved since the battles of Neuve Chapelle and Loos was the hand grenade. By the time of the Somme most battalions were equipped with the reliable standard-pattern Mills grenade.[26] However, this weapon still suffered one great disadvantage: unlike the German 'egg grenade' it was too heavy to throw far and it lacked the explosive charge to incapacitate the inhabitants of the deep German dugouts.

As against these meagre improvements upon 1915, a form of protection for the infantry which had proved efficacious once during that year would not be present along most of the front on 1 July 1916. We have already seen that Rawlinson, in the light of his Loos experience, had suggested to Haig in his initial plan of 3 April that smoke be employed along the entire front of attack on the Somme. Astonishingly, that was the last that was heard of this proposal. What seems to have happened is that Rawlinson allowed corps and divisional commanders to make their own decision regarding the use of smoke. Thus the two men in authority (Rawlinson and Haig) who had witnessed the effectiveness of smoke at Loos delegated responsibility for its employment on 1 July to men without any experience of its use on the Western Front.

In the outcome, the decision generally went against employing smoke to

---

[24] Bidwell and Graham, *Fire-Power*, p. 122 and 'Notes On The Lessons Of The Operations On The Somme Regards Infantry Attack Formations And The Employment Of Specialists', Fourth Army Papers vol. 17.

[25] Maxse used Lewis guns in this way in 18 Division. See General I. Maxse, 'The Battle of the Somme' (unpublished manuscript), Maxse Papers 69/53/6.

[26] Bidwell and Graham, *Fire-Power*, p. 125.

cover the infantry assault. Some commanders apparently were influenced by their artillery advisers who, especially in the south, warned that the clear observation currently enjoyed over the enemy's positions would be sacrificed if smoke were to be used.[27] The likelihood that the infantry would be sacrificed in the absence of smoke was apparently disregarded. In the event, smoke was, in the main, employed only to screen villages such as Fricourt and la Boisselle and the Ancre valley which were not to be taken by direct assault.[28]

If smoke had been used generally on 1 July 1916 to screen the infantry in no-man's-land, what was likely to have been its effectiveness? The experience of a division which took part in the diversionary attack on Gommecourt is instructive. The 56 Division was to attack the southern face of the Gommecourt salient. In order to draw attention to the impending attack, no attempt at surprise was made in this sector. The enemy facing the British were alert and prepared. German artillery began shelling the British assembly trenches three hours before the attack was due. Yet notwithstanding these handicaps, 56 Division *under the cover of a smokescreen* captured the German front line 'with comparatively little loss'.[29]

It would be unwise to place undue emphasis on this single example. Local conditions may have influenced the effectiveness of smoke. So the neighbouring 46 Division, attacking the north face of the Gommecourt salient, found that the wind blew the smoke back on their own lines, so denying the attacking troops concealment when they were less than halfway across no-man's-land. Nevertheless 46 Division were able to enter the German line at most places. (The heavy casualties eventually suffered by both divisions resulted from the failure of the counter-battery fire to subdue the German guns, with the result that the first waves of attackers could not be reinforced or supplied in the face of strong counterattacks.)

The use of smoke, it is safe to say, would not have provided a panacea on 1 July. However, it can hardly be doubted that its general employment would have lessened the casualties inflicted by German machine-guns on the British troops in no-man's-land. It is a heavy indictment of Rawlinson's exercise of command that he failed to impose on his subordinates the wisdom that he had derived from the otherwise unhappy experience at Loos. As events would shortly reveal, this negligence on his part was occurring in circumstances where the infantry on 1 July would need every possible aid available.

[27] Edmonds, *1916* vol. 1, p. 325.

[28] For Fricourt see Edmonds, *1916* vol. 1, p. 348; for la Boisselle, J. Shakespear, *The Thirty-Fourth Division 1915–1919* (London: Wetherby, 1921); for the Ancre valley, 36th (Ulster) Division, Weekly Summary of Operations 7/7/16, X Corps War Diary Jul–Dec 1916, WO 95/851.

[29] For Gommecourt see Edmonds, *1916* vol. 1, pp. 462–6.

III

The fact that the infantry carried no weapons capable of facilitating their crossing of no-man's-land, and would not even have the assistance of smoke to conceal their passage, could mean only one thing. Rawlinson was relying on his artillery to neutralize or destroy the enemy's defences. By the time his foot soldiers went over the top, it was anticipated that their way would have been made clear by the British bombardment.

It will be remembered that at Givenchy and at Loos Rawlinson had not considered that his artillery was sufficient to accomplish this purpose. What then were his grounds for taking a more hopeful view at the Somme? Had his guns increased in accuracy since Loos? And had they increased in number, not just absolutely but relative to the task in hand?

As regards the matter of artillery accuracy, it is indeed the case that the period between Loos and the Somme had witnessed a number of improvements. None, however, was greatly effective by the time the battle opened on 1 July. For example, from April 1916 some accurate meteorological data was being sent to the batteries by GHQ. However, the information was far from comprehensive and it was not sent frequently enough to be of substantial importance.[30]

Again, the problem of exactly locating the position of enemy targets in relation to British batteries had yet to be fully solved. Thanks to widespread trigonometrical survey it was at least possible for the British to establish exact co-ordinates for their own guns.[31] But it remained difficult to fix the location of targets within the German lines with similar accuracy. This problem was often compounded when prominent features in enemy-held territory which could have been used as survey reference points were removed by the Germans or destroyed by artillery fire. Moreover inaccurate maps were still in use, and the errors inherent in transposing aerial photographs to maps continued. Hence at the Somme the basic situation remained unchanged. The only reliable means of ensuring accuracy of fire continued to be for an FOO on the ground or in the air to observe the fall of shot and indicate corrections.

Nevertheless two methods of precisely locating enemy batteries were beginning to develop. One was flash spotting, the other sound ranging. The first depended on locating the flash of an enemy gun as it fired, the second on recording the wave of sound which followed the firing.[32] These

---

[30] Anstey, History of the Royal Artillery 1914–1918, p. 341.

[31] Great Britain: War Office: General Staff, Geographical Section, *Report on Survey on the Western Front 1914–18* (London: War Office, 1920), p. 33.

[32] See Sir Lawrence Bragg, Major-General A. H. Dawson, and Lt.-Col. H. H. Hemming, *Artillery Survey in the First World War* (London: Field Survey Association, 1971), chapters 3 and 4.

developments, which will be discussed in detail later, would in time become of considerable importance. But owing to technical problems, neither played a major role in the battle of the Somme.

One other artillery development, of considerable moment later in the war, first appeared at the Somme. This was the 'creeping barrage'. Fired by the field artillery's 18 pounder guns, it consisted of a screen of shrapnel which advanced (or crept) over the ground at a regular, predetermined pace. Its purpose was twofold. It would 'sweep' (with a hail of shrapnel) all the ground in its ambit, thus catching enemy machine-gunners who had been placed between trench lines so as to escape a barrage which jumped from one trench to another. And it would oblige the entrenched defenders to keep their heads down during those crucial moments when the attackers were advancing across no-man's-land. Indeed if the barrage was fired with sufficient skill, and the advancing infantry followed it closely enough, the enemy trenches might be overrun before their occupants could man the parapets.

Rawlinson and his artillery advisers had played a major role in the development of this tactic. At Loos the field artillery of 15 Division had fired a barrage of shrapnel which jumped from one trench line to another as the infantry attacked, in circumstances where the trench lines were so close together that the effect was practically that of a creeping barrage. This was noted by Budworth who after the battle wrote: 'A covering fire of shrapnel forms the best protection to an Infantry advance and if possible this fire should progress step by step with the advance.'[33] Rawlinson clearly heeded this lesson, and at a corps commanders' conference on 16 April he stated: 'The lifts of the artillery time tables must conform to the advances of the infantry. The infantry must be given plenty of time. The guns must "arrose" [spray as if from a hose] each objective just before the infantry assault it.'[34] Later this idea was made more explicit in Rawlinson's Tactical Notes:

Co-operation of Artillery with Infantry

The ideal is for the artillery to keep their fire immediately in front of the infantry as the latter advances, battering down all opposition with a hurricane of projectiles.[35]

Four factors prevented this innovation from reaching its full potential on 1 July. First, Rawlinson yet again left the implementation of the policy to

[33] Budworth, 'Remarks Based On Recent IV Corps Artillery Operations With An Appendix + Estimate of Ammunition Required' 6/10/15, Rawlinson Papers, 5201/33/67, NAM.

[34] 'Notes of a Conference held at Army Headquarters on the 16 April 1916' in Fourth Army Somme Preparations.

[35] 'Fourth Army Tactical Notes', p. 144.

his corps and divisional commanders, under whose control were the guns which were to fire the barrage. Some of these men (notably Morland of X Corps, Pulteney of III Corps, and the divisional commanders of VIII Corps) ignored Rawlinson's instructions and fired barrages which jumped rapidly from one trench to another. Second, in those corps (XIII and XV) where a type of creeping barrage was fired, the insufficiency of field guns in terms of yards of trench attacked meant that the shrapnel screen was thin and in some areas contained gaps. Thus sections of the German defence emerged untouched. Third, either because of the limited accuracy which could be obtained with 18 pounder guns, or because the gunners had not fully grasped the infantry protection aspect of the policy, the barrage was often started on the enemy front line. This meant that any defenders who escaped the initial burst of fire could shoot unhindered on the infantry advancing across no-man's-land. Fourth, the speed of the barrage was almost invariably too great; even in some cases where the infantry had moved into no-man's-land in order to start close to the barrage, they found themselves unable to keep pace with it and lost its protection.[36]

One factor likely to contribute notably to improved accuracy of artillery fire concerned air–artillery co-operation. Here considerable quantitative and some qualitative improvements had taken place. By 1 July, Fourth Army was supported by 68 planes, 30 of which were allotted to counter-battery spotting, 16 to spotting for trench bombardments, 9 to aerial photography, and 13 to contact patrols to monitor the advance of the infantry.[37] Thus at the Somme more planes could simultaneously direct the fire of the artillery than had been possible before.

Further, the response of the artillery to 'fleeting targets of opportunity' had grown more flexible with the introduction in June 1916 of the zone call system. Under this system the entire area to be bombarded was divided into small grids, each of which was allotted to a particular battery. When the air-observer spotted a target such as a transport column or a concentration of enemy troops passing through a particular zone, a zone call was made to the artillery which enabled the designated battery rapidly to bring the target under fire.[38]

A further source of information for the heavy artillery regarding the location of enemy targets came with the provision of five kite-balloons. Each was connected by wireless to the artillery of the corps in which it was operating.[39]

---

[36] For these matters see Anstey, History of the Royal Artillery 1914–1918, pp. 116–17.

[37] Jones, *The War In The Air* vol. 2, pp. 175–6 ; Mead, *Eye In The Air*, p. 78.

[38] Jones, *The War In The Air* vol. 2, pp. 175–6.

[39] Ibid., p. 198.

In sum, developments since Loos were rendering Rawlinson's artillery more accurate. But these developments were not very substantial, at least by 1 July. And anyway the balance sheet of change in regard to artillery accuracy was not all to the good. As the size of operations increased, new technical problems emerged and existing ones got worse.

In regard to the 18 pounder gun, prolonged bombardment quickly wore out the springs designed to return the barrel to exactly the same position after each firing. Worn springs introduced variations in the position of the barrel, so rendering ineffective the most careful calculations of range. The 4.7 inch gun, of which there were nearly 40, and which formed a significant proportion of the counter-battery guns of some of the corps, had already demonstrated alarming signs of wear during the short bombardment at Aubers Ridge. During the prolonged artillery prelude to the Somme these guns became so worn that their accuracy of fire became a matter of chance.

There were even greater problems with ammunition. Fuses for 9.2 inch howitzer shells often detached themselves in flight. As a result the shell did not explode. The fuses of 8 inch howitzer shells remained in place but often failed to ignite. There was also – for 60 pounders, 18 pounders, and 4.5 inch howitzers – the danger of fuses igniting prematurely, causing shells to destroy the guns and crews that were supposed to be firing them. Fuses for the 6 inch guns were satisfactory, but the shells themselves often varied in length by as much as 4 inches, which caused great variations in their range.[40]

Taken overall, Rawlinson had little reason to suppose that, in regard to accuracy, his artillery on the Somme would be markedly superior to that at Loos.

What then of numbers? Did Rawlinson possess so many more guns than at previous offensives that he might expect sheer weight of fire power to overwhelm the German defence? Certainly he had guns in unprecedented quantity: 1,000 field guns, 233 howitzers (6 inch and above), and 180 counter-battery guns.[41] In total this force amounted to more than twice the number of guns at Loos. More importantly, as far as trench destruction was concerned, the number of howitzers had increased fourfold. With such an imposing weight of fire power at his disposal, Rawlinson may have been tempted to conclude that he could destroy any defensive system, no matter how strong.

It is important, however, not to be mesmerized by these absolute figures.

---

[40] On problems with guns and ammunition see Edmonds, *1916* vol. 1, pp. 122–3, 356 n. 5; Anstey, History of the Royal Artillery 1914–1918, p. 112.

[41] 'Plan for Offensive by Fourth Army' 3/4/16, in IV Army Summary of Operations, WO 158/233.

Rather, it is the number of guns (and shells) relative to the task in hand that is crucial. And at the Somme the task was indeed imposing. As has already been seen, the German trenches with their many deep dugouts were formidable to an extent not hitherto encountered. Moreover, between the two main trench lines ran at least three intermediate trenches of considerable strength. Much of the intervening ground was honeycombed by a network of minor support and communication trenches. The area covered by this system varied in depth from 2,000 yards in the north to 5,000 yards in the south.

The vital question, therefore, was whether Rawlinson possessed sufficient artillery to subdue these particular defences. To guide him in his calculations, he had the experience gained at the three major battles in which he had exercised command during 1915: Neuve Chapelle, Aubers Ridge, and Loos. The artillery lessons of the first two battles were apparently fairly clear. At Neuve Chapelle a bombardment which landed 5 shells (or 300 lb. weight of shell) on every yard of trench succeeded – so long as it was accurately fired – in obliterating the German defences. At Aubers Ridge a bombardment of only two-fifths this intensity, directed against rather stronger trenches, failed to subdue the defenders. In the case of Loos the artillery lessons were less obvious, for at that battle it was a combination of artillery, gas, and smoke which had allowed the troops in some sectors to make meagre progress.

Neuve Chapelle then would seem to have been the only signpost pointing unambiguously towards success. And, it will be remembered, the strength of the Neuve Chapelle bombardment was not a matter of chance. It had resulted from experiments designed to establish exactly how many shells were needed to destroy each yard of trench. For the Somme, therefore, it would have appeared prudent to assume that only a bombardment which attained the intensity of that at Neuve Chapelle – especially in view of the increased strength of the defences now to be assailed – would have any prospect of success.

In seeking to achieve this weight of bombardment, two factors were of overriding importance. One was the total length of the successive lines of trench constructed by the enemy in the area to be overrun. As laid down in the first plan Rawlinson sent to Haig, his original intention was to attack on about a 20,000-yard front to a depth of about 1,250 yards after firing a five-day bombardment using approximately 1.5 million shells. As it happened, these calculations gave Rawlinson a shell concentration just in excess of the Neuve Chapelle figure of 300 lb. per yard of trench.[42] Here

---

[42] The weight of shells used by Fourth Army in the preliminary bombardment can be calculated by using the figures for numbers of shells in a document, 'Artillery Shells fired on 1

then seemed a sensible proposal based on a winning formula. As we know, that proposal did not survive the disfavour of Sir Douglas Haig. The latter instructed Rawlinson to attack to a depth not of 1,250 yards but, on average, of 2,500 yards. The implication of this order for Rawlinson's artillery plan was clear: by doubling the amount of trench to be attacked Haig was almost halving the intensity of the bombardment.

It would not be wonderful if Rawlinson had entered the strongest dissent from this amendment, proffering the Neuve Chapelle formula as reason for holding to his own proposal. Yet he did nothing of the sort. For this there appears a simple reason: Rawlinson had not employed the Neuve Chapelle formula as the basis of his original calculation regarding the appropriate depth of attack on the Somme. Only by chance had he reproduced it in his initial plan.

As has been indicated already, Rawlinson had used two statistical formulae in calculating the area to be attacked. One concerned the number of troops available to him. He had at his disposal 17 divisions, of which 10 or 11 would be in the front line. The received wisdom of the day was that an attacking division should occupy about 1,000 yards of trench, as anything short of this would lead to severe overcrowding. Hence it followed that he should attack on a frontage of about 20,000 yards. But this calculation did not at all take into account the nature of the obstacles confronting his forces or the problems confronting him in suppressing those obstacles.

The other statistic concerned the number of his heavy guns. Following the battle of Loos his artillery adviser, Budworth, had estimated that an offensive required one heavy howitzer per 100 yards of front. By employing a less exacting definition than Budworth's regarding what constituted a heavy howitzer (there was a difference between them as to whether a 6 inch howitzer fell into this category or only those of 8 inch and above), Rawlinson concluded that he possessed 200 such weapons and so could attack on a front of 20,000 yards.[43] This figure was more realistic than the other in that it took into account one aspect of the defences to be overcome: namely the number of yards of enemy front to be attacked. But it did not take into account the aspect that truly mattered, which was not yards of front but yards of enemy trench. At Neuve Chapelle this qualification had not applied, as the Germans had possessed only one line of trench

July 1916', Rawlinson Papers 1/6, CC, and multiplying by the appropriate weights of each type of shell. The length of trench to be attacked has been calculated by using a computer-linked digitizer on the detailed trench maps in the official history. We are grateful to the Geography Department, University of Adelaide, for guidance in the use of this technique.

[43] Budworth, 'Remarks Based On Recent IV Corps Artillery Operations'.

and therefore the yards of trench and yards of front had been identical. Nothing of the sort applied at the Somme where British forces would be assailing successive lines of trench which the bombardment must first incapacitate. Rawlinson was simply ignoring this vital consideration. The unhappy consequence was that Rawlinson was in no position to resist Haig's requirement that he double the depth of attack (and so incidentally the yardage of enemy trench under assault) because no increase in the front of attack was involved.

Rawlinson, in short, may have believed in bite and hold. But he possessed no secure way of estimating what constituted a bite, and no basis for demonstrating why an attempt at a bite might succeed where a thrust towards more grandiose goals was almost certain to fail.

The haphazard manner in which the British command arrived at the extent of the artillery's targets for the opening of the Somme campaign is not to the credit of either Haig or Rawlinson. The commander-in-chief bears a particular responsibility. He amended Rawlinson's plan in a way which was bound to diminish the intensity of the bombardment, yet appeared to disregard the potential consequences of such a change. But Rawlinson also was seriously at fault. Neither in drawing up his original plan nor in responding to Haig's amendments did he seem to be calculating the extent of his artillery resources *vis-à-vis* the length of enemy entrenchments to be assailed. That is, the lessons proclaimed by the partial successes and conclusive failures of his operations in 1915 were passing unnoticed.

As a consequence, the British command decided to send its infantry against some of the strongest defences on the Western Front in the wake of a preliminary bombardment approximately half as intense as that employed against the much sketchier German defences at Neuve Chapelle. And this was in spite of the fact that Rawlinson had already received a terrible warning as to what might happen in such circumstances. The case of Aubers Ridge may hardly seem comparable with that of 1 July 1916. For at Aubers Ridge the British artillery, confronting three lines of enemy trenches in close proximity to one another, had directed its fire only against the foremost line. Its failure to engage the second and third lines made hopeless the task of the British infantry (who were also subject to a good deal of flanking fire). But what, in the present context, is worthy of note is that the artillery fire directed on that occasion against just the first German line was (as at the Somme) approximately half as intense as that employed at Neuve Chapelle. It failed markedly to knock out its targets. The machine-guns firing from the German front line at Aubers Ridge when the bombardment ceased exacted a heavy toll on the British infantry: for example, 24 Brigade of 8 Division reported eight machine-guns as firing at it from the enemy front line.[44] The incident constituted, on a small scale, almost a fore-shadowing of the opening phase of the Somme offensive.

It must be concluded that the calamity awaiting Rawlinson's infantry on 1 July 1916 cannot be excused as an unforeseeable misfortune, such as is bound to befall an inexperienced command required to execute a leap into the unknown. It was more in the nature of a foregone conclusion.

[44] 24 Brigade: 'Report on the Offensive Operations from 8th–10th May, 1915', IV Corps War Diary May 1915, WO 95/709.

17

Round One, 1 July

I

The preliminary bombardment, which was planned to last for five days, opened on 24 June. It was crucial during this period that the weather remain fine so that the FOOs and the spotter planes could both direct the fire of the artillery and measure the results obtained. Unfortunately for the British, weather conditions were far from perfect. Of the projected five days, only one was fine.[1] The remainder had combinations of low cloud, mist, and rain. This greatly restricted aerial activity. Hence the programmes of aerial photography, of identification of German batteries, and of spotting for the heavy artillery all fell short of requirements.[2] By the 28th conditions had become so bad that Rawlinson ordered a postponement of the attack for two days.[3] Even on the 29th and 30th there were periods of low cloud and rain; nevertheless the decision was made that the attack should proceed on 1 July.

To be effective, the bombardment had to accomplish three things: it had to cut the wire in front of the German trenches; it had to destroy or neutralize the occupants of the German trench system; and it had to overwhelm German artillery which otherwise would be sweeping no-man's-land so as to halt the British infantry. Regarding the last of these, there was no likelihood that the British gunners would accomplish such a task. For one thing, the counter-battery aspect did not rate nearly as highly in the artillery's priorities as its intrinsic importance required. The absence of any counter-battery officer indicates that in this matter the British

[1] 'Fourth Army Summary of Operations, 1st July 1916', Fourth Army War Diary 5 Feb/13 July 1916, Fourth Army Papers vol. 1; X Corps War Diary 1/7/16, WO 95/851.
[2] Jones, *War In The Air* vol. 2, pp. 207–8.
[3] Rawlinson Diary 28/6/16.

command still had much to learn. Further, even had such officers been appointed, the resources at their disposal would have proved seriously inadequate. Most of the Fourth Army's 18 pounders were needed to cut the wire. Anyway, they lacked the range to reach the bulk of the German artillery, and they fired only shrapnel which was not appropriate for counter-battery work. As for the howitzers at Rawlinson's disposal, all were needed for trench destruction. Hence the most that remained for counter-battery were 128 of the 60 pounders and 40 notoriously inaccurate 4.7 inch guns. And even these were not available throughout the bombardment. In the north the 60 pounder and 4.7 inch guns of VIII and X Corps had on occasions to be used to cut the wire in front of the German second line, this being beyond the range of their 18 pounders. In the south XV Corps found that they had to use their medium-range guns for general bombardment. On the second day of the bombardment they fired only 250 shells from each of four batteries against the German guns.[4] This was a derisory amount: as the British were already aware, the Germans generally required 500 shells per battery to accomplish the destruction of one British gun.[5]

Three factors in addition to lack of guns told against Rawlinson's counter-battery endeavours. One of them, the unfavourable weather, has already been mentioned. When the RFC (Royal Flying Corps) was grounded the counter-batteries had to fire from maps which were later found to be inaccurate. Not surprisingly, few German guns were destroyed during these periods.[6]

A second factor concerned the only sound-ranging section in operation on the Fourth Army front. Until 24 June it had been useful in locating some German batteries. But once the British bombardment opened, the microphones used by the section proved unable to distinguish between the British and German batteries. This rendered the section useless for the period of the bombardment.[7]

The third factor was action by the Germans. In anticipation of a British attack, they rushed in artillery reinforcements. By 1 July these amounted to at least 17 field howitzer batteries and 36 smaller guns, probably a higher number than the British had managed to destroy by counter-battery fire.[8] Moreover, right up until 1 July a number of German batteries

[4] For the tasks given to the British artillery in the opening phase of the Somme battle see Anstey, History of the Royal Artillery 1914–1918, pp. 117–18.

[5] Diary of Lt.-Col. W. J. K. Rettie (189 Brigade, Royal Field Artillery), p. 46, ?June 1916, Royal Artillery Institution, Woolwich.

[6] Lt.-Col. C. M. T. Hogg (31 Division) to Edmonds 6/11/29, Official History Correspondence: Somme, Cab 45/189.

[7] Fourth Army, 'Hints On The Intelligence Service During Battle', Fourth Army Daily Intelligence Reports 1 Oct/16 Nov 1916, Fourth Army Papers vol. 15.

[8] Der Weltkrieg vol. 10 (Mittler: Berlin, 1936), p. 345.

remained concealed and silent, and many of these were never identified by the British. They were able to fire with deadly effect when the attack commenced.[9]

Rawlinson can have been under no illusions about the shortcomings of his counter-battery work. On the eve of battle, XIII, III, and X Corps reported hostile artillery retaliation as 'heavy', 'active', or 'moderate'.[10] The night before the attack XV Corps reported 'considerable' enemy artillery activity in the Mametz sector; and VIII Corps recorded a 'fairly active' bombardment of 4 and 29 Divisions.[11] Indeed it was the counter-battery work of his VIII Corps which most worried Rawlinson. He recorded in his diary for 28 and 29 June that the Corps 'have not been doing their counter battery work well.'[12] Events would reveal that, on the German side, 598 field guns and 246 heavier cannon survived British counter-battery fire.[13] These guns awaited the attacking infantry on 1 July.

II

Wire-cutting should have been the most easily accomplished of the British artillery's three tasks. In the first place the majority of shells available at the Somme (1 million out of approximately 1.6 million) were devoted to this purpose. Secondly the wire was the closest artillery objective and therefore the most easily observed by the FOOs. In addition raiding parties could be sent out on each night of the bombardment to report on the state of the wire and the extent to which the Germans were repairing the damage. Their findings were sent to Fourth Army Headquarters, where they were collated and published in the 'Summary of Operations' at the end of each day.

The situation they revealed appeared promising. In the south, after some initial difficulties on the front of 18 Division, XIII Corps consistently reported that the wire had been cut in front of their objectives. The XV Corps reported satisfactory results except on a section of front opposite 21 Division. The III and X Corps considered that the wire-cutting had been good except on small sections of the fronts of 34 and 32 Divisions. Once more the most serious difficulty seemed to be on VIII Corps front, where 29 Division had indicated in several reports that the wire had not been cut, and reports from 4 and 31 Divisions had revealed only partial

---

[9] Farrar-Hockley, *Somme*, p. 115.

[10] Fourth Army Summary of Operations, 1st July 1916, Fourth Army Papers vol. 1.

[11] Ibid.

[12] Rawlinson Diary 28–29/6/16. The quotation is from the entry for the 28th.

[13] *Der Weltkrieg* vol. 10, p. 349.

success.[14] Rawlinson was well aware of this, as was Haig who ordered the Army commander to investigate Hunter-Weston's artillery methods.[15] What transpired is not clear. On the 30th Haig seemed satisfied, for he commented, 'wire very well cut.'[16] But Rawlinson remained uneasy, and it was probably with regard to VIII Corps front that he wrote, 'I am not quite satisfied that all the wire has been thoroughly well cut.'[17]

Yet Rawlinson (like Haig) was clearly satisfied that wire-cutting had succeeded on most sectors of the front. Given the reports reaching him, this was not false optimism.

III

For trench destruction Rawlinson had available 233 howitzers of 6 inch calibre and above. During the course of the preliminary bombardment these guns fired 188,500 shells weighing 34.5 million pounds.[18] However, as noted earlier, this seemingly considerable weight of metal had to be distributed over a very extensive system of trenches. In consequence the bombardment, in terms of weight of shell per yard of trench attacked, possessed only half the intensity of that delivered at Neuve Chapelle.

How effective was this relatively feeble shelling in neutralizing the German trenches, the dugouts, and their occupants? During the preliminary bombardment information on this point was not easy to come by. In order to make a report, raiding parties had actually to enter the trenches and carry out a brief reconnaissance. Raiding was a risky and difficult business, the more so the further the raiding parties tried to penetrate into the German defensive system. Rawlinson therefore had better information on the German front line than on the rearward positions.

On the whole, the reports from this source were not encouraging. For the two nights preceding the battle, raiding parties from all corps reported to Fourth Army Headquarters that the Germans were alert and that at least parts of the front line were strongly held. Indeed so formidable was the German machine-gun and artillery fire in some areas that the raiding

[14] For wire-cutting reports see the Fourth Army 'Summary of Operations' from June 27 to 30; 'Wire Reports on the Night of 27/28 June' and 'Patrol Report on the Night of 28 June', Maxse Papers 69/53/6; 'Special Wire Cutting Report', VIII Corps War Diary 29/6/16, WO 95/820.

[15] Haig Diary 28/6/16.

[16] Ibid., 30/6/16.

[17] Rawlinson Diary 30/6/16.

[18] The weight of shell has been calculated from 'Artillery shells fired on 1 July 1916', Rawlinson Papers 1/6, CC. This document details the number of shells fired by each calibre of gun during the preliminary bombardment.

parties were not able even to leave their own trenches. This applied particularly in the north on the front of X and VIII Corps, but not only there: in the south, where raiding parties had consistently reported the enemy trenches 'flattened', some patrols on the nights before the attack were driven back by heavy fire, indicating that here too a significant number of enemy soldiers had survived the bombardment.[19]

There was a further source of intelligence available regarding the effects of the bombardment on the German trenches: that provided by prisoners brought in by the raiding parties. It was well known that such evidence was suspect. Prisoners had good cause to tell their captors what it was assumed they wanted to hear. It is therefore noteworthy that a proportion of the evidence from this source indicated that the bombardment was not proving effective; and that on the most optimistic view the message being provided by prisoners was decidedly ambiguous.

For example, on the basis of evidence secured from a prisoner captured on the night of the 26th on the XV Corps sector, it was concluded that although some of the trenches were badly knocked about, nevertheless:

> The dug-outs are still good. The men appear to remain in these dug-outs all the time and are completely sheltered.[20]

On the other hand statements by two prisoners from an adjoining regiment produced the view:

> our bombardment has damaged their trenches very considerably and that their company has suffered heavily, most of the casualties being due to the destruction of the dug-outs by our heavy artillery, the occupants being buried.[21]

In all, on the 29th and 30th, ten prisoners were examined on the question of dugouts. Four said that the dugouts afforded protection from the bombardment, while six claimed that the dugouts were being destroyed.[22]

Given the doubt that must attach to the more favourable reports, the most that could apparently be drawn from such evidence was that some but by no means all of the dugouts were succumbing to the bombardment. It is indicative of the frame of mind of Fourth Army Intelligence that it felt entitled to go much further. A summary on the eve of battle stated confidently:

---

[19] Fourth Army Intelligence Summaries for 29 and 30 June 1916, Fourth Army Daily Intelligence Reports 1 May/30 June 1916, Fourth Army Papers vol. 11.

[20] 'Notes from Examination of Prisoners of the 111 Reserve Infantry Regiment' in ibid.

[21] 'Examination of Ernst Birndt and Arnold Fuchs' (62 Infantry Regiment) in ibid.

[22] Fourth Army Intelligence Summary 29/6/16, Fourth Army Papers vol. 11.

From the examination of prisoners it is apparent that our artillery fire has been most effective. Most of the dug-outs in the German front line have been blown in or blocked up. Even the deep dug-outs of a Battalion HQ was not proof against our big shells.[23]

Nothing in the evidence that had come to hand provided warrant for such a conclusion. And what rendered it yet more unjustified was a further noteworthy factor – the limited sectors of the front from which the prisoners under examination were drawn. No less than seven out of the ten prisoners came from the German regiment facing XV Corps. Two others came from the regiment opposite XIII Corps and the remaining one was captured in front of X Corps.[24] That is, the prisoners were a terribly unrepresentative sample. No information at all had been provided on any dugouts north of Fricourt. Why only one prisoner was interrogated from the northern section of the front was not revealed, but presumably no others had been captured. This should have been warning enough to Fourth Army Intelligence, not only that the information on dugouts was quite incomplete, but that all was not going well with the bombardment in the north.

IV

What then was the state of Rawlinson's knowledge of the German defences on 30 June? The evidence available to him indicated three things. First, the British counter-battery programme had failed to subdue the German artillery, particularly on the front of VIII Corps. Second, wire-cutting had generally been successful, except on the VIII Corps front. Third, some dugouts in the area Fricourt–Maricourt had been destroyed but others remained intact. There was no information and therefore no grounds for confidence about dugouts north of Fricourt. That is, the artillery had certainly failed to accomplish one of its set tasks, had not clearly accomplished the second, and had largely, but not fully, accomplished the third. Yet if the attacking infantry were to have any chance of surviving the passage of no-man's-land, the British artillery needed to succeed not in just one of its tasks but in all three. There was no justification here for Rawlinson's sentiment, expressed in his diary on the eve of the infantry attack, that, except on VIII Corps front, he was 'pretty confident of success'.[25] Yet it was on no firmer basis that he sent his infantry over the top on the morning of 1 July.

[23] Ibid., 30/6/16.

[24] 'Patrols and Raids on night of 28/29 and 29/30 June 1916', Fourth Army War Diary, Fourth Army Papers vol. 1.

[25] Rawlinson Diary 30/6/16.

By the end of that day, 50,000 of the attacking troops from Fourth Army alone had become casualties, of whom 15,000 were dead.[26] Many fell victim to machine-gun and rifle fire from enemy trenches which Rawlinson's prolonged bombardment had failed to suppress. Almost as many were the victims of German artillery fire.

This last point may suggest that German gunners were blessed with more skill than their British counterparts. But that was not necessarily the case. Rather, their task was altogether more simple. They had no call to destroy barbed wire or penetrate into deep dugouts. And, given the insufficiency of Fourth Army artillery for its multiple tasks, they did not even need to knock out the British guns. The essential task confronting the German artillery was simply to deal with the attacking infantry. That could be accomplished by targetting generally on the British front line and no-man's-land from the moment the British foot soldiers left the cover of their positions. This – unlike the tasks confronting Fourth Army's gunners – lay well within the capabilities of any body of artillerymen in 1916.

V

What had been gained in return for these prodigious losses – the highest number of killed and wounded ever suffered by the British army in a single day? Only on one section of the front had Rawlinson's forces anything to show for their endeavours. On the southern sector, 18 and 30 Divisions of XIII Corps had captured all their objectives. Immediately to their left, 7 and 21 Divisions of XV Corps had penetrated well into the German defences, capturing Mametz and rendering the German position in Fricourt untenable. (It was evacuated by the Germans on 2 July.) By contrast, on the fronts of III, X, and VIII Corps, hardly a yard of German trench remained in British hands at the end of the day. For this the three corps had suffered, respectively, 11,500, 9,050, and 13,500 casualties.[27]

Disaster was most complete on the front of VIII Corps in the north. Here the corps commander had been given permission by GHQ and Fourth Army Headquarters to explode a mine under the Hawthorn Redoubt (just west of Beaumont Hamel) at 7.20 a.m., ten minutes before the main attack was launched. This proved just time enough thoroughly to alert the defenders. When the battalions of VIII Corps formed up in no-man's-land, they were met with a hail of machine-gun and rifle fire. Thousands became casualties in the first minutes of the attack.

[26] A figure of 57,470 is usually quoted. See Edmonds, *1916* vol. 1, p. 483. But this total includes the diversionary attack on Gommecourt by Third Army. The usual figure of 18,000 dead also includes the Gommecourt attack.

[27] Middlebrook, *The First Day On The Somme*, p. 266.

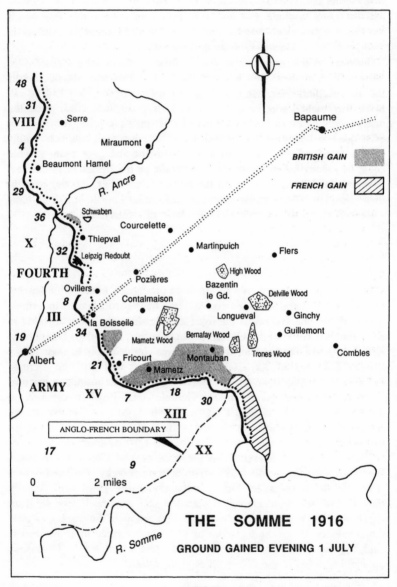

THE SOMME 1916

GROUND GAINED EVENING 1 JULY

MAP 15

Nevertheless several battalions of 4 Division and one from 31 Division managed to get across no-man's-land and break into the German defensive system. Thereupon the failure of the British counter-battery programme became evident. At about 8 a.m. German batteries in VIII Corps area brought down a hail of shells on no-man's-land and the British assembly trenches. Nothing could penetrate this curtain of fire, and so the British battalions which had gained a lodgement in the German trenches could neither be reinforced nor withdraw. Most were eventually wiped out by German counterattacks.

The experience of 29 Division was even less profitable. The Gallipoli veterans had to contend with uncut wire as well as machine-guns and shells. Hardly a man reached the German front line.[28]

It is noticeable that in VIII Corps sector even those battalions which had avoided employing a wave formation or which had endeavoured to cross no-man's-land at speed were not spared heavy casualties. The 1 Lancashire Fusiliers moved into no-man's-land before the bombardment lifted and then rushed the German positions in front of Beaumont Hamel. Within minutes they had suffered 150 dead and 319 wounded. The 1 Royal Inniskilling Fusiliers, despite advancing in columns of platoons, suffered 218 dead and 350 wounded and gained no ground.[29] Clearly, not even sophisticated infantry tactics would serve when the bombardment had failed to crush the German defenders.

Immediately to the south of VIII Corps, on the front of X Corps, 36 and 32 Divisions achieved some early successes but by the end of the day retained no substantial gains to offset their 9,000 casualties.[30] The most promising beginning on X Corps sector was made by the 36 (Ulster) Division which attacked to the south of the River Ancre. By early morning the Ulstermen had outflanked Thiepval to the north and captured the Schwaben Redoubt, a strong German defensive work. Their success was not achieved by heeding Rawlinson's tactical suggestions. The divisional commander insisted that his troops move into no-man's-land to within striking distance of the German line while the bombardment was still under way and that they rush the German position when the bombardment lifted. It was this expedient which enabled the British to carry the German front line system before its defenders could emerge from their dugouts.[31]

On the right of the Ulster Division, 97 Brigade of 32 Division employed

---

[28] For the experiences of VIII Corps see Edmonds, *1916* vol. 1, pp. 430–4, 438, 442–3.

[29] Figures taken from Bell, *Soldiers Killed*, pp. 73–4, 85–7. Infantry tactics detailed in Edmonds, *1916* vol. 1, p. 437 and Farrar-Hockley, *Somme*, p. 120.

[30] Edmonds, *1916* vol. 1, p. 421.

[31] For these operations see 36th (Ulster) Division, 'Weekly Summary of Operations', 7/7/16, X Corps War Diary WO 95/851.

similar tactics and succeeded in capturing the Leipzig Redoubt. The other attacking brigade (the 96th), by contrast, employed the conventional tactics outlined in the Fourth Army Tactical Notes. It failed completely.[32]

Once more, all attempts to render secure these early lodgements were thwarted by the fact that Rawlinson's bombardment had failed to subdue the German trench-dwellers over a wide enough length of front and his counter-battery fire had not dealt with the German artillery. As a consequence enfilade machine-gun fire from the unsubdued defenders of Thiepval was soon brought to bear against the British troops in the two captured redoubts. And German artillery fire first denied these troops reinforcements and later prevented them from being evacuated. By nightfall only a handful of the attackers still clung to a precarious position in a small section of the German front line north of Thiepval. Next day they were withdrawn.[33]

In the centre of the Fourth Army front, 8 and 34 Divisions of III Corps attacked opposite the fortified villages of Ovillers and la Boisselle. What followed was an almost unrelieved disaster. The two villages had hardly been touched by the bombardment and contained many machine-gun posts. Most of the German trench-dwellers had been protected by the deep dugouts. Many British battalions suffered heavily even before entering no-man's-land, for they were required to advance over bare ground swept by machine-gun fire in order to reach their own front line. Nor did a mine exploded under the German front line by the British aid their cause. The German infantry reached the crater first and held it throughout the day. As for III Corps's counter-battery programme, it had proved as inadequate as that of VIII Corps further north. The result was heavy casualties and no substantial penetration of the German defensive system.[34]

VI

It has not proved difficult to explain the calamitous failure on 1 July of the northern and central corps of the Fourth Army. Irrespective of the infantry tactics employed, their endeavours were doomed by the inability of the British bombardment to crush the German artillery and the occupants of the enemy trench systems.

What then is to be said about the relative success of the two southern corps (XV and XIII)? In terms of the length of front to be attacked,

[32] For the operations of 97 Brigade see Edmonds, *1916* vol. 1, pp. 400–3; for 96 Brigade, pp. 402–3.

[33] Ibid., pp. 420–1.

[34] For III Corps operations see ibid, pp. 377, 392.

they were not blessed with a larger number of guns and men than the corps to their north. Nor did the troops of XV and XIII Corps possess greater experience or (in general) employ more sophisticated infantry tactics than those on other parts of the front.

The first thing to be noted is that, in one important respect, the attack on the British right was not wholly dissimilar from that on the centre and left: casualties sustained by the attacking forces were again severe. XIII Corps suffered just over 6,000 casualties (1,500 killed) and XV Corps almost 9,000 (2,500 killed).[35] That is, the bombardment had by no means crushed or cowed the German defenders; and the attackers, advancing in broad daylight and without artificial concealment, were extremely vulnerable to machine-gun and rifle fire notwithstanding the aid of a creeping barrage.

What needs to be explained, then, is why on the southernmost part of the British front the attackers, despite heavy losses, managed to overrun the German front trenches, capture their first objectives, and hold on to what they had gained. Four reasons suggest themselves. First, the creeping barrages fired by the artillery of XIII and XV Corps were both more accurate and advanced at a slower pace than similar barrages fired on other parts of the front.[36] This, coupled with the fact that many of the brigades started out from advanced positions in no-man's-land so as immediately to follow up the barrage, meant that many of the German defenders were caught in their dugouts.[37]

Second, in one important respect the German defences in the south had less depth than those where the British attack failed. In the centre and north the deep dugouts, which were proving so impervious to artillery fire, had been constructed not only under the German front line but under several of the rearward lines as well. In the south this was not so. As a consequence most of the German troops in the latter sector, in order to take advantage of the protective dugouts, were situated well forward. Given the tactics adopted by XV and XIII Corps this meant that a high proportion of the garrisons' defenders were overrun in the first rush.

Third, in this sector – unlike most others – the command had allocated a considerable number of troops to mopping up. The result was that the Germans occupying the dugouts were not free to emerge from their shelters once the attackers had passed over and shoot them down from the rear.[38]

[35] Ibid., pp. 341, 368.

[36] Anstey, *History of the Royal Artillery 1914–1918*, pp. 116–17.

[37] 'Notes on Attacks Carried out by 7th Division in July 1916', 7 Division War Diary July–Dec 1916, WO 95/1631.

[38] Ibid.

Fourth, in the south the British 'moppers-up' and reinforcing battalions were able to reach the German trenches in comparative safety because of the feeble German artillery response. By 1 July the German artillery grouped against XV and XIII Corps had been reduced to 10 field and 13 heavy batteries, all of which had some unserviceable guns. (This total may be compared to the 68 German batteries which opposed VIII Corps's attack.) We can only speculate as to why the German artillery was so much weaker in the south. It is unlikely that British counter-battery fire had proved any more accurate and so had destroyed more German guns here than elsewhere. More probably, the bulk of the German artillery was concentrated against the British left and centre, leaving the British counter-batteries in the south with many fewer targets to eliminate. And in this task XIII Corps in particular was aided by the neighbouring French XX Corps, which attacked not only the German batteries opposite itself but also some of those facing the southern section of the British front.[39]

VII

Once battle was joined on 1 July, was Rawlinson in a position to influence the course of events, to mitigate the disasters in the north and to convert the advance in the south into something more substantial? On the morning of 1 July Rawlinson watched the entire assault from a specially constructed platform near Albert. About 8 a.m. he returned to his headquarters at Querrieu to await reports from his five corps commanders.

Fourth Army Headquarters was by now the centre of an impressive communications network. From Querrieu Rawlinson could communicate by telephone to the five corps commanders, the RFC headquarters, the Cavalry, Gough's Reserve Army, and the Sixth French Army. (The corps commanders, in turn, could communicate with their divisions, the heavy artillery, attached RFC squadrons, and kite-balloon sections.[40] Similar networks ran from divisions to brigade HQs and then to the battalion commanders in the front line.)

The problem was the perennial one faced by First World War commanders. This impressive network stopped at the jumping-off point of the attack. Once the troops had gone over the top they could only send back information by runners and over telephone lines, both of which were very vulnerable to enemy fire. On the first day of the Somme, as events turned out, communication was rather more difficult than usual because of the

[39] For these points see Edmonds, *1916* vol. 1, pp. 344, 325.
[40] See chart in III Corps War Diary Jan–June 1916, WO 95/672.

intense German artillery fire. This is not to say that Rawlinson was starved of information. During the course of the day Fourth Army HQ received over 160 telegrams from the corps HQs. But the information Rawlinson received was frequently inaccurate. Some examples will illustrate just how small were his prospects of following the course of the battle.

We have already observed the disaster on the front of VIII Corps. Hardly a man from 29 Division reached the German front line, and only isolated battalions from 31 and 4 Divisions managed to break into the German defensive system. None of these troops penetrated further than their first objective. Yet Rawlinson was told at 7.46 a.m. and again at 8.07 a.m. that all VIII Corps troops were over the German front line. The first news of a setback came at 9 a.m. when he was told that 29 Division was hung up in the German front trench. But he was assured before long (9.47 a.m.) that a fresh attack – which was 'going well' – was being made in this area. Later (11.19 a.m.) he was informed that 4 Division had reached its second objective and that 31 Division was consolidating east of Serre. However, at about the same time a note of reality began to be sounded: it was made clear that all was not well with 29 Division and that an attack by the divisional reserves was being organized at 12.30 p.m.

It was not until 2.45 p.m. that the true situation on VIII Corps's front was appreciated. Hunter-Weston then told Rawlinson that 29 Division was back in its own front line and in no condition to make a further attack, that 31 Division was also back in its front line, and that 4 Division was holding a section of the German front north of Beaumont Hamel. (In fact by this time 4 Division had been driven from the German defences.)[41]

At last possessed of accurate information, Rawlinson found that there was nothing he could do. The reserve division of VIII Corps (48) had been moved to within two miles of the front line by Hunter-Weston and was available for an attack.[42] But it was clear that the German defenders and artillery were unsubdued, that those divisions which had already attacked had suffered heavy casualties, and that there was little chance of the reserve division intervening before dusk. Rawlinson could only confirm the decisions already taken by Hunter-Weston to halt all major attacks and await the new day.

What of the situation in the south where XIII Corps had captured all,

---

[41] The preceding information is based on Fourth Army, 'Summary of Operations', WO 158/322. The file is not a summary of operations but a transcript of telegrams which passed between Rawlinson and his corps commanders during the battle. It will hereafter be referred to as 'Somme Telegrams'.

[42] 'Narrative of Operations of 1st July 1916, Showing The Situation As It Appeared To General Staff, VIII Corps From Information Received During The Day', VIII Corps War Diary WO 95/820.

and XV Corps some, of their final objectives? Information from XIII Corps, where the attack was successful, does not seem to have been more readily forthcoming than in the north. Only at 12 noon did Rawlinson know that 30 Division had succeeded along its entire line, had captured Montauban, and was consolidating. By 1.25 p.m. he was aware that 18 Division, although it had experienced more delays and suffered more casualties than 30 Division, was advancing on its final objective near Montauban Alley.[43] Here, it might be thought, was an opportunity for Rawlinson to act. On the front of XIII Corps the enemy was beaten, a fresh division was in Corps Reserve, the French – who had been completely successful on the right of the British – were willing to advance, and seven hours of daylight remained. Yet Rawlinson did not act and XIII Corps spent the remainder of the day consolidating the positions they had already captured.

For this Rawlinson has been harshly criticized. At the time, Bernafay, Trones, and Mametz woods, as well as sections of the German second line (all of which would in time be captured only at heavy cost), were held merely by small groups of enemy troops. Moreover, few German reserves were available to reinforce these positions. Certainly the German 12 Reserve Division had two battalions near Bernafay Wood by midday. But the remainder of this division, although ordered to attack between Montauban and Mametz, was by midnight still well short of the second line.[44] Had the British been able to put a fresh division into the attack, it would have stood a good chance of taking at least Caterpillar, Bernafay, and Trones woods. Perhaps even a section of the German second line between Guillemont and Bazentin le Grand would have fallen.

What was wanting was the prerequisite for such an advance: an available reserve division. For the Corps Reserve (9 Division) was not concentrated for such a movement. The corps orders, which had been approved by Rawlinson, stated that 9 Division was only to be used during the second phase of the operation; that is, only after the first objective had been consolidated and the artillery brought forward. (These activities could take as long as three days.)[45] In short, by his earlier emphasis on consolidating objectives captured, and by his caution in the timing of the second-phase advance, Rawlinson had ensured that there would be no force available to exploit a success on this part of the front. Once battle had been joined, there was nothing he could do to turn around this situation.

[43] Somme Telegrams 1/7/16.

[44] Edmonds, *1916* vol. 1, p. 345.

[45] XIII Corps Plan of Operations 29/6/16, quoted in Edmonds, *1916* vol. 1 Appendices, Appendix 21, pp. 170–1.

18

The Run-up to 14 July

I

Despite the calamity that had befallen Rawlinson's forces on 1 July, there was never any doubt that the offensive would continue. The imperatives that had occasioned the battle in the first place required that, however lamentable its opening, it should not be terminated.

The commanders chose not to ponder on what had happened. Haig remarked obtusely that 'on a sixteen-mile front of attack varying fortune must be expected!'[1] Rawlinson had the good fortune to receive inaccurate statistics regarding casualties (his first estimate put the total for 1 July at only 16,000–20,000). Anyway, Haig had offered ample reinforcements.[2]

The overriding problem was where and when to renew the attack. The events of 1 July offered no simple answer. In the south, where XIII and XV Corps had secured most of their objectives, Fourth Army was still not within striking distance of the German second line; nor had these successes gained any of the high ground of the Thiepval–Ginchy Ridge facing the British. In the north, where the German second line and the ridge were much closer to the original British line, no gains had been made.

Rawlinson had no doubt about the sector on which to renew the attack. At 10 p.m. on 1 July he issued his operation orders for the next day. They stated *inter alia*:

A large part of the German Reserve have now been drawn in and it is essential to keep up the pressure and wear out the defence. It is also necessary to secure, as early as possible, all important tactical points still in the possession of the Germans in their front line system and

[1] Haig Diary 1/7/16.
[2] Rawlinson Diary 1/7/16.

intermediate line, with a view to an ultimate attack on the German second line.[3]

This meant that the major attack by Fourth Army would be made in the north and in the centre, on the front of VIII, X, and III Corps, for here lay the 'important tactical points' in the German front and intermediate lines which barred the way to their second system of defences. In the words of the official history, 'General Rawlinson proposed to renew the attack in the centre and on his left, where it had failed, refraining for the time, from any exploitation of the success gained by his right.'[4]

Haig, who visited Rawlinson on the morning of the 2nd, was not responsive to this plan. He wanted, if possible in collaboration with the French, to exploit the success gained in the south. He was only prepared to sanction any action in the north if contact might thereby be made with troops thought to be holding out in the Schwaben Redoubt.[5] Later, after visiting Gough, Haig further downgraded the possibility of action in the north, urging Rawlinson to make his major effort on his right wing between Longueval and Bazentin le Grand.[6]

These plans received a hostile reception from Joffre. In the course of a visit on the 3rd the French commander-in-chief first urged and eventually 'ordered' Haig to attack in the north, so as to secure Thiepval and Pozières.[7] Joffre's reasoning is not altogether clear. He no doubt saw the northern attack as the most direct way of obtaining a footing on the Thiepval–Ginchy Ridge; but he was probably also concerned (while keeping the battle going) to avoid further commitment of French troops – and any attack by Haig in the south would raise the possibility of French participation.

Haig rejected Joffre's directions. By 3 July he was aware that no British troops were holding out in the German line and hence that no rescue operation in the north was called for. He had also gained an accurate appreciation of the shattered state of VIII and X Corps and realized that they were incapable of further effort. To feed new divisions into these corps would occasion delays. The only option therefore was to attack in the south,[8] whether or not the French were prepared to participate.

---

[3] Fourth Army Operation Order No. 3, 1/7/16, Fourth Army Papers vol. 7.

[4] Captain Wilfrid Miles, *Military Operations: France and Belgium, 1916* vol. 2 (London: Macmillan, 1938), p. 4.

[5] 'Visit of Commander-in-Chief to Fourth Army Headquarters at 10.30 am July, 2, 1916', Fourth Army War Diary, Fourth Army Papers vol. 1.

[6] Kiggell to Rawlinson 2/7/16 (OAD 37) quoted in ibid.

[7] Haig Diary 3/7/16.

[8] Ibid.

Rawlinson accepted Haig's view without further argument. He set to work planning an operation in the southern sector whose purpose was to gain the German second line. As preliminaries to this attack, on 3 July he issued operations orders to his XIII, XV, and III Corps for the capture of a series of intermediate objectives which included Bernafay Wood, Mametz Wood, la Boisselle, and Contalmaison. These preliminary attacks, he wrote, would secure a line 'within attacking distance' of the German second line to be assailed in mid-July.[9]

II

So between 3 and 13 July, III, XV, and XIII Corps struggled to capture the objectives which were to constitute the start line for the new attack. These were not minor operations. During this period ten divisions of the Fourth Army launched 46 attacks against the German positions. Almost 100 battalions took part, about the same number as actively participated on 1 July.[10] Casualties were high. Between 2 and 13 July three divisions (12, 19, 38) each lost over 4,000 men;[11] 17 and 23 Divisions each lost 3,500; 30 Division 2,300; and the four remaining divisions around 500 each.[12] In all, it is likely that Fourth Army suffered 25,000 casualties in reaching the start line for 14 July. (This is a higher total than would be suffered in the major attacks of 14 July and 15 September combined.)

Nor did the operations proceed according to schedule. Possession of Mametz Wood and Trones Wood was necessary to secure the flanks of the advance on 14 July. Yet on the morning of the 12th – by which time the preliminary bombardment for the major attack was already under way – neither had been captured. (They fell only on 12 and 14 July respectively.)

Despite the scale of these operations and the relatively good information available to him, Rawlinson apparently saw no role for himself in their conduct. Once having set the objectives for the three corps under his control, he made no further intervention. From one point of view this manner of proceeding was unexceptional. Arguably it was no part of an Army commander's function to involve himself in the detailed planning of

---

[9] Fourth Army Operation Orders 3/7/16 and 5/7/16, Fourth Army Papers vol. 7.

[10] These figures have been obtained by counting the number of attacks and the battalions involved in them in Miles, *1916* vol. 2.

[11] For the 38 Division see Colin Hughes, *Mametz: Lloyd George's 'Welsh Army' at the Battle of the Somme* (Gerrards Cross: Orion, 1982), p. 110; for the 12 and 19 Divisions see Miles, *1916* vol. 2, pp. 42 and 169.

[12] All figures are from Miles, *1916* vol. 2. 17 Division p. 58, 23 Division p. 57, 30 Division p. 47. The four other divisions were 7, 18, 21 and 34.

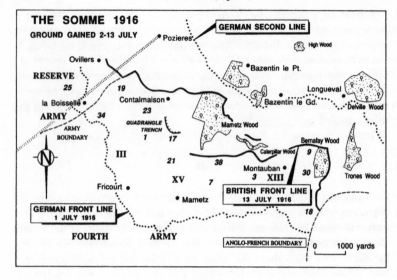

THE SOMME 1916
GROUND GAINED 2-13 JULY

GERMAN SECOND LINE

Pozieres

High Wood

Ovillers

Bazentin le Pt.

RESERVE
25

19

Longueval

la Boissellé

Contalmaison

Bazentin le Gd.

Delville Wood

ARMY
34
ARMY
BOUNDARY

23
QUADRANGLE
TRENCH
1   17

Mametz Wood

III

21

38

Bernafay Wood

Caterpillar Wood   9

XV
7

Montauban
3   XIII

30

Trones Wood

Fricourt

Mametz

BRITISH FRONT LINE
13 JULY 1916

GERMAN FRONT LINE
1 JULY 1916

18

FOURTH   ARMY

ANGLO-FRENCH BOUNDARY   0   1000 yards

MAP 16

attacks which were often being made merely by brigades. Yet from another viewpoint Rawlinson's *laissez-faire* approach came near to constituting an abdication of responsibility. Where operations were being conducted by a number of corps it appeared the job of the Army commander to play a co-ordinating role, thereby ensuring that the three corps acted not in isolation but as a unit, and that the plans of each corps were appropriate for the objectives to be achieved in the time available.

In the period 2–13 July Rawlinson's approach to command had a number of adverse effects. The most obvious was that in the majority of cases an attack made by one corps was not co-ordinated with attacks being made by other corps. Thus during this period, 23 Division of III Corps made seven attacks towards Contalmaison. On its right flank 17 Division of XV Corps made eight or nine attacks on Mametz Wood. Yet in only two of these attacks was there any attempt at co-ordination, despite the fact that one of the objectives of 17 Division, Quadrangle Support Trench, was virtually impossible to take unless Contalmaison, which dominated it, was also taken.[13]

In some cases nothing approaching the available artillery resources of the Fourth Army was used to support attacks. Thus on 7 July, when 17 and 38

[13] Information obtained from Miles, *1916* vol. 2 and Hughes, *Mametz*.

Divisions made a major attack on Mametz Wood, they were supported only by their own artillery and the heavy artillery of XV Corps.[14] The artillery of XIII Corps – which was not attacking that day – remained silent. At least some guns of the corps and divisional batteries could have leant weight to XV Corps attack. Yet no one at Fourth Army HQ intervened to secure this maximization of artillery support. It is worth noting that one factor contributing to the failure of the attack by XV Corps was an insufficiency of artillery assistance.[15]

When we view the employment of infantry during this period, the same picture emerges. No one at the top sought to ensure that the total infantry resources of Fourth Army were being employed in the most effective manner. In consequence, to take a daily average, between 3 and 12 July only 14 per cent of Fourth Army battalions in the line engaged the enemy.[16] In other words, on any one day most of the Fourth Army remained quiescent while a small number of battalions on narrow fronts were attacking complex trench systems and substantial obstacles such as Mametz Wood. These methods ensured that the attacks would be severely hampered by enfilade fire from German artillery and machine-guns situated in areas not under attack.

Even when Rawlinson's forces made their most substantial effort during this period, the picture of sporadic and unsupported efforts by British infantry still applies. The day on which the highest percentage of Fourth Army battalions in the line engaged the enemy (26 per cent, or 19 battalions out of the 72 available) was 7 July. Yet these battalions were not taking part in a single co-ordinated attack. In the main they engaged the enemy piecemeal, two or three battalions at a time, on different parts of the front and at different times of the day. The maximum number which were in action at any one time was eight, and even then their attacks were not contiguous.

If this was the case on 7 July, even more fragmented operations took place on the 8th and 9th. On the right, 30 Division attacked Trones Wood six times using only one battalion on each occasion. In the centre, two attacks were made on Mametz Wood and three on Contalmaison. None was co-ordinated with the Trones Wood operations or with one other. All failed.

What we are observing, therefore, is a succession of penny packet attacks launched with inadequate artillery preparation. When one attack failed another was immediately ordered. This virtually ensured that plans were

[14] Hughes, *Mametz*, p. 70.

[15] Ibid., p. 80.

[16] These percentages and those that follow have been derived from an analysis of the operations in Miles, *1916* vol. 2.

insufficiently thought out and hastily executed by commanders who on occasions had not even reconnoitred the ground. Most attacks were broken up by German machine-guns not located by the bombardment or firing from unbombarded sections of the line.

Certainly the capture of objectives such as Mametz Wood or Contalmaison could not have been accomplished cheaply. These were formidable obstacles, well defended by troops whose morale was good. Nevertheless it can hardly be doubted that more weighty and less frequent attacks, delivered with greater co-ordination, would have secured these objectives more expeditiously and at less cost. That these methods were not adopted was largely the responsibility of the Fourth Army commander.

III

While these operations were proceeding, planning was under way for the major attack on 14 July. One difficulty was becoming apparent. Even if successful, the preliminary operations would leave Rawlinson's forces 1,500 yards short of the German second line. It seemed unlikely that the troops attacking on 14 July would survive the crossing of a no-man's-land as wide as this – especially as it was devoid of cover and consisted of a gentle slope.

Early on, Rawlinson did not appear to be confronting this problem. And Haig – when the proposals were conveyed to him on the 5th – did not draw attention to the omission.[17] Nevertheless, in the period between 3 and 10 July, Rawlinson not only became aware of his difficulty but offered a possible solution. He proposed that, during the night preceding the attack on the German second line, his forces would reduce the gap, assembling unobserved in no-man's-land along a line marked by tapes in close proximity to the German second position. At dawn they would attack.[18] For reasons which are not clear Rawlinson did not convey this novel aspect of his plan to Haig. Before long, the matter would cause the Fourth Army commander some difficulty.

By its emphasis on concealment, Rawlinson's infantry plan for the coming attack was certainly more sophisticated than the scheme employed on 1 July. Yet too much should not be made of this. Attacking by night was neither as novel, nor as potentially decisive, as is sometimes suggested. Attempted night attacks between 2 and 13 July had met with no success. And there could be no cause for believing that the proposed night oper-

[17] Haig Diary 5/7/16.
[18] Fourth Army Summary of Events 14 July 1916, Fourth Army War Diary 14 July/31 Aug. 1916, Fourth Army Papers vol. 2.

ation on 14 July would prosper should the barbed wire remain intact and enemy machine-guns be available against British forces assembling in no-man's-land. As ever, all would depend on the ability of the British artillery to suppress the German defences long enough for the attacking infantry first to traverse no-man's-land and then to enter the enemy positions.

The key question, then, was whether the British command had learned the artillery lessons of 1 July. In preparation for the new attack, were detailed calculations being made of the exact quantities of ammunition needed to demolish the enemy defences? There is no evidence that anything of the sort was taking place. Perhaps on this occasion Rawlinson divined that the available artillery would be more than adequate for the task in hand and that no detailed calculations were needed. Yet it is rather more likely that, as on 1 July, he was simply engaged in assembling all the guns he had at his disposal and concluding that they had better be sufficient. The operation on 14 July would prove different from its predecessor because, this time, the assumption proved correct.

For the attack on 14 July, the Fourth Army had available 1,000 artillery pieces of which 311 were heavy howitzers or guns. Although this total was 500 less than for the 1 July attack, the task facing the artillery on the 14th was, proportionately, altogether less formidable.[19] On 14 July the front of attack was approximately 6,000 yards, as against 22,000 yards on 1 July. Even more significant, the German trench systems behind the front on 14 July amounted to no more than an additional 12,000 yards,[20] compared with the 300,000 yards of supporting trenches on 1 July. In total, then, the artillery on 14 July with two-thirds of the number of guns that had been at its disposal on the 1st would have to demolish only one-eighteenth of the length of trench.

Rawlinson planned for a three-day bombardment during which almost half a million shells would be fired.[21] The component of the bombardment devoted to trench destruction (that fired by the howitzers) consisted of 62,000 shells weighing about 12 million pounds.[22] This meant that 660 lb.

---

[19] Artillery statistics are taken from 'Battle of Somme: Artillery Notes and Statistics', Rawlinson Papers 5201/33/71, NAM. The reduction in the number of guns was due to the establishment of the Reserve Army under Gough.

[20] These figures have been calculated using the same method as mentioned in footnote 42, chapter 16 The map used is in Miles, *1916* vol. 2, Sketch 10 facing p. 67.

[21] See 'Fourth Army Ammunition Expenditure' in 'Somme Artillery Notes and Statistics', Rawlinson Papers 5201/33/71, NAM.

[22] No detailed figures exist for the 14 July bombardment. The number of howitzer shells fired and their weight has been obtained by assuming that the proportion of heavy howitzer shells to shells fired by the field artillery was the same as that for 1 July. As the proportion of howitzers to total number of guns in the Fourth Army was slightly higher on 14 July than it had been on 1 July (31 per cent as against 29 per cent), this seems a safe assumption.

of shell would fall on every yard of trench attacked, an intensity of fire twice that of Neuve Chapelle and five times that achieved before the 1 July attack.[23] Clearly then, the assaulting infantry would find the German trenches and their defenders in a far more impaired condition than had been the case on 1 July.

By contrast, other components of Rawlinson's artillery plan for 14 July were less satisfactory. He did not insist that the creeping barrage – so effective where it was employed on 1 July – be uniformly adopted.[24] Nor did he devote much thought to counter-battery matters, despite the heavy toll which German guns had exacted upon his troops on the opening day. It was fortunate for the attacking force that on this occasion its over-whelming preponderance of guns and shells would render these short-comings of minor import.

IV

In one respect Rawlinson's proposals for 14 July marked a retrogression on those for a fortnight earlier. For the renewed assault he envisaged a major role for the cavalry, whereas in the planning for 1 July he had been sceptical about whether the cavalry could play any useful part. The Fourth Army operations orders for 14 July stated that:

> Should the enemy's line be broken and Delville Wood and Bazentin-le-Petit be secured, the task of . . . [the 2nd Indian Cavalry Division] will be to seize High Wood and the enemy's switch line immediately on the East and West of the wood. As soon as the XV Corps can take over High Wood the Division will push forward to Flers and Eaucourt L'Abbaye thus covering the deployment of the XIII and XV Corps.[25]

These orders do no credit to Rawlinson's command. For their execution, they required the 2nd Indian Cavalry Division to make their way through the cratered area behind the British front line, cross the British trenches, negotiate no-man's-land, traverse the craters and trenches of the German second line, advance over a mile across open ground and capture a wood which dominated that ground, take a trench line situated on a reverse slope and out of sight of British artillery, and *then* advance a further one and a

---

[23] Similarly the number of shells per yard devoted to wire-cutting was about five times that used at Neuve Chapelle.

[24] Major A. F. Becke, 'The coming of the creeping barrage', *Journal of the Royal Artillery*, 58 (1931–32), p. 37.

[25] 'General idea of future plans in the event of the attack of the enemy's 2nd line between Longueval and Bazentin-le-Petit being successful', Fourth Army Papers vol. 7.

half miles and capture two large villages while at the same time covering the deployment of two Army corps. It is doubtful if so much ground could have been traversed had no enemy at all been present, whereas such a cavalry advance was almost certain to run into German infantry reserves moving forward. The result could only be a slaughter of the mounted force. Rawlinson's orders therefore only make any sense if he was expecting the enemy to flee. And if that was his expectation then the boundaries of cloud cuckoo-land should be moved down a stage from their usual location around GHQ.

As it happened, Rawlinson's orders to the cavalry were not only unrealistic but flawed in detail. The 2nd Indian Cavalry Division had been placed under the tactical command of XIII Corps. Yet the first objective assigned to the cavalry was High Wood, which was in the zone of XV Corps. Thus if an opportunity to capture High Wood ever did arise, XV Corps not XIII Corps would be in the best position to exploit it. Such orders were a sure recipe for confusion.

V

The most novel aspect of Rawlinson's plan for 14 July was the night assembly deep into no-man's-land followed by a dawn attack. Nothing, it will be recalled, had been said about it in his original operation orders, so that Haig first became aware of it when he visited Rawlinson at Querrieu on 10 July.[26]

Initially Haig made no comment upon it, and confined himself to urging Rawlinson to complete the capture of Contalmaison and Mametz and Trones Wood to secure the flanks of the main attack.[27] By the next day, however, Haig had formed a strongly negative opinion. He now refused to sanction the night attack, informing Rawlinson:

> Our troops are not highly trained and disciplined, nor are many of the staff experienced in such work, and to move two divisions in the dark over such a distance, form them up, and deliver an attack in good order and in the right direction at dawn, as proposed, would hardly be considered possible even in a peace manoeuvre.[28]

Instead Haig proposed an attack by XV Corps from around Mametz Wood, followed by a turn eastwards to roll up the German line towards Longueval. If this attack was successful XIII Corps would attack Longueval

[26] Haig Diary 10/7/16.
[27] Ibid.
[28] 'Note of discussion as to attack of Longueval Plateau and the Commander-in-Chief's decision thereon' [11/7/16] (OAD 60), Fourth Army Papers vol. 1.

next day. Although Haig gave no further details of his plan, in outline it had little to recommend it. It was to take place on a narrow front and involved the kind of complicated turning movement that Haig had so deprecated in Rawlinson's initial plan for Neuve Chapelle. The eastward attack toward Longueval also risked being taken in the flank by a German counterattack from High Wood. Finally, as Congreve (XIII Corps commander) pointed out, Haig was inviting defeat in detail.[29]

Presumably most of these arguments were levelled against Haig's plan at a meeting between Rawlinson and his corps commanders (Horne and Congreve) at 2 p.m. on the 11th. In any case as a result of that meeting Rawlinson told Kiggell that the corps commanders were both strongly in favour of the original plan, and that after a full discussion he was himself in agreement with them. He added that Horne was 'much averse' to attacking without the support of XIII Corps. Kiggell relayed these views to Haig and then spoke to Horne who reiterated his objections to Haig's plan. Haig refused to budge. Rawlinson was instructed to prepare the attack along the lines indicated by the commander-in-chief.[30]

Rawlinson passed on these orders to his corps commanders. But after a further talk with Montgomery and Horne, he decided to press Haig once more to countenance the night attack.[31]

Haig called a meeting of his own staff on the 12th to discuss what he called Rawlinson's 'amended plan'.[32] (It was in fact the same plan.) Birch, Haig's artillery adviser, who had been in touch with Congreve, assured the commander-in-chief that the British could dominate the German artillery, and after some discussion Haig agreed that Rawlinson's plan should be tried.[33] He insisted, however, that Rawlinson re-examine his counter-battery programme, that a contingency plan in case of failure be worked out, that the use of motorized machine-guns be considered (none was available), and – perhaps surprisingly – 'that large bodies of cavalry should not be employed until the situation clearly admits of it; there would be too much danger of their coming unexpectedly under heavy fire from the enemy's rallying points and being thrown back in confusion on our infantry.'[34]

Rawlinson replied to Haig that he was acting on each of these directions. Yet in at least one respect he plainly did nothing of the sort. The final cavalry plan was no less ambitious than the first. Rawlinson's orders that

[29] Congreve Diary 11/7/16, private papers.

[30] For these discussions see 'Note of discussion . . . on Longueval Plateau'.

[31] Rawlinson Diary 11/7/16.

[32] Haig Diary 12/7/16.

[33] Congreve Diary 11/7/16; Haig Diary 12/7/16.

[34] Kiggell to Montgomery 2/7/16 in IV Army Summary of Operations WO 158/234.

the cavalry were to seize what were likely to be two of the enemy's main 'rallying points', High Wood and the Switch Line, were (in spite of Haig's warning) allowed to stand.

Of far greater import to Rawlinson, in the central issue under dispute he had got his way. The night attack would go ahead.

19

Success by Night, 14 July

I

As planned by Rawlinson, the attack of 14 July was to be carried out by five divisions. From left to right, these were 21 and 7 Divisions of XV Corps, and 3, 9, and 18 Divisions of XIII Corps. The 33 Division of XV Corps was in reserve. In the first instance exploitation was to be carried out by the 2nd Indian Cavalry Division.

The overall purpose of the operation, as has been indicated, was to capture the German second line in that southern sector of the front where Rawlinson's attack had enjoyed some success on 1 July. Specifically, the task of XV Corps was to capture and consolidate Bazentin le Grand Wood, Bazentin le Petit village, and Bazentin le Petit Wood. The XIII Corps were to capture and consolidate Longueval, Delville Wood, and Bazentin le Grand village. In what amounted to a separate operation, 18 Division of XIII Corps was to capture Trones Wood. Should the enemy's line be broken, the first task of the cavalry would be to seize High Wood and the newly constructed Switch Line to the east and west of it.[1]

II

The bombardment began on the morning of the 11th, and was maintained right up until the early hours of the 14th. Its primary targets were the German trenches and wire. In the night hours just before the attack, the bombardment was maintained so as to prevent the Germans repairing defences destroyed during the day. But in the darkness its noise also proved useful in covering the assembly of 3 and 9 Divisions in their advanced positions in no-man's-land.

[1] Fourth Army Operation Order 13/7/16, Fourth Army Papers vol. 7.

At the appointed time, the movements of the infantry went smoothly. Before midnight, covering parties with Lewis guns were sent out and took up positions on the crest line. Marking parties followed, to place white tapes along the line on which the main body of troops was to assemble. Just after midnight the attacking force as a whole moved out. By 2.45 a.m. they were assembled, undetected by the enemy and with only a few casualties caused by stray German shells.[2]

At 3.20 a.m. the five minutes of intense bombardment began. At 3.25 the infantry attacked. A remarkable success awaited them. Along practically the whole line they overran the German front and support systems, the defenders fleeing where they had not been killed.[3]

What was the cause of this significant achievement? How had British forces first been able to take up positions in no-man's-land unmolested by the enemy and then manage to overrun the German front positions? The evidence leaves this matter in no doubt. All reports from divisions and corps remark on the effect of the artillery bombardment. One observer noted that the German 'front line system was unrecognisable as such, so severely had it been handled by the artillery.'[4] The wire, equally, had been demolished.

Rawlinson saw this clearly. After paying tribute to the detailed staff work needed to assemble the troops within striking distance of enemy positions in the dark, he continued:

> there is no doubt that the success of the enterprise must be attributed in a very large measure to the accuracy and volume of the artillery bombardment. The enemy's wire, as well as his front and second line trenches, were smashed to pieces. The morale of the defenders had been greatly reduced by the din and concussion of the constant explosions, and it was clear from the number of dead that were found in the trenches that he had likewise suffered heavy casualties from the artillery bombardment.[5]

In drawing these conclusions, Rawlinson was proving more perceptive than later observers, who have chosen to ascribe the success wholly to the expedient of attacking in the dark. It is quite clear that had the wire not been cut and the occupants of the German trenches not been largely

[2] J. Ewing, *History of the 9th (Scottish) Division, 1914–1919* (London: Murray, 1921), pp. 109–11.

[3] Fourth Army, 'Summary of Events, 14th July, 1916', Fourth Army Papers vol. 2.

[4] Brigadier-General H. C. Potter [Commander 9 Brigade, 3 Division] to Edmonds 20/3/30, Official History Correspondence: Somme, Cab 45/190.

[5] Rawlinson to Lady Rawlinson, Wigram, Cowans, Archibald Murray, Bagot, and Derby 18/7/16, Rawlinson Papers 5201/33/18, NAM.

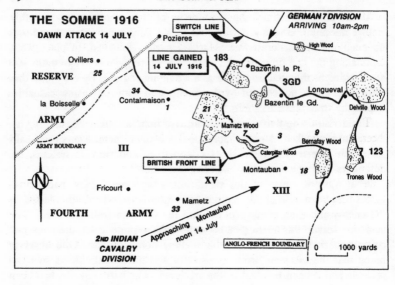

MAP 17

eliminated, a night attack would have stood little chance of succeeding. Already on the Somme in the period 2–13 July British night attacks had been swept away by pre-sighted German machine-guns and rifle fire, or had come to a halt when the attackers had encountered uncut wire. On 14 July it was the elimination of the trench-defenders by the artillery which allowed the British to assemble in no-man's-land unhindered; even the best staff work could not have protected these troops if significant numbers of German machine-gunners had survived the bombardment. And it was the destruction of the barbed wire which enabled the attackers to reach the German positions so swiftly.

What had been achieved in terms of territory changing hands? By mid-morning Trones Wood had fallen and the entire German second line from Longueval to Bazentin le Petit Wood had been overrun. Success, however, had not been total. German defenders were still holding out in the ruins of Longueval, and no advance on Delville Wood had yet proved possible.

III

The situation on the Somme front immediately following the success of the initial attack on 14 July was in some ways similar to that at Neuve Chapelle after the early break-in. The artillery on both occasions had enabled the

attackers to penetrate the main German defensive system. It will be recalled that the attempts at exploitation of the Neuve Chapelle success had
failed. Were the British better placed to exploit their initial victory on the
Somme? One or both of two factors would decide these questions. The
first was the state of the German defenders. The other was the rapidity
with which the British command could react to such opportunities for
exploitation as presented themselves.

There is little doubt that when news of the capture of what on 1 July had
been the German second line reached Rawlinson, he concluded that a real
opportunity for exploitation did exist. And during the course of the day he
attempted to capitalize on it, by employing first the cavalry and then the
infantry.

The events of 14 July soon demonstrated the unrealistic nature of
Rawlinson's cavalry plan. When the orders (from XIII Corps) to move
ahead reached the cavalry, scouts were sent forward to reconnoitre a line of
advance. They found the ground so slippery from the recent rains that the
horses could hardly stand. They also encountered a considerable problem
with unbridged trenches. Baffled, the patrols returned to Montauban,
unable to give any clear guidance as to how the cavalry was to be brought
into action.[6]

Unaware of this development, Rawlinson remained confident that a
move on High Wood by his horse-soldiers was imminent. He was supported by erroneous reports describing the cavalry patrols as an advanced
column of the division, and as being temporarily held up in negotiating the
German trench system.[7] Only around noon, by which time the cavalry had
still not appeared at the front, did Rawlinson become seriously concerned.
He did so with good cause. At that time the cavalry were still struggling
past Montauban.

Just before 1 p.m. news finally reached Rawlinson that conditions
behind the front were likely to cause considerable delay to the cavalry.
Reluctantly he abandoned (for the moment) the attempt to send the cavalry
through. The infantry of XV Corps was now ordered to capture High
Wood.[8]

In the event it was late afternoon before this movement could be attempted. Rawlinson himself contributed to the delay. For he made the
advance by XV Corps conditional on the capture of Longueval by XIII
Corps.[9] This was a curious decision. In no sense did Longueval dominate

---

[6] Terry Norman, *The Hell They Called High Wood* (London: Kimber, 1984), pp. 88–9.

[7] XIII Corps to Rawlinson (9.25 a.m.) 14/7/16, Somme Telegrams.

[8] For these messages see Fourth Army telephone messages to GHQ, 14/7/16, GHQ War
Diary July 1916, WO 95/5.

[9] Ibid.

the approaches to High Wood from the XV Corps area. Indeed almost the reverse was the case: an advance on High Wood (had it been possible) could well have rendered Longueval untenable for the Germans. In any case, at the time Rawlinson gave this order it was clear that Longueval was proving a tough nut to crack. The 9 Division had exhausted itself in numerous attacks on the village and further action had to wait on the arrival of the reserve brigade.[10] Thus Rawlinson could have deduced that by placing this condition on action by XV Corps he was really opting for no immediate advance at all.

In the event Rawlinson's decision to delay the advance hardly mattered. German intervention ensured that XV Corps were simply not in a position to carry out a forward move. Throughout the morning the enemy delivered counterattacks against XV Corps forces near the Bazentins. One of these restored to the Germans the north-west corner of Bazentin le Petit Wood and most of the village. The village was swiftly recaptured by XV Corps but (in the words of the 21 Division Narrative): 'Throughout the morning constant attempts were made to turn the enemy out of the NW Corner of Bazentin-le-Petit Wood; heavy casualties were suffered and little progress made.'[11] Attempts during the afternoon to dislodge the Germans met with no greater success. It was not until sometime between 5 p.m. and 7 p.m. that the wood could be declared clear of the enemy.[12]

It is plain why XV Corps encountered these difficulties. German reserves had arrived in numbers on the battlefield. In fact they had arrived much more rapidly than the British command had had cause to expect. The counterattacks in the early morning against 21 and 7 Divisions were made by local reserves and would have been anticipated by the British. But it so happened that on the day of the attack the Germans had decided to relieve their 183 Division, which was holding the line between Bazentin le Petit and Pozières, with their 7 Division. During the night of 13/14 July the leading columns of the latter division were just to the north of Flers. As soon as news of the British attack reached the higher German command, troops from this division were sped towards the battlefield. Elements of these formations (totalling probably 5,000 men) arrived piecemeal in the area of the Bazentins between 10 a.m. and 2 p.m. It was these troops that carried out the counterattacks which occupied XV Corps for most of the day.[13]

[10] XIII Corps to Fourth Army (1.14 p.m.), 14/7/16, Somme Telegrams.

[11] 'Operations of 21st Division, 14/7/16' Fourth Army Papers vol. 2. See also 'Operations of the 7th Division, 14/7/16' in ibid.

[12] Ibid.

[13] The information in this paragraph is taken from *Schlachten des Weltkrieges: Somme Nord* (Oldenburg: Stallung, 1927), pp. 9–36. This is an official monograph issued by the Reichsarchiv and will hereafter be referred to as Reichsarchiv, *Somme-Nord*.

In consequence, it was not until the German reserves had been repelled and British reserves had moved forward that High Wood could be attacked. (Curiously, Rawlinson's insistence that the capture of Longueval – which still had not taken place – must precede such an attack now quietly disappeared.) Only at 7 p.m. were two battalions from 7 Division and two from 33 Division in a position to advance on High Wood and the Switch Line. Unhappily, a regiment of cavalry which had reached the front in the late afternoon accompanied the attack.[14]

The cavalry were soon dealt with by German machine-gunners. The infantry, by contrast, initially made good progress. High Wood was entered at 8.40 p.m. Such progress, however, was short-lived. As 7 Division troops pressed forward they were met by heavy machine-gun and rifle fire from the Switch Line which ran through the northern end of the wood.[15] Fire from this line also stopped the forces from 33 Division who were attempting to advance to the left of the wood.[16] By nightfall, the British held a line which ran through the centre of High Wood and then turned sharply along the road to Bazentin le Petit. The Switch Line remained in German hands.

The late hour at which the attack on High Wood was delivered has occasioned severe criticism of Rawlinson's command. It is argued that High Wood lay invitingly open throughout 14 July and that, but for the commander's insistence on employing his cavalry, it could have been overrun by the infantry early in the day without encountering great resistance. The story is often told of how RFC pilots reported not once but several times that the wood was free of enemy forces, and of how the opportunity to act on these messages went begging.

This account overlooks two matters. The first is that, as just related, the German reserves occupying the area in advance of High Wood kept the British engaged for most of the afternoon. Hence an early occupancy of the wood was out of the question. The second is that evidence from the German side invalidates the reports of the RFC observers. It can well be believed that the detection from the air of entrenched German troops inside a wood was a chancy business. So it is no cause for wonder if in this instance British airmen failed to discover German defenders. Nevertheless it remains the case that these defenders were in occupancy. That is, at whatever time British forces – be they cavalry or infantry – mounted an attack, they were bound to encounter severe and ultimately prohibitive resistance.

It is necessary to stress this point on account of the misapprehension that

---

[14] 'Operations of the 7th Division, 14/7/16' and 'Operations of the 33rd Division 24/7/16', Fourth Army Papers vol. 2.

[15] Brigadier-General J. R. Minshull [Commander 91 Brigade] to Edmonds n.d., Official History Correspondence: Somme, Cab 45/136.

[16] Operations of the 33rd Division 14/7/16, Fourth Army Papers vol. 2.

has arisen concerning it. Already by the commencement of the British offensive early on the morning of 14 July, the Switch Line in the vicinity of High Wood was occupied by rather more than one battalion of German troops with supporting machine-guns.[17] So whenever the British reached this area – which they could do only by driving back the two German battalions occupying the approaches to the wood – they were bound to encounter almost 1,000 enemy troops supported by machine-guns and occupying a strongly wired position untouched by artillery fire. It is possible that an attack in divisional strength would have overwhelmed this position. But Rawlinson's XV Corps did not have this kind of reserve readily available. An attack in brigade strength – and that, realistically, was all that could have been mounted – had no chance of success.

IV

As concerns the matter of command, several noteworthy conclusions can be drawn from the events of 14 July. First, Rawlinson's scheme to overrun the former German second line by sending forward his infantry in the dark on the heels of a truly devastating bombardment was a notable piece of planning, which redounds much to his credit. Yet a qualification must be entered. In advance of the attack, Rawlinson does not appear to have recognized that it was the intensity of the bombardment – so much superior to that of 1 July – which held the key to success.

Second, Rawlinson's decisions in the aftermath of early success left much to be desired. The total ineffectiveness of his plan for cavalry exploitation ought to have been obvious to him. It merely confirmed what Rawlinson had appeared to appreciate before 1 July but which he had since chosen to forget: namely that horse-soldiers had no place as a weapon of exploitation on the Western Front. As for his decision during the day of the attack to await the fall of Longueval before advancing on High Wood, this made no sense in terms of the geographical relationship between the two objectives.

The third conclusion is paradoxical. Contrary to the general view, Rawlinson's command failures were not of marked importance. No opportunity to rush the Switch Line presented itself, whatever may have been believed by RFC observers.

In sum, the story of 14 July is a tale of significant but necessarily limited achievement accompanied by some strangely inappropriate command decisions. The latter, as it happened, did not result in any major lost opportunities.

[17] Reichsarchiv, *Somme-Nord*, p. 29.

20

The Forgotten Battles,
15 July – 14 September

I

By the evening of 14 July the position of the Fourth Army was as follows. It had breached the German second line from Bazentin le Petit Wood in the west to Longueval in the east. The Bazentins, woods and villages, were in British hands. So was Trones Wood and the southern half of Longueval. In addition some British detachments were fighting in High Wood while others were preparing to advance on Delville Wood and on the German second line around Guillemont.

This situation seemed full of hope. Yet in the months that followed little was accomplished. During the weeks from 15 July to 14 September, the British line advanced barely 1,000 yards on a front of 5 miles. So on 14 September, High Wood was yet to be captured, British troops had but a tenuous hold on Delville Wood, and Guillemont had only just fallen. And these small gains were achieved at a terrible price in British fighting men.

What presents itself in this period is not any major operation but rather a succession of small attacks designed to advance the British line at one point or another. All told in these 62 days, Fourth Army carried out some 90 operations (attacks by at least one battalion), only four of which were launched across the whole of its front.[1] That is, none of these undertakings was substantial in itself – with the result that this segment of the Somme campaign is largely missing from the history books. Yet the period as a whole amounts to a major episode. Indeed the heavy scale of casualties

[1] These figures have been obtained from a close reading of the official history, divisional histories, and other secondary sources, corrected where possible from unit war diaries. Nevertheless the figure of 90 should be regarded as approximate. At times it is not at all clear when an attack should be counted as a discrete operation or whether it was made in battalion strength. There were in addition many operations carried out only by companies or platoons which are omitted from our consideration.

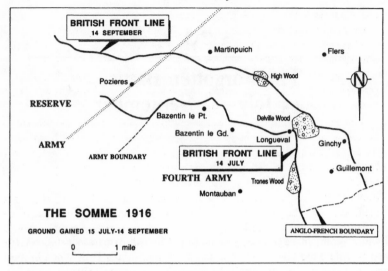

BRITISH FRONT LINE
14 SEPTEMBER

• Martinpuich   • Flers

Pozieres •   High Wood

RESERVE

Bazentin le Pt. •   Delville Wood

ARMY   Bazentin le Gd. •   Longueval   Ginchy •

ARMY BOUNDARY   BRITISH FRONT LINE
14 JULY

FOURTH ARMY   Trones Wood   • Guillemont

Montauban •

THE SOMME 1916

GROUND GAINED 15 JULY-14 SEPTEMBER   ANGLO-FRENCH BOUNDARY

0   1 mile

MAP 18

suffered overall, along with the negligible gains of territory, places this phase on an equal footing with the disastrous opening day of the Somme campaign.

It is necessary to be specific. On 1 July 1916 British forces sustained 57,000 casualties and accomplished an advance of 1 mile on a 3-mile front (that is, 3 square miles). The current orthodoxy concerning the Somme campaign is that this was a singular misfortune, quite out of keeping with subsequent stages of the battle. After 1 July, it is argued, the British made solid gains at reasonable cost.

Yet in the period 15 July to 14 September, the Fourth Army suffered 82,000 casualties while advancing only 1,000 yards on a 5-mile front (2¾ square miles).[2] That is, while capturing a somewhat smaller area than in

---

[2] The figure of 82,000 casualties must be regarded as only very approximate. Fourth Army figures for August can be set more or less accurately from the War Diary at 32,000. The Fourth Army suffered 125,000 casualties in July. It is probable that 95,000 of these were caused by operations from 1 July to 14 July leaving 30,000 for the remainder of the month. For September, total British casualties on the Somme (Fourth and Reserve Armies) were 110,000. As three battalions in four which attacked during that month came from the Fourth Army it is feasible that three out of four casualties can be assigned to that Army, that is, 80,000. But as three-quarters of all attacks during September were carried out on and after September 15, only 20,000 casualties can be assigned to the period 1–14 September. Total Fourth Army casualties for the period are, therefore, July 30,000, August 32,000, September 20,000, grand total 82,000.

the massed offensive of 1 July, the Fourth Army during six weeks of small-scale attacks sustained casualties that were 40 per cent higher.

The significance of this second phase of calamity during the Somme operations has largely gone unremarked, if only because the losses did not fall within a 12-hour time-span and so lack dramatic impact. Yet the fact remains that once again the Fourth Army was paying a prohibitive price to secure infinitesimal amounts of territory.

The overall pattern of this bewildering array of small-scale operations becomes evident with the aid of statistics. We are dealing with a period of 62 days. There were attacks on 41 of them, during which, on average, 6.5 battalions out of 84 available (5.5 per cent) engaged the enemy.[3] The maximum force employed by Rawlinson in this period occurred on 3 September when he attacked with 27 battalions out of 96 available (28 per cent). This was one of a mere five occasions when 20 or more battalions were employed in an attack. By contrast, there were twenty-eight occasions when the attack was delivered by less than 10 battalions. This may be compared with the first day of the Somme, when 120 battalions attacked out of about 160 available (75 per cent).

Another battle pattern emerges when we look at the sector of the front being assailed. On only six occasions was a continuous attack made along the entire Fourth Army front.[4] What this meant was that in most instances the operations of any one division were unsupported by flanking divisions. For example between 15 July and 14 September, twenty-one attacks were made in the Longueval–Delville Wood sector. On only four occasions were they supported on both flanks, and on eleven occasions the operations were completely unsupported. Similar statistics could be produced for other sectors of the front.

A further insight into these operations is gained by noting the experiences of one division. Table 20.1 summarizes the actions of the 1st Division. Several observations follow from this table. First, this division launched no less than thirteen attacks during these weeks, but only two of them involved more than one brigade (that is, four battalions) and most were altogether smaller. Second, in terms of the forces involved the scale of loss was decidedly high. In the ten attacks for which we have accurate figures, casualties per attack amounted to 40 per cent. (Average battalion strength has been calculated at just over 800.) Third, in not one of these

---

[3] The number of attacking battalions has been obtained from the sources listed in footnote 1. The number of 'available' battalions has been arrived at by calculating the number of divisions holding the line and multiplying by 12 battalions. It is highly unlikely of course that more than 75 per cent of these battalions would have been committed to one attack.

[4] The source for the figures in this paragraph is Miles, *1916* vol. 2.

TABLE 20.1   *First Division attacks 15 July–14 September 1916*

Date of attack		Objective	Battalions committed	Casualties
July	15	Switch Line	2	
	16	Switch Line	1	
	17	Switch Line	1	
	22/23	Switch Line	5	
	25	Munster Alley	1	
	26	Munster Alley	1	
				2625
Aug.	16	Intermediate Trench	2	
	18	Intermediate Trench	2	
	19	Intermediate Trench	2	
	24	Intermediate Trench	1	
				3336
Sept.	3	Wood Lane	3	
	8	Wood Lane	3	
	9	High Wood	5	
	10–14	no attacks		approx 1000

Source for dates, objectives and numbers of battalions committed is Miles, *1916* vol. 2. Casualty returns are taken from 'Actual Casualties by Divisions' for July and August 1916, in Fourth Army Papers vol. 2. The figure for September is an estimate based on the scale of the attacks launched. It errs, if at all, on the low side.

operations did 1 Division succeed entirely in its designated undertaking. Indeed as late as 14 September Rawlinson's forces still did not occupy all of the Switch Line or Munster Alley or Intermediate Trench or Wood Lane or High Wood.

What was true of 1 Division applies overall to the fighting on the Somme in the interval between the major battles of 14 July and 15 September. The front was by no means quiescent and yet all attacks were on a small scale. Overwhelmingly, indeed, they were delivered by one or two battalions assaulting on very narrow frontages and unsupported by action on the flanks. It is difficult to doubt that this largely accounts for the fact that the casualty rate per attack was high and the reward in terms of territory overrun was negligible.

Certainly there is a further aspect to these operations, for which nothing comparable is to be found in the events of 1 July. Rawlinson's attacks were inflicting heavy loss upon the Germans, primarily on account of the huge number of shells being fired by his artillery aided by air superiority. Between 15 July and 14 September the British fired 6.25 million shells into the German positions.[5] The German Official History does not seek to conceal the fact that the German forces were being worn down to a significant degree by such a weight of shelling delivered under the guidance of aerial observation.[6]

Another point made by the German Official History belongs here. During this period the German command held to a policy of seeking to regain by counterattack every yard of ground captured by the British. This brought upon German forces additional heavy casualties. So while during these weeks the Fourth Army carried out 90 attacks in battalion strength or above, the Germans counterattacked on 70 occasions. We have no way of estimating the price paid for the latter endeavours, but it cannot have been small.[7]

Nevertheless, it is plain that during this phase the British were conducting their campaign in a way which brought heavier loss to themselves than to their enemies, while holding out no prospect of achieving either the major victory first expected of the Somme undertaking or even such a limited victory as Rawlinson had accomplished on 14 July. Whether judged in terms of the losses his forces were sustaining, or of territory overrun, or of the dislocation wrought upon the German defensive positions, Rawlinson in these eight weeks was failing in any significant purpose. It is little cause for wonder that, by their end, his standing with Sir Douglas Haig had markedly diminished.

II

It is now necessary to look in more detail at events in the weeks succeeding Fourth Army's attack on 14 July. The partial success of that day had left Rawlinson with formidable problems. Certainly, a section of the German second line had been captured and part of the Bazentin Ridge secured. But key sections of the ridge, particularly Pozières, High Wood, and Delville Wood, remained in enemy hands. In addition the Germans were still securely in possession both of their second line from Ginchy southward and of the Switch Line which ran from Pozières through High Wood to the

---

[5] Figures derived from daily table of 'Fourth Army Ammunition Expenditure' in 'Somme Artillery Notes and Statistics', Rawlinson Papers 5201/33/71, NAM.

[6] *Der Weltkrieg* vol. 10 (Berlin: Mittler, 1936), p. 374.

[7] For German policy see ibid., p. 384. The number of German counterattacks has been derived from those mentioned in 'Somme Telegrams'.

south of Flers. The latter presented the British with a particular problem. For the most part the Switch Line was sited on a reverse slope, and so could not be seen by artillery observers in the new British front line.

In consequence, a set of imposing tasks confronted Rawlinson in the immediate aftermath of 14 July. He had to complete the capture of the ridge, which meant devising a scheme for attacking a trench system he could not directly observe. At the same time he must mount an attack on the uncaptured sections of the German second line.

Rawlinson's first action was to order the capture of those objectives of 14 July still in German hands.[8] On the left and right of the line this brought dividends. During the 15th the South African Brigade on the right captured most of Delville Wood, while on the left III Corps advanced its position to within striking distance of Pozières. But in the centre matters did not go well. Attempts to seize the Switch Line and High Wood and to secure the northern section of Longueval all failed.[9]

On the 16th Rawlinson, reviewing the problems resulting from the action of two days before, apparently decided not to persist with the attempt to clear up particular obstacles by means of small-scale operations. At a Fourth Army conference he announced that, 'as the enemy had now had time to bring up new troops, the time for isolated attacks had now finished and an organised attack on a broad front was now necessary.'[10]

These observations seem blessed with much insight. Yet quite plainly Rawlinson had not considered their implications. For he went on to propose the 18th as the date for the projected major assault, on the grounds that the French were prepared to co-operate with him by attacking north and south of the River Somme.[11] It is difficult to see how any 'organised attack on a broad front' could be mounted within, at most, a meagre 48 hours. Not for the first time, Rawlinson was demonstrating both an ability to perceive the sort of endeavour required in existing circumstances and a failure to allow that perception actually to shape his operations.

In consequence, Rawlinson's moment of insight at the Fourth Army conference on 16 July was not reflected in the events of the following days. As it happened, it was not possible to launch the supposed 'broad front' operation (which will be discussed below) until 22/23 July. In the interval, the 'isolated attacks' which Rawlinson had appeared to deprecate continued unabated.[12] So on the 16th, 9 Division attempted to complete the capture of Longueval and Delville Wood, while 1 Division sought to improve its

---

[8] Fourth Army operation order 14/7/16, Fourth Army War Diary July 1916, WO 95/431.
[9] Miles, *1916* vol. 2, pp. 90–2.
[10] Fourth Army Conference 16/7/16, Fourth Army Papers vol. 2.
[11] Ibid.
[12] Details of these operations are to be found in Miles, *1916* vol. 2, chapter IV.

position to the east of Pozières. On the 17th these operations were repeated with the addition that 34 Division attacked Pozières, one of the strongest positions in the German line, with one battalion. On the 18th, following the recapture by the Germans of sections of Longueval and Delville Wood, 3 Division carried out another attack there. The following day still further operations were attempted against Delville Wood.

On the 20th a more concerted attack was delivered against the German line from High Wood to Delville Wood, but even then no flank support was provided for the attacking 7 and 5 Divisions. This was to have unfortunate consequences for 5 Division. A small party of the 2 Royal Welch Fusiliers from this division managed to occupy a section of the Switch Line in High Wood. But they were unable to advance further or to roll up the Switch Line because of flanking fire from its unattacked sector to the west of High Wood.[13] Eventually they were driven out by German counterattacks. Lack of flank support thus helped to deny to the British their retention of a significant objective.[14]

It would be pleasant to record that, although unsuccessful, these small-scale operations between 16 and 20 July had at least stood a decent chance of success. But a report on a typical attack puts paid to any such interpretation. It concerned 53 Brigade from 18 Division, which had done so well on 1 July. On 19 July this brigade attacked Longueval and Delville Wood. It gained not a yard of ground and sustained heavy casualties. In his report the brigade commander, Brigadier-General Higginson, set out the reasons for failure. These included insufficient time for previous reconnaissance so that the exact position of the brigade itself was uncertain; insufficient time to study the plan of attack; insufficient time for artillery preparation; difficulty of communications with battalions; poor co-operation between artillery and infantry; failure to co-ordinate the infantry attack with the lifting of the barrage; the extreme difficulty of the task in hand given the intensity of the fire it encountered; the inadequate training of commands and troops for such onerous tasks; and the failure to communicate plans to neighbouring units, so that 76 Infantry Brigade on Higginson's left did not even know that his troops were going to attack.[15]

The shambles revealed by this report was not exceptional. Similar inadequacies were evident during the attacks made by almost every division, yet the Fourth Army command persisted in ordering these operations notwithstanding their unpropitious circumstances. The consequence was lament-

[13] Terry Norman, *The Hell They Called High Wood*, p. 148.

[14] Reichsarchiv, *Somme-Nord*, p. 107.

[15] Brigadier-General H. W. Higginson (OC, 53 Brigade), 'Attack on Longueval & Delville Wood. July 19th 1916', Maxse Papers, 69/53/6.

able. Between 16 and 20 July, no ground was gained and over 8,000 casualties were sustained.[16]

Meanwhile the planning of the promised 'organised attack' was dogged by misfortune and muddle. As mentioned, Rawlinson had envisaged an operation on 18 July by his three corps in conjunction with the French. Two factors delayed the operation. First, the weather deteriorated. This was of particular importance because, as we have seen, the German Switch Line was situated on a reverse slope. Aerial observation of the preliminary bombardment was therefore imperative.[17] It was not until the 21st that the weather cleared and the bombardment could commence. Second, the problems of co-ordinating the attack of the British right flank with that of the French exceeded expectations. Foch stated that his preparations would take one day longer than Rawlinson's, a position which he maintained despite the postponement of the attack.[18]

Final orders for the operation were issued only on 21 July.[19] At the strong urging of Haig, but with Rawlinson's full agreement, it was decided once more to employ the ruse of a night attack.[20] The main part of the assault was to commence at 1.30 a.m. on 23 July. On the right, however, the joint action with the French would open at an hour to be arranged by Congreve and Fayolle, and this turned out to be 3.40 a.m.

The preliminary bombardment began at 7 p.m. on the evening of 22 July. Only hours earlier, the Fourth Army commander had learned of two disturbing developments. First, at 2 p.m. the French announced that they would now not be ready to attack until some time on the 24th. Rawlinson, given the advanced stage of his preparations, was not willing to consider a further postponement. He reluctantly ordered that the attack on Guillemont should go ahead, even though it would be unsupported on its right.[21] He did not, however, bring back the starting time for XIII Corps's attack, even though its later hour had no justification except co-operation with the French.

The second disturbing development was a report from aerial observers that the Germans had dug a new and strongly manned trench 'several hundred of yards in advance of the Switch Line, roughly parallel to [the British] forward positions between Bazentin-le-Petit and High Wood.'[22]

---

[16] This figure is a rough estimate based on the experience of the 1st Division detailed in table 20.1 on p. 206.

[17] Fourth Army War Diary 17/7/16, Fourth Army Papers vol. 2.

[18] Rawlinson Diary 17/7/16; Rawlinson–Foch Conference 17/7/16, Fourth Army Papers vol. 2.

[19] Fourth Army Operation Order 21/7/16.

[20] Haig Diary 21/7/16; Rawlinson Diary 21/7/16.

[21] See Miles, *1916* vol. 2, pp. 113, 136; Rawlinson Diary 22/7/16.

[22] Jones, *War In the Air* vol. 2, p. 239.

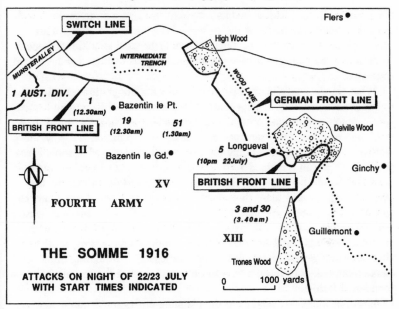

MAP 19

This fresh obstacle, later called Intermediate Trench, completely altered the tactical situation facing 19 and 51 Divisions. Rawlinson responded by ordering that this trench be captured as a preliminary operation at 12.30 a.m., after which these divisions should proceed to attack the Switch Line at the prearranged time of 1.30.[23] This meant that, while on the right the attack would commence at the later hour (3.40 a.m.) previously arranged with the French, on the centre-left there would now be two jumping-off times: 12.30 a.m. for 19 and 51 Divisions and 1.30 a.m. for 1 Division. Meanwhile it had been decided – for reasons which are obscure – that 5 Division of XV Corps, in the centre of the attack, would mount a preliminary operation to capture Wood Lane at 10 p.m. on 22 July and then attack the Switch Line at 1.30 a.m. on the 23rd.

Variations in the start-time of the attack did not cease here. The 51 Division never received the information that a new obstacle, Intermediate Trench, had been discovered lying across its line of advance and that this was to be attacked at 12.30 a.m. Hence this division, unlike 19 Division on its left, adhered to the start-time of 1.30 a.m. But on the left of 19

---

[23] Rawlinson Diary 22/7/16.

Division, 1 Division had altered its zero hour to 12.30 a.m. to conform with a flank attack being made by the Reserve Army against Pozières. This had the accidental effect that 19 Division would be attacking simultaneously with one of the divisions flanking it, although not that which Rawlinson had intended.

What we are observing is a process by which an operation intended as a 'concerted' major attack degenerated into a series of distinct and unco-ordinated minor attacks. All told, the six attacking divisions of Fourth Army had not one but four separate zero hours: 10 p.m. on 22 July for 5 Division, 12.30 a.m. on 23 July for 1 and 19 Divisions, what should have become 12.30 but remained 1.30 for the ill-informed 51 Division, and 3.40 a.m. for 3 and 30 Divisions. There was no reason to doubt that the first of these attacks would alert the whole German line and so eliminate any possible element of surprise from this assault. Clearly this was reason enough either to rethink the whole operation or anyway to delay it until its various elements could be synchronized – with at least a prospect that the French would at last be in a position to participate. Yet nothing of the kind was attempted. Rawlinson's 'concerted' attack proceeded in palpably dis-concerted fashion.

Nor were the shortcomings in the planning of the attack confined to the matter of timing. In most respects the artillery preparations compare very unfavourably to those of 14 July. On that occasion the task of the artillery had been relatively simple. Most of the German line had been under direct observation. Three days had been allowed for the bombardment, and as most of the shells were delivered in daylight it had been possible to make constant corrections. For the attack of 22/23 July none of this applied. Most of the German line was concealed behind a reverse slope. Rawlinson therefore had to rely on aerial observation to ensure accurate registration of the guns, and this could only occur in clear weather. For several days the attack had to be delayed just because such weather was wanting. When at last visibility improved the attack went in almost immediately, leaving little time for artillery registration. (Again, Rawlinson's decision to press ahead rather than wait for the French seems obtuse.)

Given all these adverse factors, it can hardly be deemed remarkable that the operation of 22/23 July proved an almost unrelieved disaster. Quite apart from Rawlinson's decision to send different units forward at a suc-cession of times, there was no reason for the Germans – given their experiences on 14 July – to be taken by surprise by a night attack. And the inadequacy of the bombardment in most sectors left the enemy's trenches and their occupants intact. Consequently even the first of the attacking divisions, the 5th, found itself up against an enemy alert and unimpaired. The attackers, advancing on Wood Lane, were illuminated by flares and then ran into wire.[24] They were eventually forced back to their own lines having sustained over 1,000 casualties.[25]

On the left of the Fourth Army front, 1 and 19 Divisions, attacking at 12.30 a.m., were caught in no-man's-land by German flares and their attacks brought to a standstill by concentrated machine-gun fire.[26]

On the right of 19 Division, 51 Division suffered a predictable disaster. Having failed to receive Rawlinson's amended instruction, they attacked out of phase with 19 Division. As the battalions advanced towards the Switch Line they were met by heavy machine-gun fire at 'close range from the eastern end of Intermediate Trench, which was well wired and held many Germans who used flares freely.'[27] The attackers, not even aware that this obstacle existed, fell back in confusion. As for the more rightward section of this division, its members found the defenders of High Wood thoroughly alerted by the earlier operations of 5 Division against Wood Lane.[28] They failed to gain any ground.[29]

On the right of 5 Division, the attack at 3.40 a.m. on Longueval and Delville Wood by 3 Division proved equally barren. Owing to the late arrival of final orders it was 2 a.m. before the ultimate plan was explained to the battalions. Then it transpired that only one map of the operational area was available. None of the officers had been over the ground, it was pitch dark, and the approach route was so cut up with trenches and shell holes that there was no possibility of keeping direction. The enemy meanwhile had been manning their defences since the commencement of the attack by 5 Division to the immediate north more than five hours earlier. As for the bombardment, it proved so feeble as to be hardly noticeable. The attack soon disintegrated, with small groups stumbling around Longueval in the dark subjected to heavy enfilade machine-gun fire from the north. Not a yard of ground was gained.[30]

On the right flank of the Fourth Army's operation, the attack by 30 Division against Guillemont also failed, but for rather different reasons. These need to be noted, both because they do not redound to Rawlinson's discredit in the way that the failures on the other sectors clearly do, and because they were to have important implications for subsequent operations in this area. In the sector around Guillemont, the British artillery

---

[24] Reichsarchiv, *Somme-Nord*, p. 159.

[25] Miles, *1916* vol. 2, pp. 136–7.

[26] Ibid., p. 138.

[27] Ibid., p. 137.

[28] Reichsarchiv, *Somme-Nord*, pp. 156–7.

[29] Miles, *1916* vol. 2, p. 137.

[30] This account is derived from a letter from an officer of the 9 Brigade (E. Thomson) to Edmonds 12/1/34 in Official History Correspondence: Somme, Cab 45/138.

had good observation over the German defences. Consequently their bombardment wrought great damage upon the German trench lines.[31]

However, in this particular area it no longer proved sufficient to target upon the enemy line. For in response to previous well-directed British bombardments the German machine-gunners were elsewhere – in shell holes clear of their trenches. As G. C. Wynne points out, this development converted a series of trenches into a 'zone or defended area, within which the front units moved as the situation demanded.' This change in German defensive arrangements meant that the British artillery now had 'no known and easily located trench line' on which to direct their fire. Instead they 'had to batter a whole area of ground, using an immense quantity of ammunition' to ensure the destruction of the German defenders.[32] The amount of ammunition required to achieve this was not available to the British in 1916.

In the most rightward sector of his attack, then, Rawlinson's failure could be attributed to the emergence of unanticipated tactical problems. Elsewhere along the front, no such explanation was available for what had been a considerable setback.

One message at least emerged clearly from this unhappy episode. Attack by night did not hold the key to success on the Somme. If unsupported by a bombardment whose intensity was appropriate to the circumstances, a forward move in the dark would fail as assuredly as an attempted advance in the light. Rawlinson, to his credit, had perceived this truth even following his success on 14 July. To his discredit, his failure to act on this perception drove home its message a mere eight days later.

Daylight on 23 July found the Fourth Army commander confronted with the consequences of failure. He immediately ordered the capture of Delville Wood and the northern section of Longueval,[33] on this occasion employing forces commensurate with the strength of the resistance to be subdued. So on 27 July two brigades were sent against these objectives, supported by the entire artillery resources of XV and XIII Corps, a total of 368 guns.[34] Such an accumulation of artillery was truly formidable. While the scattered form of the German defences precludes a precise calculation of the intensity of the bombardment, the round figures are sufficiently revealing. Some 125,000 shells, weighing 4.5 million pounds, were fired. This constituted a more intensive bombardment than that of 14 July.[35] The

---

[31] Reichsarchiv, *Somme-Nord*, p. 188.

[32] Wynne, *If Germany Attacks*, p. 123. See also Reichsarchiv, *Somme-Nord*, p. 188.

[33] 'Appreciation Of The Situation By the Commander of the Fourth Army, 24 July', in Miles, *1916* vol. 2, Appendices, Appendix 12, pp. 32–3.

[34] Conference at Fourth Army HQ 25/7/16, Fourth Army War Diary 25/7/16, AWM 26/10/241/27. The number of guns is taken from Rawlinson's Diary 27/7/16.

[35] 'Battle of Somme: Artillery Notes and Statistics,' Rawlinson Papers 5201/33/71 NAM.

German accounts leave no doubt about the ferocity of the British bombardment and the heavy casualties it inflicted. Delville Wood is described as being full of wrecked machine-guns and dead and wounded men.[36] As a result the British 2 Division was able to occupy most of the Wood and 5 Division most of Longueval.[37] After two further days of ferocious shelling the capture of the village was completed.[38] The real message of 14 July had been reaffirmed.

III

Most unfortunately, simultaneously with his Delville Wood success Rawlinson was engaged in planning a rerun of the barren experience of 22/23 July. He agreed with Foch that an Anglo-French attack be made towards Guillemont and Maurepas. And he further agreed to extend the front of attack by undertaking 'as many offensive operations as possible on the rest of the Fourth Army front on the same day.'[39] In so saying Rawlinson was committing himself, in addition to the main endeavour, to a set of subsidiary and isolated attacks: against Intermediate Trench, Wood Lane, and the orchards to the north of Longueval.[40] These three attacks were to go in at 6.10 p.m. on 30 July. This was a markedly different zero hour from that of the main effort, which they were supposedly supporting but which would be commencing more than 13 hours earlier (4.45 a.m. on 30 July).[41]

Not surprisingly neither the Anglo-French attack nor the isolated and unco-ordinated supporting attacks enjoyed a happier fate than those of 22/23 July which they so closely resembled. Rawlinson's forces went forward in the same old way and were stopped in the same old way. The artillery bombardment was, for the frontages under attack, even less adequate than it had been a week before. The only permanent gains made by Fourth Army were on the front of 19 Division, where a small section of Intermediate Trench was taken. This trivial acquisition cost the British 5,000 casualties.[42]

To sum up, the period from 15 to 30 July was one in which the Fourth Army delivered a succession of small-scale attacks, largely fruitless and

---

[36] Reichsarchiv, *Somme-Nord*, p. 177.

[37] Miles, *1916* vol. 2, p. 158.

[38] Ibid., p. 160.

[39] Foch–Rawlinson telephone conversation 27/7/16, Fourth Army War Diary 27/7/16, AWM 26/12/41/37.

[40] Fourth Army Operation Order, 28/7/16, Fourth Army Papers vol. 2.

[41] Continuation of the above order in ibid.

[42] Estimated figure. The 30 Division alone suffered 2,800 casualties. See Miles, *1916* vol. 2, p. 166, n. 3.

seemingly at odds with the commander's clear expression of intent. How do we account for this gulf between the motive and the act? Two reasons suggest themselves. First, Rawlinson allowed minor operations to be embarked upon independently when they were intended to secure particular objectives he had already designated. In other words, he was failing to direct these activities occurring on his own Army front. Second, when on two occasions (22/23 July and 30 July) Rawlinson embarked on what were intended to be large-scale efforts, these degenerated – thanks to the uncoordinated starting-times of the various elements involved – into a sequence of minor attacks. Hence yet again Fourth Army was acting in a manner at odds with the commander's expressed intention.

IV

Notwithstanding these barren endeavours, as July ended Rawlinson seemed determined to press on. At a corps commanders' conference on 31 July, he stated that XIII Corps was to prepare once more to assail Guillemont. Further, 'the policy to be adopted by III and XV Corps was to be offensive, troops to press forward with a view to the capture of the Switch line.'[43]

It might appear that Guillemont, a fortified village in that section of the German second line still resisting conquest, was only likely to succumb to an assault on the scale of 14 July. Instead, Rawlinson here reaffirmed his so far ill-rewarded policy whereby attacks would be occurring all the time, all his forces would – at one stage or another – be engaged in attacking, but no attack would involve sufficient guns or troops to attain its objectives.

Haig, it is evident, was becoming disenchanted with this course of events. After the failure on 23 July he had told Rawlinson that his plan was to '*consolidate*' Fourth Army's left and centre, and to improve the position on the right.[44] Following the abortive action of 30 July Haig stated yet more firmly that Fourth Army should hold on its left and centre, and should press forward on its right:

> I reminded Rawlinson that my plan is to do everything possible to bring the French on my right forward into line. At present their troops are echeloned back in rear of my right. The British front to the north (that is on the line Longueval–Bazentin–Pozières) must there be *stationary*.[45]

[43] Fourth Army Conference, 31/7/16, Fourth Army Papers vol. 2.
[44] Haig Diary 23/7/16. Haig's emphasis.
[45] Ibid. 30/7/16 (emphasis added).

This seemed a clear statement of policy: Rawlinson should be directing his endeavours to aiding the French to get forward on Fourth Army's right. This would eliminate the sharp Delville Wood–Longueval salient.

Three days later Haig produced a document amplifying this policy. It deserves to be quoted at length:

> (i) The first necessity at the moment is to help the French forward on our right flank. For this we must capture Guillemont, Falfemont Farm and Ginchy as soon as possible. These places cannot be taken, however – with due regard to economy of the means available – without careful and methodical preparation. The necessary preparations must be pushed on without delay, and the attack will be launched when the responsible Commanders on the spot are satisfied that everything possible has been done to ensure success.
>
> (ii) While pushing on preparations for the attack on the places mentioned in (i) no serious attack is to be made on the front now held by the XV and III Corps (extending from Delville Wood to 'Munster Alley'). Preparations for a subsequent attack on this front must, however, be carried on with energy and method . . . The decision as to when a serious offensive is to be undertaken on this front is reserved by the Commander-in-Chief.[46]

The second paragraph is unambiguous. Rawlinson should make no serious attacks on his left and centre. And although he should prepare for a subsequent offensive there, only the commander-in-chief could authorize its actual initiation.

The first paragraph, at least as far as method is concerned, is a less happy production. Haig tells Rawlinson that he must attack on the right flank 'as soon as possible', 'push[ing] on' with the necessary preparations 'without delay'. But Rawlinson is also warned that his objectives cannot be taken 'without careful and methodical preparation' and that the attack must only go in when 'the responsible Commanders on the spot are satisfied that everything possible has been done to ensure success.' As if the inherent contradiction between these two aspects were not enough, Haig then throws in the chilling stipulation that 'due regard' must be given to 'economy of the means available' – as certain a prescription for failure in offensive operations on the Western Front as could be imagined. Nevertheless, the import of Haig's first paragraph could not be doubted. The commander-in-chief was requiring Rawlinson to direct his endeavours to his right wing with the purpose of bringing forward the French.

---

[46] Haig to Rawlinson and Gough (OAD 91) 2/8/16, quoted in Miles, *1916* vol. 2, Appendices, Appendix 13, p. 35.

TABLE 20.2 Number of battalions employed in operations during the period 1–24 August on the Somme

Objective	1	2	3	4	5	6	7	8	9	10	11	12	13	14	15	16	17	18	19	20	21	22	23	24
Switch Line/Intermediate Trench/West of High Wood	1	1	–	1	–	3	–	–	–	–	1	5	–	–	–	2	3	2	2	–	–	–	–	1
High Wood	–	–	–	–	–	–	–	–	–	–	–	–	–	–	–	–	–	1.5	–	–	–	–	–	–
Wood Lane	–	–	–	2	–	–	–	–	–	–	–	–	–	–	–	–	–	3	–	–	1	–	–	4
Longueval/Delville Wood	–	–	–	–	–	–	3	–	–	–	–	–	–	–	–	–	–	4	–	–	1	–	–	4
Ginchy	–	–	–	–	–	–	–	–	–	–	–	–	–	–	–	–	–	2	–	–	3	–	–	–
Guillemont	–	–	–	–	–	–	–	6	–	–	–	–	–	–	–	–	1	2	–	–	–	–	–	–
South of Guillemont	–	–	–	–	–	–	–	–	–	–	–	–	–	–	–	4	2	2	–	–	–	–	–	–
Right flank in co-op. with French	–	–	–	–	–	–	–	–	–	–	–	–	–	–	–	–	–	1	–	–	2	–	–	–
Total	1	1	–	3	–	3	3	6	–	–	1	5	–	–	–	6	6	17.5	2	–	7	–	–	9

Astonishingly, nothing in Rawlinson's conduct of operations changed as a consequence of Haig's pep talks and memoranda. Between 1 and 25 August – when torrential rain halted attacks for a week – the Fourth Army continued to launch a succession of small-scale operations directed more to its left and centre than to its right. Table 20.2 makes the course of events clear.

Three things are especially evident from this table. One is the frequency of the operations. On 14 days out of 24, attacks of at least battalion strength were delivered. (There were also a great many attacks at company level or less not recorded here.)[47] The second is the small scale of the operations. Only on one day (18 August) out of the 14 was an attack delivered on a broad front and at divisional strength. The third aspect is the apparent disregard of Haig's instruction that 'the first necessity' was to concentrate on Rawlinson's rightward sector. In the period 1–24 August, 47.5 battalions in all were involved in twenty-five attacks on the left and centre of Fourth Army's front. By contrast, 25 battalions delivered ten attacks in the sector adjacent to the French. It is little wonder that as August wore on Haig began evincing clear signs of impatience with his Fourth Army commander.

V

Haig's displeasure was aggravated by the fact that, on the few occasions when Rawlinson did choose to act in the sector designated by his chief, he did not acquit himself well. In the first half of August Fourth Army troops only once, on the 8th, were directed against Guillemont. The outcome was not happy. Although this was Rawlinson's third assault on the village, the plan (in the words of the official history) 'differed little from those of the previous attacks.'[48] A member of the attacking division (the 55th) later identified the reasons for the total failure of the assault: first, there was no support provided on the flanks; and second, with the positioning of the German machine-guns clear of the trenches the artillery preparation was not effective. He wrote:

> Corps and Higher Commanders refused to believe that Guillemont could not be taken by an isolated attack. They did not realize that the terrain lent itself specially to a strong machine gun defence. These guns were located on the flanks away from the trench systems, and consequently in positions impossible to locate and destroy before an

---

[47] See for example the III Corps Summary of Operations, August 1916, in III Corps War Diary, Aug–Dec 1916, WO 95/674.

[48] Miles, *1916* vol. 2, p. 177.

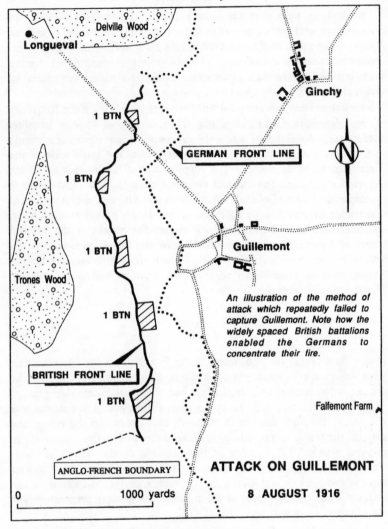

Delville Wood

Longueval

Ginchy

1 BTN

GERMAN FRONT LINE

N

1 BTN

1 BTN

Guillemont

Trones Wood

An illustration of the method of attack which repeatedly failed to capture Guillemont. Note how the widely spaced British battalions enabled the Germans to concentrate their fire.

1 BTN

BRITISH FRONT LINE

1 BTN

Falfemont Farm

ANGLO-FRENCH BOUNDARY

ATTACK ON GUILLEMONT

0   1000 yards

8 AUGUST 1916

Note: in addition, one battalion was in reserve.

MAP 20

attack ... In addition an isolated attack allowed the Germans to concentrate the whole of their artillery in that sector for the defence of Guillemont.[49]

[49] ? Cochrane to Edmonds 8/1/?, Official History Correspondence: Somme, Cab 45/132.

Rawlinson shied away from these considerations. He preferred to lay responsibility for the failure on his long-suffering rank and file. The lack of success, he wrote, 'was mainly due to the want of go and inferior training of the infantry.'[50] Haig took a different view. He was convinced that responsibility for failure lay further up the hierarchy than where the Fourth Army commander was seeking to place it. He believed that Rawlinson, by simply indicating to his subordinate commanders the objectives to be assailed and leaving them to devise the actual operations, was falling short of his responsibilities.

So Haig dispatched Kiggell and Davidson to Fourth Army Head-quarters with a stern message. It was that 'the repeated failures to capture Guillemont have convinced the Commander-in-Chief that the method of attack adopted requires careful and full reconsideration.'[51] Haig insisted that Rawlinson should do two things. He should discuss the problem of capturing Guillemont with officers – down to brigade level if necessary – who had already been involved in attacking it. And he should then, after careful consideration, *himself* draw up a plan for the next attack.[52] Haig even gave Rawlinson a strong indication of the form the operation should take. It should consist of an attack 'on a very wide front', from the Somme to High Wood, 'so as to prevent the enemy from placing a barrage which might stop us if we attacked on a small front.'[53]

In some respects the plan for his next operation, on 18 August, did show that Rawlinson was taking Haig's lecture to heart. He played a co-ordinating role. He avoided the error, so evident on 23 and 30 July, of having different units attacking at different times: his whole front jumped off at 2.45 p.m. But in two vital matters Rawlinson's orders showed no advance. The preliminary bombardment, although more weighty than those fired on 23 and 30 July, was inadequate for the task in hand now that an area rather than a line had to be suppressed. And once more the infantry attacked in widely separated small units.

Yet again the attack failed. Some ground was gained on either side of Delville Wood and a few trenches in front of Guillemont were wrested from the Germans. But the cost was prohibitive; the battalions of 3 Division alone suffered 68 per cent casualties.[54]

Once more a Fourth Army operation had met with little success.

---

[50] Rawlinson Diary 8/8/16.

[51] All quotations in this paragraph are from 'Note of an interview at Querrieu, at 11.00 am, 9th August, 1916, between [Rawlinson, Kiggell, Montgomery and Davidson]'. Fourth Army Papers vol. 2.

[52] Ibid.

[53] Haig Diary 12/8/16.

[54] Miles, *1916* vol. 2, p. 193.

Wood Lane, High Wood, and Guillemont remained in German hands. Rawlinson's response was to order an immediate resumption of the kind of operation that had failed so conspicuously on four occasions. But Haig was now much readier to intervene.

VI

On 19 August, the commander-in-chief sent Rawlinson a directive telling him to prepare for a major attack in mid-September along the whole front. (This directive would bear fruit in the well-remembered operation of 15 September.) The object of this big offensive would be to capture, in the sector Morval to Le Sars, the enemy's last system of prepared defences. But in order that this length of front might be attacked with any chance of success, a good start line must be established. This meant that, in advance of 15 September, Fourth Army had to secure the strongpoints of High Wood, Ginchy, Guillemont, and Falfemont Farm. Haig urged that operations to achieve these ends be commenced at once.[55]

Clearly, however, the commander-in-chief had no confidence that the type of attacks recently delivered by the Fourth Army would achieve his objectives. His judgement upon those operations, in truth, was damning. 'The only conclusion that can be drawn from the repeated failure of attacks on Guillemont', he told Rawlinson, 'is that something is wanting in the methods employed.'[56] Haig went on to make crystal clear what this 'something' was. Rawlinson's attacks had been delivered on excessively narrow frontages, had employed insufficient forces, and had lacked oversight by Rawlinson himself. For Fourth Army's next endeavour, Haig wrote:

> The attack must be a general one, engaging the enemy simultaneously along the whole front to be captured, and a sufficient force must be employed, in proper proportion to the extent of front, to beat down all opposition.[57]

He suggested to Rawlinson that two and a half divisions be used to attack Guillemont, a force sufficient to deliver a continuous attack along the whole front.

Haig also indicated that his directive of 9 August requiring of Rawlinson a more active role in formulating the plan had not been taken sufficiently to heart. He gave Rawlinson some basic instruction in the duties of an Army commander. He agreed that: 'In actual *execution* of plans, when control by

[55] GHQ to Fourth Army (OAD 116) 19/8/16, AWM 26/9/4/41.
[56] GHQ to Fourth Army (OAD 123) 24/8/16, Fourth Army Papers vol. 5.
[57] Ibid.

higher Commanders is impossible, subordinates on the spot must act on their own initiative, and they must be trained to do so.' But during the preliminary stages, responsibility did not rest with subordinates; 'in *preparation*' for battle, Haig laid down, 'close supervision by higher Commanders is not only possible but is their duty, to such extent as they find necessary to ensure that everything is done that can be done to ensure success. This close supervision is especially necessary in the case of a comparatively new army. It is not "interference" but a legitimate and necessary exercise of the functions of a Commander on whom the ultimate responsibility for success or failure lies.' As if this were not sufficiently to the point, Haig drove the message home. 'It appears to the Commander-in-Chief that some misconception exists in the Army as to the object and limitations of the principle of the initiative of subordinates, and it is essential that this misconception should be corrected at once, where it does exist.'[58]

So far, in this boys'-own-guide on how to command an Army, Haig had been making good sense. But, almost characteristically, he then put all this useful instruction at risk by seeking to deny Rawlinson sufficient time to implement the necessary changes. 'Not a moment must be lost', he instructed the Fourth Army commander, in carrying out the new attack.[59] This was an invitation to disaster. Undue haste was simply incompatible with the changes in Fourth Army practices desired by Haig.

At this point a factor beyond the control of Haig and Rawlinson intervened to save the Fourth Army from another hasty, ill-considered operation. The weather, which had been reasonably fine in mid-August, deteriorated on the 25th. From that day there followed a week of heavy rain, rendering operations impossible.[60] The attack was finally rescheduled for 3 September. Thus Rawlinson and his staff secured an additional ten days in which to plan their next attack.

The interval was put to particularly good use in the case of Guillemont – although only at the cost of reducing the attack on the left of the sector (which included High Wood) to something of a diversion. Between 25 August and 2 September a grid of trenches was dug by night into no-man's-land north-west of Guillemont so the village could now be assaulted from a flank.[61] At the same time Rawlinson was assembling a force of 27 battalions for the attack. This meant that it would be possible to launch a continuous offensive along the designated front, and to concentrate 20

[58] Ibid.
[59] Ibid.
[60] For weather conditions see the Fourth Army War Diary for the relevant days.
[61] Captain J. A. C. Pennyquick to Edmonds 30/10/35, Official History Correspondence: Somme, Cab 45/136.

battalions (nearly two divisions) against the rightward sector which included Guillemont, Ginchy, and Falfemont Farm. Only in the vital matter of artillery did the operation launched on 3 September prove no advance on what had gone before. Indeed the number of shells (400,000) used on this occasion was no greater than that employed on 18 August,[62] while the length of trench under attack was a good deal more extensive. And as it happened, artillery support promised by the French for those Fourth Army troops assailing Falfemont Farm was, on the day, not forthcoming. Without informing their allies, the French turned their guns on a German attack occurring to the south.[63] Hence the German machine-gunners in the Combles valley who dominated the British positions remained unsuppressed.[64]

Lack of artillery support may be deemed responsible for the fact that, at the end of 3 September, three out of Rawlinson's four principal objectives in this attempt to secure the mid-September start line remained in German hands: High Wood, Ginchy, and Falfemont Farm. Nevertheless, the decision to attack on a broad front served one positive purpose. It obliged the Germans also to spread their artillery widely, so denying them the opportunity (which they had employed so effectively on earlier occasions) to pound from the flanks the British forces assaulting Guillemont. And here at least Rawlinson did score a success.

The operation against Guillemont was also assisted by the preparations, carried out during the period of bad weather, which removed the necessity for a frontal assault on the town. The village was captured by 20 Division (with an attached brigade from 16 Division) attacking from the north. The enfilading German machine-gunners were themselves taken in the flank and within three hours the British were consolidating to the east of the village.[65] To the south of Guillemont the attack by 5 Division also caught the German machine-gunners in the flank and an advance beyond the village was made. (An added bonus in this area was that the artillery had managed to obliterate the German positions.)[67]

In a day of mixed fortune, 3 September had seen a major stronghold in the German second system overrun. And in that there were no strong German defences to the east of Guillemont, the British success here held out the opportunity for further advance – as long as it was undertaken

---

[62] 'Somme: Artillery Notes and Statistics'.

[63] Lyn Macdonald, *Somme* (London: Michael Joseph, 1983), p. 249.

[64] Miles, *1916* vol. 2, p. 252.

[65] Ibid., p. 255.

[66] Ibid., pp. 252–3.

[67] For this incident see 5 Division to XIV Corps 5/9/16 and Fourth Army Summary of Operations for 5/9/16 in Fourth Army Papers vol. 3.

before the enemy had the chance to consolidate. Urgent messages were received from commanders on the spot promising significant gains if fresh troops were pushed in. Rawlinson, who happened to be visiting the relevant corps commander at the time, ordered an immediate advance.[67] As a result, troops from XIV Corps occupied a wood to the east of Guillemont virtually without opposition.[68]

This phase of the campaign did not cease here. Rawlinson was convinced that one more push by 7 Division, which had been unable to capture Ginchy, would bring him that prize also. So on 4, 5, and 6 September that unfortunate division (which had already suffered prohibitive casualties) was thrust into a series of hastily prepared, narrow-front attacks. Ginchy did not fall. And 7 Division was reduced to so shattered a condition that it had to be removed from the order of battle for the mid-September offensive.[69]

By 7 September Rawlinson was reconciled to assaulting Ginchy by the methods employed against Guillemont four days earlier. A broad-front attack was organized. After an extremely heavy bombardment Ginchy was attacked by eight battalions from 16 Division. Notwithstanding heavy casualties, the attack succeeded. With the exceptions of High Wood (where yet another attack failed on 9 September) and Falfemont Farm, the start line for the 15 September offensive now lay in British hands.

VII

It is difficult to find a rationale for Rawlinson's conduct during the eight weeks from 15 July to 14 September. We must speculate that he saw the operations as being of so minor a nature, for such clear and limited objectives, as not to require him to impose any pattern of conduct on his subordinate commanders. They were left to undertake the capture of places which had lain within the objectives of the major operation on 14 July. Consequently Rawlinson took no action to terminate the piecemeal attacks which occurred subsequent to his pronouncement on 16 July that such attacks were no longer appropriate. And he did nothing to enforce Haig's judgement of late July and early August that the left and centre of his front 'must therefore be stationary'.

This does not mean that Rawlinson was unaware of what was going on. His diary for these weeks records events in considerable detail. But his entries read like the work of an observer, not those of a commander who

---

[68] Ibid.
[69] C. T. Atkinson, *The Seventh Division 1914–1918* (London: Murray, 1927), p. 318.

saw it as his responsibility to direct and even inspire the course of events.

The consequences were twofold. For the Fourth Army, these weeks proved costly and ill-rewarded. For Rawlinson, this method of exercising (or failing to exercise) command attracted the mounting disfavour of the commander-in-chief.

New Weapons and Old,
15–30 September

I

By 12 September the Fourth Army, with two significant exceptions, had reached the start line for Haig's proposed new major attack. (The exceptions were Falfemont Farm – which had now passed into the French sector – and High Wood.) Confronting Rawlinson's forces was a succession of three German trench systems. It will indicate the laborious progress of the British forces during two and a half months of campaigning that for some of its length, the first of these lines consisted of what back on 1 July had been the German third position.[1] In addition, the Germans had constructed a new defensive work of some strength known as the Quadrilateral, to the north of Combles.

How were these defences to be penetrated? On 28 August Rawlinson sent his first proposals to Haig. In essence Rawlinson's plan was a restatement of the step-by-step approach first advocated for 1 July. Each German trench system was to be attacked in a separate operation. There was to be a pause of about 24 hours between operations, during which consolidation of the positions captured would take place and the artillery brought forward for the next attack.

For several reasons Rawlinson did not consider it 'a practical operation' to attempt the capture of more than one German defensive system in a single blow. First, only in the area immediately to the south of Martinpuich did the British line have good observation for the artillery over the rearward German positions. Second, to the east of Martinpuich the distance

[1] The first line ran from Combles through Flers to High Wood and Martinpuich; the second from Flers to Eaucourt L'Abbaye and Le Sars; the third in front of Morval, Lesboeufs, Guedecourt to the Butte de Warlencourt.

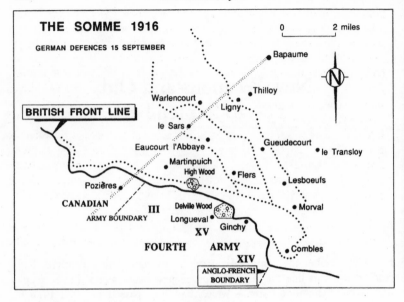

MAP 21

between the first and second German systems extended to 3,000 yards, a formidable distance considering the difficulty of maintaining artillery support for advancing troops, and taking into consideration 'the large concentration of hostile artillery in front of us.' Third, the most distant German line was out of range of the 'large majority' of British guns and howitzers. Thus Rawlinson's reasons for rejecting an all-out attack were substantially the same as those which had led him to reject this approach on 1 July.[2]

For the mid-September attack, however, a new weapon of war would lie to Rawlinson's hand. He would have at his disposal 50 tanks. The First World War tank was essentially an armoured machine-gun or light artillery carrier, potentially able in the face of small arms fire to cross trench lines, crush barbed wire, and engage enemy trench garrisons. It might seem that the presence of so novel a weapon gave Rawlinson cause to employ a more daring plan of attack.

Rawlinson concluded otherwise. Having visited tank headquarters at St Requier on 26 August and having studied GHQ memoranda on tanks, he was aware that the Mark 1 tank was a very imperfect weapon.[3] Over rough

[2] Rawlinson to GHQ 28/8/16, Fourth Army Papers vol. 5.

[3] Rawlinson Diary 26/8/16. GHQ produced three memoranda on tanks before the September battle: 'OAD 111 of 16/8/16', 'Notes on Tank Organization And Equipment',

ground it could advance at only 55 yards per minute (2 miles per hour).[4] The tank, therefore, would be slower than the infantry. Further, the first models were decidedly prone to mechanical failure. (Two out of the six demonstrated to Rawlinson had broken down.)[5] The large size of the tanks and their slow speed made them exceptionally vulnerable to artillery fire.[6] In addition, Rawlinson was able to observe that the first tank crews were 'green' and lacking in practice.[7]

Nevertheless, it was not at all the case that Rawlinson resisted the introduction of tanks or concluded that they had no place in the coming battle. On the contrary he expressed himself 'On the whole . . . rather favourably impressed.'[8] He promptly incorporated tanks into his battle plan and in one sector gave them a key role. What he was not prepared to do was to see the tank as a weapon of breakthrough or even the means of quelling a sequence of enemy defences.

In keeping with this thinking Rawlinson distributed small numbers of tanks to each of the attacking corps for the purpose of capturing specific German strongpoints which were likely to hold up the attack or prove costly to take. These tanks were expected to precede the infantry and subdue the strongpoints in advance of the waves of troops. In addition, Rawlinson concentrated a larger number of tanks with the object of capturing the village of Flers. This aspect was a key point of the whole plan, for if Flers fell it was thought that the German second position could be rolled up from the south-east.

In short, Rawlinson expected the tanks in the opening stages of the battle both to enable him to capture a village of considerable tactical importance and to reduce casualties in the main attack. He therefore reasoned that with relatively fresh troops the interval between each attack could be reduced to 24 hours. Tanks would thus speed up the whole operation which would in turn keep the Germans off balance until all their defensive positions had been captured.

Rawlinson's plan contained one curious feature which suggests that, far from underestimating the potentials of the tank, he had failed to grasp its limitations. All the operations outlined in his plan were to take place at night. Admittedly Rawlinson was relying on bright moonlight to allow the tanks to operate. But even moonlight would not have provided enough

---

and 'Preliminary Notes on Tactical Employment of Tanks'. All three are printed in Miles *1916* vol. 2, Appendices, Appendix 15, pp. 39–45.

[4] GHQ, 'Notes on Tank Organization and Equipment'.

[5] Rawlinson Diary 26/8/16.

[6] GHQ, 'Notes on Tank Organization and Equipment'.

[7] Rawlinson Diary 26/8/16.

[8] Ibid.

illumination for the tank commanders to keep direction, to avoid falling into communication trenches, and, most importantly, to distinguish friend from foe. As it stood this aspect of Rawlinson's plan threatened to turn his considered approach to the use of tanks into a shambles.[9]

II

When formulating his plan, Rawlinson was well aware that his decision to proceed step-by-step might not prove congenial to the commander-in-chief. He noted in his diary, 'D.H. won't like this but I am sure it is right. If we attempt too much we run the risk of doing nothing.'[10]

His anticipation of Haig's response proved well founded. On receipt of the plan Haig commented:

> studied Rawlinson's proposals for the September attack and for the use of the Tanks. In my opinion, he is not making enough of the situation with the deterioration and all-round loss of moral[e] of the enemy troops. I think we should make an attack as strong and as violent as possible, and plan to go as far as possible.[11]

Two days later Kiggell embodied these thoughts in a memorandum to Rawlinson:

> with reference to your [plan] ... the commander-in-chief considers that the situation is likely to be favourable for an operation planned on bolder lines.
>
> Accordingly he desires that the 'tanks' may be used boldly and success pressed in order to demoralize the enemy and, if possible, capture his guns.[12]

Rawlinson's response is significant. On other occasions (most notably before the 14 July operation) he had resisted basic amendments to his plan, and had done so with a good prospect of extracting concessions from Haig. But matters had changed by early September. Now Rawlinson was in no position to put up a spirited resistance: as became evident when he capitulated immediately to the commander-in-chief and incorporated all Haig's suggestions into a new plan. The reason for this surrender is not far to seek. Rawlinson's conduct of operations in August, as we

---

[9] Rawlinson's views on tanks are incorporated in Rawlinson to GHQ 28/8/16, Fourth Army Papers vol. 5.

[10] Rawlinson Diary 28/8/16.

[11] Haig Diary 29/8/16.

[12] Kiggell to Rawlinson 31/8/16, Fourth Army Papers vol. 3.

have seen, had not inspired confidence and had eventually earned him a stern lecture from Haig on the duties of an Army commander. Clearly, Rawlinson felt that he lacked the resources to engage his superior in a protracted debate on tactics – hence his speedy capitulation.

How then did Haig envisage the battle? He wanted almost every fresh division placed in the front line. They would make a speedy advance, capturing all three German lines and so opening the way for the five divisions of cavalry that would be massed behind the British front. There would be no pauses, just one violent attack. Once the cavalry had broken through they would establish a flank on the right of the attack, so enabling the infantry to roll up the German positions to the north. The tanks would be used much in the way suggested by Rawlinson except in two respects. They, along with the infantry, would press on to the German third line without any halts. And they would not be used at night. The main attack would be carried out in the half-light of dawn.[13]

In this last respect Haig's conception was clearly superior to Rawlinson's. But for the rest, the commander-in-chief's plan was severely flawed. There was the patent absurdity of expecting the cavalry to advance ten miles through the shattered remains of three German trench systems and then form an effective flank guard unhindered by German reserves. In respect to the infantry also, Haig's sweeping amendments to Rawlinson's plan possessed the potential for serious consequences. Haig was committing most of the Fourth Army to the initial attack. This involved a drastic thinning-down in the reserves which would be available to exploit whatever gains might be made. Corps reserves now consisted of only three divisions (20, 21, 1), all of which had been through the Somme mill during August. As Rawlinson pointed out 'we shall have no reserves in hand but tired troops.'[14]

Finally, there was the matter of artillery. A major deficiency in Haig's scheme – correctly identified by Rawlinson – concerned 'the range of the more distant objective [the German third line] in reference to artillery.'[15] That is, the German third line was beyond the range of the British guns. Haig's response was to stipulate that the artillery be brought forward as soon as the German first line had been captured. (Significantly, he did not appear to think that the tanks – assuming they could get so far – would make good any deficiencies in the artillery assault on the third position.) Such a proposal was hardly a solution at all. It was doubtful if the infantry could relay reliable information back to the artillery in time to ensure that the guns would be in a position to follow on the heels of their next

[13] Rawlinson to GHQ 31/8/16, Fourth Army Papers vol. 2.

[14] Rawlinson Diary 30/8/16.

[15] Fourth Army Conference 31/8/16, Rawlinson Papers 1/6, CC.

move. Anyway, the state of the ground – honeycombed with trenches and cratered by shells – would deny the guns any speedy passage.[16] And once the artillery had been brought forward, the gun-layers would confront a problem for which there was no solution in 1916, that of quickly registering the guns on new targets.

In short, it seemed very likely that if the infantry did manage to reach the outskirts of the German third line, they would find its defences largely intact and would be without artillery support to deal with them. However, Haig's amendment to Rawlinson's plan had reduced the likelihood that the infantry would get so far. Now that the three stages of the German defensive network were to be assailed in one operation, the preliminary bombardment would have to account for – in so far as it was capable of reaching – many more yards of enemy trench than Rawlinson had envisaged. (This of course assumes that Rawlinson possessed the additional shells to fire a further bombardment prior to each stage of his step-by-step advance; and that he intended to get his guns forward and register them upon each set of German defences before sending his infantry into the next phase of the attack. On these matters the surviving documents provide no guidance.) No attempt was made by Haig to provide the greater volume of guns and shells which would be necessary at the outset to deal with these additional lengths of enemy defences. In short, by rejecting Rawlinson's step-by-step approach Haig was running the risk – already referred to by the Fourth Army commander – of achieving nothing by trying to achieve everything.

It is important to lay bare the essential difference between Rawlinson and Haig in their approach to the battle. Haig planned for a decisive operation that would shorten the war. All his directives – the need to capture the three German systems at a blow, the heavy infantry concentrations, the extension of the radius of operation of the tanks, and above all the massing of great numbers of cavalry – flowed from this premise. Rawlinson by contrast planned merely to capture the German defensive positions. He was sceptical that his attack, whatever plan was employed, would so shatter the enemy's powers of resistance as to facilitate cavalry exploitation. Nor did he consider that German morale would collapse.

It is also necessary to emphasize areas of agreement between the two commanders. Neither saw the tank as a weapon of exploitation. The most that either expected of the new weapon was that it might subdue strongpoints and capture fortified villages in close proximity to the front. The difference between them as regards the tank lay only in the fact that Haig expected it to engage obstacles to a greater depth than did Rawlinson.

[16] Ibid.

III

If Haig, without specifying the point, amended the artillery aspect of Rawlinson's plan quite markedly, and Rawlinson allowed this change to occur without resistance, then this can be no cause for amazement. For although neither man seemed to believe that the appearance of the tank obviated the need for a sufficiency of artillery, one looks in vain for a serious consideration of the quantities of ammunition required to enable tanks and infantry to perform their tasks.

Once more, Rawlinson appears simply to have assembled as many guns and shells as lay to hand and hoped that these would suffice. Fourth Army records disclose no calculations about the weight of bombardment considered necessary to subdue the German defences under attack. And Haig appears to have done no sums when he arbitrarily increased the obstacles which must, at the outset, be included among the targets.

Over the three days preliminary to the attack, 828,000 shells were thrown at the German defences.[17] These shells weighed approximately 30 million pounds, including 15.5 million pounds devoted to trench destruction.[18] It cannot be said with certainty against which parts of the German defences these shells were directed. But we do have Rawlinson's testimony that the third German trench system lay beyond the range of the 'large majority' of British guns.[19] So it is reasonable to assume that all but the heaviest British guns confined their activities to the first and second German systems. It is therefore legitimate to conclude that the bombardment fired 280 lb. of shell for every yard of German defences in these two lines (55,000 yards of trench, 15.5 million pounds of shell.)[20] This intensity of bombardment is approximately equal to that of Neuve Chapelle, twice that employed on 1 July, but less than half that for 14 July.

It must be presumed that the British commanders recognized the vital role which artillery had to play in this operation. Yet here we find them agreeing to a bombardment which in terms of the revised method of defence employed by the Germans was not of such an intensity as to ensure the attack a reasonable chance of success. It is a sorry commentary on the command's tardiness in responding to the key lessons taught by

[17] 'Battle of Somme: Artillery Notes and Statistics', Table 3, Rawlinson Papers 5201/33/71 NAM.

[18] These figures assume that the preliminary bombardment for 15 September employed a similar mix of shells to that for 1 July.

[19] Rawlinson to GHQ 28/8/16, Fourth Army Papers vol. 5.

[20] The length of trench has been calculated by the same method employed for the other battles.

battles so far that this crucial element in offensive action was the subject of so little attention and calculation.

A further aspect of the planning for 15 September underlines this strange reluctance to acknowledge the vital role of artillery in subduing the enemy. Some of the best-defended sections under attack, while included in the preliminary bombardment, were not to be subjected to the creeping barrage – notwithstanding the large role which this had come to assume in enabling the infantry to get forward. These were the sections being assaulted not only by infantry but by tanks.

The tanks provided Fourth Army's artillery with a problem. It was assumed that the armoured vehicles would run ahead of the infantry and eliminate such obstacles as barbed wire and machine-gun posts. But if Rawlinson's gunners fired a creeping barrage just ahead of the infantry it would imperil the tanks. The Fourth Army commander 'solved' this problem by decreeing that corridors should be left in the creeping barrage down which the tanks could proceed. Given that the tanks would travel in groups, these corridors would be at least 100 yards wide. And the unbombarded defences against which they would be advancing constituted, by Rawlinson's choosing, the most formidable sections of the German defence.[21]

If this constituted a solution to the problem of protecting his tanks from his own artillery, in other respects it left much to be desired. At best, the tanks would only manage to deal with the strongpoints when they got within close range of them. The strongpoints, by contrast – given that they were being spared the creeping barrage – could exact their toll on the attacking infantry from the moment the latter left their trenches. Further, it was even questionable whether the tanks would go ahead of the infantry. Given the desultory speed of which armoured vehicles were capable, the infantry – unless they were prepared to dawdle across no-man's-land and endure all the losses consequent upon such a proceeding – were likely to precede the tanks in their progress towards the strongpoints. But they would do so without the support of a creeping barrage.

Therefore, the appearance of the tank on 15 September did not provide a large body of British infantrymen with an additional form of protection and support. Ironically, it denied them the established sustenance of the creeping barrage and replaced it with a vulnerable substitute of doubtful efficacy. The dubious merit of such an expedient did not long pass unremarked in the higher circles of the British command. Three weeks after the first appearance of the tank on the battlefield, Kiggell, Haig's Chief

[21] Fourth Army Conference 31/8/16, Rawlinson Papers 1/6, CC.

of Staff, wrote a note on 'the use of tanks'. More than once, while not explicitly condemning the manner of their employment on 15 September, he called it into question. So the note began:

> In the present stage of their development [tanks] must be regarded as entirely accessory to the ordinary methods of attack, i.e., to the advance of the infantry in close co-operation with Artillery.

Kiggell then went on to grapple with the problem of how far in advance of the infantry it was wise to start the tanks at the commencement of an attack. He reached no firm conclusion, except that

> as [tanks] are merely accessory to the combined action of the infantry and artillery it would not be justifiable to take any risk of interfering with that combination or of bringing about a risk of failure of the infantry attack through not affording our men the protection of our artillery barrage or by bringing down on them prematurely the enemy's barrage.[22]

Rawlinson on 15 September had manifestly failed, in respect of the objectives being assailed by the tanks, to 'afford our men the protection of our artillery barrage.'

IV

The foregoing discussion reveals that the bombardment which preceded the 15 September attack was unlikely, on account of both its limited quantity and the manner of its employment, to reproduce the swift initial success of 14 July. Were there other factors which might make good the deficiencies of this bombardment? For example, were the British employing improved artillery techniques? And were they doing so against an enemy whose defences were less effective and whose morale had severely declined?

No new artillery techniques were developed in time for the 15 September battle. But at least the techniques available were now being widely employed. By September the General Staff had recommended to all attacking divisions that the creeping barrage be used as a means of infantry protection and as a method of killing German machine-gunners lurking in shell holes between trench lines.[23] As a result, except in respect to the tank lanes just mentioned, all divisions in the Fourth Army used creeping barrages

---

[22] Kiggell to Rawlinson 5/10/16 (OAD 169), AWM 51 [The Heyes Papers] Bundle 31.
[23] See General Staff pamphlet SS119, *Preliminary Notes on the Tactical Lessons of the Recent Operations*, September 1916.

on 15 September. Further, it appears that two refinements in technique had been introduced at the corps level. These concerned the rate of advance of the barrage and the density of shells in it.

Creeping barrages used in the early phase of the Somme battle had advanced at 150 yards per minute and had consisted of one or two rounds of shrapnel per minute from each 18 pounder gun.[24] The attacks delivered in July and August had shown generally that this was inadequate in two respects. The rate of advance was too fast for the infantry to keep close behind the barrage. And the spray of shrapnel was not of a sufficient density to ensure the elimination of the machine-gunners sheltering in shell holes. So for the coming battle the creeping barrage was slowed to a rate of 50 yards per minute and the intensity increased to 3 rounds per minute.[25] (It may be noted that these changes were not optimal. Later, such barrages were slowed to 33 and sometimes 25 yards per minute and the intensity increased to 4 rounds per minute.[26] Nevertheless the refinements instituted for the 15 September attack rendered the creeping barrage on this occasion the most formidable yet encountered by the Germans.)

What of the German defences? Certainly they gave the appearance of being less formidable than those encountered in the July battles. The first two defensive systems to be assailed had already been subjected to a great deal of fire during July and August. By mid-September they had been reduced to a series of shell holes with no interconnecting trenches and no dugouts.[27] The third line was in rather better condition but it contained few dugouts and was much shallower than was usual for a major German position.[28] Many attempts were made by the Germans to improve their defences. Most were thwarted by incessant British artillery fire.[29]

Was it the case then that these defences were in such a state of decrepitude that Rawlinson could be certain of overwhelming them with the artillery at his disposal? Experience should have cautioned him that this was not so. The fighting around Guillemont in August had demonstrated that defences consisting mainly of shell holes were notoriously difficult

---

[24] X Corps, 'Questions relating to an initial attack after lengthy preparation', 16/8/16, Montgomery-Massingberd Papers, Folder 47.

[25] XV Corps Artillery Operation Order No. 47, 13/9/16, quoted in Miles, *1916* vol. 2, Appendices, Appendix 25.

[26] Lt.-Col. A. F. Brooke, 'The evolution of artillery in the Great War, Part VI, Evolution of Artillery Tactics (2)', *Journal of The Royal Artillery*, 53 (1926–27), pp. 236–7.

[27] Major H. Etzer, *Das K. B. 9, Infanterie Regiment Wrede* (Munich: Schick, 1928), p. 86; Captain J. Rieger, *Das K. B. 17, Infanterie Regiment Orff* (Munich: Schick, 1927), p. 45. Other Bavarian regimental histories contain similar descriptions of the defences in this period.

[28] *Das K.B. 14, Infanterie Regiment Hartmann* (Munich: 1931), p. 176.

[29] Ibid., p. 169.

to subdue. It had been discovered that for a bombardment to be effective in those conditions whole areas had to be deluged with shells – a much more formidable undertaking than attacking single-line defences. Yet the lesson of August had apparently gone unheeded. For Rawlinson was preparing to attack the German defences with a bombardment of similar intensity to that which had been used to overcome the relatively feeble single-line trench at Neuve Chapelle.

German morale is not open to simple assessment. Haig judged that the enemy forces were on the brink of collapse. But he had been making such claims since the opening of the campaign, and more than once had been proved decisively wrong. Whatever the undoubted toll being levied on the enemy, their powers of resistance during the fighting of August and early September had shown no signs of weakening. This is not to say that the morale of German units facing the British on 15 September was universally good. Some of the Bavarian regiments in the line had been involved in the severe fighting around Ginchy, Delville Wood, and High Wood during the first two weeks of September. Three in particular had suffered heavy casualties.[30] And it seems possible that this experience lowered their morale. On 10 September one of these regiments described the mood in the battalions as 'depressed'.[31] (So on 15 September, not only were battalions from all three regiments overrun but large numbers of prisoners were taken – often an indication of poor morale.)[32] On the other hand the majority of the Bavarian regiments facing the British had either just entered the line or were in close support. Their troops were fresh and morale was good.[33] Perhaps in making their assessment of the enemy, British Intelligence had once more made the error of generalizing about morale from a small sample of German prisoners.

V

The bombardment for the great attack opened on 12 September. The weather, although fine in the morning, deteriorated later in the day when heavy showers fell. The rain persisted through most of the 13th, greatly hampering the aircraft which were spotting for the artillery and so – though few accounts mention this – reducing the effectiveness of the bombard-

---

[30] See *K.B. 14*, pp. 174–8; *K.B. 9*, p. 92; Major A. Ritter, *Das K.B. 18, Infanterie Regiment Prinz Ludwig Ferdinand* (Munich: Bayerisches Kriegsarchiv, 1926), pp. 154–9.

[31] *K.B. 18*, p. 151.

[32] See *K.B. 18*, p. 160; *K.B. 9*, p. 92; *K.B. 14*, p. 183.

[33] See for example the account in *Das K.B. 10, Infanterie Regiment König* (Munich: Bayerisches Kriegsarchiv, 1925), pp. 245–52.

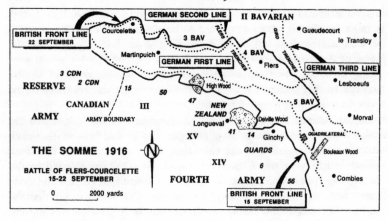

MAP 22

ment. However, on the 14th the weather cleared and an uninterrupted day's shooting was possible.[34]

By the evening of the 14th the nine infantry divisions which were to carry out the initial attack were in the line. They were distributed as follows (from left to right):

III Corps (Pulteney)	15, 50, 47
XV Corps (Horne)	New Zealand, 41, 14
XIV Corps (Cavan)	Guards, 6, 56

In support of Fourth Army's endeavour, on its left the 2 Canadian Division of the Reserve Army would attack Courcelette, while on the right the Sixth French Army would undertake subsidiary operations from Combles to the south of the River Somme.[35]

The morning of the 15th dawned bright and clear. At 6.20 some 50 battalions of British infantry rose out of their trenches and headed towards the German line. An airman recorded the scene:

> When we climbed up to the lines, we found the whole front seemingly covered with a layer of dirty cotton-wool – the smoking shellbursts. Across this were dark lanes, drawn as it might be by a child's stubby finger in dirty snow. Here no shells were falling. Through these lanes lumbered the Tanks.[36]

[34] For weather conditions see Haig Diary 12, 13, 14 September 1916.

[35] Miles, *1916* vol. 2, p. 290.

[36] Cecil Lewis, *Sagittarius Rising* (London: Corgi, 1969) (reprint of 1936 edition), pp. 102–3.

For this airman, the entry of the tank into the battle represented for the British a significant accretion of power. But for the troops on the ground, the 'dark lanes' where 'no shells were falling' had an altogether different significance. Except in one case, the lumbering tanks were soon out-distanced by the advancing infantry. This left the latter exposed to fire from enemy strongpoints which the tanks were supposed to conquer early in the battle. Ironically, therefore, the tanks in this phase of the action – thanks to the artillery arrangements Rawlinson had made for them – hindered rather than assisted the attempts of the British infantry to get forward.

The enemy's unsubdued machine-gunners exacted a fearful toll on the Fourth Army. On the right flank the 56, 6, and Guards divisions (XIV Corps) were attacking from Combles to Ginchy. In this sector the tanks had been directed on three important strongpoints: Bouleaux Wood, the Quadrilateral between the British front line and the German first position, and the Triangle, a series of trenches in the German front line. Consequently, gaps of 100 yards in the barrage had been left for the tanks at these points.[37] As soon as the troops of the corps began their advance murderous enfilade machine-gun fire opened on the Guards and 56 Divisions from the Quadrilateral.[38] The troops of 6 Division, which was attacking the Quadrilateral frontally, were cut down in even greater numbers.[39] Thirteen of the fifteen tanks for which the gaps in the barrage had been left failed to appear.[40] So it is not surprising that the attacks of 56 and 6 Divisions broke down completely.

On the left of XIV Corps, matters went better. The preliminary bombardment had left few of the defenders there in a condition to resist. Consequently, despite enfilade fire and the tenacity of the remaining German troops, the Guards captured the enemy front line and moved on towards the trenches protecting Lesboeufs. But at this stage their attack ran out of steam. It was now mid-morning and their battalions were much reduced in number as well as being under heavy German artillery fire. (British counter-battery fire was no more successful on 15 September than it had been on other occasions during the Somme battle.) They were also unsupported on the right due to the failure of 6 Division, and in the featureless wilderness to which the battlefield had been re-

---

[37] Amendments to XIV Corps Artillery Operation Order No. 19, 13/9/16 in Attack on Guillemont, Orders and Instructions, WO 158/419.

[38] Miles, *1916* vol. 2, pp. 309–12; C. Headlam, *History of the Guards Division in the Great War* vol. 1 (London: Murray, 1924), p. 152.

[39] T. O. Marden, *A Short History of the 6th Division, August 1914–March 1919* (London: Rees, 1920), p. 22.

[40] Miles, *1916* vol. 2, pp. 309–11.

duced they were uncertain of the whereabouts of their next objective. In these circumstances Cavan decided, with Rawlinson's concurrence, that no further attacks should be made until 56 and 6 Divisions could advance and reinforcements be sent to the Guards.[41]

In the centre, in front of Delville Wood and Longueval, the three divisions of XV Corps (14, 41, NZ) made the greatest advances of the day. Flers and some trenches beyond were overrun. It was also in this sector that the tanks proved most effective. Twelve of the seventeen allotted went into action,[42] and these effected the break-in. In the attack of 41 Division, 7 tanks arrived at the German front line two minutes ahead of the infantry. They shot up what remained of the German garrison who understandably 'showed very little fight, and mostly surrendered or fled.'[43] Two battalions of the Bavarians in fact disintegrated, over 500 prisoners being taken in the course of the morning.[44] The panic initiated by the tanks caused the German infantry to retire rapidly into Flers pursued by the troops of 41 Division (who were now somewhat in advance of the tanks). These troops found, however, that the wire protecting the trenches immediately to the south of Flers had not been cut. They waited therefore for the tanks which flattened the wire and led them into the village, in the process crushing machine-gun nests in several houses. By 10 a.m. Flers was in British hands.[45]

To the right and left of 41 Division, significant advances were also being made. On the right the tanks failed to arrive, and initially 14 Division suffered heavy casualties from unsuppressed machine-guns.[46] But then the panic which had developed among the German defenders of Flers began to spread into this sector. Consequently 14 Division was able to advance and establish contact with 41 Division to the east of Flers.[47]

On the left, the New Zealanders also had to go forward without the assistance of tanks, all of which were late. So these troops too, in the initial phase, suffered heavily from machine-gun fire, in this instance directed from High Wood.[48] Nevertheless, the preliminary bombardment in this sector had 'terribly battered and wrecked' the German defences. Further, sections of the New Zealanders were supported by a creeping

[41] 'Fourth Army Summary of Operations, 15 September, 1916', Fourth Army Papers vol. 3.

[42] Miles, *1916* vol. 2, pp. 320–1.

[43] 'Operations of 41st Division, 15/9/16', Fourth Army Papers vol. 3.

[44] *K. B. 9*, pp. 91–2.

[45] 'Operations of 41st Division, 15/9/16'.

[46] *K. B. 14*, p. 179.

[47] Miles, *1916* vol. 2, pp. 319–21.

[48] 'Operations of The New Zealand Division, 15th September, 1916', Fourth Army Papers vol. 3.

barrage to which they clung close. So, if at heavy cost, an advance was managed as far as Flers Trench to the west of the village.[49] There the attackers encountered uncut wire and were pinned down until two tanks appeared and smashed several paths through for the infantry. A further advance was then made to a line north-west of Flers village.[50] Thereby the whole of the second of the three German systems in the area around Flers passed into British hands.

No such successes attended the efforts of III Corps on the left of the British line. Tanks did assist 15 Division in capturing Martinpuich. But fire from High Wood prevented 50 and 47 Divisions from making substantial advances. This situation had largely arisen because of the obtuseness of General Pulteney, the corps commander. Pulteney, against expert advice (and it might be thought against all reason), concluded that his tanks would quickly capture High Wood 'because they will have cover all the way.'[51] Consequently the tank corridor was expanded on this section of the front to include the whole of High Wood. Not surprisingly the tanks proved quite unable to assist the attack on the wood, with the result that the infantry (47 Division) were subjected to a hail of fire from the German first line in the northern section.[52] It was not until the wood had been subjected to a heavy trench mortar bombardment and outflanked by the New Zealanders on the right and 50 Division on the left that it finally fell – two months after its intended capture on 14 July. Further advances on the flanks eventually allowed 47 Division to reach the east edge of Martinpuich and link up with the flanking divisions.[53]

It was therefore only in the centre of the Fourth Army attack, in the area around Flers, that the British had made significant progress. Yet even here there was no real prospect of further advance. The gains won by the three divisions of XV Corps had not been made without cost. The 41 Division had probably lost half its strength; 14 Division possibly not much less.[54] The New Zealand Division had suffered rather fewer casualties, but its troops were much scattered and intermixed with those

[49] Colonel H. Stewart, *The New Zealand Division 1916–1919: A Popular History Based on Historical Records* (Auckland: Whitcombe and Tombs, 1921), pp. 74–7.

[50] 'Operations of The New Zealand Division, 15th September, 1916'.

[51] 'Notes of Conference held at Heilly, 10 September, 1916', Fourth Army Papers vol. 6. Colonel Elles, a tank commander, advised against using tanks in a wood.

[52] Miles, *1916* vol. 2, pp. 332–3.

[53] Ibid., pp. 335–6.

[54] Ibid., p. 344. The official historian is curiously reticent about British casualties on 15 September, confining himself to the statement that the majority of battalions lost 300–400 men. This figure is approximately 40–50 per cent of the strength of an average battalion during this phase of the Somme battle.

of 41 Division in Flers.[55] And because of Haig's decision to place all his divisions in the front line, there were no reserves.

Other factors militated against any further advance. From around noon the German artillery, which seems to have emerged relatively unscathed from its encounter with the British counter-batteries, began to place a bombardment on Flers and the surrounding defences[56] (the range of which was of course accurately known to the Germans). Furthermore, it was clear to Rawlinson from reports received that practically all the tanks were out of action.[57] Finally, the bulk of the British artillery had not been able to advance quickly enough to subject the third German line to a systematic or accurate bombardment. The wire protecting this line was therefore intact and it was strongly held by German reserves which had begun to arrive on the battlefield from midday.[58] At 6.25 p.m. Rawlinson called off the battle for the day. He decreed that the German third line should receive a 'good' bombardment and that operations against it would be resumed on the 16th.[59]

VI

How then are we to sum up the events of 15 September? Measured against the operations of 15 July to 14 September the attack had been reasonably successful. Of the three German lines under attack on this day, the first had been captured on a front of 9,000 yards, and 4,000 yards of the second line around Flers were in British hands – a good base from which to attack the remainder of this line. Also German strongpoints such as High Wood and the Switch Line which had held up the British for over two months had fallen. At last Fourth Army had completed the capture of the Bazentin Ridge and had good observation over the rearward German positions. Finally, in the centre, the Fourth Army was well situated for an attack on the third German position.

But this last element serves to underline what the battle had not achieved. The German third line was still intact. German morale had not disintegrated. The five divisions of British cavalry remained in their billets. No promise of breakthrough beckoned.

---

[55] Stewart, *The New Zealand Division*, gives the casualties for the 15th as approximately 2,000 See pp. 82, 87.

[56] 'Operations of 41 Division, 15/9/16'.

[57] Fourth Army Telephone Messages to Advanced GHQ, 15/9/16 (4 p.m. message), GHQ War Diary September 1916, WO 95/7.

[58] Miles, *1916* vol. 2, p. 341.

[59] Fourth Army Telephone Messages to Advanced GHQ, 15/9/16 (6.25 p.m. message), GHQ War Diary September 1916, WO 95/7.

TABLE 21.1 *Casualties on 15 September on the Somme*

Division	Officers	Other ranks	Total
15	89	1765	1854
50	43	1164	1207
47			[4000]
New Zealand	80	2500	2580
41			[3000]
14			[4500]
Guards	150	4000	4150
6	100	3500	3600
56	185	4300	4485
Total			29376

The table has been compiled from various regimental histories and estimates based on the relative intensity of the fighting in which the divisions had been involved.

Further, Rawlinson's modest success had not been bought at a modest cost. Despite the coyness of the British official account on the subject of casualties, it is possible to establish a rough total for 15 September (see table 21.1).

Although in absolute terms this was but half the number of casualties sustained on 1 July, as a proportion of the force engaged (approximately 50 per cent of the attacking battalions) it was not substantially less than that suffered on the first day. Certainly the area of ground gained on 15 September was just over twice that overrun on 1 July (6 square miles as against 2¾ square miles). But this remained modest even as the reward of a bite and hold operation and insignificant in terms of the objectives to which Haig had aspired; namely, to unhinge the German defences and open the way for a great sweep by the cavalry.

The heavy casualties suffered on 15 September can, to a significant extent, be traced to two flaws in the British plan. The first was the method devised by Rawlinson to protect the tanks from his own artillery by leaving gaps in the creeping barrage. It has already been shown how this left German machine-gunners in the strongpoints free to wreak havoc among the attacking infantry. It needs to be borne in mind that the tank was a new weapon, so that methods had still to be devised for blending it into the existing weapons system. Yet so much had been learned about the crucial role of ample artillery support in any attempted infantry advance that it is difficult to find warrant for a decision which denied to the foot soldiers in these sectors the aid of a creeping barrage.

The second flaw is almost an extension of the first. Hard experience had demonstrated to the British command that it was the power of the artillery, relative to the defences it was assailing, which spelt success or failure for an attack. Yet in respect to 15 September neither commander addressed himself wholeheartedly to this matter. Rawlinson's initial plan, it is true, probably included a sufficiency of artillery. But this was hardly a consequence of design. Hence the Fourth Army commander did not employ this key consideration as a ground for resisting the much grander scheme which Haig pressed on him.

As for the commander-in-chief, he virtually eliminated the possibility of gaining a substantial success at modest cost when he insisted on spreading the artillery over two defensive zones instead of one and required both infantry and cavalry to break through a third zone which was not even within range of most British guns. This was a sure prescription for an unsubdued defence and heavy casualties among the attackers.

This leaves us with a final question concerning the rival plans put forward by Rawlinson and Haig. Does the outcome of 15 September prove one to have been clearly more appropriate than the other? Two things must be said against any notion of superior wisdom on Rawlinson's part. One, already mentioned, is his proposal to launch the tanks at night. The other is the fact that, at least at Flers, British forces did advance further than they would have done in his proposed first phase (whatever might have happened thereafter). By the same token, a large thing must be said against any notion of Haig's superior wisdom. The artillery dispersal required under Haig's plan helped to ensure that what his forces did achieve – which was not in fact much – would be bought most dearly. It is possible to believe that had Rawlinson's plan (transferred to daylight) been adopted, the Fourth Army in his first phase would have made a reasonable advance for a modest price and would then have been in a condition to repeat this transaction, thus accomplishing a better overall result at a more appropriate cost.

If this conclusion redounds somewhat to Sir Henry's credit as against Sir Douglas's, in the most crucial respect neither emerges well. For on the key matter of artillery concentration each failed to put forward the sort of considered proposal which the battle seemed to require. To say this is not to be wise after the event. The Somme battles of July and August had proved highly instructive. But neither Haig nor Rawlinson seemed to be taking their lessons to heart. The only extenuating consideration which may be suggested is that both commanders were so mesmerized by the approaching debut of the tanks that they concluded that these rendered inappropriate the lessons of previous operations. Yet it is hard to see that such optimism was warranted by what had been observed of tanks during their trials. To build on the known appeared in the circumstances a more responsible course than to essay a leap in the dark.

VII

At 8 p.m. on 15 September, Rawlinson issued his orders for the following day. They showed little appreciation of the heavy casualties suffered by his divisions, or the intermixture of units on the battlefield, or the lack of reserves, or the difficulty of organizing at short notice a systematic artillery bombardment of the German third line. So Rawlinson required an attack at 9.25 a.m. all along the line, to be 'pushed home with the utmost vigour' so as 'to enable the Cavalry Corps to push through to its objectives and complete the enemy's defeat.'[60]

The unreality of this directive hardly calls for comment. Suffice it to say that no concerted attack took place at all on the 16th. On the front of XIV Corps only the Guards attacked, Cavan considering his other divisions to be in no position to carry out Rawlinson's instructions. Events soon showed that he could well have reached this conclusion for the Guards as well. It took 3 Guards Brigade until 1.30 p.m. – some 4 hours and 5 minutes after zero – to collect and reorganize their troops. By then, it need hardly be said, the artillery barrage had long since moved on. Meanwhile rain which began to fall on the evening of the 15th had turned the ground into a quagmire. Advancing without artillery support the Guards ran into heavy German machine-gun fire from the third line. A small amount of ground of no consequence was gained at heavy loss.

Other ineffectual attacks took place on the remainder of the British front. The 64 Brigade (attached to 41 Division) missed the barrage because they started too late, 142 Brigade (47 Division) because they started too early. The New Zealanders began their attack but then cancelled it because of the obvious lack of progress on their flanks. The results of the day were small gains for inordinate losses.[61]

Rawlinson was eager to renew the attack as soon as possible, but the climate and the French intervened to frustrate him. The weather, having been unpropitious on the 16th, deteriorated on the following day. Rain, mist, and low cloud not only served to reduce the fighting capacity of the infantry but greatly inhibited the ability of the artillery to prepare for a new assault. The cloud made aerial spotting impossible and this prevented the heavy artillery from registering on the German line.[62] In addition the

---

[60] Fourth Army Operation Order 15/9/16, Fourth Army Papers vol. 8.

[61] For these operations see Miles, *1916* vol. 2, pp. 345–52.

[62] Ibid., pp. 354–5.

mud prevented many guns from being brought forward, while others that were in position sank in their gunpits.[63]

What clinched the postponement of the renewed attack was the attitude of the French. The operations of the French Sixth Army on the 15th had nowhere met with success.[64] On the 16th Fayolle declared that no new attack could be mounted until the troops and artillery in the line were relieved. After discussions between Rawlinson, Haig, and the French it was decided that operations should be postponed until 21 September when a major attack would be made on the third German line in conjunction with French operations to the south and an attempt by the Reserve Army to capture Thiepval. In the meantime attacks would be limited to those necessary to gain a good start line for the 21st.[65]

As a consequence minor operations with limited goals were substituted for hasty, ill-considered large-scale attacks. On the 18th, 6 Division finally captured the Quadrilateral. Between the 19th and the 22nd the Germans abandoned their line to the north of High Wood and fell back to a position eastwards of Martinpuich. During this time the New Zealand Division gained ground to the north of Flers.[66]

While these operations were under way plans were being made for the concerted attack on the German third position. These plans were to differ in two important respects from those for 15 September. First, the objectives were limited to the capture of one German trench system. This meant that the preliminary bombardment would be concentrated on a single German line. Second, the proposed employment of tanks was less ambitious. Tanks would not now accompany or lead the infantry assault. They would be held back to assist in the capture of Morval and Lesboeufs villages[67] after the trench system had fallen. Consequently, along the front of attack the creeping barrage would once again be providing uninterrupted protection for the infantry.

It is clear, however, that this altered role for the tanks, with its happy consequence *vis-à-vis* the creeping barrage, did not result from any reappraisal of the tank tactics employed on 15 September. Rather, the French were insisting on an afternoon attack in order to have several hours of daylight in which better to observe their bombardment.[68] Rawlinson considered that it would be impossible to conceal the tanks close to the front line from dawn until zero hour at 12.35 p.m. They would therefore

[63] Stewart, *The New Zealand Division*, p. 90.

[64] Miles, *1916* vol. 2, p. 348.

[65] Fourth Army Conference 17/9/16, Fourth Army Papers vol. 6.

[66] For these operations see Miles, *1916* vol. 2, pp. 356–60.

[67] Fourth Army Conference 19/9/16, Fourth Army Papers vol. 6.

[68] Miles, *1916* vol. 2, p. 370.

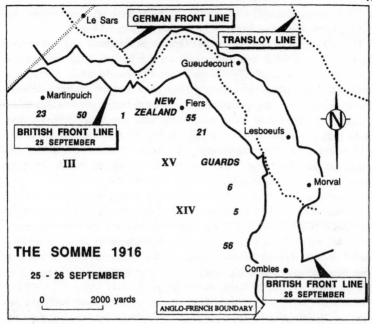

GERMAN FRONT LINE

TRANSLOY LINE

Le Sars

Gueudecourt •

Martinpuich •

NEW
ZEALAND • Flers

BRITISH FRONT LINE
25 SEPTEMBER

23   50   1   55

21   Lesboeufs •

III   XV   GUARDS

6

XIV   5

THE SOMME 1916   56

Combles •

25 - 26 SEPTEMBER

BRITISH FRONT LINE
26 SEPTEMBER

0   2000 yards

ANGLO-FRENCH BOUNDARY

Morval •

MAP 23

have to be kept well back in reserve and then employed to capture the villages in a later phase of the battle.[69]

Bad weather delayed the attack until the 25th and the preliminary bombardment opened on the morning of the 24th. Its power was formidable. In two days the British threw approximately 400,000 shells weighing about 7.5 million pounds into not more than 18,000 yards of trench.[70] The bombardment therefore achieved a concentration of about 400 lb. of shell for every yard of trench attacked. This was 40 per cent heavier than the bombardment of 15 September. As for the defences which received this weight of shell, they were more rudimentary than either the first or second German trench systems of 15 September. Compared with these, the German third system had shallower trenches and thinner wire. In

---

[69] Fourth Army Conference 19/9/16.

[70] Somme Artillery Notes and Statistics, Table C. This table gives the number of shells used. The weight of shell devoted to trench destruction is based on the figure for 15 September and adjusted for the lesser number of shells. The length of trench attacked has been calculated by the usual method.

addition the incessant British attacks since the 15th and the weather had prevented the Germans from strengthening their third line.

The operations of late September (known as the battle of Morval) were the most successful British operations on the Somme since 14 July. On the right the attack of XIV Corps 'went like clockwork.'[71] The troops advanced close behind the creeping barrage to find the German defences largely flattened by the preliminary bombardment. In some cases whole German battalions had been practically annihilated and the survivors either retired rapidly or surrendered. By late afternoon – and in advance of any intervention the tanks might have made – the entire German third system on the front of XIV Corps as well as the villages of Lesboeufs and Morval were in British hands.

Similar success attended the attack of XV Corps on the left. Here, a trench line to the west of Gueudecourt was captured. That village, however, did not fall on the 25th. Opposite Gueudecourt the attacking troops ran into belts of uncut wire. Nor had the bombardment seriously touched Gird Support Trench to the south of the village.[72] Repeated attacks were beaten back and it was eventually decided that a fresh assault on Gueudecourt must be mounted on the 26th.[73]

No tanks played a significant role on the 25th. In most cases the advance had been too swift for them to be brought into action. On the 26th, however, a single tank in co-operation with the infantry captured Gird Support Trench forcing the surrender of 370 enemy troops. It transpired that these prisoners were the sole defenders of Gueudecourt. The village was found to be unoccupied when patrols entered it in the afternoon.

To the south, the last of the fortified villages near the German third line fell without a blow. The advance on the 25th had placed Combles in jeopardy from the north and south. So on the 26th the Germans evacuated it. The objectives which Haig had laid down for the operation of 15 September had now been attained.

VIII

Did this mean that the next phase of the 15 September plan could now be put into effect: that open country lay ahead and Rawlinson's cavalry might be sent in? Predictably enough, this was not the case. While the battles were in full swing, air reconnaissance had revealed the existence

---

[71] XIV Corps, Progress of Operations: Out-Going Wires 25/9/16, XIV Corps War Diary Sept–Dec 1916, WO 95/911.

[72] For these operations see Miles, *1916* vol. 2, pp. 376–80.

[73] Fourth Army Operation Orders 25/9/16, Fourth Army Papers vol. 3.

of a strong fourth German line between Thilloy and Le Transloy. Moreover, work had commenced on a fifth line in front of Bapaume and a sixth three miles further back. These lines too would have to be overrun before action by the cavalry could be contemplated.[74]

The question to be considered by Rawlinson was whether, given the rains of late September, time remained to mount a fresh series of attacks before the campaigning season for the year came to an end.

The events of 25–26 September, taken in conjunction with those of 15 September, place beyond doubt what held the key to a successful advance on the Western Front – anyway at this stage of the war. Most accounts miss this crucial point as a result of being mesmerized by the debut of the tank. They divide between those who argue that the new weapon was used ill and so achieved less than its potential, and those who believe that it was used as well as circumstances (and numbers) allowed. Both accounts overlook the fact that tanks, particularly in the small numbers available in 1916, lacked the capacity seriously to affect the course of events. Useful though the tank might prove as an ancillary weapon, it could neither spearhead an attack nor punch such a hole in the enemy line as to open the way for a major advance. Least of all was it any sort of substitute for the artillery.

As ever, artillery was the key element in accounting for the successes and failures of middle to late September. To succeed, the objectives of an advance must lie within artillery range, the movement of infantry and tanks must conform to artillery action, and the quantities of shells employed must approximate the intensity of 14 July. Foot soldiers denied ample artillery protection would gain little or nothing and sustain inordinate loss. The cavalry could play no part in all this.

Saying this may induce a sense of *déjà vu*, traceable to events as far back as March 1915. Certainly the Somme campaign was unveiling an important artillery development with the emergence of the creeping barrage, and disclosing a promising ancillary weapon in the form of the tank. Yet overall it was reaffirming the message which Neuve Chapelle had brought home to Rawlinson. The one hopeful course of action was bite and hold; that is, advance limited to the range of the artillery. The question still remained whether the British command was prepared to base its operations on so circumscribed a method.

---

[74] See Miles, *1916* vol. 2, pp. 382–4; Jones, *War in the Air* vol. 2, pp. 285–7.

22

Mud and Muddle, October–November

I

The capture of a substantial portion of the German third line in late September appeared to Sir Douglas Haig the prelude to great events. The defences facing his troops were clearly of a lesser strength than those already captured. The enemy was in some disarray. Grandiose plans began at GHQ to convert disarray into rout. On 29 September these plans were communicated to Rawlinson. He was informed that Fourth Army operations were to be part of a general attack by all British forces south of Gommecourt. So the Reserve Army was to capture the remainder of the Thiepval Spur, Serre, and Beaumont Hamel, while Third Army on the left secured the high ground to the east of Gommecourt. The Fourth Army, meanwhile, should first aim for the Transloy Line and then go on to capture the ridge near Beaumetz, Marcoing, and Cambrai.[1]

It would be interesting to know Rawlinson's response to these orders. Perhaps it was to call for a bigger map. For the place names mentioned by Haig did not appear on any of the operational maps then in use by the Fourth Army. Beaumetz was in fact located 8 miles to the east of Flers, Marcoing was a further 8 miles distant, and Cambrai was 4 miles north-east of Marcoing. Thus Haig was postulating an advance of 20 miles, five times the distance so far achieved by the Fourth Army in a campaign of three months.

Whatever Rawlinson's private thoughts about advancing on Cambrai, his response to these instructions was to plan an attack to fulfil the first part of GHQ's orders; that is, the capture of the Transloy Line. Initially this task must have seemed a reasonable prospect. On 1 October Fourth

[1] Miles, *1916* vol. 2, p. 427; Haig Diary 1/10/16.

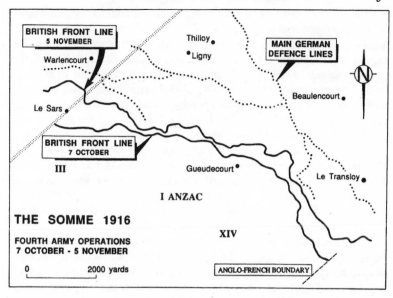

BRITISH FRONT LINE
5 NOVEMBER

Thilloy

Ligny

MAIN GERMAN
DEFENCE LINES

Warlencourt

Beaulencourt

Le Sars

BRITISH FRONT LINE
7 OCTOBER

III

Gueudecourt

Le Transloy

I ANZAC

THE SOMME 1916

XIV

FOURTH ARMY OPERATIONS
7 OCTOBER - 5 NOVEMBER

0   2000 yards

ANGLO-FRENCH BOUNDARY

MAP 24

Army, on the left of their line, made what in Somme terms was a considerable advance to the east of Le Sars.[2] German opposition seemed to be weakening.

But late that same day rain began to fall. It continued for the next four days. The whole battle area quickly turned into a sea of mud. Air observation for the artillery became impossible. The operation had to be postponed first to the 6th and then to the 7th. Rawlinson was doubtful whether the operation should be launched at all, characterizing an attack in which his air and artillery superiority could not be utilized as 'suicidal'.[3] Improving weather on the 6th and, no doubt, pressure from Haig – who informed Rawlinson on this day that he intended to keep on attacking all through the winter – reluctantly convinced the Fourth Army commander that the attack should be 'risked' on the 7th.[4]

The course of the battle confirmed Rawlinson's misgivings. Except for the capture of Le Sars on the left, no significant gains were made. By the end of the day four of the six attacking divisions were back in their own trenches.[5]

[2] Miles, *1916* vol. 2, pp. 429–31.
[3] Rawlinson Diary 5/10/16.
[4] Ibid. 6/10/16.
[5] Miles, *1916* vol. 2, pp. 434–8.

Four factors, three of which were quickly identified by Rawlinson, occasioned this defeat on 7 October. The first, of course, was the weather. Mud was now making any infantry attack a hazardous experience, for in the mire it was impossible to maintain a steady advance close behind the creeping barrage. Even more disastrous was the effect of poor visibility on artillery support for the infantry. The lack of aerial spotting had rendered ineffective much of the preliminary bombardment. Therefore the attacking troops, as they struggled through the mire, encountered uncut wire, unsubdued defenders, and heavy German artillery fire.

A second factor compounded the problems created by the weather. Having completed the seizure of the Martinpuich–Morval Ridge on 15 September, Fourth Army was now advancing on to the lower slopes of a valley. Its artillery had thereby lost the advantage of observation over the German lines. The enemy from the rising ground on either side of Bapaume once more overlooked the British positions.

The third factor concerned the Germans. As Rawlinson pointed out to Kiggell soon after the battle, the 'fighting qualities' of the troops opposed to Fourth Army seemed to have improved.[6] What Rawlinson was observing was the passing of the crisis which had overtaken the Germans in late September. The British success from the 25th to the 27th had left the German First Army holding the line between Le Transloy and Warlencourt with six understrength divisions. And such reinforcing battalions as became available to the German command were fed into the battle piecemeal. The result was a jumble of intermixed units which militated against a coherent defence. In addition the German trench lines were weak, often without wire, and with few dugouts.[7] This was the 'disarray' identified by Fourth Army Intelligence officers on which Haig had pinned his hopes for a breakthrough.[8] But by the time the British were ready to attack, the circumstances of the enemy had much improved. Between 30 September and 13 October the six exhausted divisions between Le Transloy and the Ancre were replaced by seven divisions taken from the general reserve and from quiet sections of the front.[9] Further, by 8 October the artillery resources of the German First Army had increased by 23 heavy batteries while 36 worn-out batteries had been replaced.[10] It was contingents of these fresh troops with their enhanced artillery that halted Rawlinson's attack on 7 October.

[6] For Rawlinson's observations see his diary for 9 and 12 October 1916.

[7] *Der Weltkreig* vol. 11 (Berlin: Mittler, 1938), pp. 80–1.

[8] Fourth Army Precis of Operations and Intelligence October 1st – October 15th, 1916, Fourth Army Intelligence Summaries 20 Aug/16 Nov 1916, Fourth Army Papers vol. 9.

[9] *Der Weltkreig* vol. 11, pp. 80–1.

[10] Miles, *1916* vol. 2, p. 455.

The fourth factor concerned a change in German defensive tactics. British operations on 15 and 25 September had amply demonstrated to the Germans the devastating effect of the creeping barrage – especially on the machine-gunners placed between the trench lines. So for the October battles the Germans withdrew their machine-guns to positions still just within range of the British front line but beyond the area on which the creeping barrage usually fell.[11] Thus on 7 October the German machine-gunners entirely escaped the effect of the creeping barrage and were able to inflict heavy loss by means of long-range fire on the attacking troops. In spite of its significance for the British, this change in German tactics was not identified in any of the battle reports concerning 7 October.[12] Rawlinson's next operation would be launched in ignorance of this new peril.

The timing of that attack was again decided by the weather. Rain on the 8th and 9th was followed by two dull but fine days on the 10th and 11th. Despite the fact that low cloud again prevented aerial observation for the artillery, five divisions of the Fourth Army attacked on 12 October.[13] Their objectives were the same as those on the 7th.[14] The results were also the same. Hardly a yard of ground was gained.

This second failure to take the Transloy Line led to much soul-searching at Fourth Army Headquarters. On the 13th Rawlinson called a conference of corps commanders to discuss the causes of failure and possible remedies. The improved quality of the German troops and the effect of the weather in hampering artillery support for Rawlinson's forces were again identified as major factors in the defeat. But on this occasion the effect of machine-gun fire 'beyond our first objective and therefore out of our barrage zone' was also noted.[15] The conference concluded that in future they must wait for 'good aerial observation' in order to secure a 'proper bombardment' and that the distant machine-gun fire must be dealt with by extending the creeping barrage and/or by firing a smoke barrage beyond the objectives of the attack.

The conference also decided that the next major attack would take place on 18 October. In order to drive home the decisions which had been reached, Rawlinson stressed in his orders to his corps commanders the need to subdue the distant German machine-guns: 'In regulating the

---

[11] 'Notes on Conference held at Heilly at 3 pm on the 13th October 1916', AWM 45, Bundle 31.

[12] Fourth Army, 'Summary of Operations, 7th October, 1916', Fourth Army War Diary 1 Oct/16 Nov 1916, Fourth Army Papers vol. 4.

[13] Haig Diary 14/10/16.

[14] Fourth Army Operation Order 8/10/16, Fourth Army Papers vol. 4.

[15] Notes on conference at Heilly 13/10/16.

details of the barrage, Corps must consider the importance of dealing with machine guns in rear, or to the flanks, of the objectives.'[16]

The attack duly went ahead on the 18th. It was a complete failure. The bombardment had largely missed the German defences, the British counter-batteries had failed to locate the enemy artillery, and the attacking troops suffered heavily from long-range machine-gun fire.

What had gone wrong? The main explanation is depressingly familiar. On the 18th the British used exactly those methods which had failed on the 7th and 12th. In not one instance were the recommendations made by Rawlinson's conference on the 13th implemented. No smoke barrage was fired, the creeping barrage was not extended to the rearmost German areas, and good conditions for aerial observation had not been present in the days before the attack. Why had the higher echelons of the Fourth Army ignored the recommendations of their own conference?

In the matter of smoke shells there is a simple explanation: it was not a feasible recommendation. Smoke shell was still in the experimental stage. Small quantities existed but nothing like the amount needed to blanket, for a considerable period, a large area behind the German front.

There is no firm evidence to account for the failure to extend the creeping barrage as far as the German machine-guns. Three speculations, however, may be offered. First, the Fourth Army may have lacked the quantity of ammunition required to fire a creeping barrage beyond the first objective. Second, enough ammunition may have existed at the depots but conditions on the battlefield prevented it from reaching the guns. Some evidence to support this speculation exists in Rawlinson's diary. On 13 October he wrote: 'I am anxious about getting Artillery ammunition. If rain comes we shall be in difficulties until our Decauville [light] railways are through which will not be until the 20th.'[17] A third explanation is that the corps commanders chose to ignore Rawlinson's artillery instructions – either because there was insufficient time to develop a new artillery plan or because they failed to understand the importance of the new German tactics.

What of Rawlinson's decision to launch the attack after a period of poor weather (there was only one clear day between the 12th and the 18th), given that the conference had decided that no attacks should take place without a prolonged period of aerial spotting? The most probable explanation is quite simple: yet again Rawlinson was bowing to Haig's well-known wish to prosecute the offensive.

---

[16] Fourth Army Operation Order 13/10/16, Fourth Army Operation Orders and Instructions 1 Oct/16 Nov 1916, Fourth Army Papers vol. 8.

[17] Rawlinson Diary 13/10/16.

II

By now it should have been obvious even to Haig that he lacked clear means to overcome the obstacles confronting his forces. Only long spells of fine weather (a remote prospect in the second half of October) would enable the artillery to neutralize or destroy the German defences to an extent which would allow the infantry to get forward. The new German defensive tactics could only be countered by large quantities of ammunition, which either were not available or could not be brought up to the front because of the weather. That is, the conditions for even a minor success were not present on the Fourth Army's front.

Unfortunately for their troops, neither Haig nor Rawlinson drew these conclusions. Haig claimed that as long as the French continued to attack, it was the duty of Fourth Army to provide flank protection.[18] A more important consideration, pretty clearly, was his reluctance to halt the battle without having obtained even the objectives designated for capture on the first day.

Rawlinson's reasons for wanting the battle to continue were more prosaic. In carrying out the orders of the British command at great cost to themselves, his troops had fought their way to the bottom of a low-lying valley. Rawlinson came to the unremarkable conclusion that 'to remain for the Winter in this position' was 'most undesirable'.[19] But thereby he begged an important question. Undesirable it might be to remain on low ground throughout the winter. But did the British command have it within its power to improve this position? That Rawlinson, after the experiences of 7, 12, and 18 October, could without deep reflection or detailed exposition answer in the affirmative constitutes a heavy indictment of his competence. Yet this was the answer he came to, thereby committing the hapless Fourth Army to another series of attacks.

The results of those operations can quickly be summarized. The Fourth Army attacked the Transloy Line on three occasions in late October, on the 23rd, 28th and 29th. Not a yard of ground was gained. Nor did these endeavours prove of any worth in assisting the French to get forward.

The prospects for future operations were now extremely bleak. Incessant rain had turned the battlefield into a quagmire. Only with the greatest difficulty could ammunition for the guns and food and water for the troops reach the front. The mud confined all traffic supplying the Fourth Army to a single narrow road from Longueval to Flers. The German artillery soon became aware of this. So every two minutes the road

[18] Miles, *1916* vol. 2, p. 458.
[19] 'Conference at Heilly 18/10/16', Fourth Army Papers vol. 6.

in the vicinity of Flers was the recipient of a salvo of 5.9 inch shells.[20]

The consequent conditions for the troops in the front line were laid bare by a GHQ staff officer, Lord Gort. (By 1940 he was the commander of the British army.) After a visit to the front Gort passed on to Haig a number of comments. These describe men 'living on cold food and standing up to their knees in mud and water', afflicted by trench foot and in too poor a physical condition successfully to conduct an attack. Those moving up to the front were reduced to 'a state of physical exhaustion in a very short time' by the condition of the road. And so all-encompassing was the mud that troops making an attack had to 'help each other out of the fire trenches as they cannot get out unaided.'[21] Another source described attacking infantry as not only unable to keep up with their own creeping barrage but as being reduced to almost stationary targets in no-man's-land for the enemy machine-gunners.[22]

Haig, notwithstanding, was determined to maintain the offensive. For 5 November he ordered what would be the seventh British attack on the Transloy Line, even giving Rawlinson objectives beyond that point: 'I told him that when Le Transloy is captured, arrangements must be made to push on at once to Beaulencourt in co-operation with the French. The XIV Corps had only planned to take Le Transloy.'[23]

The revelation that even the capture of Le Transloy would not end the ordeal of the troops provoked a minor revolt – not, it should be noted, from Rawlinson but from the corps commander responsible for carrying out the attack. Lord Cavan, the commander of XIV Corps, wrote to Rawlinson in terms not often employed to their superiors among high-ranking officers on the Western Front:

> With a full and complete sense of my responsibility I feel it my bounden duty to put in writing my considered opinion as to the attack ordered to take place on Nov 5th . . .
> An advance [on Le Transloy] from my present position with the troops at my disposal has practically no chance of success on account of the heavy enfilade fire of machine guns and artillery from the north, and the enormous distance we have to advance against a strongly prepared position, owing to the failure to advance our line in the recent operations . . .

[20] Captain R. O. Russell, *The History of the 11th (Lewisham) Battalion, The Queens Own, Royal West Kent Regiment* (London: Lewisham Newspaper Company, 1934), p. 78.

[21] 'Report by Major Gort 3/11/16', AWM 45, Bundle 31.

[22] Lt.-Col. J. H. Boraston and Captn. Cyril E. O. Bax, *The Eighth Division in War, 1914–1918* (London: Medici Society, 1926), pp. 87–8.

[23] Haig Diary 22/10/16.

I perfectly acknowledge the necessity of not leaving the French left in the air [and] ... I assert my readiness to sacrifice the British right rather than jeopardise the French ... but I feel that I am bound to ask if this is the intention, for a sacrifice it must be. It does not appear that a failure would much assist the French, and there is a danger of this attack shaking the confidence of the men and officers in their commanders.

No one who has not visited the front trenches can really know the state of exhaustion to which the men are reduced.[24]

Even this missive, with its suggestion that the higher command were neglecting to acquaint themselves with the situation at the front, did not alter the determination of Haig and Rawlinson. In reply to Cavan, Rawlinson emphasized 'the importance of meeting our obligations with the French.' And he insisted that a minor attack scheduled for later that day (3 November) should be allowed to proceed as it 'would form a useful test of what might be expected to be accomplished on the 5th.'[25]

The attack on the afternoon of the 3rd did indeed prove a 'useful test': it accomplished nothing at all. Rawlinson was not deterred. He concluded that the cause of failure was a want of vigour on the part of XIV Corps headquarters, and he decreed that the attack on the 5th would proceed as planned. Cavan, however, was not yet ready to submit. He insisted that he would not attack until Rawlinson had seen conditions at the front for himself.[26] Cavan won his point. As he later recalled, after viewing the front line 'R was equally convinced ... that an attack was impossible.'[27] And Rawlinson was able to persuade Haig that operations to assist the French should be scaled down to trench raids and artillery support.[28]

Yet in the event, Cavan's commendable display of plain speaking availed his forces nothing. After an interview with Foch, Haig reversed his decision. The operation on the 5th was to go ahead after all.[29] The Fourth Army was thus committed to the attack of 5 November despite the advice of the Army commander and the corps commander whose task it was to carry it out. To make matters worse, the plan promulgated by Haig made no tactical sense. The XIV Corps were ordered to mount two attacks by widely separated formations. This allowed the Germans in the intervening ground

---

[24] Cavan to Rawlinson 3/11/16, AWM 45, Bundle 31.

[25] Haig to Rawlinson (OAD 205). This is an untitled, undated document summarizing letters relating to the attack on 5 November in Fourth Army Papers vol. 5.

[26] Rawlinson Diary 3/11/16.

[27] Cavan to Edmonds 9/4/36, Official History Correspondence: Somme, Cab 45/132.

[28] Haig to Rawlinson (OAD 205).

[29] Ibid.

to bring to bear devastating enfilade machine-gun fire on the hapless troops. That is, Haig was requiring a repetition of precisely that type of attack which had caused him, two months previously, to warn Rawlinson that 'something was wanting in the methods employed.' The operation failed at a cost of 2,000 casualties.[30]

III

The British had now assailed the Transloy Line on seven occasions. They had been defeated by the weather, the new German tactics, and the ineptitude of their own plans. It does no credit to the British command that yet more assaults would have been attempted had not a new factor intervened. This was manpower. Since mid-September Rawlinson had been complaining of a shortage of fresh troops. GHQ in response had usually managed to scrape together one or two divisions from other sectors of the front. By the beginning of October that process was exhausted. Since July all 51 British divisions on the Western Front had fought on the Somme. By October British infantry strength had fallen from 689,000 to 576,000. These losses could not immediately be made good. The depots and base camps contained only 23,000 men. The implications of this manpower shortage for Rawlinson's divisions were serious. First, units too long in the line could not be replaced by fresh divisions from reserve. Second, his understrength battalions (reduced from a nominal 800 to 350) could not be replenished.[31]

This situation would have been bad enough for troops just holding the line. But Rawlinson's forces were repeatedly engaged in delivering ill-rewarded attacks. And, as their commander was beginning to realize, his operations were taking a disproportionately heavy toll of those men he could least afford to lose – officers and various specialists (for example, Lewis gunners). These men were needed to train the new drafts expected early in 1917. Rawlinson made these points forcefully in a memorandum to Haig which concluded:

> It is, therefore, in my opinion, most desirable to strictly limit our offensive operations to those necessary for improving [the] position of our front system and not to engage in any extended enterprises which do not fulfil this purpose. Otherwise there is a grave risk that

---

[30] C. E. W. Bean, *The Australian Imperial Force in France 1916* (Sydney: Angus and Robertson, 1939), p. 915. Bean estimates the casualties suffered by the Australians as 819 and those of 50 Division as 700. We have estimated the casualties of 33 Division as about 500.

[31] Miles, *1916* vol. 2, p. 536.

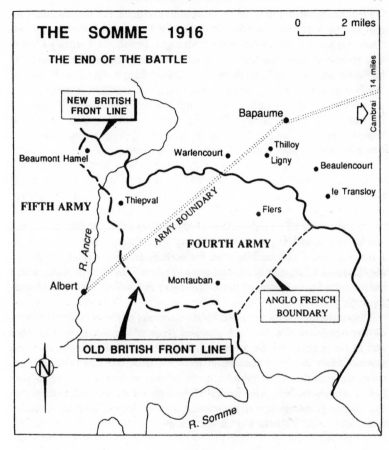

MAP 25

by attempting too much during the Winter we may fail in matters of far greater importance next Spring.[32]

Rawlinson's letter arrived at GHQ at an opportune moment. Since the beginning of the month Haig had been preparing for an inter-Allied conference at Chantilly, the purpose of which was to discuss the 1917 spring offensive. Here was a powerful warning that, unless the battle of the Somme was stopped, at least one of his Armies would be in no state to participate.

[32] Rawlinson to GHQ 7/11/16, Fourth Army Papers vol. 5.

Haig hesitated. He wanted to be able to maximize the British contribution on the Western Front in 1917. But he had no wish for the Somme campaign to terminate with the futile struggles before the Transloy Line. It was Hubert Gough, commander of what had been the Reserve Army but had now become the Fifth Army, who solved Haig's dilemma. In a well-planned operation on 13 November, carried out over firm ground and in the absence of supply difficulties, Gough captured Beaumont Hamel and the remainder of the Thiepval–Ginchy Ridge.[33] Three days later Haig brought the battle of the Somme to an end. He could now proceed to Chantilly with at least a minor success to his credit.

IV

So it transpired that at the close of the battle, after all, Rawlinson had not needed those larger maps detailing the whereabouts of Beaumetz, Marcoing, and Cambrai. Not even his preliminary objective of 1 October, the Transloy Line, had been vouchsafed to him. The Fourth Army would indeed spend the abysmal winter of 1916–17 in a valley, not on commanding high ground.

Responsibility for the lamentable last six weeks of the Somme campaign, during which the Fourth Army attacked repeatedly in hopeless conditions and to no effect, rests far more with Haig than with Rawlinson. But this was not likely to rescue Rawlinson from the disfavour into which he had fallen on account of his misadventures in August and reluctance to plan boldly in September. Nor would Haig forget that the only success in the barren period between 1 October and 15 November had been accomplished not by Rawlinson but by Gough.

---

[33] See Miles, *1916* vol. 2, chapter XVIII.

PART V

LIMBO AND RETURN

23

On the Sidelines,
January 1917–January 1918

I

The year 1917 started well for Sir Henry Rawlinson. It opened with his promotion – 'well deserved' according to Lord Derby, the new Secretary of State for War – to full general. 'I could not tell you before', Derby wrote (with an excess of negatives), 'but there was never any question of your not getting it.'[1] Rawlinson took considerable satisfaction. In his diary for 1 January he observed that he was alone in being promoted to the rank of general, and that this placed him over the heads of practically all the Lieutenant-Generals; he was now next in the list below Wully Robertson. 'From Capt. to Full Genl in 17 years is not bad going after being in 3 Form at Eton too[;] so there is hope for every one.'[2]

Almost as gratifying, at the year's turning Rawlinson became the subject of favourable attention from the Press.[3] The cause of it was Haig's 'great despatch' on the Somme campaign. In it Rawlinson figured as 'the hero' (*Yorkshire Evening News*), as 'a genius of the Somme battle' (*Daily Despatch*), and as 'Haig's Right-Hand man' (*The Graphic*). The *Pall Mall Gazette*, in a piece that singled out for attention the night attack of 14 July, wrote of 'The Rise of Rawlinson', while *Town Topics* related 'The Triumph of Rawlinson', who had outlived 'the extraordinary unjust impression created about him.' Several other journals took the latter line, commenting on Rawlinson's recovery (with Haig's and Kitchener's support) from the adversity of Sir John French's publicly expressed disapproval. According to the *Daily Sketch*, should the full story ever see the light of how Haig

---

[1] Derby to Rawlinson 29/12/16, Rawlinson Papers 5201/33/38, NAM.
[2] Rawlinson Diary 1/1/17.
[3] Rawlinson's file of press cuttings is in NAM 5201/33/38–42.

insisted on giving Rawlinson his chance, it would make a curious tale: 'for Sir Henry has had to make headway in face not only of the enemy, but of a strange deprecation in some unexpected quarters.' The completeness of Rawlinson's triumph seemed not in doubt. 'Today', opined the *Sunday Herald* in the aftermath of the Somme despatch, 'Sir Henry Rawlinson's name is in the mouths of all men.'

Nothing that followed for Rawlinson during 1917 fulfilled the promise of this happy opening. Before long he would be writing about the Cinderella role assigned to his Army. And as the year progressed he must have felt a good deal of a Cinderella figure himself. In part, this was because, during the first half of 1917, the ordering of British strategy passed out of the hands of Sir Douglas Haig. It became instead the brainchild of Britain's new prime minister. It so happened that Lloyd George did not hold British military commanders in high regard; a rule to which Rawlinson was no exception. (Back in June 1916, while Lloyd George was in the process of succeeding Kitchener at the War Office, he had spoken disparagingly of Rawlinson. In private conversations with C. P. Scott, editor of the liberal *Manchester Guardian*, Lloyd George had attributed Rawlinson's promotions – 'after repeated failures' – to 'personal and professional favouritism'. And he claimed that it was 'currently said in the army that every time he ['old Rawly'] lost an engagement he received a step in promotion. He only had to lose one more in order to be Commander-in-Chief.')[4]

Lloyd George's ascendancy over Haig was not the only factor that took Rawlinson out of the limelight in 1917. As it happened, Haig proved less than committed to viewing Rawlinson as the 'genius of the Somme battle' and his 'Right-Hand man'. He may well have been aware that, with Lloyd George now his ultimate master, he himself would not necessarily survive too many 'triumphs' of the Somme ilk. Certainly, for this or another reason, he kept open the question of which among his Army commanders would direct the next major campaign he was to devise. Rawlinson – possibly misled by Haig – was to prove slow to recognize this fact.

II

Had there been no change in the French high command at the start of 1917, Rawlinson's forces would have been fully occupied once the campaigning season began. Haig and Joffre had devised plans for a continuation in the spring of the Somme campaign, but on an extended front and with a

---

[4] C. P. Scott's Diary for 6–8 June and 13–17 June 1916, in Trevor Wilson (ed.), *The Political Diaries of C. P. Scott 1911–1928* (London: Collins, 1970), pp. 217, 219.

quiescent sector in the centre. This would have given Rawlinson the opportunity to continue what was deemed the good work of his 1916 operations, although with a diminished role for Fourth Army compared with the part to be played by the Fifth and Third Armies on its left.

But Joffre was ousted in December 1916. His successor, Nivelle, put forward a different plan of campaign which received the immediate endorsement of Lloyd George. It reserved the main offensive operations for the French forces in the Champagne. And although it contained a British component, this did not include the Fourth Army. In Rawlinson's area, the British were to take over additional miles of front from the French, thereby stretching Fourth Army so thin that it lost any offensive capacity. The attacking role for the British was assigned to the Fifth, Third, and First Armies, in particular to Allenby's Third Army and the Canadian divisions of First Army. Rawlinson was required to do only two things. He was to take over the sector of the front connecting Fifth Army on his left with the French forces on his right. And, as those forces went onto the offensive, Fourth Army was to deliver with its diminished artillery resources a bombardment which it was hoped would convince the enemy that an attack was imminent on this sector also. It was this minor participation which caused Rawlinson to write of the Cinderella role assigned to his Army.

If decisions by the new Allied leadership early in 1917 required no forward movement on Rawlinson's front, action by the Germans soon did. In late February the enemy facing Fifth Army began a large retirement, and in mid-March they commenced falling back an even further distance on Fourth Army's front. Rawlinson makes his first diary reference to this development late in February. He suspected a German trap. The enemy might be falling back over territory to which they had first laid waste so as to lure the British forward into a communications desert. Then, from a most advantageous position, they would round on their pursuers. As during the ensuing weeks the German retreat proceeded without regard to the British response, Rawlinson came to appreciate that they were not laying a trap. The enemy really were abandoning territory which they had managed to deny the British army during the Somme offensive, with their possible stopping point the Hindenburg Line – a truly formidable defensive system which they were in the process of constructing.

Nevertheless, Rawlinson saw the prospect of a German retreat on his sector as holding out dangers as well as opportunities. The enemy were first devastating the ground over which they were retreating, so providing any pursuers with severe communication and supply problems. Rawlinson concluded that the Germans might well launch a big counterattack from the Hindenburg Line, expecting to find the advancing British forces both in a disorganized state and without sufficient food and ammunition. He

determined therefore to keep touch with the retreating enemy only with
advance guards and cavalry, whose task it would be to cover the construction
by his forces of roads and railways. He would retain his existing front line
as his main line of resistance and only send his principal body of troops
forward when a new strong position had been provided for them. In the
first instance this position would be the line of the River Somme, where it
ran parallel to his front, and the Canal du Nord where it extended in the
same direction.[5]

It has been suggested that, by his display of caution, Rawlinson lost an
opportunity to fall upon a retreating enemy in open country. Yet there is
little substance to this. It took the main body of German troops only two to
three days of marching to reach the security of their prepared defences.
Hence all that was offering for the British to fall upon were 'strong rear
guards'. The latter had behind them sound communications, something
bound to be denied to any Fourth Army forces attempting a rapid pursuit.
And on much of Rawlinson's front the enemy had the advantage that they
were falling back across the River Somme and destroying the bridges as
they went. This placed a hasty pursuit – or indeed any sort of pursuit as
distinct from a methodical advance over empty territory – out of the
question for much of Rawlinson's Army.

A report by Fourth Army's General Staff reveals how constricted were
the opportunities offered by the episode of the German withdrawal.[6] The
report firmly maintained that the enemy's retirement was the fruit of Allied
action: that it was the product of the offensive on the Somme in the
summer and autumn of 1916 and the pressure maintained in the ensuing
winter. Yet the report found it necessary to stress that the enemy 'was
unbroken and was making a long and carefully prepared and very deliberate
retirement... There was no question of pursuing a demoralised enemy.'

The Fourth Army, according to this report, had ample warning of the
coming withdrawal and time to make preliminary arrangements for the
advance. But it was hampered by bad weather, by lack of labour to repair
roads and railways, and by a shortage of transport 'aggravated by a deficiency of nearly 6,000 horses in the Army.' In these circumstances the
policy of the Army commander had been to 'advance by bounds from one
line of resistance to another', so as to eliminate the danger of a successful
counterattack by the enemy and to ensure supplies for the advanced troops.

By 9 April the Fourth Army, with its heavy artillery and – at long range –
some of its field artillery, was within shelling distance of the Hindenburg
Line. So its guns were able to make their meagre diversionary contribution

[5] For these points see Captain Cyril Falls, *Military Operations France and Belgium, 1917* vol. 1
(London: Macmillan, 1940).
[6] Fourth Army, 'Notes on Recent Operations' n.d., AWM 26/10/179/22.

to the battle of Arras being launched further north in support of Nivelle's offensive. As for the period of unplanned advance in the open, it was now at an end; and the counter-strike by the Germans from the fastness of the Hindenburg Line, anticipated by Rawlinson, did not occur. Consequently a period of relative quiescence settled upon Rawlinson's front.

III

Exclusion from an active part in the British contribution to Nivelle's offensive in April and May 1917 may have been a disappointment to Rawlinson, but it would prove no great deprivation. For Nivelle's offensive itself failed decisively. And although Haig's supporting attack at Arras enjoyed some early success, overall it developed into a sorry business. An initial advance – including the capture of Vimy Ridge – was followed by a protracted and ill-rewarded slogging match at heavy cost in British lives.

Far greater disappointment than inactivity during the Nivelle episode was at hand for Rawlinson. It had been understood all along that Haig had a preferred option to the attack out of Arras. He hankered after a great campaign in Flanders. It was to be launched north-east from the Ypres salient, driving towards the sea and rolling up the enemy's flank along the Belgian coast. For the first part of 1917, Haig had been forced to forgo this scheme on account of his government's decision to back Nivelle. But he had stipulated that should Nivelle's enterprise fall short of expectations, then his own operation in the north would supplant it.

From an early stage Rawlinson was confident that, should the Ypres campaign materialize, he would have charge of it. On 27 January he recorded in his diary an account of a conference between Haig and his Army commanders. Haig had expressed the wish that Rawlinson travel to the Ypres salient (in company with Uniacke as artillery expert) to plan the big attack to be made there later in the year. Reflecting on this two days later Rawlinson observed, 'I feel highly honoured at being given command of the big effort of 1917.'

Haig's diary reference to this conference, it may be noted, does not mention the matter of command. Perhaps, already, he was – at least sub-consciously – hedging his bets. Yet Rawlinson was not inventing. Letters which Kiggell wrote on Haig's behalf that day make it plain that Rawlinson was to have a big role in directing the Ypres offensive. Plumer – who had long commanded the Second Army in the Ypres salient and so was the obvious candidate to conduct an offensive there – was informed: 'As you know, Rawlinson is to take charge of the northern part of the operations on your front. The Commander-in-Chief wishes him to reconnoitre the front which he will command at an early date and to get into touch with you as to the preparations.'[7] Simultaneously Kiggell wrote to Gough, commanding Fifth Army, informing him that Haig was putting Rawlinson in charge 'of a portion of the operations on the northern front if these come off.'[8] Haig's decision would have two consequences for Gough. Uniacke, Gough's artillery director, would be transferred to Rawlinson for this operation, 'as Uniacke knows the ground well.' Secondly, the existing front of Fourth Army (which would continue to be a quiet sector) would be placed under Gough in addition to the section of front he was already commanding – at least until some of it was taken over by the French. Budworth, who was at present Rawlinson's artillery director, and who was familiar with the Fourth Army front, would be transferred to Gough.[9]

Plainly these letters foreshadowed a situation in which Gough would be in charge of a decidedly inactive sector, and Plumer would not be the main contributor to an offensive conducted from the Ypres salient. The man in charge of what – should it materialize – would be the Third Battle of Ypres (though only the first offensive conducted there by the British) would be Rawlinson.

The Fourth Army commander duly visited the Ypres salient at the beginning of February and fixed the place for his headquarters and those of his corps. It was not, however, an entirely satisfactory tour. Rawlinson and Plumer reached no agreement concerning the dividing line between the proposed Fourth and Second Armies, and no unanimity regarding objectives. The matter then went into abeyance. Rawlinson returned south to follow up the German retreat and make his token contribution to the Arras offensive.

In no time it became evident that Nivelle's grand design was a barren undertaking, and that correspondingly the northern offensive was becoming a distinct possibility. But something else was becoming evident. Haig was reconsidering the matter of who should direct it. Rawlinson noted in his diary for 17 April that, with Nivelle's offensive seeming to have failed and Haig considering an immediate switch to the north, it was not certain who would command there. He rather feared it would be Gough, with himself remaining on the Somme at least for the summer.

A conversation with Haig eight days later seemed to confirm this. Rawlinson claimed to be 'glad': 'The prospect of another big attack is very refreshing but the defences are v strong.'[10] But he could not maintain this

[7] Kiggell to Plumer 27/1/17, Kiggell Papers vol. 78, Liddell Hart Centre, King's College, London.

[8] Kiggell to Gough 27/1/17, Kiggell Papers vol. 77.

[9] Ibid.

[10] Rawlinson Diary 25/4/17.

pose of equanimity. Following a meeting on 7 May when Haig announced to his Army commanders that the northern campaign would indeed be going ahead, Rawlinson admitted to being 'very much disgusted and disappointed' on learning that Gough 'is to have the command of this Northern part of the attack and that when I have been relieved down here I am to go into reserve.'

> This is rather a blow for I had been looking forward to that northern attack even though it is a difficult one. D.H. said nothing to me direct about it nor did Kiggell so I only heard it by accident in discussing matters with Tavish [Davidson] afterwards.[11]

Rawlinson spent much of the next day agonizing over why he and his staff were to be shunted into reserve. He managed some preposterous surmises. For one, he concluded that Haig could not have been a free agent in making his decision and must have been pressured by Robertson, the Chief of Imperial General Staff (CIGS), acting from some ulterior motive. Perhaps, he speculated, the 'Home Authorities' were facing a North Sea defeat of the British fleet followed by a German invasion of England, in which case they would need an Army staff on hand to direct the resistance. 'It is possible they are reserving IV Army staff for this.'[12]

Seeking a more authoritative view, Rawlinson wrote to Kiggell.[13] He remarked that he had heard from Davidson 'incidentally' that he was not to have charge of the northern army as previously contemplated. 'I confess to some disappointment, having been looking forward to the operation ever since Fourth Army became the Cinderella of the piece.' Kiggell in reply was comforting but specious. Rawlinson had no need to worry about a job: 'the Chief' had various schemes in mind. The reason Haig had gone back on his previous decision was that, as the Arras offensive proceeded, its drive towards Cambrai would pinch out the Fifth Army and so deprive Gough of employment. Kiggell had to admit that such an outcome seemed unlikely, but 'the Chief' thought it best to adhere to the arrangements whereby Gough would go north.

This was hardly convincing. If the offensive out of Arras had ever made such progress as to threaten Cambrai, then – irrespective of how Nivelle

---

[11] Ibid. 7/5/17. Maurice, in his life of Rawlinson, quotes a different version of the last sentence, presumably derived from a letter by Rawlinson which has not survived: 'D.H. said nothing to me directly about it and, of course I said nothing to him, though for a moment I was tempted to remind him that he had told me I was to have it.' See Maurice, *Rawlinson* p. 190.

[12] Ibid. 8/5/17.

[13] Rawlinson to Kiggell 8/5/17 and Kiggell to Rawlinson 9/5/17, Kiggell Papers vol. 78, Liddell Hart Centre, King's College, London.

was getting on – the British effort would have remained in that region
and the northern offensive set aside. The reason why Rawlinson was
being passed over for a man of such mixed accomplishments as Gough
stemmed from quite other considerations. Rawlinson doubtless guessed
them, although it was not until the campaign in Flanders was more than a
month old and failing in its larger objectives that he received an authoritative
account. He recorded in his diary for 6 September:

> Archie [Montgomery] tells me that he wormed out of Butler[14] the
> reason why D.H. put Goughy in to do the attack instead of me. It
> was because he thought Goughy the best man he could choose for
> the *pursuit*. Now I hear that Goughy has in many ways been a failure
> and that both Corps and Divn Comdrs are complaining. I told Kig it
> would be so before the offensive began. [Rawlinson's emphasis]

It was certainly the case that, in advance of the offensive, Rawlinson had
yet again been advocating the principles of bite and hold. Conversing with
Robertson on 29 June he had urged 'the desirability of holding on to
Goughys coat tails and ordering him only to undertake the limited objective
and not going beyond the range of his guns.'[15] At dinner with Haig four
days later he had shown similar boldness, pressing Haig to make Gough
undertake a *deliberate* offensive without the wild 'hurroosh' he was so fond
of and which led to so much disappointment.

> The rule is that they must not go beyond the range of their guns or
> they will be driven back by counter attacks. I am not sure that D.H.
> will insist on this with sufficient strength and I fear that if he does not
> the attack may fail with v heavy losses.[16]

Rawlinson would learn in due course that Gough had been driven to adopt
his point of view. On 5 August, with the Third Ypres offensive not quite a
week old, Rawlinson, after lunching with Gough, recorded in his diary: 'He
is converted from the "hurroosh" and now accepts the limited objective as
the normal tactics.'

IV

Gough's conversion, of course, was as good as an admission that the
Third Ypres offensive was already failing in its larger objectives. What

---

[14] Lt.-Gen. Sir Richard Butler, Deputy Chief of the General Staff, BEF.
[15] Rawlinson Diary 29/6/17.
[16] Ibid. 3/7/17.

Rawlinson did not seem to be noticing was that this put paid to his own hopes of useful employment in the second half of 1917. It will be recalled that, in the reply he received to his letter of lament to Kiggell on 8 May, Rawlinson had at least gained an assurance that he had no need to worry about a job: Haig had various schemes in mind. Two days later he secured more concrete information. Davidson flew over to lunch bearing 'several messages from D.H., to the effect that I should be required for very important amphibious operations on Gough's left along the coast, if things went well.'[17] That is, as Gough broke out from the Ypres salient and headed towards the Channel ports, Rawlinson was to direct both a drive up the coast and a landing of forces from the sea behind the German lines between Ostend and the mouth of the River Yser.

For any of this to have substance, 'things' with Gough would have to go exceedingly well indeed. Otherwise Rawlinson might find himself launching an amphibious operation fraught with the utmost peril and capable of being defeated before support could arrive. There was the further consideration that, unless he achieved complete surprise and great initial success, he might well find the enemy breaching the dikes and flooding the area where he was supposed to operate.

Despite this unpropitious prospect, from mid-May 1917 Rawlinson entered into lengthy explorations with Admiral Bacon (commander of the Dover Patrol) regarding the proposed landing from the sea. Expressions like 'pontoons', 'tides', 'horseboats', 'barges', 'smoke demonstrations', and 'landing places' figure in these discussions. Much effort was given to testing the capacity of tanks to land in shallow water and mount a sea wall. A further portion of Rawlinson's energy had to be devoted to remonstrating with General Du Cane, who had been appointed (against Rawlinson's will) as commander of the troops designated to make the landing. Du Cane, plainly, had little faith in the undertaking, telling Rawlinson that the guns would be better employed supporting Gough. On 21 July Rawlinson told Du Cane bluntly that he was spending too much time on administration and not enough on beating the enemy. As he recorded in his diary: 'We nearly had high words but I kept my temper as did he ... I let him know that I was not very satisfied with the way things were going generally.'

All this was wasted effort. Quite apart from the hazardous nature of the undertaking, the circumstances for putting it to the test never arose. As early as 2 August – the Third Ypres operation having commenced on 31 July – Rawlinson was receiving a negative account of the progress being made and commenting: 'This looks bad.' Four days later he learned that Haig was contemplating a 'further considerable delay' for his landing from

[17] Ibid. 10/5/17.

the sea, even though this might postpone it to the autumn when a break in the weather would render it impossible. 'I find v little to do just now', Rawlinson lamented, 'beyond visits and inspections.'

Frustration served to sap Rawlinson's judgement. It had been axiomatic that the amphibious operation would only be feasible if Gough's offensive managed to make substantial progress towards the coast. Yet in a memorandum on 22 August, Rawlinson urged that the operation be attempted between 5 and 8 September ('the only possible [days] for a landing on the coast') not because Fifth Army was getting on well but because its progress 'has not been as rapid as was hoped.'[18] The attack from the sea, then, would be intended to divert German forces away from Gough.

The high command was not impressed. At a conference on 22 August Haig stated firmly that: 'from a military point of view he was not prepared to undertake the combined naval and military operations until the conditions already postulated had arisen, viz., that the enemy had been seriously defeated, the Passchendaele–Staden Ridge occupied, and the enemy's positions on the coast seriously threatened.'[19] Next day Kiggell bluntly informed Rawlinson that an attempted landing in September would not be worth the candle. The chief danger lay in 'the antagonism of the War Council' who would seize on any disaster 'as conclusive evidence that D.H. was not fit for his position and would insist on his removal and the transference of 10 or 12 Divns to Italy. Such a policy would probably lose us the war and if the failure of a coast landing should result in anything of the kind it is far better not to undertake it.'[20]

In the ensuing months, as Rawlinson looked on helplessly, the coastal operation was by turn ruled out of court, resuscitated, and finally buried. His laments over his own inactivity mounted. 'I do not find much to occupy my time', he wrote on 8 September, 'so have leisure to do a bit of reading'; and on 16 October, 'I find it rather hard to get through the day and generally have to organise an expedition somewhere to kill time.'[21] His best hope early in October was that he and his staff might take over from Gough, who had been demoted from overall command of the Ypres operation in favour of Plumer, and who was the subject of much disapproval. But Gough survived as an Army commander for a while longer.

What rescued Rawlinson from idleness, quite unexpectedly, was the setback suffered by the Italian army late in October. The British government insisted on sending several divisions to Italy to help restore the situation. Briefly Rawlinson thought that he might have command ('though

I confess I am not desperate keen about the job');[22] then he learned that Plumer was to go there and that he would take over as head of Second Army – 'This is rather a surprise.' The task of assuming charge, in the midst of a campaign and in unfamiliar territory, of a force of 7 corps and 21 divisions was daunting. He wrote in his diary for 9 November:

> I have had a busy day in the office taking over all the details of this huge army of 750,000 men. The Railways, Roads, Art[iller]y, Engineers[,] reliefs, training areas etc are a labarynth [*sic*] of detail which one cannot absorb in a moment but I am thankful to say that Plumer is leaving me most of his staff to teach my people how to run the show before he requires them for Italy.

The next day Davidson telephoned 'that I am to take over V Army Front as well and Goughy goes down south.' That would leave him commanding between 900,000 and one million men – 'Rather a big thing.'

So Rawlinson was called on to preside over the miserable last actions of the Passchendaele campaign and to reflect on its meagre accomplishments. Having been excluded from all part in the undertaking he could afford to be dispassionate:

> I went round the Divns at Ypres and on the Canal bank ... all seem pretty happy but complain of mud and difficulty of comm[unications]. There is no cover for the men in the forward areas and the low lying parts of the mud and shell holes are appalling – it is worse than the Somme was last year and we shall have heavy losses from sickness.[23]

'Ypres' he noted on 27 November (a few days before sending two divisions into a quite futile attack) 'was one huge pool of liquid coffee.' At an Army commanders' conference on 7 December he learned that the manpower situation was 'really very serious', that the Germans would soon have large reinforcements from the Russian front, and that in consequence 'by the end of Feby we are likely to have quite a lively time.' He recorded in his diary: 'Any how we shall be thrown on the defensive and shall have to fight for our lives as we did at first Ypres. Not a pleasant prospect. D.H. quite realises this and gave us a dissertation on the defensive.' Rawlinson discussed this 'change of policy' with Montgomery next day. He deemed Passchendaele 'at present a really untenable position against a properly organised attack', and he summoned a conference of corps commanders to discuss falling back on a 'straight and more defensible' line. As he put it in a memorandum of 10 December, the existing position was 'defective, not

[22] Ibid. 28/10/17.
[23] Ibid. 12/11/17.

to say dangerous', constituting a salient against which the enemy could concentrate his large artillery pieces on two-thirds of the arc.

> Nothing we can hope to do can make the line now held a really satisfactory defensive position. We must therefore be prepared to withdraw from it, if the Germans show signs of a serious and sustained offensive on this front, or if an attack elsewhere necessitates the withdrawal of more troops from the front of Second Army.[24]

In anticipation of a German offensive, Rawlinson spent much of January 1918 placing the Ypres front in a state of preparedness. Having found, a year and a half before, the preparations of Hunter-Weston's VIII Corps for the attack on the Somme less than satisfactory, he now found himself taking a similar view of their defensive arrangements: 'I was not at all pleased with the progress that had been made and told H[unter]-W[eston] so.'[25] Matters were not much more satisfactory with IX Corps, and Rawlinson engaged in some plain speaking: 'if things are not right in another fortnight I shall have some blood.'[26] But at least as regards ammunition supplies, Second Army would not stand naked before its enemies, for as Rawlinson noted in his diary on 30 January: 'We have more amn than we have room for. The Q.M.G. has just asked us to prepare storage for another 45,000 tons.'

V

The year 1917 had been deeply unsatisfactory for Rawlinson: he had commanded no major operation on the Western Front. It had also been an unsatisfactory year for the BEF, but for a different reason. Time and again the forces of Britain, along with those of its principal ally, had striven to drive their adversaries from the soil of France and Belgium. Yet at the end of 1917 the Germans still stood on conquered territory and the British were frantically preparing to withstand a mighty German offensive.

Despite this seeming evidence of futility, was it the case that Haig's offensives of 1917 had been quite without accomplishment? Or had they yielded some gains, and provided lessons on the correct manner of waging offensives – lessons which one day the British army, and even Rawlinson, might have a chance to employ with advantage? To place Rawlinson's career during the culminating phases of the war in perspective, it is

[24] Memorandum by Rawlinson 10/12/17, Rawlinson Papers 1/10, CC.
[25] Rawlinson Diary 2/1/18.
[26] Ibid. 5/1/18.

necessary to attempt a summation of the British army's experiences in 1917. This is not easy. For until the campaigns fought by the BEF in 1917 have been subjected to close inquiry, it is difficult to write about them with confidence.[27] Yet notwithstanding this caveat, it seems fairly safe to offer the following observations.

The year 1917 had seen Haig's armies launch four offensives – at Arras, Messines, Ypres, and Cambrai – and the French one great operation on the Aisne (the Nivelle offensive). Not all had been unqualified disasters. When the objective had been strictly limited, and when the opposition had been subjected to massive artillery bombardment delivered with a high degree of sophistication (as in the cases of Vimy Ridge, Messines, the September and early October battles of Third Ypres, and the first day of Cambrai), a modest but striking success had been achieved at tolerable cost. But where more ambitious goals had been aimed for and the support provided by the artillery been correspondingly reduced (as was the case for the British at Arras and during the opening phase of Third Ypres, and for the French in the Nivelle operation), the attack had proven barren and the losses prohibitive.

The lessons of 1917, then, appeared to be that initial success was possible, but it did not carry with it the promise of great prizes beyond. This message had been driven home when Plumer sought unavailingly to build on his early success at Messines, and when Byng tried to extend his first strike at Cambrai by sending in the tanks and then the cavalry to widen the breach.

In time – although not until 1918 was well advanced – Rawlinson would have an opportunity to benefit from the lessons of 1917. Two large questions would then present themselves. Would he regard the British army's experiences in 1917 as confirmation of the bite and hold operations he had so often advocated and so seldom carried out? And had the commander-in-chief been converted to this manner of proceeding? – a matter of some importance, given that otherwise any lessons provided by the events of 1917, and any appreciation of them on Rawlinson's part, might count for nothing.

---

[27] The present writers are currently engaged on a study of the Flanders campaign of 1917. Although at an early stage, it already promises to require a reassessment of several well-established views.

24

Return to Command, February–June 1918

I

Whatever the difficulties of functioning as Plumer's replacement in late 1917 and the opening weeks of 1918, Rawlinson must have felt at home as commander of an actual Army with a real task to perform. But the appointment ceased as abruptly as it had begun, and Rawlinson re-entered the world of war as make-believe.

In mid-February 1918 Rawlinson found himself summoned to occupy a quite unfamiliar role. Lloyd George, in the course of his efforts to circumvent Britain's military authorities, had overseen the creation at Versailles of a Supreme War Council. One of its elements was an Executive War Board of military members, with Henry Wilson as the British representative. In early 1918 Lloyd George at last jockeyed Wully Robertson out of his post as CIGS and replaced him with Wilson, leaving a vacancy in the body at Versailles. Haig swiftly proposed Rawlinson as its occupant, with Plumer returning from Italy and resuming command in Flanders.

This appointment caused Rawlinson to become, for the first time since January 1917, the object of a deal of comment in the press.[1] The *National News* on 24 February 1918 offered a long article on 'Our Representative at Versailles' and also a profile. Rawlinson was described as a

> soldierly-looking man, rather like Lord Kitchener, with a mass of decorations and a bluff and cheerful manner which has much impressed visitors to the seat of operations. He has ingratiated himself with every politician who has been over to France, and it is understood that General Foch particularly likes him. In his choice of words [by which was presumably meant his facility with words] he is the

---

[1] For the following extracts from the press see Rawlinson Papers 5201/33–39, NAM.

antithesis of Sir William Robertson, but his fluency in the French language is not so glib as that of Sir Henry Wilson.

The *Manchester Guardian* on 24 February wrote of him as 'of course' one of Britain's best-known generals, whose relations with the French had always been cordial. 'His use of the French language is described as not really good, but as good as anybody else's.'

Perhaps most flattering was the comment by the London correspondent of the well-regarded *Glasgow Herald*. On 19 February he observed that, whatever criticisms might be heard of the Versailles Council, none could be raised against the fitness of Rawlinson to represent Britain's military interests on that highly important body. Nor was Rawlinson, as had been urged against Henry Wilson, 'a comparatively unknown man'. (The quotation is not attributed, but it cannot have been pleasing to Wilson.) On the contrary – in the judgement of this writer – there was no British general on the Western Front, with the single exception of Haig, better known than Rawlinson to the British public. Probably to a greater extent than any other corps or Army commander, Rawlinson's record of service was – up to the spring of 1917 – the history of Britain's campaigns in the West.

All of this must have been very reassuring to Rawlinson, not least after the period of despond through which his career had been passing. But on a wider perspective, it suggests how markedly the Army commanders who had been directing operations in Rawlinson's absence – Allenby, Horne, Gough, Plumer, and Byng – had failed to excite the interest or approval of the British public; in itself a comment on the barrenness of the undertakings of a year in which Rawlinson, to his fortune, had been thrust to the sidelines.

II

Rawlinson's task at Versailles would be largely negative. The Executive War Board had been given the authority to create a General Reserve consisting of divisions drawn from the various Allied armies. Thereby the board as a whole and Foch as its president might gain a substantial control over strategy. With his forces already depleted by the Ypres campaign and the transfers to Italy in late 1917, Haig was determined to surrender none of his remaining divisions to the General Reserve. Rawlinson's job would be to ensure that the British contribution consisted only of divisions returned from Italy or drawn from places yet further afield, such as Salonika. Rawlinson was initially startled by the prospect of his appointment to Versailles. But he speedily concluded that he was well qualified.

He had extensive knowledge of the Western Front from Verdun to the sea. He got on well with both Haig and Wilson. And he enjoyed good relations with Foch.

Service at Versailles in the next few weeks would tax some of these relations. Rawlinson found that Henry Wilson, who had been eager to build up the Executive War Board as long as he was its British representative, was now concerned to downgrade it. 'It looks', Rawlinson wrote in his diary for 25 February, 'as if he were playing a low down game over this[,] chiefly because he has moved to London.'

Rawlinson also found himself at odds with Foch, who argued that without a General Reserve the Executive War Board could not function even in an advisory capacity. Rawlinson sometimes argued that the board had a large role to play in devising strategy, and even talked as if Haig might come round to providing troops for a reserve. But fundamentally he was Haig's man and would exercise no pressure in this direction. And his predominant view was that it was preferable to let the respective commanders-in-chief of the British and French armies (Haig and Pétain) 'carry on as they were'. General Spiers observed Rawlinson in action at the Executive Board and reported on 11 March to Sir Sidney Clive, the head of the British mission at French GHQ:

> Rawly does not intend to say much, being a new boy on the Committee; he considers that the C's in C [Haig and Pétain] being of one mind, are in an unassailable position; and he intends to do his best to prevent their views being sat on.[2]

Yet notwithstanding Rawlinson's overriding commitment to Haig during his month at Versailles, once more he could not resist taking on the colouring of his new position. For one thing, his views on the war started to become unnervingly global. With enemy forces massing on the Western Front, Rawlinson began waxing much concerned about the German threat to Persia and to 'the East' generally. He envisaged the enemy, after completing their conquest of Russia, 'so organising Central Asia that they may have a good chance of turning us out of India.' Much, therefore, would depend on what happened in Persia, and he felt certain Britain ought to send considerable forces there to gain possession of Teheran or to turn out the Germans if they had got there first.[3]

Almost as strangely, Rawlinson lent a sympathetic ear on 20 February to the views of the Minister of Munitions, Winston Churchill, on what should be done with the British forces now in Italy. Instead of their being

---

[2] Diary of Sir Sidney Clive, Clive Papers, Liddell Hart Centre, King's College, London.
[3] Rawlinson Diary 18/3/18.

withdrawn to France, on account of the approaching German offensive, Churchill argued that they should go onto the attack in Italy. Rawlinson commented in his diary: 'In a measure he is right. We are all of us too much inclined to remain on the passive defence on the western front in view of the assembly of so strong a force of Bosches and this is to my mind fatal.' Offence, Rawlinson concluded, was the best form of defence, and they should be planning a succession of limited attacks as a response to a German onslaught: 'In Italy we might easily do a push on the lower Piave and get a success there quite cheap.'[4] That the Germans might be delighted to concede successes to the British in Italy while themselves undertaking the conquest of Western Europe appeared to be escaping Sir Henry's attention.

In accordance with these notions, Rawlinson was prepared to resist bringing back to the Western Front all of the British forces which had been rushed to Italy in November. (On this matter he even found a soul mate in Plumer, who was no doubt influenced by his recent sojourn in Italy.) To make up the numbers in the West, Rawlinson toyed with the idea of transferring *Italian* divisions to the French sector of the Western Front and thereby enabling the French to take back some of the line which had been recently transferred to the British.[5]

The Germans swiftly brought to a halt these bizarre speculations. On 21 March they unleashed a massive strike in the very region where Rawlinson's proposed comings-and-goings would have been taking place. The very next day – apparently unconscious of what he had been saying less than a week earlier – Rawlinson was writing to Derby that they must get back all the troops they could from Italy (and Palestine). Otherwise, he warned, it would be too late.[6]

III

The opening of the German offensive on the Western Front on 21 March found Rawlinson returning to Versailles from Italy. The purpose of his visit had been to discuss, on behalf of the Executive War Board, the formation of the General Reserve out of British and French divisions presently in Italy.[7] Events at the front overtook Rawlinson. Within days, not only the General Reserve but the Supreme War Council itself had been rendered irrelevant by the onrush of German forces between St Quentin and Arras.

[4] Ibid. 20/2/18.
[5] Ibid. 16–17/3/18.
[6] Rawlinson to Derby 22/3/18, Rawlinson Papers 5201/33/72, NAM.
[7] Rawlinson Diary 14/3/18.

Initially, as the overextended Fifth Army under Gough fell back in some disorder, Rawlinson was no more than an alarmed spectator. In his diary he commented: 'Not good days on the battlefront.' Amiens, he felt certain, was the Germans' objective, and if they gained it they would divide the British and French armies and could then throw their whole weight against whichever adversary they chose.[8]

Yet Rawlinson was about to discover that events so damaging to one part of Britain's forces were working to his personal advantage. For almost a year, he had been relegated to the peripheries of command on the Western Front. Ludendorff's massive thrust against the Fifth Army would change this. It may have been Haig's responsibility that the British army in this sector was deplorably weak, but it was Gough who was called on to pay the price. On 26 March the CIGS (Henry Wilson) informed Rawlinson that, in consequence of the setback on Fifth Army's front, Gough was to be sent home. Rawlinson recorded: 'I am to reconstitute the 4 Army [as an administrative structure] to take over and reorganise the remnants of the V Army.'[9] Rawlinson's qualifications for the post were evident enough. However variable his performance during 1916, he had gained much experience in command of an Army. There was no likelihood that he would panic in face of present adversities. And in personal terms, it was bound to be satisfactory to Haig that Rawlinson's career depended so largely on his chief's good graces and yet that Rawlinson was an old (if at this moment somewhat strained) friend of the recently appointed CIGS – someone with whom Haig was determined to cultivate good relations.

IV

Rawlinson, with Montgomery as COS and Budworth as artillery commander, took up his new post on 28 March. After a talk with Gough, Rawlinson commented:

> The situation is serious. The V Army troops are beat to the world and no French reinforcements are yet in sight. If the Bosche attack heavily tomorrow I fear he will break our last line of defence in front of Amiens and the place will fall.[10]

The situation Rawlinson found was indeed serious. His new Army consisted of little more than five weak divisions of XIX Corps (Watts).

---

[8] Ibid. 22, 23, 24 March.
[9] Ibid. 26/3/18.
[10] Ibid. 28/3/18.

These were holding a precarious line to the south of the Somme near Villers Bretonneux. Most of these divisions had been in action since the commencement of the German offensive. Some idea of the state to which they had been reduced can be seen in table 24.1, which shows that the total manpower of these five divisions had fallen below the nominal fighting strength of a single British division (10,000 men). It was not to be expected that XIX Corps would long withstand further severe German assaults.

TABLE 24.1 *Estimated fighting strength of Fifth Army when Rawlinson took command, 30 March 1918*

Division	Estimated fighting strength
39	800
66	880
50	3000
8	2600
24	1800
Total	9080

Source Table headed 'March 30th 1918', in Rawlinson Papers, 1/10, Churchill College, Cambridge

Gough, recognizing this, had prepared a second defensive line covering Villers Bretonneux between Hamel and Demuin. But, as Rawlinson soon discovered, this line too was held by a pitifully weak force: two under-strength reserve divisions of XIX Corps (16 and 61) with about 3,000 men between them, and 'Carey's Force', an improvised group of tunnellers, engineers, and stragglers numbering about 4,000.[11] In immediate reserve all that could be called upon were three divisions of XVIII Corps (18, 24, 8) recently relieved by the French divisions to the south. These divisions also had been in the line since 21 March and were no stronger than those of XIX Corps.[12]

Before his departure Gough had taken some further actions. Three divisions of the Cavalry Corps were being rushed to the front, with 1 Cavalry Division entering the line to the south of the Somme on 29

[11] Gough, 'Troops in V Army', 27/3/18, Rawlinson Papers, 5201/33/77, NAM.

[12] Brigadier-General Sir James Edmonds, *Military Operations: France and Belgium, 1918* vol. 2 (London: Macmillan, 1937), pp. 43, 50.

March.[13] In addition a brigade was detached from 3 Australian Division, which was operating to the north of the Somme, and sent to the vicinity of Villers Bretonneux. But all told these reinforcements amounted to only the equivalent of just over one infantry division.

On assuming command Rawlinson cast about for further reinforcements. He sent an urgent appeal to Foch:

> unless fresh troops are sent here in the next two days, I doubt whether the remnants of the British XIX Corps which now hold the line to the east of Villers Bretonneux can maintain their positions . . . I feel anxious for the safety of Amiens, and desire strongly to impress on you the danger of the place if the enemy renews his attack from the east before fresh troops are available.[14]

Foch had nothing to give. The French themselves were under heavy German pressure. Coincidental with Rawlinson's request they were forced out of the important centre of Montdidier. Paris lay only 50 miles beyond.

Thus the situation confronting Rawlinson appeared altogether bleak. Yet his fears of the imminent fall of Amiens did not come to pass. Gradually the German advance on the front of his Army slowed. Admittedly on the 29th, XIX Corps withdrew to the positions held by Carey's Force in front of Villers Bretonneux, but it did so of its own volition. And this would prove the last substantial withdrawal made by Rawlinson's Army. The British line stabilized in front of Villers Bretonneux for almost a month. Rawlinson was quick to take credit for this development. On a copy of the papers handed to him by Gough on 27 March he noted: 'The units [of the V Army] were in a state of lamentable confusion and demoralisation and in full retreat before the advancing German Army. It was a difficult task to stay the hostile advance and save Amiens but by superhuman efforts we managed to do it.'[15]

This comment is understandable. Indeed Rawlinson must have welcomed the sensation of once more successfully commanding in battle. Yet the truth was that there was virtually no relationship between his accession to the direction of the Fifth Army sector and the halting of the German advance. Rather, events on the German side of the line were determining that in the last days of March the drive towards Amiens would grind to a halt.

As an inspection of map 26 will show, from about 27 March – one day

[13] Ibid., p. 25.

[14] Rawlinson to Foch 28/3/18, Rawlinson Papers 1/10, CC.

[15] Undated note on documents headed, 'Papers Handed Over To Me By Gough', 27/3/18, Rawlinson Papers 5201/33/17, NAM.

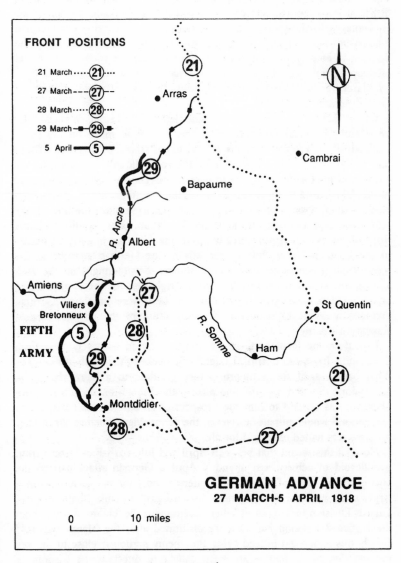

FRONT POSITIONS

21 March ·····(21)····
27 March ----(27)---
28 March ·····(28)·····
29 March ---(29)---
5 April ----(5)----

Arras

Cambrai

(29)

Bapaume

R. Ancre

Albert

Amiens

Villers
Bretonneux

FIFTH
ARMY

(5)

(27)

(28)

St Quentin

R. Somme

Ham

(29)

(21)

Montdidier

(28)

(27)

GERMAN ADVANCE
27 MARCH–5 APRIL 1918

0   10 miles

MAP 26

before Rawlinson took command – the enemy advance on the Somme was beginning to lose momentum. Evidently the leading German infantry divisions were approaching exhaustion. Yet, paradoxically, the problems encountered in transporting their ammunition were causing the German infantry to outrun their artillery support. Further, consequent upon the decision to employ storm troopers as the spearhead of costly if successful offensive operations, the enemy had lost many of their best men. And from 27 March further progress must lie across the inhospitable wilderness of the old Somme battlefield.

Other factors on the German side lightened Rawlinson's task. By 28 March the main German effort was not being made on his front. Ludendorff, in keeping with his refusal to set strategic objectives ('Don't talk to me of strategy. I hack a hole, the rest follows'), was allowing the advance of his Eighteenth Army to become directionless. Gaps still existed in the Allied front to the south where French reinforcements, coming into battle without their artillery, had not managed to stabilize the line. It was into these gaps that the attackers moved – thus widening still further a front of attack which was already stretching German infantry resources to the limit, and also shifting the axis of the German advance to the south-west, which meant away from Amiens. Bewilderingly, on the 28th Ludendorff swung his main effort to his right, against the British Third and First Armies at Arras. Consequently there were simply no German divisions available to maintain the momentum of the advance against Rawlinson's Army.

Hereafter, the focus of German attention moved decisively away from the Somme front. On 9 April, Ludendorff attacked the British in Flanders. That battle raged for a month before grinding to a halt, whereupon Ludendorff directed his attention against the French on the Chemin des Dames. This opened to him the prospect of an advance on Paris, which Ludendorff would pursue as far as the River Marne before his forces' progress was halted once and for all.

None of this meant that between April and July 1918 Rawlinson's front was devoid of activity. On 4 and 5 April a German attack carried the enemy to the edge of Villers Bretonneux. And later in the month, in a larger scale operation incorporating mustard gas and tanks, the German 4 Guards Division forced out of Villers Bretonneux the 'children' with whom the British 8 Division had been reconstituted after the March retreat.[16] Briefly this attack did indeed bring the enemy perilously close to the key rail junction of Amiens – an event calling in question the wisdom of Ludendorff's decision to make his main endeavour elsewhere. But in

---

[16] Rawlinson to Henry Wilson 24/4/18, Rawlinson Papers 5201/73/44, NAM.

consequence of that decision, the Germans were in no position to capitalize on this near-success. On the day following the fall of Villers Bretonneux, Rawlinson ordered an immediate counterattack.[17] This operation, carried out by two brigades of 5 Australian Division and one of 18 Division, drove the Germans from Villers Bretonneux and halted for good their progress on the Amiens front.[18]

Rawlinson, of course, could not know precisely when the Germans would abandon their attempt to capture Amiens. Indeed there were indications that their offensive might be resumed at any time.[19] GHQ responded to this possibility by at last providing reinforcements – 47 Division and four divisions of the Australian Corps. By the middle of May these divisions were in the line and 18 and 58 Divisions of the III Corps had been replenished.[20]

Rawlinson meanwhile was engaged in improving the defences on his front. In so doing he took careful note of the methods used by the Germans to achieve their successes on 21 March. He laid it down that the forward zone, which embraced the area within 2,000 yards of the front line, should be held thinly, with machine-guns in dugouts substituting where possible for quantities of riflemen. In the rear of this zone he located formations of forces (infantry, tanks, and machine-gun companies) capable of delivering local counterattacks immediately the enemy bombardment lifted. Further back would lie a second and a third zone, each with two or more trench lines. These would be well wired and contain dugouts sheltering substantial counterattack forces. The main strength of the artillery was so situated as to enable a heavy barrage to be placed in front of the forward zone.[21]

Rawlinson kept careful watch over these activities. In the six-week period from 5 May to 13 June he made 17 inspections of the defences being constructed by the corps and divisions of what had now become the Fourth Army. Their progress he recorded in his diary.[22] Finally, on 13 June he was able to conclude that should the enemy attack, 'We are ready.'[23] Rawlinson's assiduousness, as we shall observe shortly, would prove in marked contrast to what was happening on the other side of the line.

---

[17] Annexe to Fourth Army War Diary 24/4/18, Fourth Army Papers vol. 41.

[18] Fourth Army Summary of Operations 24/4/18, Fourth Army War Diary 27 Mar/30 Apr 1918, in ibid.

[19] Fourth Army Intelligence Report 2/5/18, AWM 26/12/349/3.

[20] GHQ, Headquarters of Formations as located on 12 May 1918, AWM 26/12/345/14.

[21] See three papers by Rawlinson: 'Policy on the Fourth Army Front', 28/4/18; 'Artillery Policy' 28/4/18; 'Memorandum by Rawlinson' 31/5/18 in Fourth Army Papers vol. 42.

[22] Rawlinson's Short Note Diary provides an overview of his activities during this period.

[23] Rawlinson Short Note Diary 13/6/18.

PART VI

VICTORY

25

A Formula for Success,
June–July 1918

I

Rawlinson, as we have seen in the last chapter, was restored to command over a major sector of the Western Front in 1918 on account of his considerable experience as chief of an Army. And he promptly revealed his qualities by his attention to readying his forces against any renewal of the German assault. But nothing in his past actions or present diligence marked Rawlinson out as a man who would soon be presiding over a succession of triumphs on the battlefield. A challenge confronts the historian in relating the events of July to November 1918. How do we account for what, on a first view, appears to be a mighty transformation in Rawlinson's level of accomplishment? That is, the operations carried out by Fourth Army in the second half of 1918, bringing the Great War to its climax and providing Rawlinson with his finest hour, transcend any expectations that might have been formed from his conduct of battle up to this point. Are we to look to Rawlinson's performance, or to other areas altogether, for an explanation? This question will inform our consideration of these events.

II

By the beginning of June, it was becoming clear to some in Fourth Army command that the circumstances on their front were changing. Far from being capable of a further offensive, the Germans facing Rawlinson were highly vulnerable to counterattack. The Australian Corps in particular were discovering that the German troops in this sector were not the formidable fighters of the March offensive. On 10 June an Australian division carried out a large-scale raid in the Morlancourt area. The result was a great

success. The Germans were driven from their trenches with relative ease.[1]
As a result of this operation and other raids carried out to the south of the
River Somme, Australian Corps Intelligence came to the conclusion that
the enemy troops facing them were of very 'poor quality'.[2] They also
discovered that the German defences and supplies were inadequate: 'wire
weak'; 'apparently little [work being done] on front line'; 'rations are very
bad and scarce.'[3]

This situation reflected a number of significant developments on the
German side. First, those elite groups who had survived the offensives
of March and April had been removed in May to deliver a blow against
the French. Their replacements were of a much lower calibre. Second,
the German high command had entered a state of suspended animation
concerning the Amiens sector. They were loath to abandon Amiens as an
objective, yet they had no fresh reserves available with which to renew
the attack. So they neither made preparations to attack again nor provided
labour (which was in short supply) for the construction of effective defences.
(Perhaps they considered the British to have lost all offensive capability.)
The commanders on the spot failed to make good this situation by taking
the initiative themselves in the construction of defences. Thus on the
Amiens front there was no German counterpart to Rawlinson's devoted
oversight of the provision of an effective system of protection. This presented Rawlinson with the opportunity to undertake a different kind of
operation altogether.

III

Responding to this promising situation, Rawlinson (among others on the
British side) began seriously to plan a counteroffensive. Yet no sooner
had the planning begun than he found himself confronting a quite unprecedented problem. The British were running out of men. An average
battalion on the Fourth Army front now contained 650 instead of the
standard 900 men. And from the end of 1917 British divisions consisted
only of 9 instead of 12 battalions. So a 1918 division might contain a mere

---

[1] C. E. W. Bean, *Official History of Australia in the War of 1914–18*, vol. 6: *The Australian
Imperial Force in France During The Allied Offensive, 1918* (Sydney: Angus and Robertson, 1942),
p. 240. (Hereafter, Bean, *Australian Official History* vol. 6.)

[2] Blamey to Divisional Commanders 12/6/18, Australian Corps Intelligence Summary
12/6/18, AWM 26/12/362/8.

[3] Australian Corps Intelligence Summary 10–11/6/18 and 15–16/6/18, AWM 26/12/
362/8 and 9.

6,000 riflemen, compared to the 10,000–12,000 to be found in a 1916 division.[4]

What made this situation unprecedented was that it constituted no temporary problem – of the kind, for example, that Rawlinson had faced in the winter of 1916–17. Then it had been a matter of waiting for the drafts of 1917 to replenish the shattered Somme divisions. Now there would be no fresh influx of men. Even with conscription in Britain extended to men up to 50 years of age, wastage would exceed replacement for the foreseeable future. Eventually divisions would have to be broken up. The British army was a wasting asset.

How, under these conditions, could a succession of offensives be prosecuted? Pétain, many months before, had proposed one solution – to wait for the Americans. This was not agreeable to a British command increasingly aware of tempting weak spots in the enemy's defences and unable to persuade America's military leaders forthwith to provide soldiers for the assault.

For Rawlinson, as for Britain's other military chiefs, the solution lay elsewhere: in the prodigious accomplishments of their nation's heavy industry. Already, the home front was proving capable not only of replacing the enormous number of guns lost in the March retreat but of adding to their quantity. So by July the British army had more artillery at its disposal than had been available before 21 March. At the same time British factories were delivering mounting numbers of tanks (of superior quality), machineguns, Lewis guns, trench mortars, smoke, gas, and above all high explosive shells. Consequently the means of delivering a different sort of offensive, in which fire power would more than make good Britain's diminishing resources of manpower, was indeed available to commanders on the Western Front.

Rawlinson produced a sketch of this amended style of warfare in a paper written for GHQ in June. He suggested that if the British army was to return to the offensive 'bearing in mind the limitations of our man-power' it would be necessary to develop

> all possible mechanical devices in order to increase the offensive power of our divisions. The only two directions in which such development can be reasonably expected are (1) the increase of machineguns, Lewis guns, and automatic rifles, and (2) the increase of numbers and functions of tanks.[5]

---

[4] 'Composition of a British Division 1918', Supreme War Council Papers, Cab 25/94.
[5] Rawlinson, 'Increase in our Offensive Power by Additions of Machine and Lewis Guns' Rawlinson Papers 5201/33/77, NAM.

He went on to suggest an improvement in the quantity of machine-guns allotted to divisions (64 Lewis guns per battalion instead of 20) and enhanced tank production so as to provide 36 tanks to each division taking part in an attack.[6]

The restriction of Rawlinson's comments to light weapons and tanks, and in particular the omission of any reference to heavy artillery and high explosives, must be deemed surprising. Perhaps Rawlinson was taking for granted the decisive lessons concerning the employment of massed artillery which had been established beyond question during the successful episodes of 1917; namely, the first day of Arras, the seizure of Messines Ridge, and Plumer's three attacks in the middle phase of Third Ypres. But it may also be the case that, even now, Rawlinson would need to pay special heed to the advice of his artillery officers when he was planning his operations.

Overall, it may be concluded that Rawlinson was learning, under dire necessity, the crucial lesson which was still eluding the German high command: that fire power, not manpower, must hold the key to success in battle. Whether he had fully realized that artillery was the paramount form of fire power, on which must rest all prospects of successful command, is not quite so certain.

IV

It has already been noticed that, by mid-1918, when Rawlinson was moving once more to the attack, a number of important developments in artillery techniques lay at his disposal. These had been applied in several operations of 1917 – operations in which Rawlinson's only role had been that of spectator.

Nineteen-seventeen is remembered as a bleak and barren year for the British army on the Western Front. For this there is good cause. Yet, as has already been pointed out, in the present context what needs to be stressed is that the year which witnessed the unduly prolonged attacks at Arras and Passchendaele was noteworthy for something else – the limited yet striking successes accomplished by the British army thanks to the employment of new artillery techniques. What lay ahead for Rawlinson from mid-1918 was a repetition and refinement of the positive aspects of the campaigns of 1917.

The last occasion on which artillery developments were discussed in detail was in relation to the battle of Neuve Chapelle. It will be recalled that in March 1915 there was a multitude of factors which could affect the

[6] Ibid.

accuracy of guns and the ability of gunners to locate the position of targets within enemy lines. During 1916, despite such artillery refinements as the creeping barrage, nothing had been done to overcome these basic problems. However, 1917 was witness to great improvements in British artillery techniques.

Regarding guns, variations in range caused by worn barrels were now offset by appropriate adjustments to each gun immediately before a major battle.[7] Equally, variations in shell weights were identified at the munitions factories and batches of shells with identical weights dispatched to the front.[8]

Meteorological factors – wind speed, temperature, atmospheric pressure – which could all affect the flight of a shell were taken into account as a matter of course. By the end of 1917 at least six meteorological readings per day were sent to the gunners from weather stations close behind the front.[9]

In addition, all British guns were now located accurately on the surface of the earth by trigonometrical survey. Thereby artillerymen could be supplied with accurate, up-to-date maps of all sectors of the Western Front.[10]

But ensuring that guns would fire accurately was only half the story. For artillery to attain full effectiveness, the position of its targets within the German lines also had to be established with some precision. In 1917 two new techniques and the refinement of an existing technique made certain that this information would be available on most occasions.

The more important of the new techniques was sound ranging. This was based on the principle that sound waves from the firing of a gun travel outwards like ripples from a pond into which a stone has been dropped. These 'air-ripples' could then be picked up by a sequence of microphones placed behind the British front. The time taken by the ripples to reach each microphone formed the basis on which the position of the gun which had fired the shell could be calculated with some accuracy. The principle of sound ranging had been discovered as early as 1915, but it had taken until 1917 to develop a microphone responsive only to the low-frequency sound of the distant discharge of a gun.[11]

A less accurate technique of gun location derived from observing the

[7] Brooke, 'Evolution of Artillery In The Great War: III The Evolution of Artillery Equipment', *Journal of the Royal Artillery*, 52 (1925–26), p. 50.

[8] Severn, *The Gambardier*, p. 95.

[9] Anstey, History of the Royal Artillery 1914–18, p. 341.

[10] Major John Penrose, 'Survey for batteries', *Journal of the Royal Artillery*, 49 (1922–23), p. 270.

[11] See the section on sound ranging by Bragg in *Artillery Survey in the First World War*.

flash resultant on the firing of the weapon. If this flash was witnessed from a number of positions within the British lines, its whereabouts could be established by plotting on a map the bearings taken by each of the observers. Their point of intersection indicated the position of the gun.[12]

Sound ranging and flash spotting were important developments. But both had a number of shortcomings. The former depended on wind to carry the sound of the firing of a German gun as far as the British line. Given that the prevailing wind in northern France is westerly, this did not always occur. Also, the delicate equipment and miles of cable used by a sound-ranging section meant that the technique was difficult to use in mobile warfare – a particular drawback during successful operations. Flash spotting required good visibility and often could only be carried out successfully at night, when flashes were more easily seen.[13]

Surpassing these in importance were refinements introduced into aerial photography. By 1917 most of the difficulties which had earlier impaired the accuracy of this form of information had been overcome. When transposing photographs onto maps, allowance was now made for the curvature of the earth and the height from which the photograph was taken. Cameras had much improved, and the clearer pictures which they produced were being subjected to increasingly sophisticated analysis by staff experienced in identifying small and camouflaged targets.[14] Of course the use of aerial photography depended on the maintenance of air superiority. It was Rawlinson's good fortune that this factor could be taken for granted along the British front in 1918.

One organizational matter should be noted. We have no certain information about the manner in which the new artillery techniques were introduced or who it was that first made the discoveries. We can assume that experts and specialists at various intermediate levels of authority were responsible. Back in 1915 and 1916, no mechanism had existed by which such innovations could become generally known. Hence they often remained the preserve of a single division or corps. By 1917 GHQ were issuing pamphlets which disseminated all new techniques to Armies, corps, and divisions. Moreover, these pamphlets were periodically updated so that, for example, 'Interpretation of Aerial Photographs' appeared in many editions between 1917 and 1918.[15] So there was no danger that Rawlinson, on resuming command, would, along with his staff, be unaware of the latest technical developments.

---

[12] See the section on flash spotting by Lt.-Colonel H. H. Hemming in ibid.
[13] Guy Hartcup, *The War of Invention: Scientific Developments 1914–18* (London: Brassey, 1988), p. 75.
[14] Ibid., p. 76.
[15] See various editions of this publication in the Australian War Memorial Library.

What did all this amount to? It meant that, before a major battle, the position of most enemy guns could be located by aerial photography, sound ranging, and flash spotting. These locations could then be accurately transposed onto up-to-date maps. British artillerymen now also knew accurately the position of their own guns, and were firing weapons to which sophisticated adjustments had been made that took account of wear, shell variations, and weather conditions at the time of firing. Hence the guns could be ranged with precision on their German counterparts. And this could now be done merely by measuring on a map the bearings and distances between the British and enemy batteries. No ranging shots were needed to establish this relationship. As a result batteries could remain silent until zero hour. When they suddenly sprang into life, there would be every likelihood that their shells would on most occasions find their targets. Surprise, as Rawlinson was about to demonstrate, could thus be reintroduced into battle.

V

The first of Rawlinson's victorious battles was a fairly minor affair, an attack by two brigades to straighten the line held by the Australian Corps in front of the village of Hamel. Three factors convinced Rawlinson that the Germans were vulnerable to counterattack on this sector. The first was the continuing reports from the Australian Corps of the poor state of German defences opposite Fourth Army and the low morale of the troops manning them. The second was the confirmation of these reports provided by the success of Australian raiding operations at Morlancourt and elsewhere. The third was the arrival of the Mark V tank.

This vehicle was a modification of the Mark IVs used at Cambrai which were themselves modifications of the Mark I first employed by Rawlinson on the Somme. The Mark V had several advantages over its predecessors: it was slightly faster than the Mark I and the Mark IV (4.6 m.p.h. against 3.7 m.p.h.); it could be driven by one man instead of four; the fuel tanks were placed outside the cabin and protected by armour; and it had greater endurance, thanks to better insulation for the crews and larger fuel tanks.[16] The most important advantage, however, lay in all-round reliability. The Mark V was not as prone to breakdown as its predecessors.

With these three considerations in mind Rawlinson invited Monash (the newly appointed commander of the Australian Corps) and Courage, the

[16] R. E. Jones, G. E. Rarey and R. J. Icks, *The Fighting Tanks From 1916 to 1933* (Old Greenwich, Connecticut: W.E. Publishers, 1969 – reissue of 1933 ed.), pp. 5, 16, 31.

commander of the tanks attached to Fourth Army, to devise an operation against Hamel village.[17] Their proposals, which arrived at Fourth Army HQ on 21 June, proved strikingly similar. They stressed the element of surprise, to be achieved by silently registering the guns in accordance with the new artillery methods detailed above. So at zero hour the bombardment provided by more than 600 guns would descend upon the unsuspecting German batteries as well as upon strongpoints in Hamel village and Vaire Wood. Simultaneously some 50 to 60 tanks would roll forward covered by a barrage which would move 300 yards in front of them. Behind the tanks would come two brigades of Australian infantry whose ultimate objective would lie some 2,000 yards from the start line. They would then be relieved by two reserve brigades which would consolidate the positions captured. The whole operation was to take about 100 minutes.[18]

The plans of Monash and Courage were to a large extent based on the British experience at Cambrai late in 1917, where tanks had been used in conjunction with a predicted artillery barrage. In one important respect, however, Monash suggested a departure from the Cambrai model. His own corps shared, though to a slightly lesser degree, the manpower shortages of the rest of the British army. The Australian Corps was more than 8,000 men below strength.[19] An operation incurring heavy casualties might cause an entire division to be broken up – a serious consideration in a national force of only five divisions.

To avoid this possibility Monash suggested limiting the number of brigades to be used in the operation to two and spreading them thinly across the entire 7,000 yards of front.[20] The fire power allotted to the attacking formations – 600 guns, 60 tanks, and increased numbers of Lewis guns and machine-guns – would compensate for the lack of men.[21]

This was in marked contrast to the situation at Cambrai where the infantry was still relatively thick on the ground. Thus two brigades at Cambrai would on average have attacked on an 800-yard front.[22] At Hamel this length of front was to be increased fourfold. That is, Monash was endorsing the emphasis on fire power as against manpower which Rawlinson had enunciated in his document in June, but highlighting the importance of artillery as against other forms of weaponry which had been lacking in Rawlinson's exposition.

---

[17] Rawlinson Diary 18/6/18.

[18] Tank Corps Hamel Plan 21/6/18, Monash Papers, AWM DRL3, 2316, Book 18; Australian Corps: 'Hamel Offensive', 21/6/18, AWM 26/10/36i/2.

[19] Rawlinson to GHQ 23/6/18, AWM 26/10/350/5.

[20] Australian Corps: 'Hamel Offensive', 21/6/18.

[21] Ibid.

[22] At Cambrai, at zero hour, 16 brigades attacked on a 6-mile front.

So in the weeks preceding the climactic battles of the Great War, the education of the Fourth Army commander continued apace. Monash was laying down the precise volumes of artillery needed to deliver a crushing blow upon the enemy, while Courage was performing a similar function regarding the quantity of tanks. But the process of education did not stop here. Indeed Monash and Courage were among those receiving wisdom as well as dispensing it. For one of the principal merits of the Hamel plan emanated neither from them nor from Rawlinson but from yet lower levels of command. This concerned the provision of a creeping barrage for the infantry.

Rawlinson and Monash, drawing upon the experience of Cambrai, did not propose giving this form of protection to the foot soldiers. The heavy artillery was to fire a barrage 300 yards in front of the tanks which would be rolling forward in advance of the infantry. It was expected that this barrage and the tanks would between them eliminate most opposition, so that the infantry coming up behind them would proceed unmolested. This reasoning did not recommend itself to the Australian lower order commanders. Blamey, COS to Monash, and Sinclair-MacLagan, the infantry commander who was to carry out the attack, had been present at the ill-fated battle of Bullecourt in 1917. On that occasion, as a result of poor staff work and mechanical unreliability, the majority of tanks had simply not arrived to support the infantry, yet on their account the foot soldiers had been denied the protection of a creeping barrage. Blamey and MacLagan firmly represented to Monash that the infantry and tanks should advance together close behind a creeping barrage fired by the field artillery. As for the heavy artillery barrage which Monash had proposed firing just in advance of the tanks, that would be delivered on likely centres of resistance behind the German front, thereby offering additional protection.[23] These proposals were immediately accepted by both Monash and Rawlinson.[24]

It would be easy to overlook the importance of the refinements here incorporated into the original plan. For it could be argued that, even without such thorough preparation derived from so many sources, a victory at Hamel was a likely outcome – owing simply to the parlous conditions of the adversaries being subjected to attack. In the near vicinity of Hamel there were approximately 2,500 German infantrymen from three divisions all of which had been identified by the Australian Corps Intelligence as low

[23] Paper by Blamey 22/6/18, AWM 26/10/361/2; 4 Division Conference, Monash Papers.
[24] P. A. Pedersen, *Monash as Military Commander* (Melbourne: Melbourne University Press, 1985), p. 227.

grade and with poor morale.[25] The German defences consisted merely of a single line trench and some shell holes, with little wire protection, no dugouts, and no communications trenches.[26] It is unlikely that forces so placed could have withstood a considerably lesser weight of assault than that which was now to be directed against them.

But that is not the crucial point. What matters is that Rawlinson, not least thanks to the initiatives of Monash and Courage and the intervention of Blamey and MacLagan, was now developing methods of attack which stood a substantial chance of subduing – at tolerable cost to his infantry – *whatever* defences the enemy placed in their path. This point needs to be stressed. Under the initial Hamel plan, as devised by Monash and accepted by Rawlinson, some German machine-gunners would almost certainly have survived the barrage and escaped the attention of the tanks. They could then have taken heavy toll of the infantry coming forward unprotected in the wake of the armoured vehicles, even though their resistance would in time have been subdued. The amended plan denied the enemy even this much opportunity. In order to engage the British infantry, the German machine-gun posts had to survive in succession first a bombardment from the heavy guns, then a field artillery barrage, and finally an assault delivered by tanks and infantry acting in concert. This greatly enhanced the British infantry's chances of survival.

VI

All this planning came to fruition at 3.10 a.m. – zero hour for the battle of Hamel – on 4 July.[27] Appropriately, given the date, Rawlinson had managed (if only after some struggle with the American command) to incorporate several American battalions into the attack. The artillery plan worked perfectly. Two-thirds of the 302 heavy guns blanketed the German batteries as the infantry and tanks moved off, silencing 'for some hours after zero the hostile artillery on the main battle front.'[28] In most instances, the deadly combination of the creeping barrage followed closely by the tanks and infantry made short work of the enemy defenders.[29] And in those

[25] Australian Corps: 'Estimate of German strength opposite Hamel 22/6/18', AWM 26/10/361/2.

[26] Sir James E. Edmonds, *Military Operations: France and Belgium, 1918* vol. 3 (London: Macmillan, 1937), p. 198.

[27] Rawlinson, 'Operations By The Australian Corps Against Hamel, Bois de Hamel and Bois de Vaires July 4th 1918', Rawlinson Papers 5201/33/77, NAM.

[28] Ibid.

[29] Ibid. Some shells fell short causing casualties to the Australian troops.

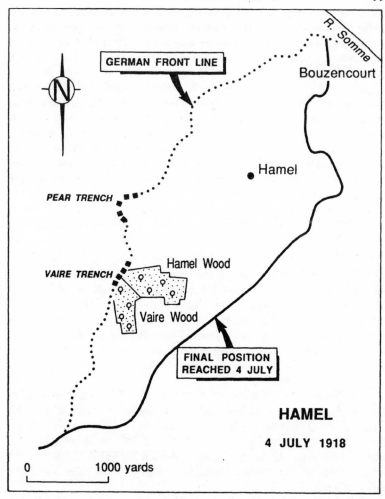

GERMAN FRONT LINE

R. Somme

Bouzencourt

Hamel

PEAR TRENCH

VAIRE TRENCH

Hamel Wood

Vaire Wood

FINAL POSITION
REACHED 4 JULY

HAMEL

4 JULY 1918

0   1000 yards

MAP 27

instances where the tanks did not get forward, the German strongpoints were subdued by a combination of Lewis guns and rifle grenades.[30]

Only one hold-up occurred. This was at Pear Trench. Here the barrage had started beyond the German defences, and the tanks detailed for this section lost their way in the mist. In consequence the trench had to be

[30] Ibid.

taken by frontal assault in the old way, resulting in considerable casualties to the Australians.[31] No better illustration could be provided of the key role that must be assigned to the new methods if a British army running low in infantry was to achieve victories at less than prohibitive cost.

Notwithstanding their hold-up at Pear Trench, by 5 a.m. the two brigades sent in at Hamel were digging in on the whole line of their final objective. The operation had cost about 1,000 casualties (850 Australians, 150 Americans). In return most of the German garrison of 2,500 men had been put out of action: over 1,000 were prisoners and another 1,000 were dead or wounded.[32] The new methods had been entirely vindicated. The questions which remained to be answered were, first, could they now be repeated on a larger scale, and, second, would they prove effective against a more powerful defensive system.

VII

The manner in which the plans for the Hamel operation had reached their final form is illuminating in the overall story of Rawlinson's exercise of command, and goes a long way towards answering the question posed at the start of this chapter. For what we are seeing, in microcosm, is the way in which the role of Army commander was being adapted to the circumstances of war on the Western Front. Put briefly, Rawlinson was becoming less and less the creator of great operations. Rather, his role was diminishing to that of a manager drawing forth and co-ordinating the endeavours of others.

Thus, what is emerging from our exploration of Rawlinson's exercise of command, as it proceeded from the terrible failures of 1 July 1916 to the victories of two years later, is not just the story of a man who eventually got better at his job. That is one aspect of the tale. But the major aspect lies outside Rawlinson. As the complexity of the war expanded, the nature and extent of his job significantly contracted. Thereby it fell more within the limits of his competence.

The operation at Hamel, if only a minor engagement, is noteworthy as revealing the fortunate outcome of this transition. For what occurred there was not just a display of the enhanced weaponry and technical expertise which, at many levels, now lay at Fourth Army's disposal. It was also a demonstration of those many facets of planning which were now passing out of the orbit of the Army commander and into the hands of a considerable array of experts.

[31] Edmonds, *1918* vol. 3, p. 206.
[32] 'Capture of Hamel and Hamel Ridge by the Australian Corps' n.d., AWM 26/10/361/3.

26

Amiens: The Plan

I

In the light of his success at Hamel, Rawlinson's mind turned to putting into effect plans for a larger operation which had been gestating since May but had fallen into abeyance. These plans concerned an attack out of Amiens designed to render that crucial rail centre immune from further menace by the enemy.

Rawlinson had good reason to believe that the situation of the Germans in this sector was not comfortable. Information which came to hand in the aftermath of the Hamel success confirmed the message of that battle: that the German defences in this sector were not in good condition and that nothing was being done to improve them. Raiding parties of Australian troops on 7, 8, 9, 11–12, 13–14, and 16 July entered considerable sections of German line with very little loss. What this process of 'peaceful penetration' appeared to demonstrate was that the enemy were doing nothing to strengthen their trenches and wire, and that the morale of those holding these sketchy defences continued low.

One report by the Australian Corps is of particular note, as indicating that the deficiencies among the enemy were not confined to their frontline troops. According to this report, such new defence work as was being undertaken by the Germans was 'so haphazard as to lead to the conclusion that [it was] dictated entirely by local considerations and not by a general plan.'[1] In other words, no one among the upper echelons of the German forces facing Fourth Army was performing the task to which Rawlinson had applied himself so diligently in May and June: that of ensuring the construction of defences to a coherent overall scheme. At least in this

[1] Australian Corps Intelligence Report 1/8/18, AWM 26/12/472/2.

instance, when confronted by a menacing situation the German command structure was showing less initiative and purpose than the British.

II

The tardiness of the enemy introduced an element of haste into Rawlinson's preparations. As mentioned, it had taken him most of May and June to produce secure defences for the localities into which his army had been driven. He did not propose to allow the enemy, who had also come into new and sketchy positions (if by happier means), to render their defences secure. Hence the timespan between the decision to launch an attack out of Amiens and its execution was only three weeks. This may be contrasted with the three months of planning which had preceded 1 July 1916. The undertaking of 8 August 1918 was altogether more complex, given the developments in artillery techniques and the necessity of co-ordinating all arms so that they would move simultaneously. Nevertheless, such was the highly developed state of the British army that three weeks proved sufficient.

Rawlinson completed his scheme for transmission to GHQ on 17 July.[2] The attack was to be carried out by 11 divisions on a 19,000-yard front, from Morlancourt (to the north of the River Somme) to Demuin (south of the river).

The advance was to be in three stages. The first objective was the German front line and beyond it to a distance 1,000–2,500 yards, the inner Amiens defence line constructed by the French in 1916. Four divisions were assigned to securing this objective: a British division operating north of the Somme, and two Australian divisions and one Canadian division operating south of the river. These troops, on reaching their objective, would halt and consolidate.

A further four divisions, of identical national composition to the first, would then leapfrog through them to capture the second objective. This lay 3,000 yards beyond the first. It encompassed no particular German defensive line and the reason for its selection is not very evident. (Perhaps Rawlinson reasoned that troops could not be expected to advance any further without a pause.) Anyway, the halt here was intended to be brief. Once the position had been consolidated, the same troops would advance to the third stage. This involved a forward move of about 1,000 yards to capture the outer Amiens defence line. Simultaneously, in the Canadian

---

[2] For details in the following paragraphs see: Rawlinson to GHQ, 17/7/18, Rawlinson Papers 5201/33/77, NAM.

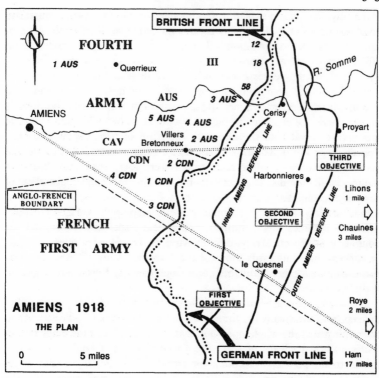

MAP 28

sector, two further divisions would secure the high ground on the southern flank of the main attack. The offensive would then be halted.

Several points here deserve comment. In Rawlinson's scheme, there was to be no complementary advance by the French on the right of the British. Perhaps reflecting on his Somme experiences, Rawlinson concluded that the problems of co-ordinating a combined offensive were just too imposing.

Secondly, a new feature of this plan was the arrangement whereby divisions detailed to capture the first objective would not be involved in the capture of the second. This resulted from the experience of Cambrai. There it had been discovered that by the time they had reached the first line, the troops making the initial assault were reaching exhaustion. GHQ drew the conclusion that for future attacks fresh troops would be needed to advance beyond the first objective. Rawlinson, revealing continuing adaptability, accepted this conclusion.

Thirdly, Rawlinson's plan was characterized by an almost obsessive emphasis on secrecy. The Army commander went so far as to remark that 'the success of the operation will depend to a very great extent... on effecting a complete surprise.'[3] To ensure it, he adopted stringent measures. Initially only corps commanders were informed of the forthcoming attack. Divisional commanders were apprised of it only on 30 July, and infantry brigadiers even later.[4] Again, approach marches by reinforcing infantry and artillery were to be made only at night,[5] and the Canadians were not to come into the line until the night of 6/7 August.[6] Further, Fourth Army Headquarters issued a series of firm instructions concerned with the preservation of secrecy: troops were threatened with dire consequences if they discussed the operation in public;[7] and registration of guns was prohibited except in so far as this lay within the compass of normal artillery activity.[8] Deception was also employed. Work on rearward defensive schemes was continued,[9] while near Arras (that is, beyond the boundaries of Fourth Army) dummy wireless stations were operated so as to conceal the southwards move of the Canadian Corps.[10] At every pre-battle conference held with his corps commanders, Rawlinson reiterated the need for secrecy.

A comment on this is called for. The extent to which Rawlinson managed to keep from the enemy the time and place of the attack is indicative of the skill with which the whole operation was conducted. And the emphasis on secrecy was one means of achieving a vital objective. Certainly, even had the Germans possessed accurate foreknowledge of the attack they could not have greatly improved their defences in the time available, and if they had responded by increasing the numbers of infantry in their forward positions this could only have added to their losses. But what they could have done with advance warning was to relocate their artillery on the eve of the attack, and so have thwarted the effectiveness of British counter-battery fire. For Amiens, therefore, secrecy was of the utmost importance.

[3] Rawlinson to GHQ 17/7/18.

[4] Notes of a Conference 29/7/18 in 'Extracts From Letters And Conferences Concerning The Operations of August 8th, 1918', AWM 26/12/472/2. (Hereafter, Letters and Conferences Concerning Amiens.)

[5] Maj.-Gen. C. E. D. Budworth, 'Fourth Army Artillery in the Battle of Amiens, August 8th, 1918', Royal Artillery Institution Library, MD 1186. (Hereafter, 'Fourth Army Artillery in the Battle of Amiens'.)

[6] Colonel G. W. L. Nicholson, *The Canadian Expeditionary Force 1914–1919* (Ottawa: Queen's Printer, 1962), p. 391. (Hereafter *Canadian Official History*.)

[7] Fourth Army General Instructions – Secrecy – 2/8/18, AWM 26/12/472/1.

[8] 'Fourth Army Artillery in the Battle of Amiens'.

[9] Fourth Army General Instructions – Secrecy.

[10] Nicholson, *Canadian Official History*, p. 389.

The plan did not go unamended. One considerable change was imposed by the (nominally, at least) highest military authority of all: Field-Marshal Ferdinand Foch, generalissimo of the Allied forces. Apprised of the attack, he firmly informed Haig that the French on the British right must be assigned a role. Haig passed on this directive to Rawlinson. Rawlinson, perforce, bowed to necessity. On the day, French participation would contribute little to the success or failure of the operation.

Haig also made last-minute amendments. He had approved Rawlinson's first plan without comment, and had seemed equally happy with some revisions which reached him on 31 July. We may contrast this behaviour with his attitude before and during the Somme campaign of 1916, when he intervened frequently and in detail during the planning process. No doubt in the aftermath of the Hamel operation he was more confident that the Fourth Army knew its business. But it was also the case that, as the British army at every level became a more complex, sophisticated, and above all specialist organization, any detailed intervention by the commander-in-chief became increasingly inappropriate. Haig's job, like Rawlinson's, was – it may be suggested – diminishing not expanding as the forces under his direction grew in expertise and complexity. And Haig, again like Rawlinson, proved far more effective as a commander once the sphere of his activities began to diminish to an extent that brought them within the limits of his capabilities.

Nevertheless, in some respects the old Haig lived on, intervening when it was not appropriate to do so and imposing changes that were not required. With the approach of battle he became – as so often in the past – ever more optimistic about the outcome of the operation and convinced that Rawlinson was suffering from over-caution. So on 5 August, with the attack not 72 hours distant, Haig visited Rawlinson and told him that he should look beyond capturing the inner Amiens defence line. Once that objective had been seized and placed in a state of defence: 'reserves must be pushed on to capture the line Chaulnes–Roye. The general direction of the advance is to be on Ham.'[11] Roye, it may be noticed, was 5 miles beyond Rawlinson's final objective and Ham some 15 miles beyond that. That is, Haig was extending Rawlinson's depth of operations from 7 miles to 27.

In the past, such interventions by Haig had caused drastic dislocation to Rawlinson's plans. On several occasions the Fourth Army commander had been obliged to spread his artillery fire thinly so as to encompass the additional objectives which Haig had introduced – sometimes with dis-astrous consequences for the attempts to reach even his initial goals.

[11] Haig Diary 5/8/18.

Happily, for at least the opening phase of the Amiens operation, Haig's intervention lacked such damaging implications. The additional objectives he had designated happened to be so distant that there was no point in diverting artillery against them. That is, there would on this occasion be no dispersal of effort away from the objectives which Rawlinson had originally proposed.

For the subsequent stages of the battle, however, Haig's intervention would prove more damaging. The Fourth Army was now committed to continue the struggle without pause until it had reached the distant towns of Roye and Ham. There would be no period of consolidation, and no regrouping of infantry and artillery so as to deal effectively with enemy reserves. So, the longer the battle progressed the more likely it was that the Fourth Army would find itself engaging the enemy under unfavourable circumstances.

Rawlinson too, in the weeks following his initial plan of 17 July, admitted some amendments, although not in the drastic manner of Foch and Haig. These concerned the leapfrogging manoeuvres to be undertaken by III Corps and the Canadians. Instead of being carried out by divisions as originally planned, they were to be executed by smaller units (brigades) in the interests of simplicity.

Other changes to which Rawlinson consented concerned the tanks and the cavalry. Not surprisingly in the light of the success at Hamel, for the Amiens operation Rawlinson had assigned a considerable role to tanks as supporters of the infantry. Six battalions of heavy tanks (constituting 196 vehicles), along with 30 supply tanks and 48 light tanks, were allocated to this task. To capture the first objective they and the infantry would advance together behind a creeping barrage; to capture the second and third, the tanks accompanied by mobile artillery would be in the van with the infantry following somewhat behind.[12]

Another aspect of Rawlinson's initial scheme made much less sense. Astonishingly, given all experience since the early weeks of the war, the Cavalry Corps were included in the plan. It was proposed that, should sufficient disorganization develop in the German ranks, the cavalry were to sweep through the gap, capture the German artillery, and then wheel right to threaten the Germans facing the French First Army.[13] Needless to say there was little chance of such a gap making its appearance; nor, should it do so, was the cavalry likely to survive an incursion into it. Probably by this stage of the war Rawlinson was including this aspect simply as a sop to Haig, knowing that it was very likely the commander-in-chief would insist

[12] Rawlinson to GHQ 17/7/18.
[13] Ibid.

on it and very unlikely that any opportunity to employ the cavalry would occur.

Both these aspects of the plan underwent some change in the run-up to the Amiens battle. Fuller (temporarily in command of the Tank Corps) told Rawlinson that for so major an operation many more tanks than the proposed six battalions would be needed. He suggested that the entire Tank Corps of twelve battalions (ten heavy and two light) should participate – a leap from 274 vehicles all told to 552.[14] This made a good deal of sense. The increased quantity of tanks allowed for the allocation of a small number to form a reserve. And with this volume of tanks operating, it followed that even though a fair number would, as usual, fail to reach the battlefield owing to mechanical breakdown, a sufficient body would participate to assist the infantry at every stage of the day's operations. Rawlinson accepted Fuller's proposal, thereby converting Amiens into the largest tank battle of the war.

A further suggestion by Fuller was altogether more bizarre. He feared that, however overwhelming the British assault, the enemy might manage to withdraw their guns and infantry before the attacking forces could get forward to capture them. So he proposed that his light tanks be used in conjunction with the cavalry to speed the advance to the final objective and thwart any attempted German retirement. Rawlinson agreed. In so doing he was transforming the whippet tanks into a form of cavalry acting in conjunction with the mounted soldiers.[15]

This proposal made no sense at all. The two elements, light tanks and men on horseback, had nothing in common. Should the cavalry actually break through into open country, their speed of advance (until they encountered enemy machine-gunners) would greatly exceed the 4 miles per hour of the whippets. If the cavalry slowed their progress in order to remain in tandem with the tanks, they would be losing whatever opportunity presented itself for exploiting success. At the same time they would be placing themselves at a risk from which the whippets would not necessarily be able to protect them. For tanks could only deal with pockets of resistance – such as machine-gun posts – at close range, by which time the cavalry would probably have sustained heavy loss. Yet Rawlinson immediately adopted Fuller's proposal – with unfortunate consequences on the first day of the battle.

The planning for the battle of Amiens, then, seemed in some respects unhappily reminiscent of schemes over which Rawlinson had presided two years earlier: schemes which had yielded little reward at grievous cost. For

---

[14] Fuller to Fourth Army 23/7/18, Fourth Army Papers vol. 49.
[15] Ibid.

what we appear to be witnessing is a familiar mixture, compounded on the one hand of common sense and the application of lessons thoroughly learned, on the other of irresponsible flights of fancy sitting cheek by jowl with a stubborn resistance to the wisdom that the war had cruelly taught.

But the similarity between the planning for this operation and that for many episodes of the Somme campaign in 1916 is only superficial. First, and quite crucially, the Amiens scheme had not been devised in response to pressure to produce an offensive even when no appropriate operation was offering. Its origin was to be found in a glowing opportunity that was plainly beckoning. And second, in practically all the areas that really mattered, hard-learned lessons and mounting expertise were being applied in a manner bound to prove effective. As for those areas where old-style commanders looked stubbornly backwards and new-style technocrats re-fused to relate their visions to the realities on the ground, these were entirely marginal. They would not, in any significant degree, impede the accomplishments of the day.

In sum, 8 August 1918 under Rawlinson's command would not – or to be quite specific *could* not – turn into a replay of 1 July 1916.

27

The Implements

I

The variety of weapons and accessories to battle employed on 8 August 1918, and the manner in which they were co-ordinated, gives this operation a decidedly modern appearance. Indeed it can be argued that at last the British army was employing a true weapons system, with interlocking roles assigned to tanks, aeroplanes, a variety of forms of communication, artillery, infantry, and even horse-soldiers. Only with the most thorough co-operation between the various elements would the attack achieve its maximum effect. By the same token, a serious failure in interaction – particularly between the more vital elements – might imperil the whole undertaking.

Yet it is still the case that some of the implements which had become part of the British army's stock in trade could contribute only marginally to a successful outcome or would contribute only if the operation fulfilled the highest of expectations. The cavalry, for example, would only play a part if Haig's wildest dreams came true; Rawlinson's more modest purposes could be accomplished without them.

Aircraft were plainly more important than this, yet still not of the foremost importance. For the day, the Allies had assembled in the sector of the attack a formidable superiority in number of aeroplanes. Whereas most German squadrons remained tied to the Champagne sector, with the result that they could muster only 365 aeroplanes in the vicinity of Amiens, the British had 800 aircraft to support the attack and the French in excess of 1,000. Further, it is an indication of the increasing sophistication of British preparations for battle that a separate air-plan was submitted to Haig. It provided, in the run-up to the attack, that the Royal Air Force (as it had become on 1 April 1918) should contribute substantially to achieving Rawlinson's object of surprise by driving away any German aircraft seeking to reconnoitre over British lines. Once battle was joined the RAF would undertake other tasks. Some squadrons would fly contact patrols, so alerting the high command to the progress of the infantry and indicating where artillery support was needed. Others would drop supplies of ammunition to troops advancing on the forward objectives, or, as opportunities arose, harass enemy troops and batteries beyond artillery range. And for the first time in war, aircraft in certain sectors would seek to drop smoke bombs so as to screen advancing British infantry from the observation of the enemy.[1]

All of this was of considerable potential value, and evidence of the increasing use of creative imagination in the conduct of battles. But the truly valuable contribution of aircraft remained their role as ancillaries to the two principal elements in the whole undertaking – the elements which retained their pre-eminence in all of the Western Front's great endeavours from the war's opening to its close – infantry and artillery.

The attack by Fourth Army out of Amiens was to be delivered by ten divisions of infantry, with a further division in reserve. This was just about as many divisions as had attacked on 1 July 1916, but it involved by no means the same number of men. On the first day of the Somme, ten divisions had contained roughly 100,000 men. Two years and a multitude of casualties later, they comprised only half that number. This is important given that the front of attack on 8 August 1918 was roughly the same as on 1 July 1916. In other words, compared to the Somme, half the number of men would be attacking the same length of front. Would the later attack fail then, not for the reasons of two years before, but from a simple want of numbers?

The answer would prove to be in the negative. Lack of numbers did not constitute a bar to success. Some of the reasons concern the condition of the enemy, to which reference has already been made: the sketchy defences and inadequate weaponry at their disposal, and the low morale which befalls troops aware of inadequate attention and preparation by their own high command. Other reasons for the Fourth Army's success lie on the British side of the front and concern the forces carrying out the attack: the manner of their employment, and the resources at their disposal.

First, the attack formations adopted by Rawlinson's corps commanders ensured that the troops would not advance shoulder to shoulder as so often on 1 July 1916. Rather, they would attack in widely separated columns. Thus they would present a dispersed target to enemy machine-guns and artillery.[2]

---

[1] S. F. Wise, *Canadian Airmen and the First World War: The Official History of the Royal Canadian Air Force* vol. I (Toronto: University of Toronto Press, 1980), pp. 521–7.

[2] Bean, *Australian Official History* vol. 6, p. 530; Nicholson, *Canadian Official History*, p. 398.

Second, Rawlinson – almost certainly recalling 1 July 1916 – ordered that equipment carried by the troops be reduced to a bare minimum.[3] This enhanced rapidity of movement, which was likely to be important especially for the second wave of troops advancing beyond the first objective without the protection of the creeping barrage.

Third, and even more important, the 500 men in a 1918 battalion packed a considerably heavier punch in terms of firepower than did the 1,000-strong infantry battalion of two years earlier. A 1916 battalion, apart from its rifles which were well-nigh useless in trench warfare, might have had at its disposal 4 Lewis guns and one or two light trench mortars. This may be contrasted with 1918, when each battalion included 30 Lewis guns, 8 light trench mortars,[4] and at least 16 rifle-grenadiers.[5] In addition, a battalion in the vanguard of the advance would enjoy the support of at least 6 tanks.

What is noteworthy about all these weapons is that, unlike the rifle, they were wholly suited to dealing with the major obstacles (other than the enemy's artillery) likely to be encountered by the infantry as they went forward, especially the enemy's machine-gun strongpoints surrounded by barbed wire or encased in concrete. These positions could now be dealt with at medium range (200 yards or so) by trench mortar or rifle grenade detachments, or they could be taken in the flank by teams of Lewis gunners working around them, or they could be crushed by the tanks. (Needless to say, on many occasions enemy machine-gunners would find themselves having to contend with a combination of these weapons.)

Yet the principal implements which would enable Rawlinson's depleted force of foot soldiers to get forward – as twice their number had so signally failed to do two years before – would not be Lewis guns or mortars or even tanks. Now more than ever it would be the artillery: those long black arms – as Wilfred Owen described them – 'slowly lifted up . . . towering towards Heaven, about to curse.'

II

Rawlinson's plan had not specified the amount of artillery necessary to facilitate the infantry's attack. At the Somme that would generally have meant that no such calculation was being made; whatever artillery lay to

---

[3] Nicholson, *Canadian Official History*, p. 398.
[4] Captain A. D. Ellis, *The Story of the Fifth Australian Division* (London: Hodder and Stoughton, n.d.), pp. 3–4.
[5] Bean, *Australian Official History* vol. 6, p. 37.

hand would be assembled and deemed sufficient. Nothing of the sort was true at the time of Amiens. By 1918 innovations and refinements in artillery methods ensured that the sorts of calculation vital to opening a way for the infantry were being undertaken as a matter of course. This was not just a case of the British commanders learning from their past mistakes. More significantly, the new artillery methods by their very nature would make good any deficiencies on the part of the commanders.

Back in July 1916 the task of the artillery had been to fire a sufficiency of shells to destroy a section of trench. As a way of facilitating an advance by the infantry this was deficient in two respects. Artillery fire might immobilize trench defenders for a relatively brief period, but it could not totally eliminate them. And a bombardment which dealt only with the enemy's trenches left his artillery intact, with terrible implications for the attacking infantry.

It is indicative of the advances which Britain's artillerymen had made between 1916 and 1918 that, for Amiens, the artillery plan did not even include trench destruction. Rather, the field artillery would fire a creeping barrage which was unlikely to kill, but stood a good chance of neutralizing, the German trench-dwellers for a short period; long enough, it was calculated, for approaching British infantry to fall on their adversaries before the latter could man their weapons. Simultaneously the heavy artillery would unleash what should prove a devastating counter-battery bombardment. On the most hopeful view this would destroy the German guns. On the least hopeful it would render the enemy artillerymen incapable of serving them for the duration of the attack. By these means the two most deadly opponents of an infantry operation – the machine-gun and the artillery piece – would be so diminished in effectiveness that they might cease to be capable of repelling Fourth Army's advance.

By 1918, as it happened, the numbers of guns and shells needed for these two vital tasks – creeping barrage and counter-battery – were always calculated. This more scientific approach to gunnery had come about gradually. Concerning the creeping barrage, already during the Somme campaign Fourth Army had been trying to calculate the optimum number of shells required per gun per minute, and the optimum rate at which the barrage should advance; and during 1917 this process had been continued, principally by Third Army during the battle of Arras and by Second Army during the offensive at Ypres. So by 1918 it had been concluded that for adequate infantry protection the requirements were as follows: one gun for each 25 yards of trench under attack, each gun firing 4 rounds of shrapnel or high explosive per minute; the rate of advance of the barrage being 25 yards per minute.[6] This was the pattern adopted at Amiens, but with a further refinement. The barrage advanced a bit more quickly in the early stages of the attack, when progress was easiest, and slowed down as the advance proceeded and enemy resistance hardened.[7]

This formula raised artillery planning – once a matter of guesswork or the employment of whatever weapons and shells lay to hand – to the level of a mathematical equation. For a creeping barrage, the number of guns required was decided by long division: the number of yards of front to be attacked divided by 25. (A figure representing only one dimension happened to be appropriate, as the guns had only to cover the length of front over which the infantry were advancing.) The volume of shells needed was a matter of multiplication: the number of guns times the number of rounds per minute times the number of minutes during which the barrage was to be fired. (The last figure would be based on a calculation of the length of time required for the infantry to reach the first objective – this being the furthest distance that the creeping barrage could attain.)

We have evidence that for Amiens this sort of calculation was actually made. So the Australian Corps's records state:

> The extent of the Corps frontage for the operation is approximately 7000 yards. In order to cover this effectively by a barrage[,] eighteen Field Artillery Brigades will be required.[8]

And the plan goes on to state that, because there were more than enough weapons for this purpose, some guns could be removed from the creeping barrage to support the second phase of the attack without rendering inadequate the protection being provided for the troops advancing on the first objective.

Even without this evidence of calculation, the figures speak for themselves. At Amiens the Fourth Army attacked on a front of 19,000 yards – a figure that should be reduced to 16,000 for the creeping barrage which would not be employed on the northern defensive flank or the swamplands of the Somme. Using the formula of one field gun per 25 yards of front and 4 rounds per minute for an assault lasting 2 hours, the number of field guns required would be 640 and the number of shells 300,000. On the day, Fourth Army erred on the side of generosity; nearer 700 field guns were employed and 350,000 shells fired. (The number of field guns actu-

---

[6] Lt.-Col. A. F. Brooke, 'The evolution of artillery in the Great War', *Journal of the Royal Artillery*, 53 (1926–27), pp. 236–7.

[7] 'Fourth Army Artillery in the Battle of Amiens'.

[8] Australian Corps Amiens Plan, 31/7/18, AWM 26/12/361/4.

ally available, it is worth noting, was 1,236; the number of shells 700,000. Nothing reveals more starkly the contrast between diminishing resources of manpower and a superabundance of weapons and ammunition.)[9]

For counter-battery fire, artillery calculations took a different form. In 1916, when Rawlinson had last overseen a major offensive, counter-battery programmes had been relatively ineffectual for three reasons: there were never enough heavy guns; it was not possible to locate most of the enemy's artillery pieces; and even when the German batteries could be identified, the chances of scoring a hit were small. By 1918 these problems scarcely existed. Great numbers of heavy guns were now available. The introduction of sound ranging and flash spotting, and the marked improvement – both in quality and quantity – of aerial reconnaissance, facilitated the pinpointing of enemy batteries. And the new artillery methods gave the British gunners every prospect of bringing their shells down on their targets.

Fourth Army HQ took care to ensure that the improved artillery techniques were uniformly adopted by corps and divisional gunners. GHQ circulars distributed down to divisional level carried the message of these developments. And to drive home the serious view that Fourth Army artillery staff took of this matter, all corps were circulated with clear directives:

> In all Corps definite orders will be issued to the Artillery enforcing the observance of all precautions such as:-
>
> (i) Testing of all sights by officers immediately previous to Zero day.
> (ii) The duties of Section Commanders and the use of clinometers in connection with checking laying [of guns on the target] during operations.
> (iii) Close attention to corrections for atmospheric errors, etc.
> (iv) The careful sorting of all ammunition.
>
> The importance of the closest supervision in the above matters is to be impressed upon all Brigade Commanders.[10]

In addition the Army calibration range ensured that guns were adjusted individually for wear immediately before the operations.[11]

So, by the eve of the attack at Amiens, 95 per cent of enemy guns (504 out of 530) within the Fourth Army's zone of operations had been correctly

---

[9] 'Fourth Army Artillery in the Battle of Amiens'.

[10] Fourth Army Artillery Instructions No. 1, 2/8/18, Fourth Army Papers vol. 50.

[11] 'Fourth Army Artillery in the Battle of Amiens'.

identified.[12] This enabled an appropriate number of guns to be assigned to engaging the German artillery at zero, and a sufficient quantity of shells to be supplied to keep the enemy batteries neutralized during the advance of the infantry. Again, the figures speak for themselves. Facing Fourth Army were 530 guns, that is, about 108 batteries. The British had 677 heavy guns, two-thirds of which (that is, 450) could be employed against them – that is, four British guns continually engaging one enemy battery. Ammunition supplies were equally lavish. In the case of Fourth Army's 60 pounders, each gun had available four rounds to dispatch at its target every minute for a period of four hours.[13] As a formula for victory, this could hardly have been bettered.

[12] Fourth Army Fortnightly Artillery Reports for July and August, Fourth Army War Diary July and August 1918, Fourth Army Papers, vols 43 and 44.
[13] See 'Fourth Army Artillery in the Battle of Amiens.'

28

8 August 1918

I

On the immediate front of battle on 8 August, an equal number of British and German divisions confronted each other. Facing the eleven attacking divisions of Rawlinson's Fourth Army stood seven divisions from the German Second and Eighteenth Armies, with a further four divisions in reserve.[1] Yet despite this appearance of parity, the British enjoyed a substantial superiority in manpower. A Fourth Army division encompassed about 7,000 men, to a total of 75,000 for the eleven divisions engaged. No German division exceeded 4,000 men, and some fell below 3,000. So even including the four reserve divisions, there were but 37,000 Germans in the near vicinity of the battle zone. Nor was Rawlinson unaware of this agreeable situation. Fourth Army Intelligence had managed to gauge the depleted strengths of the German divisions almost to the last man.[2]

Rawlinson, further, had cause to know that the enemy's positions were not secure against attack. In most areas the German side of the front consisted of a series of shallow trenches, not all of them wired. Supporting these were but few communication trenches and dugouts and no organized defence lines in rear areas. Given the walkover at Hamel, and the pressure exerted thereafter by the 'peaceful penetration' operations of the Australian Corps, the enemy had been given fair warning to look to their defences. Yet it appeared that the response at all levels of the German command in the weeks before Amiens was one of complacency and indolence. According to the reports of British raiding parties: 'work in forward defences still

[1] In the German front lines were the 14 Bavarian, 225, 117, 41, 13, 108 and 27 divisions; in reserve the 109, 54, 43R, and 107 divisions. See maps in AWM 26/12/472/3.
[2] 'Numbers of Rifles and Machine Guns in German Divisions Holding The Line from Albert to Thinnes (inc) July 28th, 1918', in Letters and Conferences Concerning Amiens.

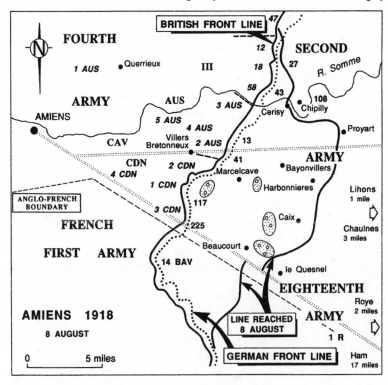

MAP 29

remains practically nil';[3] when new work was discovered it was found to be haphazard, not part of a programme intended systematically to improve the German positions.[4]

This combination of torpor and overconfidence extended to the very summit of the German army. On 5 August, Rupprecht (commander of the Army Group facing Fourth Army) reported that in general he was satisfied with conditions on his front. The situation was quiet, morale was good.[5] Ludendorff also was complacent (or hopelessly ill-informed about conditions at the front). On 4 August he issued a tactical memorandum which stated:

---

[3] Fourth Army War Diary July 1918, Fourth Army Papers vol. 43.

[4] Australian Corps Intelligence Report 1/8/18, AWM 26/12/472/2.

[5] *Der Weltkrieg* vol. 14 (Berlin: Mittler, 1944), p. 551.

At this present moment we occupy everywhere positions which have been very strongly fortified, and we have, I am convinced, effected a judicious organization in depth of the infantry and artillery. Henceforward, we can await every hostile attack with the greater confidence ... we should wish for nothing better than to see the enemy launch an offensive.[6]

His wish, whether or not it was seriously meant, was about to be granted.

II

On the British side, the concentration of men, machines, weapons, and horses began on the night of 29/30 July. The next few days witnessed the arrival of over 1,000 additional guns with their ammunition, three divisions of cavalry, and 450 tanks. One aspect of the logistics of this undertaking deserves mention: each of the three tank brigades required a reserve of 80,000 gallons of petrol, 20,000 pounds of grease, and 20,000 gallons of oil.

The last arrivals were the divisions of the Canadian Corps. They began moving into the back areas on 30 July. But so important was it to conceal their whereabouts from the enemy that they did not enter the front line until eight days later: indeed just two hours before zero. In total, 290 trains were employed in bringing the reinforcements and supplies to Amiens.[7]

The battle opened at 4.20 a.m. on 8 August. What happened in the ensuing 12 hours was remarkable. By mid-afternoon all objectives, except in the extreme south and north of the operation, were in British hands. The leapfrogging of formations went according to plan. The cost was relatively low: 9,000 British casualties. The rewards were high: Fourth Army advanced 8 miles on a 15,000-yard front, captured over 400 guns, and inflicted on the enemy 27,000 casualties, 12,000 of whom were prisoners.[8] That is, by day's end the best part of six German divisions had ceased to exist.

Once battle was joined, Rawlinson (whose major contribution had been made weeks before) had little part to play. Except in the case of III Corps – to which reference will be made shortly – reports reaching Fourth Army

---

[6] Brigadier-General Sir James Edmonds, *Military Operations: France and Belgium, 1918* vol. 4 (London: HMSO, 1947), p. 38.
[7] The information in this paragraph is taken from an article by Lt.-General Sir Archibald Montgomery-Massingberd, '8th August, 1918', in *Journal of the Royal Artillery*, 55 (1928), pp. 13–37.
[8] Edmonds, *1918* vol. 4, pp. 84–5.

Headquarters were in the main accurate, an indication that the communications system was functioning efficiently. What they revealed was that most things were going extremely well, and that in consequence no intervention by the high command was called for. Rawlinson's only part was to monitor the progress of his troops and consider the options offering for subsequent stages of the battle. Nevertheless, in a study of command it is important to elucidate the factors crucial to Fourth Army's success. For a key question presents itself. Had Rawlinson and his subordinates at last produced a winning formula? Or had their triumph on this occasion been dependent on blunders and negligence on the part of the enemy?

In important respects, as has already been indicated, the defenders were ill-equipped to withstand this particular assault. Not only were they wanting in manpower but in some localities they played into the hands of the attackers by crowding infantry into the front line.[9] Moreover, they had constructed no defensive system behind their front, and even the strong-points situated in woods and villages were not mutually supporting.

Yet it would be difficult to assert that these factors made the difference between defeat and victory. A larger number of German infantrymen in the same defensive positions would probably have meant heavier German casualties rather than more effective resistance. Stronger and better-integrated German defences would certainly have meant a slower British advance, but there is no reason for believing that an advance would not have been accomplished. The experience of Cambrai provides perspective here. The defences at Cambrai were altogether stronger than those at Amiens, and yet until the end of the day they failed to halt Third Army – which, it may be noted, was employing only the inferior Mark IV tank. The fact was that on 8 August 1918 the British had at their disposal the wherewithal to overcome any defences that the Germans might have constructed in the time available. A more vigorous response to the approaching offensive might have lessened the extent of the Germans' defeat, but that was all.

A word must also be said on the matter of morale, if only because some authorities regard this as the key factor in the British success. Two points need to be made. If German morale was not what it had been back in 1916, neither was British. Despite the relative superiority of the attacking forces to the defending on 8 August 1918, it was still the case that Rawlinson's forces had variously been through such morale-dampening experiences as Arras, Bullecourt, Third Ypres, and the March retreat. In truth, the participants on both sides at Amiens had been drained by the years of trench warfare and bloody offensives.

---

[9] Bean, *Australian Official History* vol. 6, pp. 536–7.

In any case, explaining victory and defeat at Amiens in terms of morale misses the real nature of the transaction. High morale could avail German artillerymen little when assailed by such an onslaught of high explosive as was delivered by the British counter-battery programme, or help German machine-gunners when set upon by a combination of tanks, mortars, and rifle grenades in the aftermath of a creeping barrage. Writing after the war, the authors of the German official account came by stages to recognize this. At the outset they seemed ready to settle for the conventional explanations of failure: indifferent troops and a collapsing home front. But at the last this did not satisfy. So they went on to acknowledge the part played by a further factor: the skilful tactics employed by the British. They noted that there were fresh German formations, such as 117 Division, in the line at Amiens, yet these were no more able to withstand the British attack than more battle-weary soldiers. They also observed that when key elements of the British weapons system failed – for example, when tanks sometimes crucial to success broke down – then even worn-out German troops managed to stabilize the front.[10] The conclusion is inescapable. The Germans, however parlous their circumstances, were defeated by superior fire-power tactics, which even their best troops could not withstand.

III

In sum, in vital respects the Fourth Army's planners were applying the means of victory. Pre-eminent among these was the counter-battery programme. It hardly needs to be stressed that, had the German artillery survived the bombardment unscathed, it could have exacted a fearful toll on the advancing infantry and tanks. This would have been especially true in the later stages of the attack when British forces came within range of the entire complement of German guns.

In the event, German artillery (except in the north, for reasons shortly to be discussed) was crushed.[11] The British divisions on the southern sector of the front described the enemy barrage as 'very weak and, as the attack progressed [it] ceased altogether.'[12] It was a victory less over the German guns, most of which remained intact, than over the German gunners, who were simply rendered incapable of operating their weapons. This is made clear in Fourth Army's post-battle report:

[10] For the German account see *Der Weltkrieg* vol. 14, Chapter VIII, pp. 549–67. For the lessons of the battle, including the experience of 117 Division, see pp. 564–7.

[11] Fourth Australian Division: 'Report of Operations – August 7th to August 10th, 1918', AWM 26/12/546/6.

[12] Third Australian Division: 'Narrative of Operations, 8th August to 13th August 1918', AWM 26/12/528/9.

Some guns had been hit and some dumps of ammunition blown up, but . . . in the majority of cases, the detachments had evidently either been driven from their guns or had failed to man them. Some guns were captured with camouflage material over them, and muzzle and breech covers still on. Where attempts had been made to keep the guns in action or to limber up, the havoc wrought amongst personnel and horses was generally great, and afforded excellent testimony to the accuracy of the fire and the destructive effect of the shells.[13]

As further evidence that it was the German gunners, rather than their guns, that fell victim to the British bombardment, it is noteworthy that some 450 out of a probable 500 German guns operating to the south of the Somme were captured intact.[14]

The significance of this virtual elimination of the enemy artillery scarcely needs to be stressed. British tanks and infantry could proceed behind the creeping barrage unhindered by this potentially formidable adversary.

The second key factor enabling Rawlinson's troops to get forward was surprise. This flowed in part from British dominance in the air which denied the enemy the chance to oversee Fourth Army's preparations; in part from the gunners' ability to fire a predicted barrage and so not advertise the imminence of the attack; and in part from the climatic conditions which obtained on the morning of the battle.

Thanks to surprise, the attacking infantry were able to overwhelm many of the frontline enemy garrisons before the latter were even aware that an offensive was under way.[15] Some authorities have argued that the crucial factor in bringing this about was a heavy early-morning fog, which reduced visibility in most areas to a few feet. This view must be qualified. Certainly, the fog did contribute to the infantry's ability sometimes to arrive unannounced at the German front line, and thereby it helped to reduce Fourth Army's casualties and increase their bag of prisoners. But the element of surprise did not in essence depend on chance factors. Command of the air and the ability to delay the bombardment until the moment the advance began were sufficient to ensure that, be it in mist or bright sunlight, the enemy would not receive sufficient notice that an attack was on hand. (Again, the experience of Cambrai is instructive. Without the aid of fog but by means of a predicted bombardment and air superiority the

---

[13] 'Fourth Army Artillery in the Battle of Amiens'.

[14] Ibid.

[15] For such instances see Nicholson, *Canadian Official History* pp. 399–401, Bean, *Australian Official History* vol. 6, pp. 532–40; Second Australian Division: 'Narrative of Operations, 8th August to 13th August, 1918', AWM 26/12/528/9.

British had caught their enemies off guard and had even penetrated the formidable Hindenburg Line.)

In the second and subsequent stages of the advance on this memorable 8 August, neither surprise nor fog would be present to aid the attackers. An even more noteworthy absentee would be the creeping barrage, for British forces were now proceeding beyond the range of their field artillery. Yet the advance managed to continue.

Fundamental to everything, of course, was the continued suppression of the German artillery by Fourth Army's heavy guns. But that left German infantry, and in particular German machine-gun strongpoints, to be dealt with. In the event, the tanks along with the close-support weapons of the infantry – Lewis guns, trench mortars, and rifle grenades – were sufficient to overcome these.

The lifting of the fog was a positive advantage at this stage. The sight of a mass of 400 tanks trundling towards them was plainly too imposing a sight for numbers of German troops – who, it should be recalled, were hardly expecting to be set upon at this early stage of the conflict. A great many of them fled or surrendered.[16] Indeed, the two hours of 8 August 1918 during which British forces at Amiens advanced from their first to their second objectives constituted for the tanks their most compelling moment of the whole war. The crushing blow delivered to the defenders' capacity and will to resist by the unfamiliarity and sheer volume of tanks would not, in like degree, be repeated from this day to the ending of the war.

Not all resistance crumbled. But the Germans who at this phase chose to stand and fight found themselves outclassed by the combination of armoured vehicles with infantry employing an effective range of close-support weapons.[17] The most formidable opposition offered by the Germans at this stage came from those garrisons located in the many woods and villages which stood between the Fourth Army troops and their objectives. (This was particularly the case in the Canadian sector.) On the Somme two years earlier, any one of these obstacles might have delayed the infantry for considerable periods of time. Now, however, the British had the weapons needed to deal with them. In the case of both woods and villages, the almost invariable practice of the Canadians and Australians was to outflank the obstacles with tanks working in co-operation with infantry, and then to attack them from all sides with as much fire power as lay to hand.[18] Thereby the strongpoints were mopped up one by one.

---

[16] Edmonds, *1918* vol. 4, p. 48; Second Australian Division Narrative.

[17] Nicholson, *Canadian Official History*, p. 400; Fifth Australian Division: 'Report on Operations', AWM 26/12/559/6.

[18] For examples see Edmonds, *1918* vol. 4, pp. 48–50; Bean, *Australian Official History* vol. 6, p. 535.

On occasions, certainly, some elements in the British weapons system fell short. Tanks failed to arrive to support the infantry, or field artillery in the process of being brought forward was not available when the attack went in. What is notable, however, is that even in these instances there was always a sufficiency of fire power at the disposal of the infantry to beat down the strongest opposition.[19]

In a measure, of course, this success was evidence of the quality of the infantry carrying out the attack. The Australian and Canadian divisions were relatively fresh and made up in the main of battle-hardened veterans. There was no lack of determination on their part to get to grips with the enemy. Yet too much should not be made of this aspect. At the battle of the Somme in 1916 the attacking infantry were not wanting in courage or enthusiasm. It availed them little as long as they lacked weapons and tactics appropriate to deal with their opponents. At Amiens in 1918 the weapons, and a serviceable plan, were to hand. Certainly the Australians and Canadians employed both skilfully. But without these implements, and in the absence of the technical expertise of the artillerymen, progress, as in 1916, would have been meagre and would have been dearly bought.

IV

Above we posed the question: were Rawlinson and the forces under his command on 8 August 1918 applying a winning formula, or was their success dependent on the blunders of their enemies? The answer is now evident. A more efficient adversary in better spirits might not have yielded so much; he would certainly have been obliged to yield.

Certain things, it needs to be added, did not go all that well for Fourth Army on 8 August 1918. The attempt to employ whippet tanks in co-operation with the cavalry was a predictable fiasco. In most areas the cavalry soon outdistanced the tanks and proceeded on their own. Fortunately for the horse-soldiers, by this stage most German resistance had collapsed. Hence they managed to occupy some sections of the final objective unimpeded. In other areas, however, their attempt to advance unescorted resulted in heavy casualties at the hands of German machine-guns.[20] In any case the attempted combination of ill-matched arms failed dismally. It ended – as Edmonds discreetly put it – with 'a certain amount of mutual recrimination'.[21]

In the extreme south 4 Canadian Division failed to capture all of its

[19] For an example of infantry alone acting successfully against a German strongpoint see Nicholson, *Canadian Official History*, p. 400.

[20] Edmonds, *1918* vol. 4, p. 51.

[21] Ibid., p. 53.

objectives. What thwarted it was the arrival of two regiments of the 1 German Reserve Division – an event not anticipated by Fourth Army Intelligence. This German division was located just west of Roye when the battle opened, and with great dispatch placed two of its regiments in front of Le Quesnel by 8.30 a.m.[22] By the time the Canadians arrived (about 3 p.m.)[23] the regiment was dug in and even supported by a number of field guns which had managed to get forward. The Canadians were beyond the protection of their own artillery, had few tanks, and were at the end of a long march.[24] Under these conditions it is not surprising that the enemy did not relinquish the Le Quesnel sector of the front.

The Australians also experienced some difficulty, not on their main front of attack where a successful raid by armoured cars added to the disorganization of the German defence,[25] but on their extreme left flank, along the southern bank of the River Somme. There 4 Australian Division, advancing over the marshes of the Somme, found themselves heavily fired upon by machine-guns and artillery from the north of the river. Further progress here proved impossible. So a reserve brigade was brought forward and a defensive flank formed facing the river.[26]

What this setback revealed was that all had not gone well with the attack of III Corps. The Chipilly Spur, whence came the German fire so damaging to the Australians, was the principal objective of III Corps's 58 Division. Plainly it had not succumbed to their attack.

Much, in truth, had gone wrong for the British forces to the north of the Somme, and by the end of the day they were still short of their first objectives. From the outset they had been dogged by ill-luck. Two days before the opening of the attack, two of the III Corps divisions (18 and 58) had been heavily attacked by a fresh German division (the 27th) and driven back 500 yards.[27] On the following day – that is, 7 August – they had counterattacked and retaken most of the lost ground, but this operation had left the two divisions in poor condition for an offensive within 24 hours. Further, the Germans in this sector were expecting a renewal of the engagement and so were on the alert when the main attack began.[28]

Nor were III Corps operating in the manageable conditions which obtained to their south. The ground over which the advance was to be made

[22] Edmonds, *1918* vol. 4, p. 91.

[23] Ibid., p. 57.

[24] Nicholson, *Canadian Official History*, p. 405.

[25] Fifth Australian Division Report on Operations.

[26] Fourth Australian Division Report on Operations.

[27] III Corps War Diary 6/8/18, WO 95/680.

[28] Edmonds, *1918* vol. 4, p. 76.

was indented by numerous small ravines[29] which hampered the movement of infantry and were a particular obstacle to tanks. In any case III Corps had only been allocated 36 tanks, in contrast to the 288 all told (operating in more suitable territory) at the disposal of the Canadians and the Australians. This meant that III Corps were for the most part trying to advance without the tank support contributing so largely to success south of the Somme.[30]

Furthermore, apparently all did not go well with the counter-battery programme in this sector. For it was the case that the Germans managed to support their troops with 'ample' artillery fire.[31] Perhaps counter-battery intelligence had failed to learn of the existence of the batteries belonging to the newly arrived German 27 Division, or had simply lacked sufficient time in which to pinpoint them.

Finally, the two assault divisions of III Corps[32] were anything but well equipped for their task. As mentioned, they had just been through two days of hard fighting and see-sawing fortunes. But this was only the culmination of a positive saga of hardships. Both divisions had been almost destroyed in the March retreat. The reinforced 58 Division had then suffered anew in the fighting around Villers Bretonneux in April, and had lost 3,000 men.[33] Both divisions had been rebuilt (cobbled together might be a more accurate description) with the rawest of conscripts brought hastily from Britain in the post-March panic. The troops so acquired had been allotted to various divisions on no more considered a basis than the date on which they had arrived in France. Coming as they did from all parts of the United Kingdom, they possessed none of the coherence of the locally recruited 'pals' divisions of 1916 – a coherence which, to a significant degree, was still a feature of the Canadian and Australian divisions. The training of these new arrivals following their descent upon France had at best been sketchy, and such experienced soldiers as they found in their units were still recuperating from the experience of retreat. In sum, there was good reason to question the readiness of these III Corps divisions for battle in particularly testing circumstances and with inadequate tank support.

In the context of military command, these varied explanations of the relative failure of operations north of the Somme on 8 August raise an important question. Rawlinson was not ignorant of the condition of III Corps's divisions. He was also aware of the difficult terrain over which they must advance, and their paucity of tank support. Further, he had admitted

[29] Ibid., p. 74.

[30] Ibid., p. 77.

[31] Ibid., p. 76.

[32] The third division was merely to form a defensive flank to the north.

[33] Edmonds, *1918* vol. 4, p. 75.

to severe reservations about the competence of Butler, the commander of III Corps.[34] (Rawlinson's doubts were not without substance. Butler was suffering from overstrain and would be relieved temporarily on 11 August.)[35]

Given these circumstances, there seemed good grounds for acquiring fresh divisions for III Corps or even for bringing an entirely new corps into the area. There would have been no problem about this. The British had at least some divisions on the Western Front which had escaped involvement in the March retreat. There was also no lack of corps staff to substitute for the exhausted Butler. Certainly none of this would have guaranteed success north of the Somme, given the effects of the German attack on the eve of battle, the unsuitability of the terrain for a swift advance, and the paucity of tanks there. But Rawlinson had a responsibility not to compound these difficulties by assigning this phase of the operation to worn-down or inexperienced divisions.

Rawlinson failed in this aspect of his task. No doubt his attention was focused on the south of the Somme, where the main operation would be conducted and the prospects seemed so good. But in selling short the flanking operation to the north, Rawlinson was doing a disservice not just to III Corps but to the Australians on the south bank of the river, who were required to advance in an area dominated from their left.

Fortunately for the operation as a whole, this misjudgement by the command did not weigh too heavily. The Australian advance proved so rapid that the hold-up on the left wing, while causing unnecessary casualties, did not enable the enemy south of the Somme to rally. Soon the Australians, preceded by the Canadians, were within sight of their third and final objective for the day: something more formidable than a line on a map, which was all that the second objective had amounted to, but not very much more formidable. The third objective consisted of trenches originally dug by the French and now considerably decayed, which the Germans since capturing had done little to restore. This had the incidental consequence for the defenders that the parapets faced the wrong way and the barbed wire lay on the far side from where any attack would be coming. The momentum, the battle skills, and the combination of weapons which had brought Fourth Army's forces this far would not be halted by obstacles as rudimentary as these. In short order, the third objective fell into the attacker's grasp.

---

[34] See Rawlinson's diary for 18/7/18, 6/8/18.
[35] Edmonds, *1918* vol. 4, p. 151.

29

The Following Days

I

As a generalization, even where the first day of a major attack on the Western Front went well, the second and subsequent days proved hazardous. In the case of Amiens this was particularly so, just because the initial advance had enjoyed such success. So far forward had the front line gone that only a small complement of the heavy artillery could be brought into position for the next day, and none of these guns had been registered on particular targets. It is unnecessary to reiterate the obstacles awaiting an attack unsupported by accurate counter-battery fire.

The situation regarding field artillery was little better. Some guns were not yet in place. Barrage plans had to be developed in haste. Good communications between advancing infantry and the guns no longer obtained. Consequently there was uncertainty in the gun lines about the precise whereabouts of the infantry they were supposed to be assisting.

Inadequacies in artillery support were not the only obstacles to a repetition on 9 August of the success of the day before. A majority of tanks were at this moment out of action – some permanently, thanks to destruction by enemy artillery, others temporarily, on account of mechanical failure. And even where tanks remained serviceable, their crews were succumbing to exhaustion. Moreover, the elimination of tanks was not spread evenly along the front: some units retained considerable tank support, others none at all.

The situation of the infantry was also more precarious by 9 August. Their elaborate communications system ceased at what had been their front line of the day before, so that the further they advanced the more uncertain was the flow of information. Thus communications still passed freely between Rawlinson, his corps commanders, and the commanders of divisions. But divisional commanders were frequently unable to contact the headquarters of their brigades, on whose co-ordinated action the next successful move must depend.

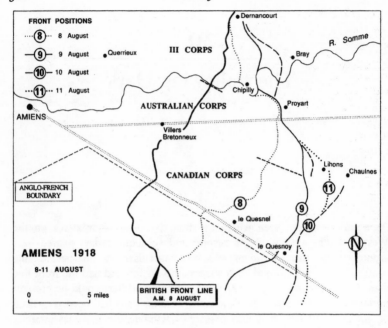

MAP 30

Causes for concern did not cease here. There was the mounting weariness of even successful infantry. And there was the disjunction between the Australian Corps south of the Somme and III Corps to its north.

Despite all these negative aspects Rawlinson did not hesitate to order a renewal of the advance on the morning of 9 August. During the 8th much information had reached him regarding the chaotic conditions behind the German lines. This made it easy for him to conclude that, whatever Fourth Army's problems, it enjoyed a marked advantage over its adversaries. Anyway Rawlinson was not in a position to disregard Haig's firmly expressed view that the operation should continue until the line Ham–Roye was reached.

II

Orders for renewal of the attack were not dispatched from Querrieu until sometime after midnight on the night of 8/9 August,[1] leaving Rawlinson's

---

[1] The Third Australian Division received the order from Monash at 3 a.m. on the 9th.

commanders very little time in which to organize this renewed advance. This gap of at least six hours between achievement by the infantry of their final objectives on the 8th and the dispatch of orders for an attack the following morning is much to be deplored – not least because its likeliest cause (as Montgomery admits)[2] was the fact that the staff were too busy congratulating themselves on their victory forthwith to turn their minds to fresh operations.

Rawlinson's orders were for Fourth Army to 'push forward tomorrow and establish itself on the general line Roye–Chaulnes–Bray-sur-Somme–Dernancourt.'[3] The advance was to occur in three stages. First to move would be the Canadian Corps and the right of the Australian Corps. Then III Corps, who were to make good their failure on the 8th, would advance to a position adjacent to the left wing of the Australians. That would facilitate an advance by the remainder of Monash's forces. The start-times would be decided upon by the corps commanders. Currie would give the go-ahead for the Canadians and the Australian right. As far as his left was concerned, Monash would wait upon the progress of III Corps north of the Somme.[4]

In these circumstances a coherent attack would be difficult to achieve in any case, but Rawlinson and his staff managed to complicate matters further as far as the Canadians were concerned by denying them promised reinforcements. Before the battle Currie had been told that 32 Division was to be placed at his disposal for operations subsequent to 8 August. Only late on the 8th or early on the morning of the 9th did he discover that this would not be the case.[5] The reason is uncertain. The 32 Division's War Diary states that the division had been placed so far back that it could not be brought forward in time. The Canadian Official History believes that Montgomery countermanded Rawlinson's order so that 32 Division would be available for subsequent operations.[6] Whatever the reason, this shillyshallying obliged the Canadians to rearrange their attack formations at the last minute, with consequent indecision, uncertainty, and even a measure of chaos.

The problems facing Fourth Army on the morning of 9 August did not end here. Frontline units received their orders late and at differing times. Lateral communications between the Canadian brigades, even from within the same division, proved difficult, on account of the uncertain location of

[2] General Sir A. Montgomery-Massingberd, '8th August, 1918'.

[3] Fourth Army Operation Order 8/8/18, AWM 26/12/472/2.

[4] Ibid.

[5] Nicholson, *Canadian Official History*, p. 410.

[6] 'Report on Operations of 32nd Division, August 10th and 11th 1918', 32 Division War Diary June 1918–October 1919, WO 95/2372; Nicholson, *Canadian Official History*, p. 410.

headquarters. This also generated uncertainty among the right wing of the Australian Corps, who were awaiting Currie's order to attack. As for the Australian left, it could not find out whether or not the attack of III Corps was under way.

Other factors exacerbated this lack of co-ordination among the attacking forces. Some divisions decided at the last minute to delay attacking until tank and artillery support was to hand; then – in its absence – went ahead with the operation anyway. And at least one force of Canadians held off advancing while awaiting an adequate supply of small arms ammunition.[7]

As a result, sixteen attacking brigades employed thirteen different start-times. Among the Canadians and the Australians, the only co-ordinated attacks were by 6 Canadian and 15 Australian Brigades at 11 a.m. and by 7 and 5 Australian Brigades at about 4 p.m. In the III Corps sector, three brigades and most of a fourth went forward at 5.30 p.m. All other attacks were unsupported on both flanks.

With regards to the provision of assistance from the artillery, we have information for thirteen brigades. Five received no artillery support, five received some, and three received support that was so far ahead of them as to be of no assistance. The situation regarding tanks was no more satisfactory. Six brigades received no tank support, three received none initially but some later, and seven received it from the start. Nowhere was the supply of tanks ample. The largest number available to any brigade was fourteen. In total less than fifty tanks supported Fourth Army's attacks when they opened. Only one brigade (1 Canadian) possessed tank and artillery support at the commencement of its operation.

All this might have been of small significance had the attacks gone in unopposed, but this was not the case. At least fourteen out of the sixteen attacking brigades were met with heavy machine-gun fire and at least ten with hostile artillery fire. Eight brigades had to contend with both forms of opposition.

These details evoke an appalling sense of *déjà vu*. We seem to be setting the scene for a replay of the sort of operation over which Rawlinson had presided so often in the course of the 1916 campaign, until Haig had been forced to tell him that there was something wanting in the methods he was employing: operations in which unco-ordinated attacks with inadequate fire support failed against the opposition of enemy machine-guns and artillery. Yet the outcome on 9 August 1918 was notably different from that of so many of the futile endeavours of 1916. On this day the Fourth Army

[7] Lt.-Col. C. E. Long, 'Ammunition supply during the Great War, with special reference to the 1st Canadian Division', *Canadian Defence Quarterly*, 5 (1928), pp. 157–8.

managed to advance about three miles, captured many prisoners, and sustained only moderate casualties.[8]

The explanation is to be found on the other side of the front. In response to the British advance on 8 August and the devastation of the enemy frontline divisions, the Germans during the evening of the 8th and the ensuing night and day had rushed in a succession of replacement divisions.[9] So by the time most Fourth Army attacks went in on 9 August they were probably up against a larger number of enemy troops than had awaited the British on the morning of the 8th. But these enemy troops were not well placed to hold off the attackers. German accounts make it clear that on 9 August most reinforcements entered the battle piecemeal rather than as coherent units.[10] Moreover, all the reinforcements, having been hurried forward in the main by truck lacked their supporting artillery. This deficiency had to be made good – to a meagre extent – by borrowing batteries from a nearby artillery school, assembling such guns as had survived the onslaught of the previous day, and resorting to such improvisations as employing anti-aircraft guns in an anti-tank role.[11] As evidence of the straits to which the Germans were reduced, only three batteries could be mustered to support a counterattack against the Australians at Lihons.[12]

This was not the full extent of the defenders' difficulties. Few of the German reinforcements knew the exact position of the front line, which anyway was changing piecemeal as the various British operations got under way. In addition, many of the supposedly fresh German units being brought into the line were in fact exhausted divisions but recently withdrawn from the front for purposes of recuperation. And even the relatively fresh troops were confronted with a demoralizing situation, as they encountered surviving elements of the divisions crushed on the preceding day and now in an advanced state of collapse.

This demoralization seemed to have spread to those elements of the German command immediately involved in the battle. By midday on the 9th the local commanders concluded that the present front could not be held and asked permission to retreat to a line Bapaume–Péronne–the Somme.[13] This was altogether too pessimistic. Like the British after 21 March, even disoriented German forces proved able, with their machine-guns and small amounts of surviving artillery, to slow down the increasingly

---

[8] Edmonds, *1918* vol 4, p. 114.
[9] Ibid., pp. 90–1.
[10] *Der Weltkrieg* vol. 14, p. 566.
[11] Ibid., p. 557.
[12] Ibid., p. 559.
[13] Ibid.

disjointed British attacks and establish a fresh line of sorts. Von Kuhl (Rupprecht's Chief of Staff) soon recognized this. After spending most of the afternoon studying the situation and contemplating the request for a major withdrawal, he rejected the proposal. He noted the incoherent nature of the British attacks and the fact that no new British divisions were being employed.[14] He also observed that attacking forces would soon find themselves in the wilderness of the old Somme battlefield.[15] There were no grounds for easing the path of the British by falling back to the Somme.

So although on 9 August the British managed an advance which, given the disordered nature of their operations, would have been accounted a major triumph in 1916, its message was not wholly reassuring. The problems confronting the attackers were mounting. The will of the German rank and file had not been irrevocably broken. And the nerve of the German high command was still holding.

III

The events of 10 August drove home these messages. In brief, operations that day were largely a recapitulation of what had happened on the 9th, but with the balance of advantage tipping yet further towards the defenders. Only one fresh division (32) was added to the British forces going into the attack, while the enemy had acquired four new divisions and some additional batteries of artillery.[16] Such attacks as Fourth Army was able to deliver (in all only ten brigades went forward during the day) proved increasingly incoherent. There were at least seven start-times for offensive movements delivered with precious little artillery or tank support. (Only 57 tanks were employed along the entire front.)[17] A significant obstacle was encountered in the form of the successive trench lines of earlier battles, still in reasonable shape and shielded by some hastily improvised wire.[18] In consequence not a great deal was accomplished. The maximum advance made by British forces on this day (it occurred in the Canadian sector) was just two miles.[19]

The significant issue to arise from this is the response of the British command. To Currie, Monash, and the divisional commanders, it was evident that they were being called on to prosecute attacks under increas-

[14] Ibid., p. 560.
[15] Ibid.
[16] Edmonds, *1918* vol. 4, p. 138.
[17] 'The Battle of Amiens', Tank Corps War Diary, June–September 1918, WO 95/94.
[18] Edmonds, *1918* vol. 4, p. 120.
[19] Ibid., p. 119.

ingly adverse conditions: that the key elements in their weapons system – particularly counter-battery fire and tanks – were steadily diminishing in number or effectiveness, and the key elements in the enemy's defences – a system of viable trenches and adequate artillery support – were being re-established. The question was whether Rawlinson (and after him Haig, and thereafter Foch) would form the same judgement and draw the appropriate conclusion.

Back in 1916, just such a situation had not at all deflected Rawlinson from allowing the offensive to proceed. Either he had directed attacks to continue or, by refraining from calling them off, he had let the struggle run its unavailing course. By 1918 he was capable of greater wisdom than this, although whether his insights would result in appropriate action remained doubtful. Contemplating Fourth Army's meagre progress on 10 August, he noted in his diary:

> hostile resistance is stiffening ... [Now] is the time to extend the battle front and put in further attacks by Armies on the flanks, [Foch] strongly advised D.H. to make the III Army attack as I suggested a week ago and I think it will be done.[20]

There was a misunderstanding here. Certainly, Foch on 10 August had agreed with Haig that Third Army (immediately to the north of Fourth Army) should advance on Bapaume. But there was no suggestion of any slackening in the endeavours required of Rawlinson's forces. Fourth Army was expected to continue its advance to the line Ham–Péronne 'and to try and get the bridgeheads on the Somme.'[21] This directive from Foch was passed by Haig to Rawlinson, who accordingly issued orders for a further advance.[22] Nevertheless it was not only Rawlinson who was beginning to doubt the wisdom of such intentions. Haig was inclining to a contrary view after visits to Currie and Lambert (commander of 32 Division), both of whom stressed the stiffening of German resistance on the Fourth Army's front.[23]

On 11 August Rawlinson strove hard to influence Haig in this direction. He informed the commander-in-chief that little progress was being made and that the Germans had put in several strong counterattacks against the Australians and Canadians.[24] This appeared to do the trick. Haig went straightway to Foch and told him that the attack would be switched to the

[20] Rawlinson Diary 10/8/18.

[21] Haig Diary 10/8/18.

[22] Fourth Army Operation Order 10/8/18, Fourth Army Operation Orders and Instructions, 1 Aug/22 Sept 1918, Fourth Army Papers vol. 50.

[23] Haig Diary 10/8/18.

[24] Rawlinson Diary 11/8/18.

front of Third Army, with Rawlinson's forces staying put until a set-piece attack could be made.[25]

This seemed to make admirable sense. What immediately followed did not. Haig – as on a number of earlier occasions – threatened to negate a sensible decision with a ridiculous corollary. Fourth Army's set-piece attack was to take place on 14 or at latest 15 August;[26] that is, in three or four days' time. So slender was Rawlinson's grasp on his own new-found wisdom (or so loath was he to challenge the judgement of his chief) that he entered no dissent from Haig's wishes.[27]

Yet there was no question of Fourth Army's being able to mount a major operation within this time-limit; no prospect, indeed, of it achieving much more than the fruitless thrusting against stiffening resistance which had been the pattern of 9 and 10 August. The elaborate system of sound ranging and flash spotting needed to establish the position of the enemy's artillery, and the ranging of British counter-batteries on the weapons so discovered, could not be accomplished in the time allowed. Furthermore, by 13 August there were hardly any serviceable tanks on Fourth Army's front.[28] There was also the question of the condition of the rank and file troops. No substantial reinforcements were being introduced to the Fourth Army sector, which meant that the new operation would have to be undertaken with essentially the same formations as had launched the great attack on 8 August and the less-rewarded endeavours of the 9th and 10th. To say that these forces were approaching exhaustion and needed a good rest would appear to require no elaboration. There could be no expectation that troops in this condition would be able, in a few days' time and without substantial tank support, to make headway against an enemy with fresh (if disorganized) divisions and increasing quantities of artillery – the latter, it should be noted, largely unsubdued by British counter-battery fire. This was a prescription for disaster.

The proposed attack by Fourth Army on 14 or 15 August never took place. The British Official History provides a graphic explanation for its nonoccurrence which has since been generally accepted. In this view, Haig on 10 August, citing Foch's authority, directed Rawlinson to continue the battle. At this Rawlinson became 'almost insubordinate' and delivered the stinging response: 'Are you commanding the British Army or is Maréchal Foch?'[29] The shaft, coming from one of his juniors and a man so normally

[25] Haig Diary 11/8/18.

[26] Ibid. 12/8/18.

[27] 'Notes of Conference held at 2nd Australian Division Headquarters, Villers Bretonneux at 3 p.m., 11th August, 1918', AWM 26/12/472/2.

[28] Tank Corps: Summary of Actions, Tank Corps Narratives Aug–Oct 1918, Fourth Army Papers vol. 65.

[29] Edmonds, *1918* vol. 4, pp. 135–6.

pliable as Rawlinson, got home to Haig and set in train the process by which he called off further immediate action on Fourth Army's front.

The documents, alas, do not bear out this gripping version of events. Neither Haig's nor Rawlinson's diary mentions any such incident; and although Haig might have chosen not to record such outspokenness from a subordinate, Rawlinson's reticence is more difficult to account for. Anyway, a more significant omission is that neither diarist so much as mentions meeting the other on this day. Yet Haig in particular was thorough in recording the names of those he encountered, and Rawlinson might be expected to remark on having met his chief even if he could not bring himself to record his own lapse into near-mutiny. What is more, events subsequent to 10 August do not bear out the account in the official history. Operations orders issued on 11 August make it clear that no decision had been made to call off the battle up to that point; and that all that was decided on the 11th was that the renewal of the offensive would be delayed until the 14th or 15th. So we are left needing to explain why the battle was not renewed even on the latter date.

Once more, Fourth Army was saved by the resolute intervention of a corps commander. On 13 August Rawlinson visited Currie. To his surprise, he found that the Canadian 'looks on the attack that has been arranged for the 15th as rather a desperate enterprise and anticipates heavy casualties.'[30] Rawlinson tried to reassure Currie, but the Canadian produced photographs of the German defences facing his corps. These, Rawlinson admitted, 'certainly show an inordinate amount of wire.'[31] And he endorsed Currie's view that 'the old systems of trenches which cover his front are a source of strength to the enemy. It would be a pity to make a failure at the end of so successful an enterprise.'[32]

Currie's intervention brought Rawlinson to the sticking point. The event was not without precedent. Back in 1916 another corps commander, Cavan, had at last rebelled at the proposal for more futile attacks. But at Amiens there were yet stronger reasons for Rawlinson to take his subordinate's views into account. In the political climate that had developed in Britain by 1918, commanders who persisted in futile endeavours were much more likely to find themselves in bad odour. Anyway, Rawlinson was conscious that this time he had commanded what he deemed 'so successful an enterprise'. This was bound to disincline him (even in order to please Haig) to tarnish a positive accomplishment by subsequent 'failure'. And perhaps yet more significant, Currie more than most corps commanders was a man whose protests could not be lightly set aside. The reason lay in

[30] Rawlinson Diary 13/8/18.
[31] Ibid. 13/8/18.
[32] Ibid.

the forces he led. They constituted a 'national army', and one of great distinction. To its credit lay the capture of Vimy Ridge and Passchendaele Ridge and the splendid deeds of 8 August. When Currie uttered expressions like 'desperate enterprise' and 'heavy casualties', these were not easy to disregard, for they might well become the strictures of a whole nation. So, having for days been uncomfortable about the continuation of the battle, Rawlinson found himself in the unusual situation where the views of a particular corps commander were almost bound to carry more weight with him than the judgement of his own commander-in-chief.

On 14 August, armed with the photographs which Currie had just employed to sway his own judgement, Rawlinson called on Haig. With this pictorial assistance he pressed Haig to postpone the operation scheduled for 15 August, at least until Byng was ready to launch Third Army's attack further north.[33] The considerations which had brought Rawlinson to this decision were bound to weigh also on Haig; he accepted the suggestion (Rawlinson noted) 'without a murmur'.[34]

Foch, by contrast, was unlikely to be swayed by Canadian sensibilities or the unwillingness of British commanders to prolong a successful operation to an unsuccessful and costly conclusion. When Haig that same day informed him of the decision, Foch 'murmured' a great deal. First he urged, then he ordered, Haig to proceed with the original plan.[35] Probably he thought he was leaning on an open door; after all, the far-fetched idea of projecting the objectives of the Amiens operation as far as the line of the Somme had originally been Haig's. If so Foch learned his error. Haig indicated in the most direct way that his ambitions were now irrevocably constricted:

> I spoke to Foch quite straightly and let him understand that *I was responsible to my Government and fellow citizens for the handling of the British forces*. F's attitude at once changed.[36]

It would be the last time that Foch would ever try to issue orders to the British commander-in-chief. The question which Rawlinson probably never directed to Haig, about who commanded the British army, had been decisively answered.

As for the battle of Amiens, it was at an end.

---

[33] Ibid. 14/8/18.
[34] Ibid.
[35] Haig Diary 14/8/18.
[36] Ibid. Haig's emphasis.

30

Pursuit

I

From the perspective of the Fourth Army, the events which succeeded the closing down of the Amiens offensive and which culminated in the action against the Hindenburg Line may be briefly summarized.

After the Currie–Rawlinson *démarche* on 14 August, Haig – as he had indicated to Foch – moved the main focus of attack to Byng's Third Army, on Rawlinson's left. That operation (the battle of Albert) began on 21 August. The next day Fourth Army moved to support Byng by acting in a flank protection role. On 23 August Rawlinson launched a more extensive attack north and south of the Somme. This succeeded in breaking through the old 1916 defensive line which the Germans were endeavouring to hold.

From this point, almost continuous attacks by Third and Fourth Armies, aided by the French on Rawlinson's right, forced the Germans back upon their hastily improvised 'Winter Line'.[1] But in the event not even this manoeuvre retrieved their situation. On 26 August the British command widened the battle further by opening an offensive on the front of First Army, to the north of Third Army. In consequence the German Winter Line was by 2 September completely outflanked: the Canadians on the left had seized a section of the Drocourt–Quéant Line, Third Army were in possession of Bapaume, and the Australian Corps under Rawlinson had driven the Germans from the Mont St Quentin–Péronne bridgehead. In consequence the German high command that day were brought to a decision they had so far adamantly resisted: to retreat to the Hindenburg Line.[2] So by 11 September the armies of Great Britain were facing the Germans in their last major defensive position in the West.

---

[1] *Der Weltkrieg* vol. 14, p. 571. This position corresponded roughly to a line Bucquoy–Maricourt–the bridgehead west of Péronne–St Christ–Noyon.

[2] Ibid., p. 586.

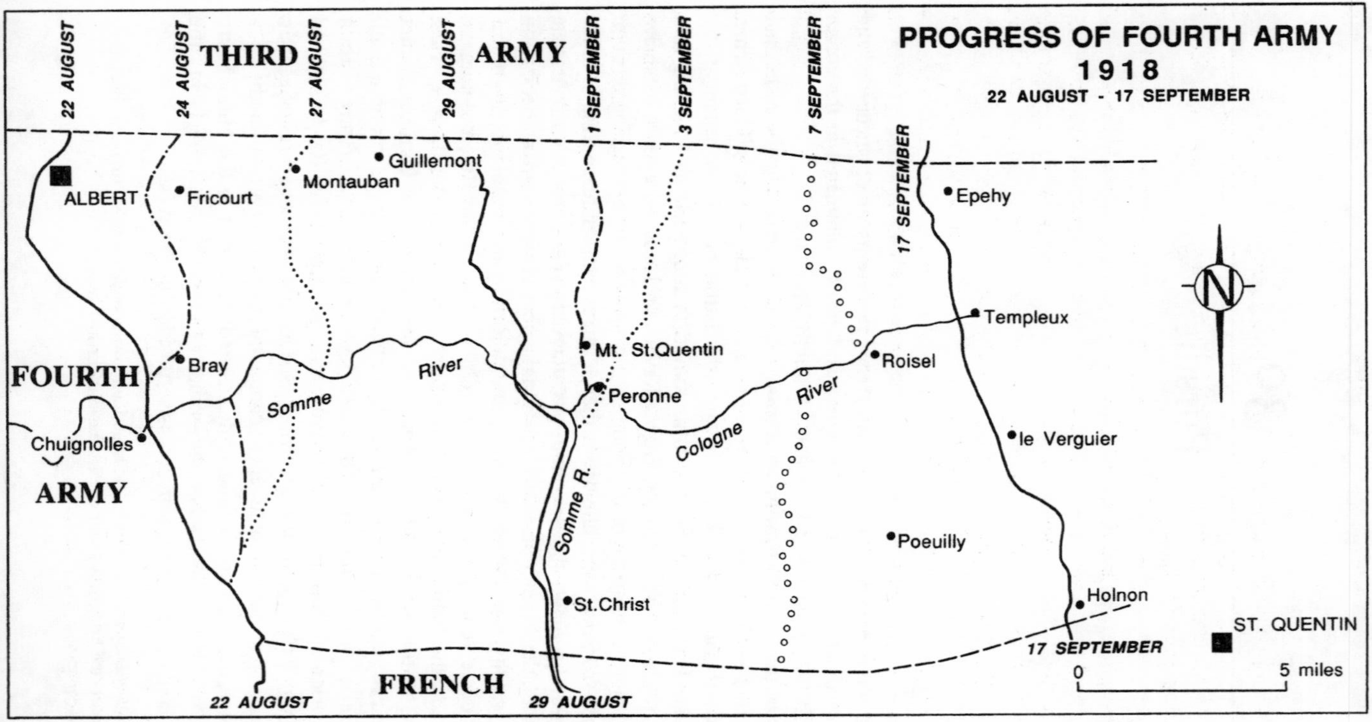
PROGRESS OF FOURTH ARMY
1918
22 AUGUST - 17 SEPTEMBER
22 AUGUST
24 AUGUST
27 AUGUST
29 AUGUST
1 SEPTEMBER
3 SEPTEMBER
7 SEPTEMBER
17 SEPTEMBER
THIRD
ARMY
FOURTH
ARMY
FRENCH
ALBERT
Fricourt
Montauban
Guillemont
Bray
Chuignolles
Somme
River
Mt. St.Quentin
Peronne
Somme R.
St.Christ
Cologne
River
Roisel
Templeux
Epehy
le Verguier
Poeuilly
Holnon
ST. QUENTIN
N
22 AUGUST
29 AUGUST
17 SEPTEMBER
0
5 miles

MAP 31

II

For the operations just related, Rawlinson's command had been somewhat reduced. On 21 August the Canadians had been returned to First Army, so that Fourth Army consisted only of III Corps and the Australian Corps plus the 32nd Division.

From the moment the Amiens battle was at last called off, Rawlinson was preparing for the attack which took place on 23 August. The pause of some eight days was vital. We have seen how the weapons system which had served Fourth Army so well on 8 August disintegrated in the following days, until by 11 August infantry advances were being attempted without adequate support from artillery and tanks. From 15 August Fourth Army was reassembling the elements which had brought about its earlier triumph. Guns were calibrated, brought forward, and registered on targets. A sound-ranging section with its miles of cable was brought into action.[3] Tanks, in so far as they were available, were mustered. And because, as on 8 August but unlike the improvised actions of the ensuing days, the gunners knew the exact positions of their own infantry, accurate creeping barrages could be provided. Unlike the Amiens attack, a great deal of wire protected much of the German defensive system. A week before the attack went in, Fourth Army's artillery began methodically to cut it.[4]

Rawlinson's role in planning the attack of 23 August was much what it had been before Hamel and Amiens. That is, it was confined to blending the requirements of the technical experts into a unified plan. As on the earlier occasions, he performed this task with competence.

The resulting operation was no walkover. There was a deal of hard fighting, with the German machine-gunners in particular holding on tenaciously.[5] But the enemy was fundamentally outmatched by the British weapons system, which a fresh German division such as the 21st was no more able to withstand than the exhausted 107 and 185 Divisions.[6] The German wire had been well cut, and the German artillery had again fallen victim to British counter-battery fire. A smoke barrage concealed the approach of the tanks (36 were available) until they closed with the trench defenders.[7] These and the creeping barrage made clear the way for the infantry. No amount of personal bravery on the part of the enemy could withstand the several elements in this potent combination.

[3] Australian Corps: 'Counter Battery Methods during the Advance, October 1918', AWM 26/12/494/2.

[4] Australian Corps: Daily Tactical Artillery Reports AWM 26/12/494/3.

[5] Pedersen, *Monash*, p. 261.

[6] Bean, *Australian Official History* vol. 6, pp. 753–4.

[7] Edmonds, *1918* vol. 4, p. 213.

The exploits of just one tank gives form and force to this generalization. The tank commander relates:

> At 4.25 a.m. on the 23rd instant, I proceeded with my Female Tank 'Mabel' No. 9382 in front of the Infantry. I made a very zig-zag course to the Wood in the south-west edge of the village of Chuignolles where I encountered an Anti-Tank gun which was eventually knocked out by the male tank commanded by 2/Lieut. Simmonds who was operating on my right. I then worked up the south side of the village heavily machine gunning all the crops and copses dislodging several enemy machine gun crews of the enemy. I next came back to the village and mopped up the enemy on the outskirts until it was clear. Then emerging from the smoke of two shells which dropped short, I found myself in the midst of a battery of whizz bangs, the gunners of same battery I at once proceeded to obliterate with good success after which I came behind another battery. I proceeded with the same operation. Then I started to take Infantry over to the high ground south of Square Wood when I was called back by an Australian Colonel to attend to some M.G. nests which had been left in the centre of the village, here I mopped up 12 M.G. nests then started to catch up the remainder of the tanks and barrage, but while at the top of a very steep bank I received a direct hit from a whizz bang in the front horns, which sent me out of control to the bottom of the bank where I found it had broken one plate of my left track. After repairing same, the barrage was finished, and Tanks were coming back to rally, so I brought my tank back to the rallying point at Amy Wood.[8]

The sum of these actions of 23 August on Fourth Army's front was as follows. North of the Somme, III Corps with 3 Australian Division on its right advanced on the flank of the main attack, which was being carried out by Third Army on its left. All objectives, including the town of Albert, were captured.[9] South of the Somme, 1 Australian Division and 32 British Division drove back three German divisions (21, 107, 185) a distance of one and a half miles, forcing them right out of the old defensive line which they had been occupying since 15 August.[10]

This progress (along with that made by the British Armies further north) convinced Haig and Rawlinson that the enemy were approaching collapse. Haig correspondingly ordered Fourth Army on to Péronne and the line of

[8] Tank Corps War Diary, June–Sept 1918, WO 95/94.

[9] Edmonds, *1918* vol. 4, p. 204.

[10] Bean, *Australian Official History* vol. 6, pp. 753–4; 'Report on Operations of the Australian Corps', AWM 26/12/490/3.

the Somme, adding: 'The pressure on the enemy must be continuous and relentless and the favourable situations, which exist to-day, developed to the full.'[11] Rawlinson passed this on to his corps commanders: 'The enemy shows more and more signs of becoming demoralized. Full advantage will be taken... to press on and give him no rest... No opportunity will be missed of making ground toward Péronne.'[12]

Nevertheless, the commander-in-chief and the Fourth Army commander were not quite of one mind. Rawlinson's enthusiasm for a 'relentless' pursuit was apparently conditional on some of his formations which had been in action since 8 August being replaced by fresh divisions. Haig, as Rawlinson learned on 25 August, did not intend to provide these replacements, his view being that any fresh units could best be allocated as reinforcements to the yet more major operations of First and Third Armies.[13] Rawlinson accepted this decision with reluctance, but also with the sensible conclusion that it denied him the wherewithal for the intended relentless pursuit of the enemy. That is, if he believed that enemy morale was failing, he did not intend to put this view to the test until he could present a decent show of strength. So he wrote in his diary:

> This change in function [Fourth Army to resume flank protection for the Third Army] will enable me to ease down the offensive[,] which I must do if I cannot get fresh troops... The Boche is in a bad way & I wish I had some fresh divisions to follow up the success[,] but D.H. hasn't got them.[14]

This conclusion had an interesting sequel. Later that day Rawlinson passed on to Monash an instruction to 'ease down' his advance and wait on events to the north.[15] Monash was reluctant to comply. He considered that the Australian Corps still had ample fighting power to force the Germans from the line of the Somme. To his own troops therefore he interpreted Rawlinson's orders in a way which ensured the continuance of offensive action.[16]

It is clear from Rawlinson's diary that he soon realized what was afoot and had no objection to giving Monash his head if significant results could be obtained.[17] This incident is often portrayed in terms of a wily corps

---

[11] GHQ, Operation Order 23/8/18 (OAD 912) GHQ Letters 1918/Feb 1919, Fourth Army Papers vol. 48.

[12] Fourth Army Telegram 24/8/18, AWM 26/12/472/6.

[13] Haig Diary 25/8/18.

[14] Rawlinson Diary 25/8/18.

[15] Pedersen, *Monash*, p. 262.

[16] Ibid., pp. 262–3.

[17] See Rawlinson Diary from 26/8/18 to 2/9/18.

commander outfoxing his obtuse superior. In fact Rawlinson's conduct redounds to his credit. In the first place, however hopeful he might be regarding the decline in the enemy's fighting powers, he jibbed at any suggestion that he should put this to the test with inadequate resources. That is, having developed a means of prosecuting battle which would overwhelm the enemy be they in good spirits or in ill, he declined to proceed by altogether riskier means on the off chance that these might suffice. Yet at the same time Rawlinson would not impose a veto on a corps commander of proven attainments who judged that the forces at his disposal were sufficient to carry out a further operation. Such good sense in both regards would have been welcome on those many occasions during this war when it proved to be conspicuously absent.

III

From 23 August to 3 September Rawlinson enjoyed the unfamiliar experience of presiding over a battlefield that moved every day. Apart from indicating the general line of advance (towards Péronne and the north–south line of the Somme), he had little call to intervene in these conditions. Actions were continuous and small in scale. Plans were improvised by divisional generals or brigadiers as the situation demanded. Often there was no time to refer these plans to corps commanders, let alone to the Army commander.

It follows that the spectacular set of small victories achieved by the Australian Corps and to a lesser extent III Corps in the eleven days under discussion were observed and applauded, but not planned, by Rawlinson. His role as approving spectator is evident in the capture of Mont St Quentin by 2 Australian Division. Monash informed Rawlinson on 30 August that the German stronghold was to be attacked with three under-strength battalions. Rawlinson was sceptical of any success being achieved with such a force, but nevertheless gave his approval.[18] The next day he recorded: 'As ... I was dressing Archie [Montgomery] rang to say that the Australians had taken Mt. St. Quentin! ... I was overjoyed. It is indeed a magnificent performance and no praise is too high for them.'[19] Once again, Rawlinson had been prepared to allow his confidence in Monash's judgement and his reluctance to disrupt a winning combination to override his own misgivings.

These Fourth Army successes of late August and early September 1918 are sometimes written down as hollow victories. It is argued that,

[18] Rawlinson Diary 30/8/18.
[19] Ibid. 31/8/18.

after 8 August, the Germans were conducting a skilful withdrawal to the Hindenburg Line, and that although they might be seeking to delay the appearance of the Fourth Army before that position they were not seriously contesting the intervening ground.

This view is not borne out by the German sources. Certainly, in the aftermath of 8 August there were some on the German side who did recommend an immediate withdrawal to the line of the Somme followed rapidly by a step back to the Hindenburg defences.[20] But, quite clearly, they were overruled by Ludendorff. The most he would consider was the preparation of the Winter Line for defence.[21] In the meantime every yard of ground must be defended – an undertaking he deemed not too difficult as the battle had stabilized.[22]

The ease with which the British broke the second German defensive line at the battle of Albert came, correspondingly, as something of a shock to Ludendorff. Even so, the most he would sanction was withdrawal to the Winter Line, which now included a sizeable bridgehead to the west of Péronne.[23] The only unforced withdrawal, therefore, was that of 26, 27, and 28 August, which brought the German forces to the position specified by Ludendorff.[24] As we have seen, it was to prove a short stay, rudely terminated by the British attacks in the Arras–Cambrai sector and Fourth Army's triumph at Mont St Quentin. Only after these chilling losses, it needs to be stressed, did Ludendorff (on 2 September) sanction a retreat to the Hindenburg Line.[25] That movement began on the night of 3/4 September and was completed by the 11th.[26]

It is evident from the foregoing that the Germans now standing on the Hindenburg Line had not come to this place by a decision on their part. They had been driven out of two defensive positions which it had been their intention to hold, one of them designated the Winter Line to establish its function as the final stopping-place for the year.

IV

The forward movement of Fourth Army, then, is not to be accounted for by the decisions of the German high command but by actions emanating

---

[20] *Der Weltkrieg* vol. 14, pp. 559–69.
[21] Ibid. See also Sir James E. Edmonds and Lt.-Col. R. Maxwell-Hyslop, *Military Operations France and Belgium, 1918* vol. 5 (London: HMSO, 1947), p. 161.
[22] Edmonds, *1918* vol. 5, p. 176.
[23] *Der Weltkrieg* vol. 14, p. 571.
[24] Edmonds, *1918* vol. 5, p. 314.
[25] *Der Weltkrieg* vol. 14, p. 586.
[26] Ibid.

from the British side of the front. On all but a few instances, attacking British infantry had proved to be in possession of sufficient fire support to overwhelm enemy resistance. From 24 August this support did not, as far as Rawlinson's troops were concerned, include any tanks, all of which were confined to the areas of Third and First Armies. Crucially, however, it did include artillery of all types. So during the approach march to Mont St Quentin the infantry recorded the spectacle of 'the Germans harried from spur to spur and trench to trench by British shells.'[27] The attack on the Mont itself was supported by some 100 field guns and 90 heavy pieces.[28]

There were, nevertheless, occasions when even the artillery could not subdue all forms of resistance and the infantry must overcome rifle and machine-gun posts. Strikingly, their own resources in fire power had now come to the point where this was not impossible. One participant relates:

> When the infantry advance was definitely checked by fire from a rifle post, a machine-gun post or, more often, from a position defended by both rifles and machine guns ... the platoon commander would assemble his section commanders and decide upon a plan. When conditions as to range and cover were suitable this plan provided for the Lewis guns taking up positions from which they could open fire on the objective when required and for the rifle and grenade sections, their number and strength varying according to the task, to select the best covered line of approach to the objective, so as to get to effective rifle-grenade range. Some of the men most skilful in the firing of the grenade could hit a large shell-hole five times out of six at one hundred yards, and do very good practice at twice that distance, or even farther ... It must be remembered that many of these men were veterans of several years' fighting experience ...
>
> The attack would then commence and it would not be long before the Germans in the post would find themselves under a heavy, accurate and destructive high-angle fire from rifle grenades. The length of time they stood this depended on the range, their moral[e] and their casualties, but generally the effect of the rifle-grenade fire was to cause the survivors to bolt. As soon as they did this the Lewis-gun sections were given their opportunity and they would open fire on the targets thus forced from cover into the open by the fire of the rifle grenadiers ...
>
> The effect of the constant repetition of this tactical manoeuvre on the moral[e] of the enemy can well be imagined. The high angle of descent of the rifle grenade searched out the garrisons of posts which

[27] Bean, *Australian Official History* vol. 6, p. 808.
[28] Ibid., p. 810.

otherwise had excellent cover and as the rifle grenadiers were beyond the range of hand grenades, and the fire often came from more than one direction, there was no effective means of reply available at once.[29]

In the dates under consideration (27 August–2 September) over 20,000 rifle grenades were issued to the 2 Australian Division.[30]

The Germans had no answer to British attacks so conducted. Their own artillery, although always present, could neither suppress the British guns nor deal effectively with fast-moving and dispersed groups of infantry. Their machine-gunners could exact a severe toll on the attackers but, as the above account makes clear, could not halt their progress. Thus it was by superior numbers of artillery pieces and the fire support they could provide and by the skilful use of fire power in the hands of the infantry that Rawlinson's Fourth Army late in September found itself approaching the climactic battle of the war.

[29] Colonel J. M. A. Durrant, 'Mont St Quentin: some aspects of the operations of the 2nd Australian Division from the 27th of August to the 2nd of September, 1918', *Army Quarterly*, 31 (1935), pp. 91–2.
[30] Ibid., p. 93.

31

Approach to the Hindenburg Line

I

The Hindenburg Line had been constructed during the winter and spring of 1916–17. In the year or so that followed, more defences had been added. Hence, by the time the Fourth Army moved to the assault in September 1918, the Hindenburg system in toto consisted of six lines constituting a defensive zone 6,000 yards deep.

The sector of the Hindenburg system confronting Fourth Army fell into two fairly distinct parts, southern and northern. In the southern part, the main defensive line had been sited to incorporate the St Quentin Canal. This feature constituted a formidable obstacle to any attacking force. Its banks possessed a decidedly steep gradient and fell away 50 feet to the water. The bed of the canal was 35 feet wide, and a series of dams maintained water or mud to a depth of over 6 feet.[1] In consequence, there was no possibility of tanks being employed to help breach this section of the defences. In the northern sector – that is, above Bellicourt – the canal ran into a tunnel and so was less of an obstacle to an attacker. To strengthen their defences here, the Germans had occupied a rise to the west of the tunnel. On this site they had constructed three trench lines, 200 yards apart, all wired and supplied with dugouts. Even the tunnel was incorporated into the defences. It was converted into an artillery-proof underground shelter capable of housing many thousands of men.

Along its entire length the main line was amply provided with concrete dugouts and machine-gun posts. Wire protecting the line was everywhere formidable and in places hundreds of yards deep.

Yet notwithstanding this achievement, the Germans who constructed

[1] Edmonds, *1918* vol. 5, p. 102.

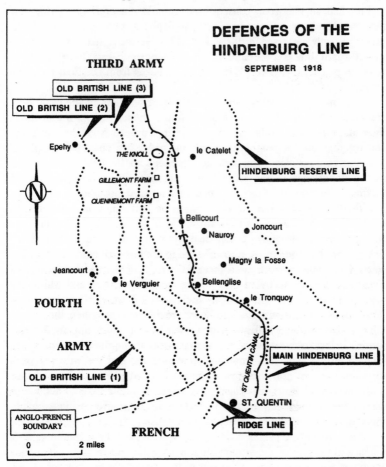

DEFENCES OF THE HINDENBURG LINE

SEPTEMBER 1918

THIRD ARMY

OLD BRITISH LINE (3)

OLD BRITISH LINE (2)

Epehy

THE KNOLL

le Catelet

HINDENBURG RESERVE LINE

GILLEMONT FARM

QUENNEMONT FARM

Bellicourt

Nauroy

Joncourt

Magny la Fosse

Jeancourt

le Verguier

Bellenglise

FOURTH

le Tronquoy

ARMY

ST QUENTIN CANAL

OLD BRITISH LINE (1)

MAIN HINDENBURG LINE

ANGLO-FRENCH BOUNDARY

ST. QUENTIN

FRENCH

RIDGE LINE

0   2 miles

MAP 32

the system soon became aware that it was not without flaw. Initially they had intended, following their experiences on the Somme, to place the main Hindenburg Line on a reverse slope, which they had concluded gave the best protection from hostile artillery fire. But – although claiming that this was indeed what they had done – the outcome had been otherwise. They had become so attracted by the support which the canal would offer any body of defenders that they had placed the main positions there. So now they were effectually defending, not the reverse slope of a ridge, but a valley line.

This had an important consequence. Should the overlooking ridge fall into the hands of an attacker, the Hindenburg Line proper would lie under directly observed artillery fire. The Germans needed, therefore, to safeguard the considerable ridge running south-east from Epehy in order to protect their main Hindenburg defences from the Fourth Army's artillery.[2]

Hence no sooner had the main Hindenburg position on the canal been completed than the German planners found themselves having to direct their attention to the ridge that lay above it. To begin with they set about constructing an 'outpost line' along the ridge. It consisted simply of machine-gun positions and was not intended to be held in force. But as the importance of the ridge more and more impressed itself on the German planners, they strengthened this forward position by equipping it with dugouts and wire. It was now to be garrisoned in strength, and every effort would be made to retain it. To all appearances, therefore, two strong defensive structures rather than one now confronted the British.

Yet even this came to seem insufficient to the German command. To the west of the ridge were located three lines of trenches which Rawlinson's Fourth Army had occupied back in the summer of 1917 and which had been overrun by the Germans in the course of their March offensive. The German command went to some trouble to strengthen them, particularly by fortifying villages within them. Even when upgraded, these former British trenches were not strong positions by the standards of the Hindenburg system: they contained few dugouts, and the wire remained to the east of the trenches where the British had placed it. Nevertheless they constituted obstacles which any attackers would have to subdue as a preliminary to coming to grips with the main defensive positions: that is, the ridge and then the Hindenburg system proper.[3]

In the aftermath of their defeat at Amiens, the Germans sought to increase the depth of the Hindenburg system even further by constructing a support and reserve line to the east of the main defensive position. However, neither was complete by the time the British assault got under way.

II

If the Hindenburg defences were indeed powerful, were they more than that? Were they invulnerable? From the British point of view, four elements in the situation gave cause for hope.

[2] For a discussion of these issues and a description of the Hindenburg Line defences see 'Notes on the Siegfried Line – German Defence Scheme', AWM 26/12/490/6. Siegfried was the German name for the defences.

[3] Fourth Army, 'Appreciation of the Situation, 10th September 1918', AWM 26/12/475/1.

First, it should be noted that the basic layout of the Hindenburg defences was linear, on the pattern adopted in anticipation of the British campaign on the Somme in 1916. Yet it was the fact that such defences had fallen to the attackers in the course of the Somme campaign, if only at fearful cost. Indeed the type of defence which had given the British most trouble in the later stages of the Somme campaign had occurred after the initial German trench lines had been obliterated by British artillery, forcing the defenders to resort to a chequerboard pattern of mutually supporting strongpoints. By the time of the Third Battle of Ypres (July–November 1917) the Germans had become thoroughly aware of this, and during that campaign they had employed this system to telling effect. But by then the main sections of the Hindenburg system had been constructed on linear principles. Nor in the months following Third Ypres did the Germans have cause to update the Hindenburg system. For their whole endeavour between January and July 1918 had been devoted to an offensive which would leave the Hindenburg Line far behind.

Admittedly, in the aftermath of Amiens, some attempt was made by the Germans to introduce Third Ypres principles to the Hindenburg defences. This took the form of the construction of 'miniature forts' between the main system and the ridge.[4] But by the time the German command was driven to recognize that they might soon be obliged to make a stand on the Hindenburg positions, the labour, the materials, and the time required for systematic work were simply not available.

There was a second element of hope in the situation as far as Rawlinson's forces were concerned. As the complexity and extent of the Hindenburg defences had grown, they were making excessive demands on German resources in manpower and even more in fire power – especially machine-guns and artillery. This placed the German command in a dilemma. Should it concentrate on one part of the Hindenburg system as against others, and if so on which? It was evident that, if the ridge fell, then the entire defences of the main line would be subject to directly observed artillery fire. Indeed it was the growing awareness during 1917 that, to quote a German appreciation of the main Hindenburg positions, 'the siting of guns is rendered very difficult' and 'the artillery conditions for the attacker are not unfavourable' which had driven the German planners to redirect their attention towards the ridge.[5] It seemed to follow that the ridge should receive the lion's share of German manpower and fire power in anticipation of the coming British assault. Yet the German command had invested so much of its endeavour in the main system based on

---

[4] Wynne, *If Germany Attacks*, p. 147.
[5] 'Artillery Appreciation of the Various Divisional Sectors of the Siegfried Line' (translation of a German document) in Fourth Army Papers vol. 53.

the St Quentin Canal that it was loath now to try and make the reverse slope of the ridge its primary defensive position. So it resorted to an un-happy compromise, whereby scarce resources were divided between the ridge and the main line. They were thus producing two separate positions neither of which was certainly defensible against a devoted assault.

The third factor providing the British with a prospect of success was one which their enemies had no cause to anticipate. In the Amiens attack on 8 August, the Australians had captured the plans, not of the entire Hindenburg system, but of that section of it which embraced the canal from Bellicourt to St Quentin. The captured documents came complete with maps which displayed the precise location of trenches, wire, dug-outs, battery positions, artillery observation points, sound-ranging posts, telephone and wireless systems, headquarters, billets, and rearward instal-lations.[6] The scheme was dated February 1917. But the maps were un-likely to have become outmoded in the ensuing 18 months, for in the interim the Germans had – with cause – been devoting their attention to other sections of the Western Front. And by the time they realized that the Hindenburg system would soon become a contested area, the speed of the British advance allowed them no opportunity – even had they recog-nized the need – to alter these elaborately constructed arrangements.

These potential weaknesses of the Hindenburg system did not escape the attention of British planners. The appreciations that were soon pro-duced by Fourth Army authorities in the light of the captured documents devote much attention to the shortcomings of the Hindenburg system and the means whereby the maximum advantage might be taken of them.[7]

But a fourth consideration transcends all these. The British were now employing such massive quantities of artillery in so co-ordinated and skilful a manner that it is not certain any defensive positions could have withstood them. If the Hindenburg system had been more up to date, if the Germans had concentrated their resources on either the ridge or the main line, and if the British had lacked the bonus provided by the captured documents, then the task confronting Fourth Army would indeed have been more formidable. It does not follow that it would have lain beyond their powers.

Certainly the British were now short of men, and could not afford the human price they had paid for their advance on the Somme in 1916. But this was not required, Fourth Army now possessed abundant weaponry

[6] 'German Defence Scheme: St. Quentin Sector of the Siegfried Line', AWM 26/12/490/6.

[7] See, for example, 'Hindenburg Line – Captured Document – Appreciation by Captain J. Chapman, 5th Australian Division', AWM 26/12/473/3; and 'Fourth Army Appreciation of the Situation, 10th September 1918.'

and the expertise to employ it effectively against the most sophisticated defences offering at that time. Fortune favoured the British in their attack on the Hindenburg Line. But fortune was on the side of big battalions possessing the wherewithal to get forward even without it.

III

In the light of these considerations, Rawlinson proposed to Haig that, notwithstanding the fact that Fourth Army's divisions were understrength and wearied by over a month of near-constant campaigning, an immediate attack on the Hindenburg system was feasible. The German positions on the ridge (the 'outpost line' as it was still sometimes called, although quite erroneously) would be attacked in a first, distinct operation. Only when it had fallen would the main Hindenburg Line be assailed.[8]

Haig readily agreed, and with some cause. He and Foch were planning a series of blows along a great section of the Western Front, which would keep German artillery and infantry resources fully stretched and deny the enemy the opportunity to concentrate guns against the Fourth Army's advance.

Despite Rawlinson's confidence, serious difficulties confronted the Fourth Army in attacking even the ridge position. As far as the infantry were concerned, Rawlinson's divisions were (as we have just noted) tired and understrength. Eight divisions were to be used in the attack.[9] No less than five of them had been in action more or less continuously since 8 August. Of the remainder, two had recently been reconstituted after being almost destroyed in March. Only one division was fresh, and it was but newly arrived on the Western Front from the Middle East.

In respect to numbers, all Fourth Army divisions were well below establishment. The battalions of the Australian divisions averaged 390 men and officers.[10] The divisions of III and IX Corps, with nine battalions to the Australians' twelve, were even weaker. In all, it is probable that the eight attacking divisions of the Fourth Army could muster no more than 40,000 troops – of whom only two-thirds, or 27,000, would initially go over the top.[11] Nor, for the attack on the ridge, would these men receive substantial tank support. Of the 150 tanks in the Fourth

---

[8] Rawlinson to Haig 11/9/18, AWM 26/12/473/4.

[9] From north to south these were 58, 12, 18, and 74 (III Corps), 1 and 4 Australian (Australian Corps), and 1 and 6 (IX Corps).

[10] Bean, *Australian Official History* vol. 6, p. 896.

[11] Usually two brigades out of three in a division were used in the initial attack.

Army area no less than 130 were unfit for battle.[12] That is, along a front of 20,000 yards a beggarly 20 tanks would be present to assist the infantry.

These were considerable shortcomings, given that the Fourth Army would be assaulting the strongest defences it had so far encountered in 1918. In his note to Haig, Rawlinson had proposed attacking four trench lines: the three old British positions of 1917 and the ridge itself. As Rawlinson himself noted, while the first three of these lines might not present much difficulty, the fourth was 'a well-prepared defensive system with dugouts and good wire, and is no longer an outpost line.'[13]

Nor would the attackers have any advantage in infantry numbers. The ridge was defended by twelve German divisions with two more in reserve.[14] Given the state of German manpower, it is unlikely that any of these formations contained more than 2,500 men.[15] Yet this still gave the Germans about 30,000 men with 5,000 in reserve; a rough equality with the attackers.

But whatever the handicaps under which Fourth Army might labour when delivering this assault, in one all-important respect its resources would clearly prove sufficient unto the day – artillery. The infantry would be supported by 1,500 guns, of which 1,000 were field pieces and 500 heavy.[16] This would enable a creeping barrage to be fired across the whole front of attack, allow two-thirds of the heavy artillery to concentrate on counter-battery work, and still provide a surplus for dealing with particular strongpoints.[17]

The two corps with the greatest experience in Western Front fighting (the Australian and III Corps) decided to supplement the creeping barrage with a machine-gun barrage.[18] In the Australian Corps this meant that every machine-gun not earmarked to accompany the infantry advance (250 in all) would fire at zero.[19] It was hoped that this hail of machine-gun bullets delivered indirectly over the heads of the advancing infantry would at least in part make good the absence of tanks employing machine-guns.

[12] 'Situation of Tanks and Crews', 18 September 1918 in Tank Corps War Diary, June–Sept 1918, WO 95/94.

[13] Rawlinson to Haig 11/9/18.

[14] Edmonds, *1918* vol. 5, p. 476.

[15] The Fourth Army Intelligence Report of 8/9/18 estimates that no German division contained more than 2,500 men. See AWM 26/12/473/3.

[16] Edmonds, *1918* vol. 5, p. 477.

[17] For example see IX Corps, 'Artillery Instructions Series A, 14/9/18', IX Corps Operation Orders, 7 Sept/31 Oct 1918, Fourth Army Papers vol. 72.

[18] III Corps Operation Order 15/9/18, III Corps Operation Orders 22 Aug/20 Oct 1918, Fourth Army Papers vol. 67; 'Report on Operations of the Australian Corps'.

[19] Pedersen, *Monash*, p. 274.

The planning of the battle conformed to the pattern now made familiar by success. As Monash later commented: 'The contemplated battle presented only a few novel features. The methods of the Corps were becoming stereotyped, and by this time we all began to understand each other so well that most of what I had to say could almost be taken for granted.'[20]

Yet if circumstances no longer called for great initiative among the upper echelons of command, there were some respects in which Rawlinson either acted inappropriately or did not act at all when the situation seemed to require his intervention. As an example of inappropriate action one may instance the matter of the start lines laid down in the barrage and bombardment maps for the attack of 18 September. Presumably on account of overconfidence, these maps – drawn up about a week before the event – assumed a start line which had yet to be captured. For IX Corps, in the southernmost sector, it involved gaining ground to a depth of 4,000 yards, while for the Australians in the centre an advance of several hundred yards was required.[21] In the event the Australians and most of IX Corps managed to gain the start line before the offensive opened.[22] But that proved not to be the case with 6 Division of IX Corps, which would suffer severely as a result; and anyway such a practice was ill-advised, as the attempt to repeat it ten days later would make abundantly clear.

Concerning Rawlinson's failure to intervene when action by him seemed called for, two instances suggest themselves. We have seen that for 18 September the two more experienced corps under Rawlinson's command proposed to supplement the artillery barrage – and incidentally help to compensate for the paucity of tanks – by employing all available machine-guns to fire a barrage over the heads of the advancing infantry. The less experienced IX Corps did not include this provision in its plan. No one at Fourth Army HQ saw fit to draw the corps commander's attention to this tactic or to impress upon him its considerable merits.

An even more striking failure on Rawlinson's part concerns his attitude to the leadership of III Corps. It had already become evident before the battle of Amiens that Rawlinson felt little confidence in Butler, the corps commander. Shortly after 8 August Butler suffered a nervous collapse and was replaced temporarily by de Lisle. Nevertheless on the eve of the battles for the Hindenburg Line Butler was permitted to return. Yet this was no indication that Rawlinson felt more confidence in the recuperated Butler than in the worn-down version. After a visit to III Corps HQ on 16 September he noted in his diary:

[20] Ibid., pp. 273–4.
[21] Edmonds, *1918* vol. 5, p. 475.
[22] Ibid., p. 476; Pedersen, *Monash*, p. 274.

I am pretty sure the Aust & IX Corps will do their jobs but am not so confident about the III Corps ... They do not seem to fix up their plans with the same precision as the other Corps & I think Butler does not keep his Div Cmdrs in order enough. I suppose he has not the practical experience to make decisions and to shut them up when they begin talking rot. If they make a mess of this show I shall have to talk seriously to Butler for it will be his fault.[23]

This is an extraordinary statement. Here we see Rawlinson anticipating a failure on the part of III Corps and identifying its cause in advance. Yet there is no suggestion that as Fourth Army commander he bore any responsibility for permitting Butler to resume his post or to continue in it. Nor does Rawlinson appear to have thought that he should convey to Butler forthwith – rather than after it was too late to do anything about it – his misgivings concerning the conditions of III Corps command. This diary entry reads like the comments of an observer with no power to influence events rather than those of the man having ultimate responsibility for what occurred within the Fourth Army structure. That attitude of detachment on Rawlinson's part had been evident on occasions enough during the Somme campaign of 1916. It is startling that, after so lengthy a learning experience and with the Great War in its closing stages, he had yet to gain a securer grasp on his responsibilities.

IV

The attack on the so-called 'outpost line' took place at 5.20 a.m. on 18 September in drizzling rain and thick mist.[24] The day proved one of mixed fortunes for the Fourth Army. In the centre, the attack by the Australian Corps succeeded. By the end of the day the Australians had overrun the three old British defensive lines and the German positions on the ridge. From their final lodgements they overlooked the main Hindenburg defences from the canal south of Bellenglise to the tunnel north of Bellicourt.

On the flanks of the Australian Corps success had been partial. So 74 Division in the north and 1 Division in the south had both captured small sections of the ridge line. On the extreme flanks of the attack not even the first objectives had been captured. These failures were in part caused by special circumstances. In the south IX Corps were subjected to heavy

[23] Rawlinson Diary 16/9/18.
[24] Fourth Australian Division: 'Report of Operations 10th–20th September, 1918', AWM 26/12/547/4.

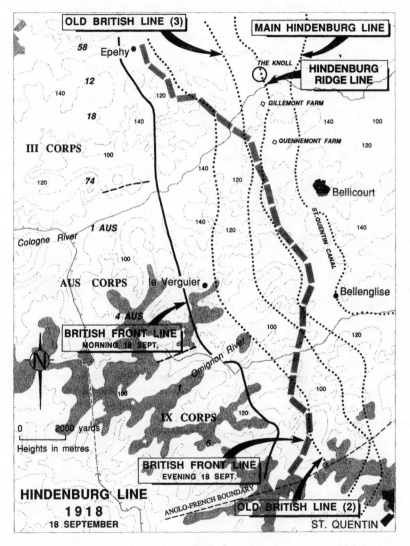

OLD BRITISH LINE (3)

MAIN HINDENBURG LINE

58

Epehy

THE KNOLL

HINDENBURG RIDGE LINE

12

140

18

140

120

◇ GILLEMONT FARM

III CORPS

100

140

140

100

◇ QUENNEMONT FARM

120

120

74

120

140

120

Bellicourt

1 AUS

140

Cologne River

100

ST. QUENTIN CANAL

AUS CORPS

le Verguier

Bellenglise

4 AUS

BRITISH FRONT LINE
MORNING 18 SEPT.

100

Omignon River

120

N

100

IX CORPS

120

0   2000 yards

6

100

Heights in metres

BRITISH FRONT LINE
EVENING 18 SEPT.

HINDENBURG LINE
1918
18 SEPTEMBER

ANGLO-FRENCH BOUNDARY

OLD BRITISH LINE (2)

ST. QUENTIN

MAP 33

enfilade fire when a French attack to their right failed to materialize. In the north III Corps had to subdue particularly strong defences, in the form of a string of villages and trenches well supplied with dugouts. In addition they were facing a fresh German division which had entered the line on the eve of battle.[25]

Apart from these special circumstances, some general observations about the operations of 18 September may be made.

First, British counter-battery fire in a set-piece attack was now so accurate that it could neutralize most German retaliatory fire. Those reports on 18 September which mention German artillery at all merely state that its reply was 'light and scattered, causing few casualties'.[26]

Second, the operations on the front of the Australian Corps demonstrated that strong trench lines, in some cases protected by intact wire, could be taken provided that the attacking divisions followed close behind an accurately fired barrage. Furthermore, under these conditions German troops were now as likely to surrender as to fight. Two quotations taken from an account of the battle by the 4th Australian Division confirm these points.

> Owing to the density of our barrage the enemy 'went to earth' and the Infantry followed so close to it that in many cases the Germans surrendered without offering much resistance.

> One of the chief points in the success of the operation against [our final objective] was the fact that many platoons crossed the hostile wire under the cover of the barrage, and were into the hostile trenches almost immediately after the barrage lifted. Only the extreme accuracy of fire of our Field Artillery enabled us to do this.[27]

Other factors contributed to the Australian success. As an additional form of artillery, the machine-gun barrage proved effective: according to the Australian report, several German officers related that 'it was impossible for anyone to put their heads above the parapet without being shot.'[28] And the tactical handling of small units along with the combination of arms (Lewis guns, rifle grenades, trench mortars) was once again a feature of Australian operations; by these means the fortified

---

[25] For IX Corps see Edmonds, *1918* vol. 5, p. 478; for III Corps, pp. 483–4.

[26] 'Report on Operation Carried out by 1st Australian Division on 18th Sept, 1918, 5/10/18', AWM 26/12/504/1.

[27] Fourth Australian Division: 'Report of Operations'.

[28] Ibid.

village of le Verguier was captured, yielding 480 prisoners, 80 machine-guns, and several pieces of field artillery.[29]

Another comment on the operations of 18 September is called for. What occurred in the area of III and IX Corps revealed that, if any of the factors which led to success on the Australian front were absent, the Germans were still capable of very stiff opposition. For example, divisions in IX and III Corps lost the barrage, in the first instance due to inexperience, in the second because of over-complicated operation orders requiring the barrage (and as a consequence the troops) to make several changes in direction. In both cases the attacking infantry were met with a hail of machine-gun fire which caused heavy casualties and halted the advance.[30] In the IX Corps sector the absence of a machine-gun barrage also gave some of the defenders a better chance to man their weapons. Clearly, in situations which gave the German defenders some hope of success, they were still prepared to fight it out. That is, in the absence of the full range of expertise which the British army was now in a position to employ in delivering their attacks, no operation was assured of success.

All this has important implications in the area of command. It is plain that the attack might have succeeded along most of the front had Rawlinson intervened to require IX Corps to fire a machine-gun barrage and III Corps to act on a less complicated and confusing plan of advance. (Only in the matter of the action, or rather inaction, of the French was the issue of success and failure beyond his control.) So on 18 September it was Monash's highly effective scheme of operations which converted what could well have been an unrewarding day into one that was moderately well rewarded.

[29] Ibid.
[30] Edmonds, *1918* vol. 5, pp. 485–6.

32

The Plan of Attack

I

By the end of 18 September the three old British defensive lines and that part of the ridge under assault from the Australians lay in Fourth Army's hands. From their final position the Australians overlooked the Hindenburg Line from the canal south of Bellenglise to Bellicourt. The entire German defences in this area (whose precise whereabouts were accurately known from the captured documents) lay exposed.

Nevertheless much remained to be done before Fourth Army could ideally launch an attack on the canal and its defences. In the north the third of the old British lines, the ridge line, and some strongly defended positions between them remained in German hands. And in the south IX Corps had the problem of co-ordinating operations with the French, who had failed to capture enemy-held territory overlooking IX Corps positions.

II

Even while the operations of 18 September were in progress, preparations were under way for the next operation – an attack on the central Hindenburg position. On this occasion, instead of the plan being drawn up by Montgomery and his staff, the job was given to Monash – an indication of the Australian's standing as a result of his unbroken record of success since 8 August, but also an acknowledgement that he had a more intimate knowledge than the Fourth Army staff of the ground to be attacked.

Monash's plan was drawn up in anticipation of total success on 18

September.[1] In the north, such success was not accomplished on that day. Consequently, to secure the start line for the next major operation, III Corps must first capture 3,000 yards of strongly defended ground. Of course Monash had drawn up his plan before III Corps had failed, and it could have been amended in the light of that circumstance. But III Corps's objectives for 18 September had been chosen for the good observation they provided over the tunnel section of the central Hindenburg Line – reason enough, it would appear, to persist in trying to capture them in advance of the new attack.

The problem for Rawlinson as it developed in the next few days was this: so comprehensively had III Corps failed on 18 September that it must have been open to doubt whether further attacks by these worn-down forces would ever succeed. On the other hand the main attack had been scheduled for the 29th. This left insufficient time to relieve III Corps, make an attack with fresh forces, and then replace those forces with the American Corps which was to be employed on the 29th. Another option would be to use the Americans for both the preliminary operation and the main attack. But that was exactly the task that had been given to III Corps before the battle of Amiens. Opinion was unanimous that this had adversely affected its performance in the main attack. Rawlinson finally adopted a compromise. He ordered III Corps to continue their operations in the hope that they would succeed – although he cannot have had great confidence in this course given that at the same time he was arranging with Haig to have Butler relieved.[2] But at the same time he advised the American Corps that they should be prepared to take over the operations from Butler if the start line had not been captured by the 27th.[3]

In the event, by 24 September III Corps were still 1,000 yards short of Monash's projected start line. The Americans were therefore ordered by Rawlinson to complete the task in the next three days.[4]

It may be wondered why, rather than wearing out the Americans in a preliminary operation, Rawlinson did not adjust the barrage plans to the line currently held. For this there was ample time. And, according to one authority, Monash suggested this option to Rawlinson. However, the latter rejected it on the grounds that it might upset the complicated plans already made.[5] This was clearly an inadequate reason, given that Monash

---

[1] Monash to Fourth Army 18/9/18, Australian Corps Operation Orders 22Sept/31 Dec 1918, Fourth Army Papers vol. 69.
[2] Rawlinson Diary 21/9/18; Haig Diary 22/9/18.
[3] Rawlinson Diary 22/9/18.
[4] Ibid. 24/9/18.
[5] Pedersen, *Monash*, p. 285.

was offering to rework all his barrage plans. More probably, Rawlinson was loath to forgo any opportunity to capture the extremely favourable start line which had been proposed. He thereby ran the risk of blunting his attack forces in this area in advance of the main operation and then finding his forces still not at the proposed jumping-off point.

III

The principal feature of Monash's plan was that he proposed to attack only the tunnel section of the Hindenburg Line, a frontage of no more than 6,000 yards. His reasoning was that here alone was it possible to use tanks – which were once again in reasonable supply, thanks mainly to the endeavours of the repair shops. Two American divisions, accompanied by 60 tanks, would assault the tunnel sector, which ran from Bellicourt in the south to Vendhuille in the north. They would capture the main line and advance beyond it to take the key villages of Nauroy and Le Catelet and their defences. The initial advance would be to a depth of 4,000 yards. Two Australian divisions, with the aid of 30 tanks, would then leapfrog through the Americans and capture the Beaurevoir Line, some 4,000 yards beyond. Here they would consolidate. The advance eastwards was to be continued by cavalry – a proposal which sits oddly with Monash's reputation as a thoroughly modern general. More realistically, the canal defences on either side of the tunnel would be unhinged by expansion north and south. Following behind the Australians, III Corps would swing left through Le Catelet and IX Corps turn right through Bellicourt.

Monash laid it down, without specifying particular numbers, that sufficient artillery should be provided to bombard the Hindenburg defences for four days, and to cover both the American and Australian operations with a creeping barrage.[6]

One major aspect of this scheme did not win Rawlinson's approval. He agreed to the proposal whereby the Americans would make the initial assault in the tunnel area and the Australians would exploit the break-in. And he did not dissent from Monash's proposed use of the cavalry as a force for exploitation. Regarding the use of tanks, he increased the proposed numbers from 90 to 162 (86 for the Americans, 76 for the Australians) and added a contingent of whippet tanks and armoured cars. On the left of the Australian–American attack, he considerably diminished the role assigned to III Corps, presumably because he did not consider them capable of playing a major part. Their task was now restricted to

[6] Monash to Fourth Army 18/9/18.

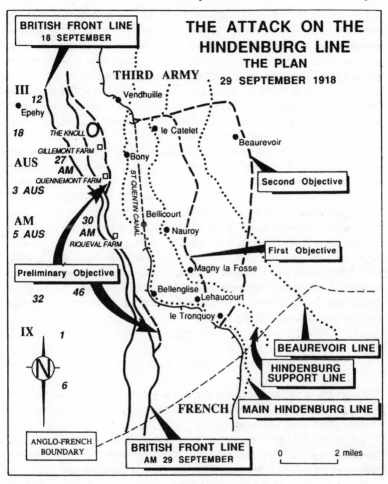

THE ATTACK ON THE
HINDENBURG LINE
THE PLAN
29 SEPTEMBER 1918

BRITISH FRONT LINE
18 SEPTEMBER

THIRD ARMY

Vendhuille

III 12
• Epehy

18   THE KNOLL
GILLEMONT FARM
AUS   27
AM
QUENNEMONT FARM
3 AUS

AM
5 AUS   30
AM
RIQUEVAL FARM

Preliminary Objective

32   46

IX   1

6

ANGLO-FRENCH
BOUNDARY

• le Catelet
Beaurevoir

• Bony

ST QUENTIN CANAL

Second Objective

Bellicourt
• Nauroy

First Objective

• Magny la Fosse

Bellenglise
Lehaucourt
le Tronquoy •

BEAUREVOIR LINE

HINDENBURG
SUPPORT LINE

MAIN HINDENBURG LINE

FRENCH

BRITISH FRONT LINE
AM 29 SEPTEMBER

0   2 miles

MAP 34

providing a flank guard for the left of the Americans attacking across
the tunnel.

Rawlinson disagreed fundamentally with Monash's scheme where it
concerned the frontage of the attack. In his judgement a front of only
6,000 yards was altogether too narrow, especially as it was flanked by
strong canal defences. When it is recalled that at Loos in 1915 a frontage
of attack of 10,000 yards had been chosen in order that at least the central

section would be free from flanking fire, it will be evident that Monash was setting up his attacking forces for very heavy casualties indeed. Rawlinson therefore almost doubled the frontage by increasing it to 10,000 yards. Under this arrangement 46 Division of IX Corps, on the right of the Americans and Australians, would assault the canal from Bellenglise to just south of Bellicourt. The 32 Division would then pass through them to capture the high ground to the east of the canal. Further south still, flank protection to these operations would be provided by 1 Division. This would have the incidental benefit of obviating a clumsy feature of Monash's plan referred to above, whereby the IX Corps would have been required to negotiate the crowded tunnel area in order to swing right and outflank the canal to the south.[7]

Rawlinson now faced the problem which Monash had sought to avoid: that of getting 46 Division across the canal, which, it will be recalled, in most places contained water or mud to a depth of 6 feet. To traverse this obstacle some 3,000 lifebelts were obtained from cross-channel steamers, 'together with light portable rafts, ladders, collapsible boats and heaving lines'.[8] Rehearsals were held on the banks of the Somme to familiarize the troops with this exotic equipment.[9] But none of this would be of great service unless exceptional measures were taken to suppress the German defences on both sides of the canal.

IV

The next phase of the planning, therefore, concerned the artillery. What type of bombardment was called for by the obstacle to be overcome? And what weight of bombardment?

Concerning the first matter, it was soon realized by Rawlinson and Monash that a predicted bombardment coinciding with the opening of the infantry attack – which had proved so effective at Cambrai and Amiens – would not be appropriate. The main Hindenburg defences were protected by huge belts of wire against which, on the 46 Division sector, tanks could not be used. In addition the banks of the St Quentin Canal needed to be broken down to ease the crossing by 46 Division. Further, it would be necessary systematically to smash in the German dugouts and to destroy

[7] For Rawlinson's amendments to Monash's plan see Rawlinson to GHQ 18/9/18, Fourth Army Papers vol. 50.

[8] 'Account of the Part Taken by the 46th Division in the Battle of Bellenglise on the 29th September, 1918', III Corps and IX Corps Narratives Aug/Oct 1918, Fourth Army Papers vol. 63.

[9] Ibid.

strategically placed machine-gun posts, command centres, and communication networks. At Amiens no such formidable defences had existed. And at Cambrai the wire had not been so thick, machine-gun emplacements and dugouts had not been present in such profusion, a multiplicity of tanks had been available, and the territory had been appropriate for the employment of armoured vehicles.

All this led inescapably to the conclusion that a lengthy preliminary bombardment would have to be fired. That meant that the element of surprise, about which Rawlinson had been so enthusiastic at Amiens, would have to be dispensed with. But at the Hindenburg Line, oddly enough, the presence or absence of surprise did not necessarily matter. Whereas at Amiens, with sufficient warning, the Germans might have relocated their guns and obliged the RAF to go looking for them, at the Hindenburg Line nothing of the sort was true. Quite apart from the fact that the enemy – such was the pressure being brought against them all along the Western Front – had no abundance of guns on the Hindenburg Line, there was no point to be served by shifting them about. As the German authorities came to recognize, once the British were on the ridge they could observe every move the enemy guns might make and adjust the aiming of their own weapons accordingly.

German foreknowledge of the coming attack, then, would not be disadvantageous if Rawlinson's bombardment carried sufficient weight to put the enemy defences out of action. But to achieve this posed a problem for Fourth Army's planners. Given the complexity of the German defences, the absence of surprise, and the inappropriateness of tanks for much of the front under attack, they simply had no recent experiences on which to draw. Indeed, and quite paradoxically, the last time Fourth Army had fired a bombardment of the sort appropriate to this occasion was some two years and three months earlier at the calamitous opening to the Somme campaign in 1916.

It will be recalled that in the run-up to the attack on 1 July 1916, Fourth Army had fired a bombardment lasting seven days and comprising 1.6 million shells with a weight of 71 million pounds.[10] This had proved woefully inadequate to crush the German defences. Now Rawlinson proposed to do something which on first appearance seemed alarmingly similar. The front of attack was only 10,000 yards on 29 September 1918 as against the 20,000 yards of 1 July 1916. But the depth of the defences was every bit as strong, and Fourth Army was firing over four days a bombardment of only 750,000 shells weighing 39 millions pounds.[11]

[10] 'Somme: Ammunition', Rawlinson Papers, 1/6, CC.

[11] Major-General Sir A. Montgomery, *The Story of the Fourth Army in the Battles of the Hundred Days, August 8th to November 11th, 1918* (London: Hodder and Stoughton, 1931),

What hope did Rawlinson have that a bombardment only as strong – given the differing lengths of front – as that which had failed so disastrously two years before would now succeed? It might seem that Fourth Army planners were lapsing into their old habit of ignoring previous experience. But this was not the case. The artillery calculations for the attack on the Hindenburg Line were soundly based, taking into account two developments in artillery since 1916: the increased efficiency of shell, and the changing nature of bombardments.

Concerning the efficiency of shell, in 1918 wire was cut using 18 pounder high explosive shell fitted with instantaneous fuses. High explosive cut much more wire per shell than the 18 pounder shrapnel shells used at the Somme. And they also had the advantage over shrapnel of not requiring extremely accurate gun-laying to achieve their purpose. In addition, in 1918 a greater effect could be expected of heavy shells in that most of those fired would actually explode. On the Somme in 1916 as many as 30 per cent of the heavier calibres had proved to be duds.

The other difference between 1916 and 1918 relates to the changed nature of bombardments in 1918. The point has been made often enough about the ineffectiveness of British counter-battery fire in 1916 compared to its devasting effect two years later. There are other improvements and modifications to be noted.

Regarding wire-cutting, at the Somme the aim had been to eliminate all the wire on the front of the attack. At the Hindenburg Line this was attempted only in the canal sector. In the tunnel sector, the artillery had only to cut lanes, which constant shelling prevented the enemy from repairing; further destruction of the wire was left to the tanks and to infantry protected by a creeping barrage.

The Somme bombardment of 1916 had attempted to do more than eliminate all the wire. It had also sought to obliterate the defenders. Nothing of the sort had proved attainable, and at Cambrai and Amiens it had not even been attempted. By 1918, that is, the artillery's objective had changed to the more modest and achievable one of just suppressing the artillery and machine-guns of the defenders for the duration of the infantry attack.

Clearly, tactics which relied on suppression of defences rather than their obliteration were a great deal more economical of shell. So in calculating the weight of bombardment necessary to achieve success at the Hindenburg Line, Rawlinson could afford to ignore the attempted obliteration bombardment at the Somme. What was now necessary was a bom-

Appendix G, 'Daily Ammunition Expenditure by the Fourth Army Aug–Nov 1918', p. 328. The weight of shell has been calculated from the types of shell used.

bardment like that employed at Amiens supplemented by a destructive element directed against the particular obstacles which the Hindenburg Line defences presented; namely, the wire, the canal, the machine-gun strongpoints, and the dugout entrances. For this purpose, in planning the attack Rawlinson had more than doubled the weight of heavy shell fired at Amiens – 27.5 million pounds would now be fired as against 12.7 million pounds on 8 August, an increase of 120 per cent. Almost all this shell would be used for one or other of four purposes: to suppress the enemy's guns, to smash down the banks of the St Quentin Canal, to destroy or neutralize the larger German dugouts by blocking their exits, and to destroy strategically placed machine-gun posts, command centres, and communication systems. The Fourth Army planners were ensuring that the operation would not fail through insufficiency of shell.

But the British artillerymen would have advantages in addition to the sheer weight of the bombardment. From their positions on the ridge they enjoyed the best observation over any major German defensive system yet attacked in the course of this war. As the Germans themselves put it:

> The artillery conditions for the attackers are not unfavourable...
> There is abundant room for siting attacking batteries...The obser-
> vation conditions for the attacker are favourable as the heights
> north-west of Bellenglise and south of Pontruet afford a compre-
> hensive view, particularly along the gently rising slope...These
> favourable observation conditions for the attacker considerably
> diminish the sites available for the defenders artillery...
>
> These circumstances – restricted area for the deployment of
> our batteries, favourable observation conditions for the attacker –
> necessitate a fairly close grouping of our artillery.[12]

This last sentence is remarkable. So good were the conditions for the attackers' artillery, the document seems to be saying, that those batteries which remained to the Germans would have to be closely grouped. This appeared to overlook the fact that thereby they became easier targets.

There was one quite novel feature in the Fourth Army's bombardment. After many setbacks the British had finally managed to manufacture mustard gas. Preliminary to the infantry attack, every mustard gas shell available would be fired at the German artillery (which had been employing similar tactics against the British since the Third Battle of Ypres).[13] Al-

---

[12] 'Artillery Appreciation of the Various Divisional Sectors of the Siegfried Line' (translation of a German document) in Fourth Army Papers vol. 53.

[13] Maj.-Gen. C. E. D. Budworth, 'Fourth Army Artillery In The Attack on The Hindenburg Line, Sept. 29 1918', AWM 26/12/474/1.

though this would hardly be of critical importance, it so happened that the Germans were running out of the materials for gas masks and protective clothing. Hence this development did constitute a further factor in impairing the ability of the German gunners to hold back the attackers.[14]

Finally – and, on the day, very significantly – special artillery arrangements were provided for IX Corps. As already noted, Rawlinson had extended the front of attack to include this force even though it was up against the canal proper – a form of defence which Monash clearly thought could not be taken by frontal assault. Rawlinson, when he took a different view, was relying on the destructive power of his artillery. Almost all the heavy guns of IX Corps and three-fifths of its field artillery were allocated to 46 Division which was to assault across the canal.[15] In addition several batteries of heavy howitzers were brought close up to the front and placed in positions where they would bring under severe enfilade fire the section of the canal to be attacked.[16] This was probably the heaviest weight of artillery fire ever to accompany the attack of a single British division in the course of the Great War.

[14] L. F. Haber, *The Poisonous Cloud: Chemical Warfare in the First World War* (Oxford: Clarendon Press, 1986), p. 229.

[15] 'Precis of Fourth Army Orders Affecting Artillery For The Attack On The Hindenburg Line, 29th Sept. 1918', AWM 26/12/474/2.

[16] 'Offensive Operations undertaken by IX Corps from 18 September to 11 November 1918', Fourth Army Papers vol. 63.

33

The Battle of the Hindenburg Line

I

The preliminary operation, intended to capture that part of Monash's proposed start line still in enemy hands, was undertaken by 54 Brigade of 27 American Division on the early morning of 27 September. In the main it failed. The troops, advancing to their objectives through a fog, apparently missed some of the strongpoints (Quennemont Farm, Gillemont Farm, and the Knoll) which were the key to the German defences in this area. When the fog lifted the defenders in these strongpoints were able to take a heavy toll on the following waves of troops. Thus, although some of the Americans were successful in reaching part of the ridge line, most were pinned down or became casualties in front of the German strongpoints.[1]

A dilemma now faced Rawlinson and Monash on this sector of the front. They could hardly start the barrage for 29 September from the original American front line for fear of hitting those troops still between that line and their objective. Rawlinson therefore decided to adhere to the original barrage plan as if the objectives of the 27th had been taken. This meant that the brigades of Americans attacking on the 29th would have to advance 1,000 yards over strongly defended ground before they found the protection of their creeping barrage – a circumstance which produced in

[1] Most accounts attribute the American failure either to poor mopping-up or to the fact that the Germans had a series of tunnels on this part of the front which allowed them to infiltrate troops behind an enemy attack. For this view see II United States Corps, 'Report on Operations, 1918', AWM 26/12/482/4. In our account we have relied on a report made by the office of the Corps of Engineers, Headquarters II Army Corps, American Expeditionary Forces 1/9/19 in AWM 26/12/482/5. An officer from this corps walked over the battlefield in 1919 and found no covered tunnels.

Monash a 'state of despair' (something not likely to be allayed by Haig's facile judgement that 'it was not a serious matter' and he should attack as arranged).[2]

II

What numbers of Germans faced the 30,000 Allied troops – six attacking divisions plus two providing flank protection – on the morning of 29 September? The enemy force amounted to seven divisions with one in close reserve; two more were a few miles back, and a further four could arrive on the battlefield within 72 hours.[3] (All this was almost exactly estimated by Fourth Army Intelligence.)[4] Little can be gleaned from the German accounts on the state of these divisions. That they were far below full strength is beyond doubt. Three battalions from a regiment of 185 Division holding the line near Bellicourt could only raise a total of 375 men.[5] The 2 Guards Division in reserve consisted of only three battalions instead of the regulation nine.[6]

Of the artillery supporting these divisions nothing is known. No German account mentions the number of guns available on this sector of the Hindenburg Line. However, there seems no reason to doubt Budworth's estimate that the German artillery was 'markedly inferior' to the 1,600 guns supporting the British.[7]

III

The British bombardment of the Hindenburg positions began on the early morning of 26 September. From then until zero hour on the 29th (5.50 a.m.) 750,000 shells (including 30,000 gas shells) were thrown at the German defences.

The effectiveness of this bombardment was variable. It benefited least 27 American Division in the north, which was making another attempt to capture the defences of the ridge line. In this area the British shells pulverized the defences of the central Hindenburg positions protecting the

[2] Haig Diary 29/9/18.

[3] Brigadier-General Sir James E. Edmonds and Lieut.-Colonel R. Maxwell-Hyslop, *Military Operations: France and Belgium, 1918* vol. 5 (London: HMSO, 1947), p. 97.

[4] Ibid.

[5] Bean, *Australian Official History* vol. 6, p. 985.

[6] Ibid., p. 995.

[7] Budworth, 'Fourth Army Artillery In The Attack On The Hindenburg Line'.

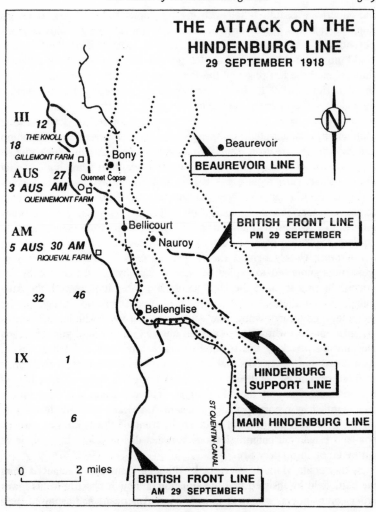

THE ATTACK ON THE
HINDENBURG LINE
29 SEPTEMBER 1918

III 12
THE KNOLL
18
GILLEMONT FARM

Bony

Beaurevoir

BEAUREVOIR LINE

AUS 27
3 AUS AM
Quennet Copse
QUENNEMONT FARM

BRITISH FRONT LINE
PM 29 SEPTEMBER

AM
5 AUS 30 AM
RIQUEVAL FARM

Bellicourt

Nauroy

32   46

Bellenglise

HINDENBURG
SUPPORT LINE

IX   1

MAIN HINDENBURG LINE

6

ST QUENTIN CANAL

0   2 miles

BRITISH FRONT LINE
AM 29 SEPTEMBER

MAP 35

northern sector of the Bellicourt tunnel. (The troops manning these defences were in the main driven underground and kept there for the duration of the bombardment.) But no bombardment fell upon the Germans
holding the strongpoints along the ridge – the Knoll, Gillemont Farm, and
Quennemont Farm – for fear of hitting the scattered groups of Americans
who had survived the attack on the 27th. Nor did the creeping barrage aid

the American assault. It fell with great accuracy on the designated start line, but this was 1,000 yards to the east of the attacking troops and well beyond the German strongpoints. In addition, what artillery the Germans could muster in this area had shifted position on the night of the 28th and thus escaped the last phase of the British counter-battery programme.[8] So the Americans went forward unprotected by a creeping barrage against defenders and artillery not subjected to barrage or bombardment.

The results were predictable. The Americans were cut down in large numbers by concentrated machine-gun fire from the German strongpoints and by artillery fire from the German rear areas. Only the thick mist in which the attack was carried out prevented losses from being higher.[9] Nor did the Americans receive much help from the thirty-four tanks which accompanied the attack. Ten ran into an old British minefield (even though the Germans had roped it off and marked it with signs, 'Achtung minenfeld');[10] eleven more received direct hits from German field artillery; and seven became ditched.[11]

Following closely behind the Americans came 3 Australian Division, which was supposed to exploit the gains made by the Americans by advancing beyond them to the Hindenburg Support Line. Instead, the Australians found themselves enmeshed with the Americans in fighting for the ridge line strongpoints. The Australians too were without the benefit of tanks, most of which were knocked out by German field guns. By early morning the attack in this sector had degenerated into isolated groups of Australians and Americans making unco-ordinated attempts to push on.[12] In these circumstances divisional headquarters could form no clear idea of the position of any of their formations. The confusion was then greatly compounded by reports placing parties of Americans variously to the east of the Bellicourt tunnel and held up in front of the ridge line strongpoints.[13] Finally all communications between divisions and brigades were cut by German artillery fire.[14]

At this point Monash intervened. Although many miles removed from the battlefield he insisted that the situation, although obscure to his lower order commanders, was clear to him. Most Americans *had* captured their

[8] Bean, *Australian Official History* vol. 6, p. 986.

[9] 'Operations Report of the 27th Division, A.E.F., covering the period Sept. 23rd to October 21st, 1918', AWM 26/12/487/2.

[10] Bean, *Australian Official History* vol. 6, p. 960.

[11] 'Report on Operations: 4th Tank Brigade September 27th to October 17th, 1918', AWM 26/12/481/3; Tank Corps Narratives, WO 95/97.

[12] 'Action Near Bony – 29th September–2nd October, 1918': Third Australian Division, AWM 26/12/530/3.

[13] Third Australian Division Telegrams 29/9/18, AWM 26/12/530/3.

[14] 'Action Near Bony'.

objectives. Only remnants of German troops lay between the Australians and the tunnel defences. Ignoring the protests of the commander of 3 Australian Division (Gellibrand), he ordered an attack for 3 p.m. to mop up these Germans.[15] This operation, conducted without artillery support, failed with heavy casualties, although Gillemont Farm was finally captured.[16] No further progress could be made until towards nightfall when the Germans, cut off from reinforcement and low on ammunition, were driven off Quennemont Farm and the western slopes of the Knoll by improvised parties of Australians and Americans.[17] The ridge position of 18 September had finally fallen, but at a cost of 5,000 casualties to the two divisions involved. And 2,000 yards ahead of them still stood the five lines of trenches and wire of the central Hindenburg defences.[18]

Immediately to the south, however, events were proceeding a good deal more smoothly. The 30 American Division, which was in the happy position of occupying its start line, had the benefit of a trench bombardment, counter-battery fire, and a creeping barrage carried out according to plan. In consequence the American infantry with their thirty-four supporting tanks were able to advance to timetable. On the left the wire had been cut and the defenders were caught in their dugouts by the Americans who swept over the trench systems and formed up to the east of the tunnel.[19] However, attempts to advance further were frustrated by heavy enfilade fire from the unsubdued Quennemont Farm on their left. So the Americans threw out a defensive flank and awaited the Australians. Further right the German wire had not been cut 'to any considerable degree', but here the tanks forced lanes through for the infantry. Bellicourt was soon captured, its defenders still stunned by the bombardment when the Americans arrived.[20] So by noon Bellicourt and the tunnel defences were largely in American hands and parties of US troops had begun an advance on Nauroy in the Hindenburg Support Line.[21]

It was now time for 5 Australian Division to advance through the Americans. In doing so the Australians at times came under severe fire from German machine-gun posts which had remained concealed during the American advance. Nevertheless they managed to go forward and by 12.20 p.m. Nauroy in the Hindenburg support system had been captured.

---

[15] Pedersen, *Monash*, p. 289.

[16] 'Action Near Bony'.

[17] Edmonds, *1918* vol. 5, pp. 108–9.

[18] 'Action Near Bony'; 'Operations Report of the 27th Division A.E.F'.

[19] '30th Division A.E.F., Report on Operations of 30th Division against Hindenburg Line September 27th–September 30th, 1918', AWM 26/12/487/3.

[20] Ibid.

[21] Montgomery, *Fourth Army*, p. 162.

But by this time all but two tanks had been knocked out and heavy enfilade fire was being encountered from the north, so little advance beyond the village was possible.

On the left of this sector, flanking fire from the still uncaptured German strongpoints on the ridge prevented 5 Australian Division from advancing much beyond the American positions. An attempt to push on in conjunction with the abortive attack made by 3 Australian Division to the north ended in costly failure. Pressure was also being exerted by the German reserves to the south, anyway until around 3 p.m. (Why it then relaxed will soon become apparent.) Particularly on account of the precarious situation to the north, the decision was taken to consolidate 5 Australian Division's position. No further advances were attempted in the tunnel sector that day.[22]

IV

The partial success in the southern sector of the Australian–American attack had partly redeemed the failure further north. The tunnel defences had been breached, Bellicourt had been captured, and the support line around Nauroy was in Allied hands. Nevertheless, had no other events taken place on the front of Fourth Army that day the position of Rawlinson's men would have been precarious. The troops in the breach were vulnerable to counterattack from the north and south of the tunnel. Had it stood alone, the Australian position around Nauroy would have formed a dangerous salient. That the success was not isolated was due to some extraordinary events on the southern part of the Fourth Army's attack.

Here, it will be recalled, due to Rawlinson's insistence, 46 Division was to assault the Hindenburg defences by attacking across the St. Quentin Canal. It is worth restating what this task entailed. In the area to be assaulted the canal was 35 feet wide, the banks on either side were up to 50 feet high and steeply sloped, the lower 10 feet of the banks were faced with brick, the canal contained water or mud to a depth of over 6 feet, and both banks of the canal were strongly wired. Before reaching the canal the attackers had to penetrate a continuous line of trenches with numerous machine-gun strongpoints. Beyond the canal there were three lines of trenches of similar strength as well as the fortified villages of Bellenglise,

[22] Third Australian Division: 'Report on Operations 29/9/18 to 2/10/18', AWM 26/12/560/6.

[23] This description of the German defences has been compiled from Edmonds, *1918* vol. 5, pp. 101–2; and Major R. E. Priestley, *Breaking the Hindenburg Line: The story of the 46th*

Magny la Fosse, and Lehaucourt.[23] These were very formidable defences.

Nevertheless, as indicated, the attackers were not without resources to deal with them. Thanks to the captured plans, the German defences in this area were known in the greatest detail. Possession of the ridge provided commanding observation over the German positions as far back as their reserve line. This artillery advantage was enhanced by the fact that at Bellenglise, the canal, though strongly defended, formed a salient vulnerable to enfilade fire. Finally, it was questionable whether any sort of defences could withstand the concentration of artillery fire – including groups of heavy howitzers placed well forward to bombard the defences on either side of the canal – which was being employed on this occasion.

In the event two further factors aided the British: on the early morning of the 29th the attackers were concealed by a very heavy fog, and so confident was the German command regarding the defences in this area that it was not anticipating an attack.[24]

Shrouded by the fog, 137 Brigade of 46 Division moved forward to seize the crossing places over the canal for the follow-up brigades. According to plan, as 46 Division advanced to the attack, on their right 1 Division captured the high ground south of Bellenglise and so guarded their flank. German artillery retaliation is not mentioned by any of the accounts, indicating that the British counter-batteries had done their job. Behind 'one of the finest barrages that the troops had ever advanced under',[25] the leading waves overran the defenders on the west side of the canal, catching most of them still in their dugouts or strongpoints. On reaching the canal the attackers made a reassuring discovery. The artillery had 'destroyed the wire on the inner bank ... and broke[n] the wall which presented sheer face to the waterway, creating a series of ramps which helped the infantry down to the water's edge.'[26] The crossing of the canal was then made with ropes, rafts, lifebelts, and the other nautical paraphernalia assembled for the task. In the north near Riqueval this process was supplemented by the capture of an intact bridge. Only in the south were serious casualties sustained at the hands of German machine-gunners who had escaped the bombardment. But the latter were too few, and too hampered by fog, to prevent a general advance, and so were quickly outflanked. Elsewhere most of the defenders were either dead or

Division (London: Fisher and Unwin, 1919), pp. 31–2.

[24] 'Account of the part taken by the 46 Division in the battle of Bellenglise on the 29th September, 1918', III and IX Corps Narratives Aug–Oct 1918, Fourth Army Papers vol. 63.

[25] Ibid.

[26] 'Offensive Operations Undertaken By IX Corps from 18th September 1918 to 11th November 1918', Fourth Army Papers vol. 63.

too stunned by the barrage to respond to the attack. In the words of the historian of the 46 Division:

> [The] sting [was] taken out of the resistance . . . by the intensity of the barrage, which had been so heavy, so well directed, and so closely followed up by our Infantry, that in many cases garrisons of enemy strong-points and trenches were unable to emerge before the positions were rushed.[27]

Some of these garrisons had been trapped in their dugouts without food for two days.

The attack did not cease with the fall of the canal. The attacking brigade and the follow-up formations regrouped behind the barrage. Then as the artillery continued with crushing intensity, the infantry advanced against the trenches east of the canal. The likely condition of their opponents may be deduced from a few statistics. It has been estimated that during each minute 126 shells from the field guns alone were falling on every 500 yards of trench. This intensity was maintained for the entire eight hours of 46 Division's attack. Therefore on any 500 yards of front, from the far bank of the canal to their final objective, the British infantry were supported by 50,000 shells.[28] Caught up in this maelstrom, the surviving Germans either fled or surrendered.

By 3 p.m. the canal from Riqueval to Le Tronquoy, the defended villages, and the central Hindenburg Line with its support system were all in the hands of 46 Division. Through it advanced 32 Division, capturing the high ground to the east of Magny, and in the process relieving pressure on the Australians to the north. The Hindenburg defences had been breached by IX Corps to a depth of 6,000 yards. Only the weak trenches and wire which constituted the Beaurevoir Line stood, in the south, between Fourth Army and open country.

V

By 3.30 p.m. Rawlinson was convinced that he had achieved success along his whole front of attack. He noted in his diary that 'All has gone very well indeed. I could not have hoped for such good results.'[29] As later reports came in he became aware that the spectacular results achieved by IX Corps had not been repeated on other sectors of the front. He was particularly harsh on the American effort.

[27] Priestly, *Breaking the Hindenburg Line*, p. 52.
[28] Ibid., p. 143.
[29] Rawlinson Diary 29/9/18.

The Americans appear to be in a state of hopeless confusion and will not I fear be able to function as a Corps so I am contemplating replacing them with the XIII Corps . . . I fear [their] casualties have been heavy but it is their own fault.[30]

This censorious account of the American troops at the Hindenburg Line became generally accepted after the war and was propagated by Montgomery and Monash in their books on the 1918 campaign. It should be disregarded. As noted earlier, the 'hopeless confusion' on the front of 27 Division, and the heavy casualties suffered by it, were the consequence of an attempt to advance against strongly defended positions without artillery protection. There were any number of precedents in this war for failure under such circumstances. On this occasion the originators of the fiasco were not the hapless American troops or their commanders but Rawlinson and Monash.

VI

During the next six days (30 September–5 October) Fourth Army completed the capture of the Hindenburg Line and advanced 6,000 yards on an 11,000-yard front to overrun the Beaurevoir Line, the last German position on this section of the front. These were substantial gains. And yet the operations do not present themselves as a series of well-ordered, methodical attacks, but as haphazard, often small-scale, unco-ordinated efforts. The uneven progress of the British advance was caused by a number of factors.

First, there was the perennial difficulty of following up a set-piece attack on the Western Front. In the aftermath of 29 September, as in the aftermath of Amiens, artillery support could not always be provided to attacking troops since their exact position was not known. Few tanks were available, and most of those that were had difficulty in making their way to the front over cratered ground. The destruction of communication networks made it difficult to co-ordinate attacks between corps or sometimes even within corps.

An example of the kind of disjointed attack that resulted is provided by the events of 2 October. In the south, 1 Division failed in all attempts to co-ordinate operations with the French on their right. As a result it did not attack at all. Further north, 6 Division launched a one-brigade attack on Sequehart at 6 a.m. Two and a half hours later a brigade from 32

---

[30] Ibid.

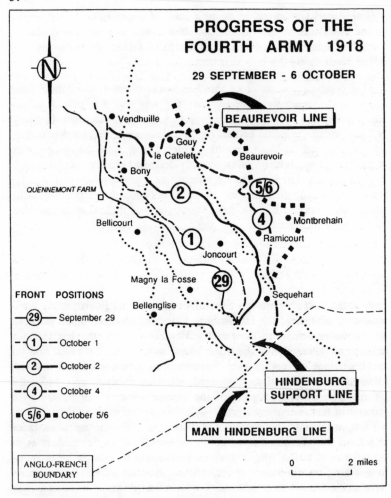

PROGRESS OF THE FOURTH ARMY 1918

29 SEPTEMBER - 6 OCTOBER

BEAUREVOIR LINE

HINDENBURG SUPPORT LINE

MAIN HINDENBURG LINE

Vendhuille
Gouy
le Catelet
Beaurevoir
Bony
QUENNEMONT FARM
Bellicourt
Montbrehain
Ramicourt
Joncourt
Magny la Fosse
Bellenglise
Sequehart

FRONT POSITIONS

—(29)— September 29
–-(1)-– October 1
–(2)– October 2
–(4)-– October 4
■(5/6)■■ October 5/6

ANGLO-FRENCH BOUNDARY

0   2 miles

MAP 36

Division attempted to capture Ramicourt. No action at all was taken by the Australian Corps on this day. All attacks failed, and artillery support fell to its lowest level throughout the whole of the battle.[31]

Other factors hampering success were peculiar to the Hindenburg Line operations. Rain fell almost continually from the night of the 29th until

[31] Edmonds, *1918* vol. 5, p. 142; for artillery support see Montgomery, *Fourth Army*, Appendix G, p. 329.

1 October. This made all movements in that period difficult and denied to the artillery the benefit of aerial spotting. In the Australian sector the uncaptured defences were the strongest faced on the second day of any Allied battle in 1918. In addition the Australians had to cope with the almost forgotten experience of heavy enfilade artillery fire from the still unlocated German batteries on their left.[32]

All these difficulties rendered the follow-up attacks hazardous and account for the scrappy nature of operations in this period. Yet, as at Amiens, other factors at times enabled substantial advances to be made on some sectors of the front. Because of the deep penetration of IX Corps on the first day of the battle, and the efforts of the Americans and Australians east of Bellicourt, the Germans had no defensive positions except the distant Beaurevoir Line on which to make a stand. In these circumstances they were vulnerable to any co-ordinated attack that could be mounted. On 1 October, operations by 5 Australian Division and 32 Division were accompanied by a heavy bombardment, a dense and accurate barrage, and tanks. The Germans, with little artillery support and no trench line to defend, were forced back some 2,000 yards, thereby relinquishing a section of the Beaurevoir Line.[33]

A slightly different example is provided by the attack of 32, 46, and 2 Australian Divisions on 3 October. Here the objective was again a section of the Beaurevoir Line, strongly wired but with an incomplete trench. In this operation the British launched a co-ordinated attack across the whole front with much-enhanced artillery cover (the heaviest in the period 30 September–5 October). So the three attacking divisions were supported by 400 field artillery pieces and the heavy artillery of three corps (IX, Australian, and the newly arrived XIII).[34] In addition 38 heavy tanks and 16 whippets accompanied the troops, the largest number mustered during this same period.[35] A considerable success was achieved. An advance of approximately 2,000 yards secured the Beaurevoir Line on an 11,000-yard front. The result once again showed the effectiveness of the British weapons system when all its elements could be brought into play.

Occasionally, progress on one part of the battlefield forced a German withdrawal in another. So at the Hindenburg Line the rapid advance of IX Corps in the south threatened to cut off those Germans to the north who had successfully held off Australian attacks against the tunnel defences. By 1 October the progress of IX Corps was such that the Germans

---

[32] Edmonds, *1918* vol. 5, p. 135.

[33] Ibid., pp. 139–40.

[34] Ibid., pp. 159, 164.

[35] Tank Corps: 'Summary of Actions', Tank Corps War Diary, WO 95/94.

were forced to withdraw to the line of the Escaut river. In this way the last of the main Hindenburg defences fell, virtually without a blow.[36]

A final factor in the British successes in this period marked a dramatic change from Amiens and allowed the Hindenburg Line operations to progress with much greater speed. In August the Germans had always had on hand enough reserves and artillery to stabilize the front, at least temporarily, thus forcing the British to halt and prepare another set-piece attack. In this way the Germans forced a pause of 12 days on the British between 12 and 23 August. By late September the situation was quite different. On the 29th the seven German divisions holding the line against Fourth Army had been dealt with severely. In particular, south of Bellicourt only scattered remnants of these formations survived. Yet because of the extent of the Foch–Haig offensive set in train on 26 September (and which by the 29th extended over a 100-mile front), no German reserves were available as reinforcements from other sectors. German commanders were instructed that they would have to do their best with local reserves.[37] As stated earlier, on the sector attacked by Fourth Army these amounted to very few. Three understrength divisions came into the line within 24 hours, but two of these amounted to no more than nine battalions in total.[38] In the next few days seven more divisions were brought up from local reserve but most of these were divisions in name only. Each consisted of only a few battalions; four had held the line between 18 and 25 September; and it seems certain that none had supporting artillery.

So by 3 October, of the seven German divisions holding the Beaurevoir Line, none had adequate artillery support, two were the remnants of divisions which had been subjected to the initial attack, four more were the remaining elements of the weak formations which had come into the line since that date, and one was fresh. The victims of continual defeat, deprived of artillery support, and without adequate numbers even to stretch across the front of attack, it is a wonder that these battered formations could manage to maintain the line. It is no matter for wonder that they were driven back with relative ease. At last the predictions that Haig had been making since 1916 seemed to be coming true. The Germans really were showing signs of disintegration.

---

[36] Bean, *Australian Official History* vol. 6, pp. 1012–13.
[37] Ibid., p. 995.
[38] Ibid., pp. 1005–6.

34

The End of the Affair

I

The accomplishments of the Fourth Army in the 60 days between the opening of the Amiens offensive on 8 August and the fall of Beaurevoir on 5 October had been remarkable. Six German defensive positions, including the strongest on the Western Front, had been overrun. And a method of proceeding against the enemy had been developed which appeared applicable in all circumstances.

The Germans now facing Rawlinson were in disarray and lacked powerful defensive positions. Hence as long as ammunition, guns, and men were available to him in sufficient quantities, the advance appeared bound to continue. Concerning guns and munitions, no problem presented itself; British industry was supplying all the army could use. Manpower was another matter. Casualties in August and September had amounted to 110,000, reinforcements to the existing divisions to only 64,000.[1] But even here there was some cause for optimism. A new corps (XIII), composed of experienced men withdrawn from Italy (25 Division) and Palestine (50 and 66 Divisions), joined the Fourth Army late in September.[2] In addition, the American II Corps was available to replace the Australians who (not surprisingly) had been withdrawn on 5 October for a lengthy rest. Again, further reinforcements for the depleted divisions remaining with Fourth Army were promised for October. (In the event reinforcements about balanced losses in October.)[3]

What the situation required, therefore, was further application of the methods devised since the opening of the offensive. Above all, the weapons

[1] Montgomery, *Fourth Army*, Appendix A, p. 275.
[2] XIII Corps Narratives October–November 1918, Fourth Army Papers vol. 64.
[3] Montgomery, *Fourth Army*, Appendix A, p. 275.

system, comprising artillery, tanks, and close-support infantry weapons must be employed to the utmost and losses among the scarce infantry kept to a minimum.

II

The first battle fought by the Fourth Army following the capture of the last vestige of the Hindenburg system reaffirmed the validity of the winning formula. On 8 October four attacking divisions (6, 30 American, 25, and 66) assailed a jumble of intermixed German formations protected neither by trenches nor wire and clinging to whatever natural features (hills, woods, villages) offered cover.[4] Even so, Rawlinson was not taking chances. Before launching the attack he pounded the luckless defenders with 350,000 shells weighing 8 million pounds.[5] Those who survived this bombardment – mainly the occupants of some defended villages – were then assailed by 94 tanks and by infantry advancing behind an 'excellent' creeping barrage.[6] All objectives were captured, and an advance to a depth of 6,000 yards was made along the whole front of attack.[7]

Three features of the operation of 8 October are worthy of note. Of prime importance is the care which British commanders were now bestowing on their infantry. Two incidents in the battle highlight this. As a result of a misunderstanding, the creeping barrage was not fired on the front of a brigade of 6 Division. The brigadier did not order his men forward, preferring to await progress of the forces to his right and left.[8] Later, when the final objective had been captured, the evident disorganization among the enemy raised the possibility of ordering a further advance. This course was not adopted. The infantry brigadiers urged – and Rawlinson agreed – that 'without further artillery support' no such attempt should be made.[9] Action was postponed until the following day.

The wisdom of their caution is underlined by the second point which emerges from the action of 8 October. When the more mobile elements among the British forces, such as whippet tanks and cavalry, ventured beyond the protective curtain of their own artillery, they were speedily dealt with by German machine-guns, anti-tank rifles, and shells.[10] That

---

[4] Fourth Army Summary of Operations, 8th October 1918, Fourth Army Papers vol. 46.
[5] Montgomery, *Fourth Army*, Appendix G, p. 330.
[6] Edmonds, *1918* vol. 5, pp. 192–5.
[7] Ibid.
[8] Ibid., p. 191.
[9] Ibid., p. 197.
[10] Montgomery, *Fourth Army*, p. 196.

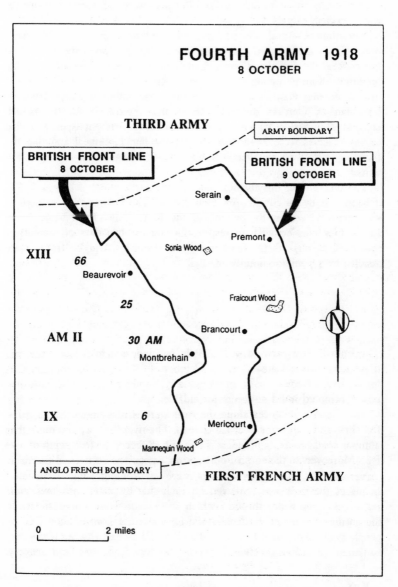

FOURTH ARMY 1918
8 OCTOBER

THIRD ARMY

BRITISH FRONT LINE
8 OCTOBER

ARMY BOUNDARY

BRITISH FRONT LINE
9 OCTOBER

Serain

Premont

XIII

66

Sonia Wood

Beaurevoir

25

Fraicourt Wood

AM II

30 AM

Brancourt

Montbrehain

IX

6

Mericourt

Mannequin Wood

ANGLO FRENCH BOUNDARY

FIRST FRENCH ARMY

N

0   2 miles

MAP 37

is, the enemy might be disorganized but they were still capable of dealing with sacrificial targets.

Nevertheless – and this is the third point to emerge from the day's operations – the devoted resistance offered by German rearguards could not conceal the fact that Fourth Army's progress was being aided by the mounting disarray among its opponents. At the end of 8 October it was discovered that Rawlinson's four divisions had captured troops from no less than 15 German divisions. Given that, pretty clearly, the British enjoyed a numerical superiority over their adversaries, it is evident that enemy reserves were being thrown into the line piecemeal and that the German staffs were making little attempt to arrange them into coherent units.[11]

The outcome of this further success by Fourth Army, accompanied as it happened by an advance on their left by Third Army, was to compel the enemy to retreat to the line of the River Selle. Even while doing so the Germans enjoyed no respite. During the two days of the retreat (9–10 October) their rearguards on Fourth Army's front were assailed by 4.7 million pounds of shell.[12]

III

The Fourth Army arrived at the Selle position, which included the fortified town of Le Cateau, on 11 October. In the space of four days its forces had advanced 10½ miles on a 7½-mile front.[13] The task that now confronted it did not seem formidable.

The German defences along the river were virtually nonexistent: a few trenches, and some wire near Le Cateau. The river itself was no more than a minor obstacle. At its broadest it was but 18 feet wide, to a depth of 3–4 feet. Moreover, to the south Fourth Army's positions outflanked the river.

Nevertheless, Rawlinson's forces were confronting some difficulties. In places the river was bordered on each side by water meadows some 100–200 yards wide, through which movement would be difficult. In the northern sector of the front stood Le Cateau, a town of about 10,000 people with solidly built houses and cellars. To its east rose a railway embankment providing excellent cover for machine-guns and field artillery.

[11] Edmonds, *1918* vol. 5, p. 210.
[12] Montgomery, *Fourth Army*, Appendix G.
[13] Ibid., p. 203.

In addition the entire Fourth Army position was overlooked by German-held ground to the east of the river.[14]

Notwithstanding these difficulties, a strong temptation must have presented itself to attempt a rush on the enemy positions before the Germans could strengthen them or bring up fresh forces. The divisions presently facing Fourth Army were known to be exhausted. Information from other parts of the front indicated that everywhere the Germans were in retreat. An advance of only a few miles by Fourth Army would enable its gunners to shell the rail junction of Avesnes, through which ran the main lateral line connecting the northern and southern sections of the German front.[15]

Rawlinson, to his credit, resisted precipitate action. His attempts to get the cavalry forward on the 8th and 9th had demonstrated that even in retreat the Germans were far from helpless. His own divisions were understrength and needed careful husbanding. A setback might harm the prospects for advance on other sectors of the front. So, following consultations with his corps commanders, he decided to prepare a set-piece attack. On the 13th he wrote:

I . . . put off the attack until the 17th so as to get all the artillery and ammunition up and make sure of penetrating the line[,] for we must not have a failure at this juncture.[16]

Rawlinson succeeded in his purpose 'to get all the artillery and ammunition up.' No fewer than 1,320 guns were brought forward,[17] and between 11 October, when the bombardment opened, and 17 October, when the attack went in, 17 million pounds of shell (only slightly less than had been fired during the artillery prelude to the much larger battle of Amiens) rained down upon the meagre German defences.[18]

The attack by the Fourth Army, assisted in the south by the First French Army, went in at 5.20 a.m. on 17 October. It was successful everywhere, the line of the Selle being forced and Le Cateau captured.[19]

Almost all the attacking divisions ascribe their success to the key element of the British weapons system, artillery. Once more the counter-battery fire had accomplished its purpose. While in the north there was

---

[14] Ibid., pp. 204–5.
[15] Ibid., p. 207.
[16] Rawlinson Diary 13/10/18.
[17] Fourth Army Summary of Operations 17/10/18, Fourth Army Papers vol. 46.
[18] Montgomery, *Fourth Army*, Appendix G.
[19] Fourth Army Summary of Operations 17/10/18.

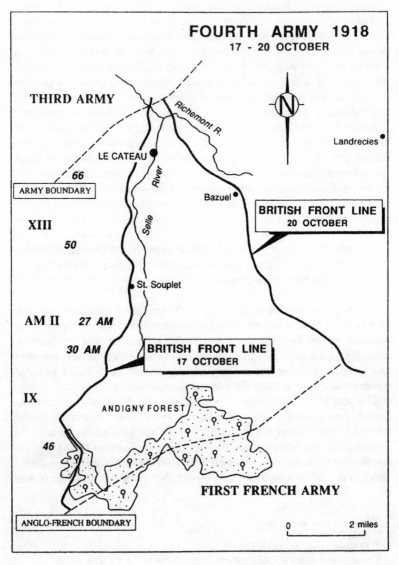

FOURTH ARMY 1918
17 - 20 OCTOBER

THIRD ARMY

Richemont R.

Landrecies

LE CATEAU

66
ARMY BOUNDARY

XIII

50

Selle River

Bazuel

BRITISH FRONT LINE
20 OCTOBER

St. Souplet

AM II   27 AM

30 AM   **BRITISH FRONT LINE**
17 OCTOBER

IX

ANDIGNY FOREST

46

FIRST FRENCH ARMY

ANGLO-FRENCH BOUNDARY

0   2 miles

MAP 38

some German artillery retaliation, it ceased soon after the commencement of the attack and thereafter was not a factor in halting the Fourth Army's advance.[20] Rawlinson's artillery was able to give direct help to the infantry. In the north where the Selle was wide enough to require bridging, the operation was carried out and the crossing made under the protection of the barrage.[21] Although the defence was often stubborn in this area, especially around Le Cateau, XIII corps noted that the 'violent bombardments to which they [the Germans] had been subjected ... sufficed to break down the resistance of the defenders.'[22]

Further south, those Germans who had survived the bombardment were simply too depleted to stop the advance, even when on occasions the attackers lost the protection of the barrage. Rupprecht noted at this time that the infantry component of any one of his divisions was, at the most, 'the equivalent to one or two battalions'.[23] It seems fair to conclude that, by the time the British artillery had wreaked its havoc, Rupprecht's nine divisions defending the Selle were reduced to not much more than scattered handfuls of men. Consequently, although some of the defenders, especially machine-gunners hidden in the villages, could take a heavy toll on the attackers, they were too few and too isolated to present a coherent defence. At times they were outflanked by parties of Lewis gunners;[24] in the south, with no river for protection, they were often as not overwhelmed by tanks.[25]

Rarely could the enemy gather enough troops even to attempt a counterattack, and when they managed to do so it usually required only the Fourth Army's artillery to disperse them. For example, one group of Germans massing against a British division were so savaged by the British gunners that only one of them reached the British positions alive.[26]

Certainly, elements other than the artillery contributed to Fourth Army's success. Fog all along the front once again aided concealment in the first phase of the attack. The bridging operations of XIII Corps were carried out with commendable skill. And similar expertize was evident in the tactics employed by Lewis gunners north of Le Cateau in beating down opposition while sections of uncut wire were being negotiated.[27] But, as ever, these infantry operations were dependent on the artillery's having

[20] See Edmonds, *1918* vol. 5, chapter XX.

[21] XIII Corps Narratives Oct–Nov 1918.

[22] Ibid.

[23] Rupprecht to Prince Max 18/10/18, quoted in Edmonds, *1918* vol. 5, p. 327.

[24] XIII Corps Narratives Oct–Nov 1918.

[25] Edmonds, *1918* vol. 5, pp. 304–5.

[26] Ibid., p. 302.

[27] XIII Corps Narratives Oct–Nov 1918.

first crushed most of the German batteries and silenced most enemy machine-guns.

IV

After continued progress on 18 and 19 October, operations on the Fourth Army's front were allowed to run down. Since 8 August Rawlinson's troops had been in the vanguard of the British advance. Now the task of driving the Germans from the line of the River Scheldt fell largely upon Third and First Armies, on Rawlinson's left. The much weakened American Corps was withdrawn from his command, so reducing Fourth Army to two corps (IX and XIII). Their main task was that of supplying flank support for the operations of the Third Army.[28]

As a first stage the battle of the Selle had to be completed. Third Army was assigned the task of forcing the line of the river north of Le Cateau, while Rawlinson's troops protected its flanks and advanced to the next water obstacle, the Sambre and Oise Canal. These operations were successfully carried out on 23 and 24 October. Little need be said about them. The British artillery fired 10 million pounds of shell at German divisions standing – as on 8 October – entirely on open ground.[29] Any centres of resistance which escaped the bombardment were dealt with by tanks, 24 of which were used in the operation.[30] Once more, in places, the fighting was severe. Once more, the Germans proved incapable of sustained resistance. By 24 October the Fourth Army had reached the Sambre and Oise Canal in the south and the Forest of Mormal in the north.

Ranwlinson immediately began planning to force the line of the canal. But as he did so the possibility was presenting itself that no such operation would be required. Some weeks earlier the German authorities – responding to Ludendorff's assurance on 28 September that the war was lost – had raised with President Wilson the matter of an armistice. Since then Ludendorff had changed his mind, but the civilian government – disregarding his views in a manner which precipitated his resignation – were by late October pressing on with armistice negotiations.

Rawlinson noted these events in his diary. He judged the German position on the Western Front now to be hopeless, but he doubted if the armistice terms ('tantamount to unconditional surrender') would be ac-

---

[28] Montgomery, *Fourth Army*, p. 230.
[29] Ibid., Appendix G.
[30] Ibid., p. 233; Edmonds, *1918* vol. 5, pp. 357–8, 361.

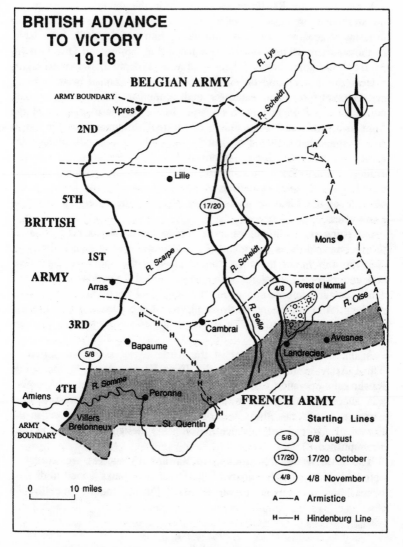

BRITISH ADVANCE
TO VICTORY
1918

BELGIAN ARMY

ARMY BOUNDARY

Ypres

2ND

R. Lys

R. Scheldt

Lille

5TH

17/20

BRITISH

1ST

R. Scarpe

R. Scheldt

Mons

ARMY

Arras

4/8

Forest of Mormal

R. Selle

R. Oise

3RD

H

H

Cambrai

Avesnes

Bapaume

Landrecies

5/8

R. Somme

4TH

Peronne

FRENCH ARMY

Amiens

Villers
Bretonneux

St. Quentin

ARMY
BOUNDARY

Starting Lines

5/8	5/8 August
17/20	17/20 October
4/8	4/8 November
A——A	Armistice
H——H	Hindenburg Line

0   10 miles

MAP 39

cepted without further fighting.[31] What was more, so promising did he consider his plans to force the canal that he hoped to put them into effect before the armistice was concluded.[32]

It says much for Rawlinson's confidence in the ability of his Army and the straitened circumstances of his opponents that he took this view. For in terms of geography the task confronting him was decidedly formidable. In the southern sector Fourth Army faced the Sambre and Oise Canal – 75 feet wide from bank to bank and with a depth of water averaging 7 feet. The low ground on either side had been flooded by the enemy, and German forces dominated the high ground to the west of the canal. No tanks could operate in this sector. In the northern segment of the front to be attacked lay the Forest of Mormal, 40 square miles in extent and, if somewhat depleted of timber, still with sections containing thick groves of trees and dense undergrowth.[33] In these areas an effective artillery bombardment, and in particular an effective creeping barrage, would prove difficult to deliver. Again, just south of the forest on the far side of the canal stood a further obstacle, the defended village of Landrecies.

Offsetting these difficulties were certain favourable aspects. None of the German positions was guarded by adequate wire or trench defences. And the only forces the enemy could place in the line were some tired and understrength divisions, with two exhausted formations in reserve.[34] Much detailed information about the canal had been gained from local residents. And most importantly of all, over 1,000 guns could be brought to bear on the canal and forest to screen the assault by the five attacking divisions.[35]

Again, no detailed account of the battle is necessary. Supported by Third Army in the north and the First French Army in the south, Rawlinson's operation which began in the early morning of 4 November was successful along the whole front. The canal was crossed from Fesmy to Landrecies, the village of Landrecies was captured, and in the Forest of Mormal an advance beyond the designated objectives was accomplished.[36]

The main factors contributing to Rawlinson's success are worthy of note. On the western boundary of the forest area, tanks helped to dispose of machine-gun nests in several villages.[37] Further south, demoralization

[31] Rawlinson Diary 3/11/18.

[32] Ibid. 28/10/18.

[33] For these details see Montgomery, *Fourth Army*, p. 242.

[34] Fourth Army Intelligence Summary 27th Oct–1 Nov 1918, AWM 26/12/475/1.

[35] Fourth Army Summary of Operations, 4th November 1918, Fourth Army Papers vol. 46.

[36] Ibid.

[37] 2nd Tank Brigade: Report on Operations: 4th November 1918, in Tank Corps Narratives Aug–Nov 1918, Fourth Army Papers vol. 65.

among the defenders of Landrecies allowed 25 Division to capture three bridges over the canal, surround the town, and force its surrender.[38] Along the remainder of the canal, skilled infantry work with improvised bridging equipment played a part in forcing several crossings.[39]

Again it was the artillery which dominated the attack and allowed the actions just described to take place relatively unhindered. The bombardment began more than a week before the actual attack. Rawlinson was concerned to achieve a tactical surprise in the canal area, and so from 25 October to 3 November restricted his artillery to 'normal firing'.[40] Even so, his limited programme delivered 12.5 million pounds of shell onto the largely unprotected defenders. Then on the day of the attack the hapless Germans were deluged with another 8.6 million pounds, one of the heaviest days of bombardment since 29 September.[41] This savage assault demoralized the defenders, protected the forces crossing the canal, and blanketed most of the German batteries. There was even an innovation in the employment of the artillery. In the Forest of Mormal whole areas or 'blocks' were deluged with fire from the heavy guns. Then the infantry worked their way around the edges of the 'blocks' and attacked any surviving defenders from every side. The fire was then lifted on to other blocks which were treated in like manner.[42]

Even so, the attackers ran into some difficulties. The German 1 Guards Reserve Division put up a stiff resistance to the north of Landrecies.[43] And unsubdued German machine-guns and artillery prevented Rawlinson's 32 Division from crossing the canal in one area.[44] What, however, is most noteworthy about these incidents is the fact that on these occasions British commanders spared their forces the futile sacrifices of years gone by. So operations against the German Guards were halted until their positions had been outflanked by troops crossing the canal to the south.[45] And the forces of 32 Division were transferred to an area where, earlier in the day, other British troops had already crossed the canal.[46] That is, even if only at the last and only after resources of infantry had fallen perilously low, the wisdom of reinforcing success rather than attempting to redeem failure was being implemented by the Fourth Army.

[38] XIII Corps Narratives Oct–Nov 1918.

[39] Fourth Army Summary of Operations 4/11/18; 32 Division: Narrative of Operations 4/11/18, AWM 26/12/484/5.

[40] Fourth Army Summary of Operations 4/11/18.

[41] For these figures see Montgomery, *Fourth Army*, Appendix G.

[42] Ibid., p. 245.

[43] Fourth Army Summary of Operations 4/11/18.

[44] 32 Division Narrative 4/11/18, IX Corps War Diary, May–Dec 1918, WO 95/837.

[45] Fourth Army Summary of Operations 4/11/18.

[46] 32 Division Narrative 4/11/18.

The battle of the Sambre and Oise Canal is noteworthy for more than the skill with which it was conducted. For it was to prove the last engagement fought by the Fourth Army. From 5 November, Rawlinson's principal task was to follow up a rapid German withdrawal and keep in touch with the German rearguards. Confronted with deteriorating weather conditions, roads becoming boggy, and an adversary departing with all the speed he could muster, even this much became difficult. So on 8 November Rawlinson formed a composite force of infantry, field artillery, armoured cars, and cavalry, under the command of Major-General Bethell (66 Division), just to maintain touch with the enemy. It was this rather motley group which received the order to cease hostilities at 1100 hours on 11 November. Bethell was informed that all defensive precautions were to be instituted 'and that there was to be no intercourse with the enemy pending further instructions.' He received no further instructions. The war was over.

V

Fourth Army, between the end of July and 11 November 1918, had won a spectacular series of victories. They had forced the Germans out of the territory overrun in the opening phase of the Ludendorff offensive. And, much more significantly, they had overwhelmed defensive positions which only a few months before might well have been deemed impregnable. In sum, since August 1918 the British had revealed that the superiority which the defensive had enjoyed over the offensive in the first three years of the war no longer applied.

Certainly it might be argued that this point had already been effectively demonstrated by the Germans in the assaults which they had launched between March and June. But Ludendorff had gained ground by expending the one commodity which neither his army nor the armies of Britain and France could afford; namely infantry. For this reason the great Ludendorff offensive had been an exercise in unmitigated folly.

Fourth Army's offensive, by contrast, was noteworthy for its entirely appropriate use of available resources. Although its objectives could not be achieved without a succession of infantry advances involving some measure of loss among foot soldiers, this aspect of battle was kept within affordable limits. Other forms of weaponry such as shells, bullets, tanks, gas, and aircraft played a greater part in destroying the powers of resistance of their adversaries and opening the way for a succession of limited, but ultimately decisive, advances.

The fact that the British were not having to pay for their successes with an insupportable levy in the lives of their infantry has largely gone unnoticed. Indeed it has often been proclaimed that these operations were extremely costly in the blood of the fighting soldiers, and that therefore there was no superiority in the methods which Rawlinson was employing over those earlier employed by Ludendorff. This is a complete misconception, as the following comparison makes clear. Back on 1 July 1916 in the disastrous opening to the battle of the Somme, the British suffered roughly 20,000 men killed. Between August and November 1918, in the course of a succession of unrelenting advances, Fourth Army sustained about 20,000 killed.[47] The contrast between the price of failure on one day in 1916 and of success in more than three months in 1918 is so marked that it may be wondered why it has gone unnoticed. The explanation is simple. Consideration has always been given not to the number of men killed but to the number of men who became 'casualties'. For the later part of 1918 that figure happened to include a substantial number who fell sick on account (primarily) of the 'Spanish' influenza epidemic which was just then sweeping not only Western Europe but the whole world. When we subtract this quite irrelevant consideration from the overall picture, we find ourselves in a position to appreciate the true nature of the success which the British army – with Rawlinson's Fourth Army in the vanguard – was accomplishing by the last phase of the war.

[47] Montgomery, *Fourth Army*, Appendix A, p. 275.

35

Conclusion

I

It is not within the province of this book to pursue Rawlinson's career beyond the victory on the Western Front. The reader may care to note that he did not pass into retirement. In mid-1919, simultaneous with receiving a baronetcy and a grant of £30,000 for his wartime endeavours, he was dispatched to Archangel in north Russia to supervise the withdrawal of British troops who had been vainly endeavouring to aid the anti-Bolshevik forces. In November 1919, safely returned to Britain, he took over the Aldershot command. And in August 1920, to his great joy and fulfilling a long-standing ambition, he was appointed commander-in-chief in India. Rawlinson was still in occupancy of that post when, in March 1925, he died unexpectedly aged only 61. Since then, Rawlinson has been largely forgotten. As stated at the outset, there was little about his personality – least of all of a scandalous nature – to keep alive any interest in him. And perhaps of greater moment in accounting for his long obscurity, the level of command at which he operated during the Great War has not been deemed of much importance.

II

Accounts of the military conduct of the First World War concentrate largely on two aspects. One is the high command. The other is the combatant soldier. This book has looked elsewhere.

Those who confine themselves to the high command take one of two views. According to the first, the men at the top proved incapable of a creative response to the challenge of this war, and so squandered the lives of their soldiers on futile undertakings. That is, they were the authors of a succession of British defeats. According to the second, the high command was engaged in a struggle which could not avoid being protracted and painful. Within these limitations, Haig masterminded victory at an appropriate – albeit terrible – cost.

At the level of the combatant soldier, the issue of whether what occurred was worthwhile or anyway necessary again presents itself. But the perspective is different. What we observe are episodes of intense suffering redeemed by the courage, good humour, capacity for endurance, and comradeship of ordinary people under stress.

This book has argued that, if we confine ourselves just to these aspects, we do not see the story as a whole. Indeed, on important occasions we do not see the essential story at all. That is, the process which would decide whether British arms succeeded or failed did not necessarily depend on the actions of the commander-in-chief or the poor bloody infantryman.

However, the point must not be exaggerated. There were crucial moments when the high command or the foot soldier helped decide the course of events. Almost certainly, Haig's army would not have been employed in the manner it was during the second half of 1917 had some other individual – say Plumer – been in overall command. And in the successful operations of 1918 it remained the case that, crucial though the role of the artillery might be in suppressing opposition and clearing the way, the infantry still had a role to play. It must advance across still-disputed ground, subdue a residue of enemy resistance, and stand upon conquered territory.

But if we confine ourselves to the decisions of the high command or the endurance of the foot soldiers, we distort what occurred on the battlefield. There were levels between the most elevated and the most lowly where choices were made and actions taken which decided whether British operations prospered or languished. One level was the mobilization of productivity on the home front. In 1918, the Ministry of Munitions provided Britain's fighting forces – predominantly in France and Belgium – with 10,700 guns and howitzers. (Comparable figures for 1917 had been 6,500; for 1916, 4,500; for 1915, 3,500.)

A second level concerns the altogether more expert way in which individual weapons were employed and in which the various types of weapon were coalesced into a single striking force. We have seen how the artillerymen (in addition to the greater quantities of guns and shells available) had developed a degree of expertise which greatly increased the effectiveness of these weapons: calibration, the employment of meteorological information, flash spotting, sound ranging, developments in aerial spotting and aerial photography, had all helped to change the nature of offensive operations. It now became possible for the artillery to suppress much of the weaponry of the defenders and provide effective cover for the attackers during the crucial stages of an advance. At the same time the artillery was being incorporated into an entire weapons system which included light and heavy machine-guns, rifle grenades and trench mortars, tanks and armoured cars, gas, smoke, and wireless telegraphy. This volume of weaponry, and the development of an administrative structure capable of placing it on the battlefield in appropriate quantities and circumstances, served to produce a strike force against which the enemy ultimately could provide no effective resistance.

The third of these intermediate levels concerned command, at various stages of the military hierarchy. For here were decided the particular tasks assigned to individual units, and here was decided the manner in which the actions of sundry units would be knitted into a larger whole.

III

This book has related the First World War career of a man who exercised command in a succession of these intermediate positions: as divisional commander, corps commander, and Army commander. Its purpose has been to reveal where opportunities for the creative use of authority plainly presented themselves, where no such opportunities were on offer, and how effectively he responded in both circumstances.

The resulting tale has proved ambiguous and far from satisfactory. One factor in particular is puzzling. Early on, Rawlinson drew conclusions from battle which seemed full of wisdom. Such insights apparently equipped him to conduct operations as advantageously as circumstances allowed. Yet nothing that followed quite fulfilled this expectation, despite episodes showing it not to be wholly unfounded.

Far from being a steady learner, Rawlinson's conduct of battles revealed no consistent advance in wisdom. At his first battle, Neuve Chapelle, he identified artillery as the key weapon and by careful calculation ensured that a sufficient quantity was available to achieve his purpose. Yet one month later at Aubers Ridge he largely neglected the artillery factor, concentrating instead on how to exploit a breach in the German line. Insufficiency of artillery ensured that no breach presented itself. It was not the case, however, that Rawlinson had forgotten the key role played by artillery in his first success. Subsequent to Aubers Ridge, at Givenchy and Loos, he lamented the lack of guns – both in terms of quantity and penetrative power – to deal effectively with the enemy defences. Indeed, smoke and gas were introduced at Loos specifically to help overcome the deficiency in artillery.

As the commander chosen for the Somme, the largest battle yet fought by the British army, Rawlinson seemed well prepared. Before Loos he had reaffirmed the primacy of artillery and had been involved in the development of an important artillery innovation in the form of the creeping barrage. At the same time he had welcomed the introduction of gas as a method of penetrating the artillery-proof dugouts of the Germans. After the battle he had waxed enthusiastic about the contribution that smoke might make in concealing the passage of his soldiers across no-man's-land.

He also seemed an appropriate choice of commander for an army which would consist largely of Kitchener divisions. At Loos he had assigned the key role of capturing Loos village to a Kitchener formation and had then witnessed the skill and flexibility with which it had gone about its task.

Given all this, Rawlinson's performance in the planning process of the Somme offensive in mid-1916 is difficult to comprehend. Once again artillery was stated to be the key to success. But, unlike Neuve Chapelle, no attempt was made to determine whether he had sufficient of this commodity to achieve the purpose of his original plan, let alone that of the more grandiose design imposed on him by Haig. And on this occasion the auxiliary weapons of Loos, gas and smoke, were absent from Rawlinson's final scheme. So the problems of the dugouts and the concealment of troops in no-man's-land, which had at least been addressed at the earlier battle, were never confronted before the Somme.

Moreover, the Kitchener divisions were now deemed by Rawlinson to be so unskilled that he recommended they adopt rigid, slow-moving battle formations in order to prevent an advance degenerating into a rabble. Also, Rawlinson failed to apply his knowledge of the efficacy of the creeping barrage. Instead he left the decision about whether or not to employ this device – as he left much else – to the discretion of inexperienced lower-order commanders. Finally, after once again advocating a limited-objective bite and hold operation, he proved sadly amenable to launching, without protest, an unlimited campaign in accordance with the ideas of the high command.

Even more puzzling was Rawlinson's performance once battle had been joined. After neglecting the artillery factor on 1 July, it might be thought that he would have ascribed such later successes as he achieved (on 14 and 27 July) to elements other than weight of shell – the ruse of the night attack in the first instance, the demoralization of the enemy in the second. But, as has been shown, this was not the case. On both occasions Rawlinson grasped that it was in truth the concentrations of artillery that had won the day. Yet never again in the course of the campaign did he employ appropriate quantities of artillery. And within a week of the 14 July operation he was proclaiming that, after all, it was attack by night that held the key to future success.

Equally erratic is his attitude to the cavalry. Before 1 July he had left his corps commanders in no doubt that he considered there was no role for mounted soldiers on the Somme. Within ten days he made cavalry an important part of his next major operation. After that he reverted to his original attitude.

One does not need to look far for other instances of such infirmity of purpose. On 16 July Rawlinson proclaimed that the time for narrow-front operations was over. He then presided over precisely this form of attack for another two months. Similarly, he was quick to agree with Haig's instructions to halt left flank operations while bringing his right into line. He then proceeded to carry out twice as many attacks on the left flank as on the right. Towards the end of the battle we find him simultaneously calling for the campaign to be terminated and prosecuting it so unrelentingly as to cause a revolt by one of his corps commanders.

In 1918, as we have observed, Rawlinson's career and his preferred method of proceeding were both vindicated. Yet his part in the march of his forces to victory was really rather modest. We do not see him seizing time by the forelock or driving events in a particular direction. Rather he presided – with reasonable efficiency and periodical lapses into the Rawlinson of the Somme – over events which were being shaped by many forces and many individuals in addition to himself.

IV

When this study of Rawlinson as Western Front commander was first conceived, it was anticipated that the work would constitute a vindication of a military figure who – along with his peers and his commander – had been disregarded or judged too harshly. What was expected was first an account of how Rawlinson found himself embroiled in a conflict unlike anything he had previously experienced and requiring of him a painful learning process. It would then be demonstrated how, over the course of four years, that learning process steadily continued.[1]

The tale which has emerged has not quite followed this pattern. There was no undeviating advance towards wisdom, and no certain demon-

---

[1] Robin Prior, in an interview over the University of Adelaide's radio station 5UV in 1984, offered this as a provisional outline of the forthcoming work. Happily no record of the broadcast seems to have survived.

stration that at the end of the day Rawlinson was master of his job. It transpired that at the outset Rawlinson was not at all ill-equipped to fight the war that presented itself. And where the war's dominant features were indeed novel and formidable, he appeared at an early stage to perceive the necessary and appropriate responses. What he then failed to do was to follow through on his insights or perfect his preferred method of operating.

In part Rawlinson's uncertain course may reflect his perilous relations with his first commander-in-chief and his dependent status *vis-à-vis* his second. But that is not the whole explanation. On occasions when there was no undue pressure from above, he revealed no certainty of purpose or commitment to the sensible course he himself had earlier delineated. And if at last matters went well for the forces under his command, this was not wholly because he had assumed mastery of himself and the situation. Two aspects largely outside Rawlinson's control played a significant part in determining the course of events in 1918. First, the parlous circumstances of the British army in matters of manpower limited crucially the way in which he was able to act. Second, expertise in the technical aspects of conducting battles had become so widespread throughout the British army, and supplies of the sorts of weaponry appropriate to this expertise had become so generous, that the importance of command in accomplishing victory had diminished absolutely. Rawlinson's contribution to the shape of events on the battlefield was altogether less, for good or ill, in 1918 than in 1916.

But that observation should not be left unqualified. Rawlinson – even at the end – had a contribution to make. During his years as Army commander he had been able to assemble a team equipped, once his Army's objectives lay within the bounds of possibility, to administer battles thoroughly and level-headedly on most occasions. And Rawlinson himself was proving ready to draw on the wisdom of talented subordinates (such as Monash) and then to amend their schemes fruitfully when this seemed called for. It will be recalled how, in the preparations for Hamel, he amended his own proposals in response to the arguments of officers below the level of corps commander; and how he expanded Monash's scheme for the Hindenburg Line when this appeared over-cautious. These actions may not have elevated Rawlinson to the ranks of an outstanding military commander. But by and large they were sufficient for the needs of the force he was leading in 1918: an Army generously equipped in weaponry (if not in manpower), assailing limited objectives, and confronting an enemy in increasingly straitened circumstances.

It is appropriate to recall here, by way of contrast, the attitude of the German command in March 1918. The grandiose objectives of the

Ludendorff offensive, and the consequent suicidal manner in which the German authorities squandered their irreplaceable infantry, reminds us that even at that late stage opportunities for folly presented themselves to commanders at every level. Even this late in the day, it was required of Rawlinson (as of Haig) to prescribe objectives and devise ways of operating which were not manifestly silly, and to provide a command structure that would facilitate his technical experts and his rank and file in accomplishing these. That much Rawlinson achieved during the climactic stages of the First World War.

Bibliography

OFFICIAL MANUSCRIPT COLLECTIONS

Cabinet Papers [Cab], Public Record Office, London
Fourth Army Papers, Imperial War Museum [IWM], London
Miscellaneous Papers, Royal Artillery Institution Library, Woolwich, London
Operational Records, Australian War Memorial [AWM], Canberra
War Office Papers [WO], Public Record Office, London

PRIVATE PAPERS

Anstey, Brigadier E. C., Royal Artillery Institution, Woolwich
Becke, Captain A. F., Royal Artillery Institution, Woolwich
Boraston, Colonel J. H., Imperial War Museum, London
Burne, Lieutenant-Colonel A. H., Royal Artillery Institution, Woolwich
Butler, Lieutenant-General R. H. K., Imperial War Museum, London
Cavan, Field Marshal Earl, Public Record Office, London
Clive, Lieutenant-General Sir Sidney, Liddell Hart Centre for Military Archives, King's College, London
Congreve, General Sir Walter, private hands
Edmonds, Brigadier-General Sir James E., Liddell Hart Centre for Military Archives, King's College, London
Haig, Field Marshal Sir Douglas, National Library of Scotland, Edinburgh
Kiggell, Lieutenant-General Sir L., Liddell Hart Centre for Military Archives, King's College, London
Kitchener, Lord, Public Record Office, London
Maxse, General Sir Ivor, Imperial War Museum, London
Monash, General Sir John, Australian War Memorial, Canberra
Montgomery-Massingberd, Field Marshal Sir A. A., Liddell Hart Centre for Military Archives, King's College, London

Rawlins, Major S. W. H., Royal Artillery Institution, Woolwich
Rawlinson, Field Marshal Sir Henry, Churchill College [CC], Cambridge
—— National Army Museum [NAM], London
Rettie, Lieutenant-Colonel W. J. K., Royal Artillery Institution, Woolwich
Robertson, Field Marshal Sir William, Liddell Hart Centre for Military Archives, King's College, London
Stephens, General Sir R., Imperial War Museum
Tudor, Major-General Sir H. H., Royal Artillery Institution, Woolwich
Wigram, Major Clive, Royal Archives, Windsor
Wilson, Field Marshal Sir Henry, Imperial War Museum

BRITISH ARMY OFFICIAL PUBLICATIONS

Great Britain: B. E. F. General Staff, *Notes For the Guidance of Meteorological Observers* (SS77) (October 1915)
—— *Preliminary Notes on the Tactical Lessons of the Recent Operations* (SS119) [late 1916]
—— *Co-operation of Aircraft with Artillery* (various editions 1916–18)
—— *Notes on the Interpretation of Aeroplane Photographs* (various editions 1916–18)
—— *Notes on the Use of Smoke* (SS175) [1917]
Great Britain: War Office, *Infantry Training Manual 1909*
—— *Range Table for 4.5" Howitzer* [1916]
—— *Range Table for 60 pr Gun* [1916]
Great Britain: War Office: General Staff, *Infantry Training (4-Company organization) 1914* (issued 10/8/14)
—— *Trench Warfare: Notes on Attack and Defence* (February 1915)
—— *Notes on Recent Operations on the Front of First, Third, Fourth and Fifth Armies* (SS158) (London: War Office, May 1917)
—— *Instructions for the Training of the British Armies in France* (SS152) (January 1918)
—— *Geographical Section, Report on Survey on the Western Front 1914–18* (London: War Office, 1920)

BOOKS AND ARTICLES

Anderson, A. T., *War Services of the 62nd West Riding Divisional Artillery* (Cambridge: Cambridge University Press, 1920)
Anderson, Lt.-Gen. Sir H., 'Lord Horne as an army commander', *Journal of the Royal Artillery*, 56 (January 1930), 407–18
Asquith, H. H., *Letters to Venetia Stanley* (selected and edited by Michael and Eleanor Brock) (London: Oxford University Press, 1982)
Atkinson, C. T., *The Queen's Own Royal West Kent Regiment, 1914–19* (London: Simpkin Marshall, 1924)
—— *The Seventh Division, 1914–18* (London: Murray, 1927)

—— *The History of the South Wales Borderers, 1914–18* (London: Medici Society, 1931)

Atteridge, A. H., *History of the 17th Northern Division* (Glasgow: Maclehose, 1929)

Austin, Lt.-Col. W. S., *The Official History of the New Zealand Rifle Brigade* (Wellington: Watkins, 1924)

Baird Smith, Lt.-Col. A. G., 'Open war', *Army Quarterly*, 5 (1922–23), 59–67

Banks, T. M., and R. A. Chell, *With the 10th Essex in France* (London: Burt and Son, 1921)

Barnett, Correlli et al., *Old Battles and New Defences: Can we Learn from Military History?* (Brassey: London, 1986)

'The Battle of the Somme: The 41st Divisional Engineers at Flers on 15th, 16th, 17th Sept 1916', *Royal Engineers Journal* (March 1920), 137–40

Baynes, John, *Morale: A Study of Men and Courage: The Second Scottish Rifles at the Battle of Neuve Chapelle 1915* (London: Cassell, 1967)

—— 'Neuve Chapelle', *Purnell History of the First World War*, vol. 2, no. 11, pp. 733–43

Bean, C. E. W., *Official History of Australia in the War of 1914–18*, vol. 4: *The Australian Imperial Force in France 1916* (Sydney: Angus and Robertson, 1939)

—— *Official History of Australia in the War of 1914–18*, vol. 6: *The Australian Imperial Force in France during the Allied Offensive, 1918* (Sydney: Angus and Robertson, 1942)

Becke, Major A. F., 'The coming of the creeping barrage', *Journal of the Royal Artillery*, 58 (1931–32), 19–42

Bell, Ernest W., *Soldiers Killed on the First Day of The Somme* (Bolton, Lancs: Bell, 1977)

Berkeley, R., *The History of the Rifle Brigade in the War of 1914–1918* (London: Rifle Brigade Club, 1927)

Bethell, Brevet-Col. B. A., *Modern Guns and Gunnery* (Woolwich: Cattermole, 1910)

Bewsher, F. W., *History of the 51st (Highland) Division, 1914–1918* (Edinburgh: Blackwood, 1921)

Bickersteth, Lt. J. B., *History of the 6th Cavalry Brigade 1914–1919* (London: Baynard Press, n.d.)

Bidwell, Shelford, 'An approach to military history', *Army Quarterly* (January 1949), 243–6

—— *Gunners at War* (London: Arrow Books, 1972)

——, and Dominick Graham, *Fire-Power: British Army Weapons and Theories of War, 1904–45* (London: Allen and Unwin, 1982)

Birch, Lt.-Gen. Sir Noel, 'Artillery development in the Great War', *Army Quarterly*, 1 (1920–21), 79–89

Blake, Robert, ed., *The Private Papers of Douglas Haig, 1914–1919* (London: Eyre and Spottiswoode, 1952)

Blaxland, Gregory, *Amiens: 1918* (London: Muller, 1968)

Body, Capt. O. G., 'Lessons of the Great War: the barrage versus concentration on selected targets', *Journal of the Royal Artillery*, 53 (1926), 59–67

Bond, Brian, ed., *Staff Officer: The Diaries of Lord Moyne, 1914–1918* (London: Leo Cooper, 1987)

Boraston, Lt.-Col. J. H., *Sir Douglas Haig's Despatches* (London: Dent, 1919)

Boraston, Lt.-Col. J. H., and Cptn. Cyril E. O. Bax, *The Eighth Division in War, 1914–1918* (London: Medici Society, 1926)

Bragg, Sir Lawrence, et al., *Artillery Survey in the First World War* (London: Field Survey Association, 1971)

'The British attack on Beaumont-Hamel', *Journal of the Royal United Services Institute*, 66 (1921), 137–41

Broad, Lt.-Col. C. N. F., 'Army intelligence and Counter-battery work', *Journal of the Royal Artillery*, 49 (1922–23), 187–98, 221–42

—— 'The development of artillery tactics 1914–18', *Journal of the Royal Artillery*, 49 (1922–23), 62–81, 127–48

Brooke, Lt.-Col. A. F., 'The evolution of artillery in the Great War', *Journal of the Royal Artillery*, 51 (1924–25), 359–72; 52 (1925–26), 37–51, 369–87

Browne, D. G., *The Tank in Action* (London: Blackwood, 1920)

Buchalet, Commandant, 'Artillery organisation', *Journal of the Royal Artillery*, 53 (1926–27), 122–36, 288–300

Buchan, John, *The History of the South African Forces in France* (London: Nelson, 1920)

Buckland, Maj.-Gen. Sir R. V. H., 'Experiences at Fourth Army headquarters: organization and work of the R.E.', *Royal Engineers Journal*, 41 (Sept 1927), 385–413

Budworth, Maj. C. E. D., 'Training and action necessary to further co-operation between artillery and infantry', *Journal of the Royal United Services Institute*, 57 (1912), 67–86

Byrne, Lt. A. E., *Official History of the Otago Regiment, N.Z.E.F. in the Great War 1914–1918* (Dunedin: Wilkie, n.d.)

Byrne, Lt. J. R., *New Zealand Artillery in the Field 1914–1918* (Auckland: Whitcombe and Tombs, 1922)

Callwell, Maj.-Gen. Sir Charles E., *Field Marshal Sir Henry Wilson: His Life and Diaries* (2 vols) (London: Cassell, 1927)

Cassar, George H., *The Tragedy of Sir John French* (Newark, NJ: University of Delaware Press, 1985)

Charlton, Peter, *Pozieres 1916, Australians on the Somme* (Sydney: Methuen/Haynes, 1986)

Charteris, Brigadier-General John, *At G.H.Q.* (London: Cassell, 1931)

—— *Field Marshal Earl Haig* (London: Cassell, 1929)

Chasseaud, Peter, 'Trench mapping: military survey and large scale mapping on the Western Front 1914–18: British experience and practice', *Stand-To* (London), 21 (1987), 29–33; 22 (1988), 6–9

Clark, Alan, *The Donkeys* (London: Hutchinson, 1961)

Colliver, Captain E. J., and Lt. B. H. Richardson, *The Forty-Third: The Story and Official History of the 43rd Battalion, A.I.F.* (Adelaide: Rigby, 1920)

Compton, Major T. E., 'The campaign in 1918 in France', *Journal of the Royal United Services Institute*, 65 (Feb 1920), 164–84

Congreve, Billy, *Armageddon Road: A V.C.'s Diary, 1914–16* (edited by Terry Norman) (London: Kimber, 1982)

Coop, J. O., *The Story of the 55th Division* (Liverpool: Daily Post, 1919)

Cooper, Bryan, *Tank Battles of World War I* (London: Ian Allen, 1974)

Cooper, Duff, *Haig* (2 vols) (London: Faber, 1935)

Croft, Major John, 'The Somme: 14 July 1916 – a great opportunity missed?', *Army Quarterly*, 116, no. 3 (July 1986), 312–21

Croft, Lt.-Col. W. D., *Three Years with the 9th (Scottish) Division* (London: Murray, 1919)

—— 'The influence of tanks upon tactics', *Journal of the Royal United Services Institute* (Feb 1922), 39–53

Crow, Duncan, ed., *AFVs of World War One* (Windsor: Profile Publications, 1970)

Crozier, Brig.-Gen. F. P., *A Brass Hat in No Man's Land* (London: Cape, 1930)

—— *The Men I Killed* (London: Michael Joseph, 1937)

Cusins, Lt.-Col. A. G. T., 'Development of army wireless during the war', *Journal of the Institute of Electrical Engineers*, 59 (July 1921), 763–70

Cutlack, F. M., *The Australians: Their Final Campaign 1918* (London: Sampson Low and Marston, 1918)

Das K.B. 10 Infanterie Regiment König (Munich: Bayerisches Kriegsarchiv, 1925)

Das K.B. 14 Infanterie Regiment Hartmann (Munich, 1931)

Davson, H. M., *The History of the 35th Division in the Great War* (London: Sifton Praed, 1927)

Dewar, George A. B., and Lt.-Col. J. H. Boraston, *Sir Douglas Haig's Command: December 19, 1915 to November 11, 1918* (2 vols) (London: Constable, 1922)

Dobbie, Col. W. G. S., 'The operations of the 1st Division on the Belgian coast in 1917', *Royal Engineers Journal* (June 1924), 185–204

Durrant, Col. J. M. A., 'Mont St Quentin: some aspects of the operations of the 2nd Australian Division from the 27th August to the 2nd of September 1918', *Army Quarterly*, 31 (1935), 86–95

Edmonds, Sir James E., *Military Operations: France and Belgium, 1914*, vol. 1 (London: Macmillan, 1933) (British Official History)

—— *Military Operations: France and Belgium, 1914*, vol. 2 (and map vol.) (London: Macmillan, 1925)

—— and Captain G. C. Wynne, *Military Operations: France and Belgium 1915*, vol. 1 (London: Macmillan, 1927)

—— *Military Operations: France and Belgium, 1915*, vol. 2 (London: Macmillan, 1928)

—— *Military Operations: France and Belgium, 1916* (1 vol. with 1 vol. of appendices) (London: Macmillan, 1932)

—— *Military Operations: France and Belgium, 1917*, vol. 2 (London: HMSO, 1948)

—— *Military Operations: France and Belgium, 1918*, vol. 2 (London: Macmillan, 1937)

—— *Military Operations: France and Belgium, 1918*, vol. 3 (London: Macmillan, 1939)

—— *Military Operations: France and Belgium, 1918*, vol. 4 (London: HMSO, 1947)

——, and Lt.-Col. R. Maxwell-Hyslop, *Military Operations: France and Belgium, 1918*, vol. 5 (London: HMSO, 1947)

—— 'The Reserves at Loos', *Journal of the Royal United Services Institute*, 81 (1936), 33–9

—— 'The Fifth Army in March 1918', *Journal of the Royal United Services Institute* (Feb 1937), 17–31

Ellis, Captain A. D., *The Story of the Fifth Australian Division* (London: Hodder and Stoughton, n.d.)

Essame, H., *The Battle for Europe 1918* (London: Batsford, 1972)

Etzer, Major H., *Das K.B. 9 Infanterie Regiment Wrede* (Munich: Schick, 1928)

Evans, M. StH., *Going Across: or, With the 9th Welsh in the Butterfly Division* (Newport, Mon: Johns, 1952)

Ewing, J., *History of the 9th (Scottish) Division, 1914–1919* (London: Murray, 1921)

Falkenhayn, General Erich von, *General Headquarters and its Critical Decisions 1914–16* (London: Hutchinson, n.d.)

Falls, Cyril, *History of the Thirty-Sixth (Ulster) Division* (London: McCaw Stevenson and Orr, 1922)

—— *Life of a Regiment*, vol. 4: *The Gordon Highlanders in the First World War, 1914–1919* (Aberdeen: Aberdeen University Press, 1958)

—— *Military Operations: France and Belgium, 1917*, vol. 1 (London: Macmillan, 1940)

Farrar-Hockley, A. H., *The Somme* (London: Batsford, 1964)

—— *Ypres 1914: Death of the Army* (London: Pan, 1970)

—— *Goughie: The Life of General Sir Hubert Gough* (London: Hart-Davis/ MacGibbon, 1975)

Foulkes, Major-General C. H., *'Gas'! The Story of the Special Brigade* (Edinburgh: Blackwood, 1936)

Fraser, David, *Allanbrooke* (London: Collins, 1982)

Fraser-Tytler, Lt.-Col. N., *Field Guns in France* (London: Hutchinson, n.d.)

French, David, 'The military background to the "shell crisis" of May 1915', *Journal of Strategic Studies*, 2 (1979), 192–205

French, Sir John, *Despatches* (London: War Office, 1915)

—— *1914* (London: Constable, 1919)

Fuller, J. F. C., *Tanks in the Great War* (London: John Murray, 1920)

Gardner, Brian, *The Big Push: The Somme 1916* (London: Sphere, 1968)

Gibbs, A. H., *The Grey Wave* (London: Hutchinson, 1920)

Giles, John, *The Somme: Then and Now* (London: After the Battle Publications, 1986)

Gillon, S., *Story of the 29th Division* (London: Nelson, 1925)

Gordon, Huntley, *The Unreturning Army: A Field-Gunner in Flanders 1917–18* (London: Dent, 1967)

Goschen, Lieut.-Colonel A. A., 'Artillery tactics', *Journal of the Royal Artillery*, 52 (1924), 254–60

Goss, J., *A Border Battalion: the history of the 7/8th Battalion King's Own Scottish Borderers* (Edinburgh: Foulis, 1920)

Gough, General Sir Hubert, *The Fifth Army* (London: Hodder and Stoughton, 1931)

Greenhous, Brereton, 'Evolution of a close ground-support role for aircraft in World War I', *Military Affairs*, 39 (Feb 1975), 22–8

—— '. . . It was chiefly a Canadian battle', *Canadian Defence Quarterly*, 18 (Autumn 1988), 73–80

Griffith, Paddy, *Forward into Battle: Infantry Tactics from Waterloo to Vietnam* (London: Antony Bird, 1982)

Haber, L. F., *The Poisonous Cloud: Chemical Warfare in the First World War* (Oxford: Clarendon Press, 1986)

Hamilton, E. W., *The First Seven Divisions: Being a Detailed Account of the Fighting from Mons to Ypres* (London: Hurst and Blackett, 1916)

Hamilton, Lt.-Col. R. G. A. (Master of Belhaven), *The War Diary of the Master of Belhaven 1914–1918* (London: John Murray, 1924)

Harrison, Major H. C., 'Calibration and ranging', *Journal of the Royal Artillery*, 47 (1920), 265–8

Hartcup, Guy, *The War of Invention: Scientific Developments 1914–18* (London: Brassey, 1988)

Haswell, Jock, *British Military Intelligence* (London: Weidenfeld and Nicolson, 1973)

Headlam, C., *History of the Guards Division in the Great War*, vol. 1 (London: Murray, 1924)

Henriques, J. Q., *War History of the 1st Battalion, Queen's Westminster Rifles, 1914–1918* (London: Medici Society, 1923)

Hickey, Captain D. E., *Rolling into Action: Memoirs of a Tank Corps Section Commander* (London: Hutchinson, n.d.)

Hogg, Ian V., *The Guns 1914–18* (London: Pan, 1973)

—— and L. F. Thurston, *British Artillery Weapons and Ammunition 1914–1918* (London: Ian Allen, 1973)

Holmes, Richard, *The Little Field-Marshal: Sir John French* (London: Cape, 1981)

Hudson, Major N., 'Trench-mortars in the Great War', *Journal of the Royal Artillery*, 47 (1920), 17–31

Hughes, Colin, *Mametz: Lloyd George's 'Welsh Army' at the Battle of the Somme* (2nd ed.) (Gerrards Cross: Orion Press, 1982)

Hussey, A. H., and D. S. Inman, *The Fifth Division in the Great War* (London: Nisbet, 1921)

Hutchison, G. S., *The Thirty-Third Division in France and Flanders, 1915–1919* (London: Waterloo, 1921)

Inglefield, V. E., *History of the Twentieth (Light) Division* (London: Nisbet, 1921)

Innes, John A., *Flash Spotters and Sound Rangers: How they Lived, Worked and Fought in the Great War* (London: Allen and Unwin, 1935)

Jervis, H. S., *The 2nd Munsters in France* (Aldershot: Gale and Polden, 1922)

Jones, H. A., *The War in the Air*, vol. 6 and 1 vol. of appendices (Oxford: Clarendon Press, 1937) (British Official History)

—— *The War in the Air*, vol. 2 (London: Hamish Hamilton, 1969). (Reprint of 1928 edn)

Jones, Nigel H., *The War Walk: A Journey along the Western Front* (London: Hale, 1983)

Jones, R. E., G. E. Rarey and R. J. Icks, *The Fighting Tanks from 1916 to 1933* (Old Greenwich, Connecticut: W. E. Publishers, 1969) (Reissue of 1933 edn)

Keegan, John, *The Face of Battle* (London: Cape, 1976)

Kennedy, E. J., *With the Immortal Seventh Division* (London: Hodder and Stoughton, 1916)

Kennedy, H. B., *War Record of the 21st London Regiment, First Surrey Rifles 1914–1919* (London: Skinner, 1928)

Kincaid-Smith, M., *The 25th Division in France and Flanders* (London: Harrison, 1920)

Kirke, Col. R. M. StG., 'Some aspects of artillery development during the First World War on the Western Front', *Journal of the Royal Artillery*, 101 (Sept 1974), 130–40

Lewis, Cecil, *Sagittarius Rising* (London: Corgi, 1969)

Liddell Hart, B. H., *The Tanks*, vol. 1: *1914–1939* (London: Cassell, 1959)

Livesay, J. F. B., *Canada's Hundred Days: With the Canadian Corps from Amiens to Mons, Aug 8–Nov 11, 1918* (Toronto: Thomas Allen, 1919)

Long, Lt.-Col. C. E., 'Ammunition supply during the Great War with special reference to the 1st Canadian Division', *Canadian Defence Quarterly*, 5 (1928), 152–9

Lowe, C. E. B., *Siege Battery 94 during the World War* (London: Werner Laurie, 1919)

Ludendorff, General E., *My War Memories 1914–1918* (London: Hutchinson, 1919)

Lupfer, Captain Timothy L., *The Dynamics of Doctrine: The Changes in German Tactical Doctrine during the First World War* (Leavenworth Papers no. 4) (Leavenworth, Kansas: Combat Studies Institute, 1981)

Lutz, Ralph Haswell, *The Causes of the German Collapse in 1918* (Stanford, CA: Stanford University Press, 1934)

McCartney-Filgate, J., *History of the 33rd Division Artillery in the War, 1914–1918* (London: Vacher, 1921)

Macdonald, Lyn, *Somme* (London: Michael Joseph, 1983)

MacIntosh, J. C., *Men and Tanks* (London: Lane, 1920)

Mackesy, Lt.-Col. J. P., 'The Battle of the Somme: R.E. preparations in the 31st divisional area', *Royal Engineers Journal* (Dec 1919), 275–8

Macksey, Kenneth, *Tank Warfare: A History of Tanks in Battle* (London: Hart-Davies, 1971)

Macleod, Major-General M. N., 'A sapper secret weapon of World War I', *Royal Engineers Journal*, 68 (1954), 275–81

Magnus, Laurie, *The West Riding Territorials in the Great War* (London: Kegan Paul, Trench, Trubner, 1920)

Maitre, Col. A., 'Evolution during the war of ideas concerning the employment of artillery', *Journal of US Artillery*, 55 (October 1921), 287–304

Marden, T. O., *A Short History of the 6th Division, Aug. 1914–March 1919* (London: Rees, 1920)

Marshall-Cornwall, General Sir James, *Haig as Military Commander* (London: Batsford, 1973)

Maude, A. H., *The 47th London Division, 1914–1919* (London: Amalgamated Press, 1922)

Maurice, Major-General Sir Frederick, *The Last Four Months: The End of the War in the West* (London: Cassell, 1919)

—— 'The Versailles Supreme War Council', *Army Quarterly*, 1 (Jan 1921), 232–40

—— *The Life of General Lord Rawlinson of Trent: From his Journals and Letters* (London: Cassell, 1928)

Mead, Peter, *The Eye in the Air: History of Air Observation and Reconnaissance for the Army 1785–1945* (London: HMSO, 1983)

Messenger, Charles, *Trench Fighting 1914–18* (London: Pan/Ballantine, 1973)

Middlebrook, Martin, *The First Day on the Somme* (London: Allen Lane, 1971)

Miles, Captain Wilfrid, *Military Operations: France and Belgium, 1916*, vol. 2 with 1 vol. of appendices (London: Macmillan, 1938)

—— *Military Operations: France and Belgium 1917*, vol. 3: *The Battle of Cambrai* (London: HMSO, 1948)

Millett, Allan R., and Williamson Murray, eds, *Military Effectiveness: The First World War* (London: Unwin Hyman, 1988)

Monash, Lt.-General Sir John, *The Australian Victories in France in 1918* (London: Hutchinson, 1920)

Montgomery, Major-General Sir A., *The Story of the Fourth Army in the Battles of the Hundred Days, August 8th to November 11th, 1918* (London: Hodder and Stoughton, 1931)

Montgomery-Massingberd, Sir A., '8th August 1918', *Journal of the Royal Artillery*, 55 (1928), 13–37

Moody, R. S. H., *Historical Records of the Buffs, East Kent Regiment* (London: Medici Society, 1923)

Munby, J. E., *A History of the 38th Division* (London: Rees, 1920)

Murphy, C. C. R., *The History of the Suffolk Regiment, 1914–1927* (London: Hutchinson, 1928)

Nichols, G. H. F., *The 18th Division in the Great War* (London: Blackwood, 1922)

Nicholson, Col. G. W. L., *The Canadian Expeditionary Force 1914–1919* (Ottawa: Queen's Printer, 1962) (Canadian Official History)

Norman, Terry, *The Hell They Called High Wood* (London: Kimber, 1984)

Oldfield, Colonel-Commandant L. C. L., 'Artillery and the lessons we have learned with regard to it in the late war', *Journal of the Royal United Services Institute*, 67 (Nov 1922), 579–99

O'Neill, H. C., *The Royal Fusiliers in the Great War* (London: Heinemann, 1922)

Orgill, Douglas, *The Tank: Studies in the Development and Use of a Weapon* (London: Heinemann, 1970)

O'Ryan, J. F., *Story of the 27th Division* (2 vols) (New York: Wynkoop, Hallenbeck, Crawford, 1921)

Pearton, Maurice, *The Knowledgeable State* (London: Burnett Books, 1982)

Pedersen, P. A., *Monash as Military Commander* (Melbourne: Melbourne University Press, 1985)

Pemberton, Brigadier A. L., *The Development of Artillery Tactics and Equipment* (London: War Office, 1950)

Penrose, Major John, 'Survey for batteries', *Journal of the Royal Artillery*, 49 (1922–3), 253–70

Pitt, Barrie, *1918: The Last Act* (London: Corgi, 1965)

Ponsonby, Lt.-Col. Charles, *West Kent (Q.O.) Yeomanry and 10th (Yeomanry) Batt. the Buffs, 1914–1919* (London: Melrose, 1920)

Portway, Donald, *Science and Mechanisation in Land Warfare* (Cambridge: Heffer, 1938)

—— *Military Science Today* (London: Oxford University Press, 1940)

Pratt, Colonel Joseph H., 'The St Quentin-Cambrai Tunnel: its use in the War', *Military Engineers Journal*, 9 (1927), 324–9

Priestley, Major R. E., *Breaking the Hindenburg Line: The story of the 46th Division* (London: Fisher and Unwin, 1919)

—— 'The evolution of intercommunication in France 1914–18', *Royal Engineers Journal* (Dec 1921), 269–75

—— *The Signal Service in the European War of 1914 to 1918 (France)* (Chatham: Mackay, 1921)

Prior, Robin, *Churchill's 'World Crisis' as History* (London: Croom Helm, 1983)

Reichsarchiv, *Schlachten des Weltkrieges: Somme Nord* (Oldenburg: Stallung, 1927)

Riegar, Captain J., *Das K.B. 17 Infanterie Regiment Orff* (Munich: Schick, 1927)

Ritter, Major A., *Das K.B. 18 Infanterie Regiment Prinz Ludwig Ferdinand* (Munich: Bayerisches Kriegsarchiv, 1926)

Ross, Captain R. B., *The Fifty-First in France* (London: Hodder and Stoughton, 1918)

Ross-of-Bladensburg, Lt.-Col. Sir John, *The Coldstream Guards 1914–1918*, vol. 1 (London: Oxford University Press, 1928)

Rowan-Robinson, Lt.-Col. H., 'The limited objective', *Army Quarterly*, 2 (1921), 119–27

Russell, A., *The Machine Gunner* (Kineton, Warwickshire: Roundwood, 1977)

Russell, Captain R. O., *The History of the 11th (Lewisham) Battalion, The Queen's Own, Royal West Kent Regiment* (London: Lewisham Newspaper Company, 1934)

Sandilands, H. R., *The 23rd Division, 1914–1919* (London: Blackwood, 1925)

Sandilands, J. W., and N. Macleod, *The History of the 7th Battalion Queen's Own Cameron Highlanders* (Stirling: Mackay, 1922)

Schaidler, Captain O., *Das K.B. 7 Infanterie Regiment Prinz Leopold* (Munich: Bayerisches Kriegsarchiv, 1922)

Schonland, Captain B. F. J., '"W/T.R.E.", An account of the work and development of field wireless sets with the armies in France', *Wireless World*, 7 (1919), 124–8, 261–7, 394–7, 452–5

Scott, Sir A. B., and P. M. Brumwell, *History of the 12th (Eastern) Division in the Great War* (London: Nisbet, 1923)

Serle, Geoffrey, *John Monash* (Melbourne: Melbourne University Press, 1982)

Severn, Mark, *The Gambardier: Giving some Account of the Heavy and Siege Artillery in France, 1914–18* (London: Benn, 1930)

Shakespear, J., *The Thirty-Fourth Division 1915–1919* (London: Wetherby, 1921)

Simpson, C. R., *History of the Lincolnshire Regiment, 1914–1918* (London: Medici Society, 1931)

Sixsmith, E. K. G., *Douglas Haig* (London: Weidenfeld and Nicolson, 1976)

Smith, A. D. B., 'Gordon Highlanders at Loos', *Aberdeen University Review*, 18 (1931), 97–112

Spears, Sir Edward, *Prelude to Victory* (London: Cape, 1939)

Stewart, Col. H., *The New Zealand Division 1916–1919: A Popular History Based on Historical Records* (Auckland: Whitcombe and Tombs, 1921)

Stewart, Major Herbert A., *From Mons to Loos: Being the Diary of a Supply Officer* (Edinburgh: Blackwood, 1916)

Stewart, J., and J. Buchan, *The Fifteenth (Scottish) Division, 1914-1919* (London: Blackwood, 1926)

Terraine, John, *Douglas Haig: The Educated Soldier* (London: Hutchinson, 1963)

—— 'Monash: Australian commander', *History Today*, 16 (1966), 12-19

—— 'Mortality and morale', *R.U.S.I. Journal*, 112 (Nov 1967), 364-9

—— *The Western Front 1914-18* (London: Arrow, 1970)

—— *To Win a War: 1918 The Year of Victory* (London: Sidgwick and Jackson, 1978)

—— *The Smoke and the Fire: Myths and Anti-Myths of War 1861-1945* (London: Sidgwick & Jackson, 1980)

—— *White Heat: The New Warfare 1914-18* (London: Sidgwick and Jackson, 1982)

——, ed., *General Jack's Diary 1914-18* (London: Eyre and Spottiswoode, 1964)

Travers, Tim, 'The offensive and the problem of innovation in British military thought 1870-1915', *Journal of Contemporary History*, 13 (1978), 531-53

—— 'Learning and decision-making on the Western Front, 1915-16: the British example', *Canadian Journal of History*, 8, no. 1 (April 1983), 87-97

—— *The Killing Ground: The British Army, the Western Front and the Emergence of Modern Warfare 1900-1918* (London: Allen and Unwin, 1987)

Trythall, Anthony John, *'Boney' Fuller: The Intellectual General 1878-1966* (London: Cassell, 1977)

Wade, A., *The War of the Guns* (London: Batsford, 1936)

Ward, C. H. D., *The 56th Division - 1st London Territorial Division* (London: Murray, 1921)

—— *The 74th (Yeomanry) Division in Syria and France* (London: Murray, 1922)

—— *Regimental Records of the Royal Welch Fusiliers*, vol. 3 *1914-1918 France and Flanders* (London: Forster Groom, 1928)

Warner, Philip, *The Battle of Loos* (London: Kimber, 1976)

Watson, Major W. H. L., *A Company of Tanks* (Edinburgh: Blackwood, 1920)

Wauchope, Major-General A. G., *A History of the Black Watch (Royal Higlanders) in the Great War, 1914-1918* (3 vols) (London: Medici Society, 1926)

Der Weltkrieg (vols. 7, 9, 10, 11, 14), (Berlin: Mittler, 1932-44) (German Official History)

Williams, Jeffery, *Byng of Vimy: General and Governor General* (London: Leo Cooper/Secker and Warburg, 1983)

Williams-Ellis, C., and A. Williams-Ellis, *The Tank Corps* (London: Country Life, 1919)

Wilson, Trevor, *The Myriad Faces of War* (Oxford: Polity, 1986)

—— ed., *The Political Diaries of C. P. Scott 1911-1928* (London: Collins, 1970)

Winterbotham, Lt.-Col. H. StJ. L., 'Geographical and survey work in France, especially in connection with artillery', *Journal of the Royal Artillery*, 46 (1919), 154-72

Wise, S. F., *Canadian Airmen and the First World War: The Official History of the Royal Canadian Air Force*, vol. 1 (Toronto: University of Toronto Press, 1980)

Wright, Major R. M., 'Machine-gun tactics and organization', *Army Quarterly*, 1 (June 1921), 290-313

Wylly, H. C., *The Border Regiment in the Great War* (Aldershot: Gale and Polden, 1924)

—— *The Green Howards in the Great War* (privately printed, 1926)

—— *History of the 1st and 2nd Battalions, the Leicestershire Regiment in the Great War* (Aldershot: Gale and Polden, 1928)

Wynne, G. C., 'The affair of the 21st and 24th Divisions at Loos, 26th September 1915', *The Fighting Forces*, 11 (1934), 30–8

—— 'Reflections on Neuve Chapelle, March 1915', *The Fighting Forces*, 12 (Dec 1935), 497–503

—— 'The chain of command', *Army Quarterly*, 36 (1938), 23–37

—— 'The Hindenburg Line', *Army Quarterly*, 37 (1938–39), 205–28

—— *If Germany Attacks: The Battle in Depth in the West* (London: Faber, 1940)

—— 'The other side of the hill: no. I: the German defence during the Battle of the Somme, July 1916, derived from German sources of information', *Army Quarterly*, 8 (April 1924), 72–83

—— 'The other side of the hill: no. III: the fight for Hill 70: 25th–26th of September, 1915', *Army Quarterly*, 8 (1924), 261–73

—— 'The other side of the hill: no. IV: Mametz Wood and Contalmaison: 9th–10th July 1916', *Army Quarterly*, 8 (Jan 1925), 245–59

—— 'The other side of the hill: no. VI: the German defence of Bernefay and Trones Woods: 2nd–14th July 1916', *Army Quarterly*, 9 (Oct 1926) 19–32; (Jan 1927), 252–60

—— 'The other side of the hill: no. IX: The Somme 15th Sept 1916', *Army Quarterly*, 26 (1933), 300–8

—— 'The other side of the hill: no. XVI: Aubers Ridge: 9th of May, 1915', *Army Quarterly*, 36 (1938), 243–8

—— 'The other side of the hill: no. XVII: Neuve Chapelle 10–12 March 1915', *Army Quarterly*, 37 (1938–39), 30–46

Wyrall, E., *The History of the Second Division, 1914–1918* (London: Nelson, 1921)

—— *The History of the King's Regiment (Liverpool)* (London: Arnold, 1928–30)

—— *The Gloucestershire Regiment in the War, 1914–1918: The records of the 1st (28th), 2nd (61st), 3rd (Special Reserve) and 4th, 5th and 6th (First Line T.A.) Battalions* (London: Methuen, 1931)

—— *The History of the 19th Division, 1914–1918* (London: Arnold, 1932)

—— *The History of the Fiftieth Division, 1914–1919* (London: Lund Humphries, 1939)

Index